San Francisco For D~~ummies~~ W9-AON-727
4th Edition

Cheat Sheet

San Francisco's Important Bus Lines

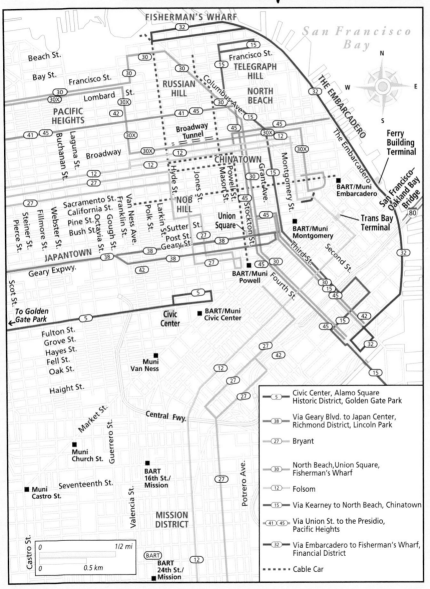

FISHERMAN'S WHARF
32

San Francisco Bay

Beach St.
Bay St.
Francisco St.
30
30X
Lombard St.
PACIFIC HEIGHTS
42
41 45
Laguna St.
Buchanan St.
Broadway
30X
27
Steiner St.
Pierce St.
Fillmore St.
Webster St.
JAPANTOWN
Geary Expwy.
Scot St.

To Golden Gate Park
5

Fulton St.
Grove St.
Hayes St.
Fell St.
Oak St.
Haight St.

Market St.
Central Fwy.
Guerrero St.

Muni Church St.
Seventeenth St.
Muni Castro St.
Castro St.

Valencia St.

BART 16th St./Mission

MISSION DISTRICT

0   1/2 mi
0   0.5 km

BART 24th St./Mission

30
30
RUSSIAN HILL
Francisco St.
Columbus Ave.
Broadway Tunnel
12
30X
12
Sacramento St.
California St.
Pine St.
Bush St.
Octavia St.
Gough St.
Franklin St.
Van Ness Ave.
Polk St.
Larkin St.
Hyde St.
Jones St.
Mason St.
Powell St.
NOB HILL
Sutter St.
Post St.
Geary St.
38
38
42
38
27
5
Civic Center

BART/Muni Civic Center

Muni Van Ness

12
27
27
27

15
15
15
TELEGRAPH HILL
NORTH BEACH
41 45
45
45
CHINATOWN
Grant Ave.
Stockton St.
Union Square
45
27
45 30
BART/Muni Powell
Fourth St.
Third St.

45
45
45
30X
12
30X
Montgomery St.
Second St.

THE EMBARCADERO
32
The Embarcadero

Ferry Building Terminal

San Francisco–Oakland Bay Bridge
80

BART/Muni Embarcadero

Trans Bay Terminal

BART/Muni Montgomery

30
15
45

42

15

32

15

27
42

12

27

Potrero Ave.

BART

12

Line	Description
5	Civic Center, Alamo Square Historic District, Golden Gate Park
38	Via Geary Blvd. to Japan Center, Richmond District, Lincoln Park
27	Bryant
30	North Beach, Union Square, Fisherman's Wharf
12	Folsom
15	Via Kearney to North Beach, Chinatown
41 45	Via Union St. to the Presidio, Pacific Heights
32	Via Embarcadero to Fisherman's Wharf, Financial District
······	Cable Car

The Napa Valley

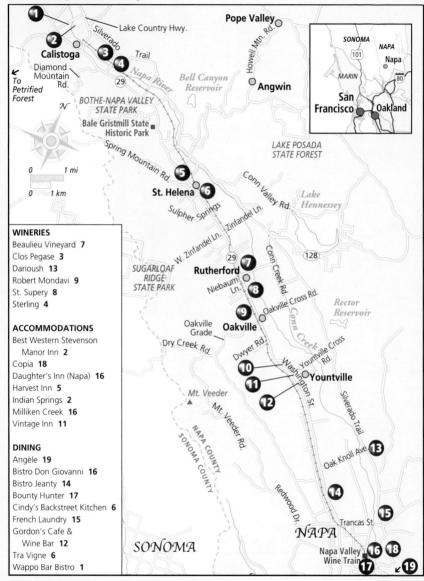

WINERIES
Beaulieu Vineyard **7**
Clos Pegase **3**
Darioush **13**
Robert Mondavi **9**
St. Supery **8**
Sterling **4**

ACCOMMODATIONS
Best Western Stevenson
    Manor Inn **2**
Copia **18**
Daughter's Inn (Napa) **16**
Harvest Inn **5**
Indian Springs **2**
Milliken Creek **16**
Vintage Inn **11**

DINING
Angèle **19**
Bistro Don Giovanni **16**
Bistro Jeanty **14**
Bounty Hunter **17**
Cindy's Backstreet Kitchen **6**
French Laundry **15**
Gordon's Cafe &
    Wine Bar **12**
Tra Vigne **6**
Wappo Bar Bistro **1**

FOR DUMMIES®

The fun and easy way™ to travel!

U.S.A.

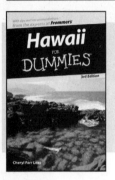

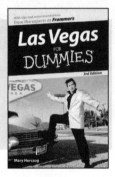

Also available:

Alaska For Dummies
Arizona For Dummies
Boston For Dummies
California For Dummies
Chicago For Dummies
Colorado & the Rockies For Dummies
Florida For Dummies
Los Angeles & Disneyland For Dummies
Maui For Dummies
National Parks of the American West For Dummies

New Orleans For Dummies
New York City For Dummies
San Francisco For Dummies
Seattle & the Olympic Peninsula For Dummies
Washington, D.C. For Dummies
RV Vacations For Dummies
Walt Disney World & Orlando For Dummies

EUROPE

Also available:

England For Dummies
Europe For Dummies
Germany For Dummies
Ireland For Dummies
London For Dummies

Paris For Dummies
Scotland For Dummies
Spain For Dummies

OTHER DESTINATIONS

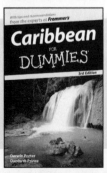

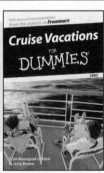

Also available:

Bahamas For Dummies
Cancun & the Yucatan For Dummies
Costa Rica For Dummies
Mexico's Beach Resorts For Dummies
Montreal & Quebec City For Dummies
Vancouver & Victoria For Dummies

Available wherever books are sold.
Go to www.dummies.com or call 1-877-762-2974 to order direct.

WILEY

San Francisco
FOR
DUMMIES®
4TH EDITION

by Paula Tevis

Wiley Publishing, Inc.

San Francisco For Dummies®, 4th Edition

Published by
Wiley Publishing, Inc.
111 River St.
Hoboken, NJ 07030-5774
www.wiley.com

WILEY

About the Author

A California native, **Paula Tevis** made many treks to San Francisco as a young girl before moving to her favorite city in 1983. After an eclectic but blessedly brief career that included stints in the computer and nonprofit sectors, she and her husband produced a couple of children in quick succession, and Paula happily relinquished the 9-to-5 world for the 24/7 one that parenting brings. Upon regaining consciousness, Paula recalled a childhood ambition and declared herself a writer. From her humble beginnings word-processing cookbook manuscripts for a local publisher, Paula metamorphosed into a freelance copy editor and soon received her first break as a professional writer with *Parenting* magazine, crafting a column on kids who cook. Over the years, she has contributed articles and essays to *Family Fun* magazine, the *San Francisco Chronicle,* Citysearch.com, *Frommer's Las Vegas, Frommer's New Orleans,* and *Variety.* She is the co-author of *California For Dummies* and author of the original *Frommer's San Francisco with Kids.*

Author's Acknowledgments

Thanks to my editor, Jennifer Anmuth, and to my dear cousins Irene Levin Dietz and Ina Levin Gyemant, who have added so much to my life in San Francisco for over 30 years. Eating in the city wouldn't be the same without Bev Chin or the guidance of Patricia Unterman; revisiting my favorite neighborhoods is an even greater pleasure with my cadre of friends, including Marjie Graham, Vicki Pate, Cynde Ahart Wood, Helene and Charles Wright, Andrea and Jeff Tobias, and Sarah Wilcox. Thanks also to Donna Joyner for her Wine Country insights. Living, no matter where, is pretty terrific and lots of fun with my husband, Mark Katz, and our very wonderful daughters, Madeleine and Lili.

Publisher's Acknowledgments

We're proud of this book; please send us your comments through our Dummies online registration form located at www.dummies.com/register/.

Some of the people who helped bring this book to market include the following:

Editorial

Editors: Jennifer Anmuth & Tim Ryan, Development Editors; Heather Wilcox, Production Editor

Copy Editor: Jennifer Connolly

Cartographer: Andrew Murphy

Senior Photo Editor: Richard Fox

Cover Photos:
Front: © J.A. Kraulis/Masterfile

Back: © James Lemass/Index Stock Imagery

Cartoons: Rich Tennant, www.the5thwave.com

Composition Services

Project Coordinator: Patrick Redmond

Layout and Graphics: Stephanie D. Jumper, Barbara Moore, Julie Trippetti

Proofreaders: David Faust, Jessica Kramer, Techbooks

Indexer: Techbooks

Publishing and Editorial for Consumer Dummies

Diane Graves Steele, Vice President and Publisher, Consumer Dummies

Joyce Pepple, Acquisitions Director, Consumer Dummies

Kristin A. Cocks, Product Development Director, Consumer Dummies

Michael Spring, Vice President and Publisher, Travel

Kelly Regan, Editorial Director, Travel

Publishing for Technology Dummies

Andy Cummings, Vice President and Publisher, Dummies Technology/ General User

Composition Services

Gerry Fahey, Vice President of Production Services

Debbie Stailey, Director of Composition Services

Contents at a Glance

Maps at a Glance

Table of Contents

Introduction

Many years ago, long before mandatory seatbelt laws, my mother would occasionally squeeze my sister Patience and me into her little red sports car and literally zoom up Highway 101 for a weekend in San Francisco. We lived 350 miles south, in Santa Barbara, but due to my mom's lead foot, we'd be cruising along the bay in no time, past a hill filled with rows of boxy pastel-colored houses, then onto the boulevard that led to our cousin Mildred's beautiful home. My desire to live in a big city (and drive really fast) no doubt developed during these trips, and many subsequent ones in my teens, but my ties to San Francisco actually extend back farther. My grandmother, Sarah, and her sister, Lottie, grew up here. At 18 and 20 years of age, they camped in Golden Gate Park after the 1906 earthquake, and in later years they lived in a series of houses in the Richmond District.

When I had the chance to move to San Francisco in 1982, I didn't think twice. My future husband and I first lived near Haight Street, then moved to a neighborhood near the Mission District and Bernal Heights. Eventually, I found myself working at one time or another around the Richmond District, Civic Center, Potrero Hill, and South of Market. I loved getting acquainted with different areas of the city, and in hindsight I realize my early, admittedly dilettantish, professional life helped prepare me for the greatest (and perhaps longest) job I've ever held — writing about San Francisco.

The San Francisco of my grandmother's day was elegant enough to attract the most famous people of its time yet still wild enough to garner an exciting reputation. The multicultural, expansive, and liberal city of today continues in that tradition, and even improves upon it. After more than 25 years of familiarity, I still continue to marvel at everything San Francisco has to offer, and I bet that after a day or two spent here, you'll do the same.

About This Book

San Francisco For Dummies, 4th Edition, is foremost a reference guide for people who intend to vacation in San Francisco and need basic, clear-cut information on how to plan and execute the best possible trip. If you like, you can begin reading from Chapter 1 and head straight through to the appendix. But if you turn directly to the restaurant chapter or to the pages on Wine Country because that's the piece that interests you at the moment, the book works just as well. I haven't included absolutely everything San Francisco has to offer in the way of attractions, hotels, restaurants, or diversions — a book that size would be too heavy to

---

Dummies Post-it® Flags

As you're reading this book, you'll find information that you'll want to reference as you plan or enjoy your trip — whether it be a new hotel, a must-see attraction, or a must-try walking tour. Mark these pages with the handy Post-it® Flags included in this book to help make your trip planning easier!

---

pack and probably too bothersome to read. What I've done is picked and chosen what I believe to be worth your time and your money while still offering enough variety to please a range of tastes, budgets, and family configurations.

Let me underscore that travel information is subject to change at any time — and in San Francisco this is especially true of restaurants as well as prices. Therefore, I suggest that you write or call ahead for confirmation when making your travel plans. The authors, editors, and publisher cannot be held responsible for the experiences of readers while traveling. Your safety is important to us, however, so we encourage you to stay alert and be aware of your surroundings. Keep a close eye on cameras, purses, and wallets, all favorite targets of thieves and pickpockets.

Conventions Used in This Book

So, San Francisco, here you come! You've picked a stunner of a destination, with a wide variety of wonderful sites to see, fabulous foods to sample, and interesting places to visit. But don't be overwhelmed. You've made a smart decision in buying *San Francisco For Dummies,* 4th Edition. This book walks you through all the nitty-gritty details to make sure that planning your trip goes smoothly and that the trip itself is memorable.

In this book, I include lists of hotels, restaurants, and attractions. As I describe each, I often include abbreviations for commonly accepted credit cards. Take a look at the following list for an explanation of each:

AE: American Express

CB: Carte Blanche

DC: Diners Club

DISC: Discover

JCB: Japan Credit Bank

MC: MasterCard

V: Visa

I've divided the hotels into two categories — my personal favorites and those that don't quite make my preferred list but still get my hearty seal of approval. Don't hesitate to consider these "runner-up" hotels if you're unable to get a room at one of my favorites or if your preferences differ from mine — the amenities that the runners-up offer and the services that each provides make all these accommodations good choices to consider as you determine where to rest your head at night.

I also include some general pricing information to help you as you decide where to unpack your bags or dine on the local cuisine. I use a system of dollar signs to show a range of costs for one night in a hotel or a meal at a restaurant (including appetizer, main course, dessert, one drink, tax, and tip). Check out the following table to decipher the dollar signs:

Cost	SF and Wine Country Hotels	SF and Wine Country Restaurants
$	$125 or less	$25 or less
$$	$126–$175	$26–$50
$$$	$176–$300	$51–$80
$$$$	$301 or more	$81 or more

Foolish Assumptions

As I wrote this book, I made some assumptions about you and what your needs may be as a traveler:

- You may be an inexperienced traveler looking for guidance on whether to take a trip to San Francisco and how to plan for it.

- You may be an experienced traveler, but you don't have a lot of time to devote to trip planning or you don't have a lot of time to spend in San Francisco. You want expert advice on how to maximize your time and enjoy a hassle-free trip.

- You're not looking for a book that discusses the history and architecture of the city, provides all the data available about San Francisco, or lists every hotel, restaurant, or attraction available to you. Instead, you're looking for a book that focuses on the places that will give you the best or uniquely San Francisco experiences.

If you fit any of these criteria, then _San Francisco For Dummies,_ 4th Edition, provides the information you're looking for!

How This Book Is Organized

Like all *For Dummies* guides, this book is organized in parts that contain anywhere from two to four chapters of related information. You don't need to start at the very beginning (though it's a good place to start); feel free to turn directly to the chapter that intrigues you the most.

Part 1: Introducing San Francisco

This part gives you an overview of San Francisco with particular attention to the lodging, dining, and touring highlights. Chapter 2 offers an overview of the city's history, and suggests some background material that will get you counting the days until your vacation begins. The calendar of events in Chapter 3 may influence your decision on when to arrive, and the text on San Francisco seasons may convince you to land when the rest of the tourists have gone home.

Part 11: Planning Your Trip to San Francisco

Because you're reading this, you probably aren't the type to just show up without an appointment — you intend to do a good bit of preplanning before your arrival. That's a good idea, and this part covers what you need to know about travel costs, with tips on how to budget and directions for getting to San Francisco, particularly if you plan to fly. Because this book is intended for a varied audience, I include specific advice for family travelers, the disabled, seniors, and gay and lesbian visitors. Then I help you decide whether to rent a car, why travel insurance may be a good idea, and how to stay in touch while you're away from home.

Part 111: Settling Into San Francisco

In an unfamiliar city, figuring out where you are can take days, but Part III saves you time by explaining how to get to town from the airport and how to get around the most important neighborhoods. A thorough discussion on local transportation options follows, including everything I know about parking — although luck and patience usually play a more important role than mere words. When it comes to figuring out where to sleep, I include a rundown of the major neighborhoods where visitors stay, offering tips on getting the most room for your money and brief but informative descriptions of my favorite hotels. A lengthy and tasty chapter on food will have you discussing the intricacies of the local food scene as if you spent all your weekends dining in these parts. And if you prefer to eat and run, you'll get a head start with a section on food to go — and I don't mean fast food.

Part 1V: Exploring San Francisco

You likely have an idea of what you want to see, and this part provides the information you need to conquer the most popular sites. Along with the big stuff, I've categorized other fun and intriguing options under lots of different interests and suggested some amusing guided tours. Many people come to the city specifically to exercise their charge cards, and my chapter on shopping will keep even the most avid consumer on his or her toes. My three- and five-day itineraries in Chapter 13 will help you focus and plan your days with all the precision you care to muster up. Got a case of wanderlust? Don't stay away long, but have a wonderful time investigating a few of the beautiful areas an hour or less from the city.

At the end of this part, I help you plan a day trip to Berkeley, an overnighter to the coast, and a getaway to Wine Country, including winery tours and a mud bath.

Part V: Living It Up after Dark: San Francisco Nightlife

As my husband says during his annual pilgrimage to JazzFest in New Orleans, "You can sleep when you're dead." But first, you need to figure out where to go after dinner, and that's what you'll discover in Part V. From opera to swing dancing to barhopping to cinema, you can always find something stimulating to do around town.

Part VI: The Part of Tens

This is where I get to lurch from the sublime (the best views) to the practical (what to do if it's raining; glorious San Francisco souvenirs under $10) and on to the ridiculous (how not to look like a tourist). But plenty of useful information is yours to be gleaned.

I also include an appendix — your Quick Concierge — containing lots of handy information you may need when traveling in San Francisco, such as phone numbers and addresses, emergency personnel or area hospitals and pharmacies, contact information for babysitters, lists of local newspapers and magazines, protocol for finding taxis, and more. Check out this appendix when searching for answers to lots of little questions that may come up as you travel.

Icons Used in This Book

These six icons appear in the margins throughout this book:

 This icon highlights money-saving tips and/or great deals.

 This icon highlights the best San Francisco has to offer in all categories — hotels, restaurants, activities, shopping, and nightlife.

 Find out useful advice on things to do and ways to schedule your time when you see the Tip icon.

Watch for the Heads Up icon to identify annoying or potentially dangerous situations, such as tourist traps, unsafe neighborhoods, budgetary
rip-offs, and other things to beware of.

 Look to the Kid Friendly icon for attractions, hotels, restaurants, and
activities that are particularly hospitable to children or people traveling
with kids.

 Part of the fun of traveling to a city other than your own is finding all the
things that you can't find anywhere else — especially when so much of
the landscape is dotted with the same old same old. This icon highlights
sights or activities that really help you get a feel for San Francisco and
why it's unique.

Where to Go from Here

Grab some sticky notes to mark the pages that you may want to refer to
later, clear your calendar, check the condition of your suitcase, and get
ready to hit the road.

Part I

Introducing
San Francisco

The 5th Wave

By Rich Tennant

In this part . . .

1 give you a taste of the Best of San Francisco, with a spotlight on the top restaurants, hotels, attractions, sights, and sounds that make up this unique city. I do my best to guide you to what is hot and new, as well as to the old standards. I tell you where to find the best San Francisco has to offer. I steer you to places both on and off the beaten path.

In the pages that follow, I also give you a brief history of San Francisco, as well as overviews of the architecture and cuisine, and finish up with a list of books and films you may enjoy as you get ready to leave your heart. . . .

Chapter 1

Discovering the Best of San Francisco

*W*ith a wink and a wave to the past, San Francisco continues to reinvent herself with all the insouciance of a pretty girl in a Mustang convertible. In her brief role as the heartbeat of the Internet economy, the city sashayed toward the 21st century with an energy and style that caused even the old-timers to gasp in admiration. Then, before there was time to dump all the stock options, the bubble burst, the old-timers scrambled to diversify their portfolios, and young commercial real-estate brokers and Web designers gave serious consideration to dental school. Fortunately, some things never change: The beautiful scenery continues to dazzle, the top-flight dining continues to garner raves, and the entertainment possibilities continue to grow in sophistication and imagination.

No matter how the economy fares, San Francisco consistently rates as one of the top tourist destinations in the world, and it's no secret why. The city's treasured cable cars provide both thrills and great views as they whiz down and around our hills; a majestically golden bridge suspends travelers over the deep blue of the bay; hidden staircases lead to lovely gardens and eye-catching homes. And where else can you savor freshly made miniature chocolate truffles, meander down the most crooked street in the world, and escape from Alcatraz — all in one action-packed day?

Summarizing San Francisco is not easy. When it comes to culture, we deliver everything from grand opera to leather-clad, fire-dancing performance artists. As for dining, we can down a burrito for lunch and polish off a multicourse designer meal for dinner — but critique both with equal passion. Our neighborhoods can more accurately be called

The Bay Area

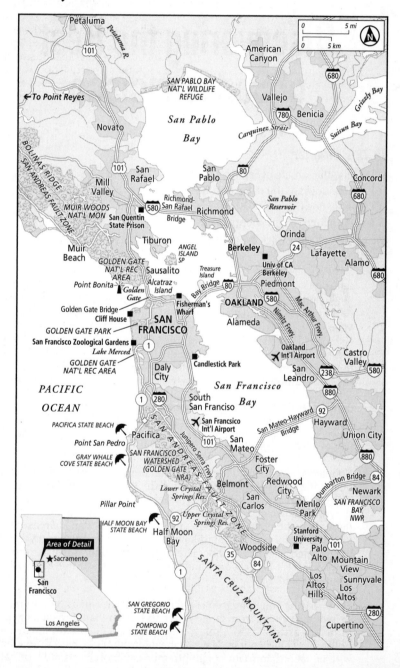

villages, each with its own retail corridor, park, and highly distinct personality. For in the face of rampant cultural homogeneity — the malling of America, so to speak — San Francisco is holding on tight to its individualism and enthusiastically applauds, or quietly salutes, those who do the same. What is consistent about the city, from the top of Telegraph Hill to the newly paved sidewalks of China Basin, is constant surprise. As you round a bend in the road, a lovely vista unexpectedly pops into your line of sight. As you savor a glass of chardonnay, a Chinese funeral cortege may suddenly glide past your cafe table, the band playing a pop classic. Or the smell of roasting coffee beans may waft down the street and completely erase any thought but where to find an espresso. Give your senses free rein to guide you through your days here, and you'll have a vacation like no other.

Because I consider the following to be the best San Francisco experiences, I've marked them with a Best of the Best icon when they appear in the rest of the book.

Best San Francisco Travel Experiences

Strolling along the Embarcadero to Aquatic Park: This is a quintessential San Francisco activity, ideally experienced on a sunny day. I love to begin near the baseball park, although exiting Muni at the **Embarcadero** (see Chapter 8) and starting there is more convenient. With the water on one side and city landmarks on the other, a leisurely walk past the piers, through **Fisherman's Wharf** (see Chapter 8), leads to **Aquatic Park** and the **Municipal Pier.** Be sure to hike all the way to the end of the pier, stopping to see what, if anything, the anglers have caught. You'll be rewarded with million-dollar bay vistas.

Shopping at the Ferry Plaza Farmers Market: Tuesday and Saturday mornings find home cooks and food lovers of all ages crowding the stalls in front and around back of the **Ferry Building** (see Chapter 12). You can sample stellar organic fruits, homemade conserves, and goat cheeses, or you can chow down on the freshest of morning pastries, bread, and heartier dishes from some of the city's well-known restaurants. This is a ritual for lots of local chefs who chat up their favorite vendors and bag the choicest morsels.

Rooting for the Giants at AT&T Park: You don't have to be a baseball fan to enjoy an afternoon or evening at this diamond of a ballpark (despite its ever-changing corporate name). Bleacher seats go on sale game days, but if you prefer something with more cachet, you can usually buy seats online from season-ticket holders (see Chapter 11). You'll find the best hot dogs around in the concession stands — load up on the sauerkraut and mustard and maybe scramble for a fly ball.

Biking in Golden Gate Park: Bike rentals are easily available along Stanyon Street and around Stow Lake (see Chapter 11). John F. Kennedy Drive, which is closed to automobile traffic on Sundays, will take you on a meandering route through this lovely slice of green. At the end of the road, head north toward Fulton Street to see the **Dutch Windmills.** In spring, the tulips here are in full, glorious bloom.

Sipping a cappuccino in North Beach: There's never a time when this isn't a great idea, but on a weekday when everyone else is at work, sitting with a newspaper and an Illy espresso defines contentment. You'll have your pick of cafes in North Beach, but I'm happy to recommend **Caffè Greco,** 423 Columbus Ave., between Vallejo and Green, which is bright and roomy and has a big selection of high-carb goodies.

The Best Hotels

Best All-Around Family Hotels: The playful and warm **Serrano Hotel,** 405 Taylor St. (☎ **866-289-6561** or 415-885-2500), can provide young families with complimentary cribs, strollers, and even booster seats; older children will be delighted to find games scattered around the public areas and goodies including mini Etch-a-Sketches in the minibar. The moderately priced **Hotel del Sol,** 3100 Webster St. (☎ **877-433-5765** or 415-921-5520), has goodies for the kids, plus a fab outdoor pool. The **Hotel Monaco,** 501 Geary St. (☎ **866-622-5284** or 415-292-0100), combines style with all the practicalities you want in an upscale hotel, such as an excellent restaurant, top-quality staff, and a spa. Although I'd never suggest that you abandon the children (for too long), you could have a massage downstairs while they hang out in the room watching a movie and enjoying room service.

Best Hotels for a Romantic Weekend: The outdoor soaking tubs at the **Hotel Vitale,** 8 Mission St. (☎ **888-890-8688** or 415-278-3700), seem to me a good place to start the fun. Then, reserve a deluxe Waterfront room and hang out the "do not disturb" sign. If you're out to impress, the spacious Bolero Penthouse suite in the **Hotel Adagio,** 550 Geary St. (☎ **800-228-8830** or 415-775-5000), includes a lovely outdoor terrace, and the hotel itself is lively.

Best View: You can be assured of a soothing view from the bay rooms at the lovely **Harbor Court Hotel,** 165 Steuart St. (☎ **866-792-6283** or 415-882-1300). Not all the rooms have great views at the **Argonaut Hotel,** 495 Jefferson St. (☎ **866-415-0704** or 415-563-0800), but request one with a window overlooking the bay for a real San Francisco treat.

Best Hotel Pool: Children under 16 aren't actually allowed in the pool at the **Huntington Hotel,** 1075 California St. (☎ **800-227-4683** or 415-474-5400), so you'll be the one to blame for splashing and making noise. If I had a category for Best Hotel Spa, the Huntington would get the nod there as well.

Best Hotel If You Have a Car: For stays around Union Square, the **Galleria Park Hotel,** 191 Sutter St. (☎ **800-792-9639** or 415-781-3060), sits over a parking garage, so the valet shouldn't take too long to retrieve your car. All the downtown hotels charge from $28 to $45 per day to park (plus tax); if you really can't live without the car, be sure to inquire about parking packages when you book your room. Parking is free at the **Cow Hollow Motor Inn & Suites,** 2190 Lombard St. (☎ **415-921-5800**), and Lombard Street takes you to the Golden Gate Bridge.

The Best Restaurants

The Best for a Romantic Meal: I like **Absinthe,** 398 Hayes St. (☎ **415-551-1590**), for the food and décor, and **Quince,** 1701 Octavia St. (☎ **415-775-8500**), which is so personable and sophisticated that eating there makes you quite fond of whomever you're with.

The Best with Kids: You can't go wrong with **Chow,** 215 Church St. (☎ **415-552-2469**), or **Park Chow,** 1240 Ninth Ave. (☎ **415-665-9912**), both of which have the same menu. The price is right; the food is non-threatening, recognizable, and tasty; and the casual atmosphere is relaxing.

The Best for a Splurge: This category is not an easy one, because there are lots of amazing kitchens to choose from, but I have no qualms about directing you to **Gary Danko,** 800 North Point St. (☎ **415-749-2060**). This place is inviting yet sophisticated, completely professional on every level, and the food is superb.

The Best Neighborhood Spots: In the Mission District, **Delfina,** 3621 18th St. (☎ **415-552-4055**), continues to please with a bright Tuscan Italian menu, while **Blue Plate,** 3218 Mission St. (☎ **415-282-6777**), feels like one of those secret finds that you want to visit again and again. Around Cow Hollow (or anywhere in the city, really), **Isa,** 3324 Steiner St. (☎ **415-567-9588**), is plainly a winner with absolutely delicious food and delightful service.

The Best for Views: Forget about the overpriced tourist traps around PIER 39 — anyway, you can't see much at night when it's dark. For the best views at bargain prices, try the **San Francisco Art Institute cafe,** 800 Chestnut St. (☎ **415-771-7020**). The scenery from **Green's,** Fort Mason, Building A, off Marina Boulevard at Buchanan Street (☎ **415-771-6222**), makes finding your way around this former military base worthwhile.

The Best Shopping

The Best for Generalists: Kids, men, brides, your mother — there's something for everyone who has excellent taste at **Dandelion,** 55 Potrero Ave. (☎ **415-436-9500**).

The Best for Books: This is more than a bookstore; **City Lights,** 261 Columbus Ave. (☎ **415-362-8193**), is representative of an era and a movement. Owner-poet Lawrence Ferlinghetti was one of the founders of the Beat movement. That it's also a terrific place to browse and buy is not completely incidental.

The Best for Kitchen and Table: You could choke on the number of shops pushing high-end knives and fancy cheese graters. A purist at heart, I remain extremely fond of **Forrest Jones,** 3274 Sacramento St. (☎ 415-567-2483), where you can find useful and pretty items at very fair prices.

The Best for People Who Consider Themselves Cool: Naturally, if you fall into this category, you won't advertise it (that wouldn't be cool now, would it?), but because even cool people have to shop, you'll find mostly everything you need for all occasions on **Haight Street** (best if you are shopping with your kids), or on even hipper **Hayes Street** (see Chapter 8).

The Best Bars and Clubs

The Best for *American Idol* Fans: They say the Hurricanes could be stronger, but you can't find better entertainment for the price of a cocktail at **The Mint Karaoke Lounge,** 1942 Market St. (☎ 415-626-4726). Given that it's in the Castro, you may want to take extra care with your appearance, especially if you're planning on taking the stage!

The Best for *Lost* Fans: The exotic décor at trendy **Bambuddha Lounge** at the Phoenix Hotel, 601 Eddy St. (☎ 415-885-5088), is matched by the sultry, sulky clientele stirring their apple martinis while awaiting small plates of Southeast Asian goodies. Word is the service is uppity, but no one will ask you to discuss your past.

The Best for *Apprentice* Fans: Should the Donald (or even the Martha) stride into town searching for attractive overachievers, he'd find at least a handful at the **Redwood Room** at the Clift Hotel, 495 Geary St. (☎ 415-775-4700).

The Best for Elvis Fans: The Southern cookin' is quite a yum — and a bargain to boot — and the vibe at blues venue **Biscuit and Blues,** 410 Mason St. (☎ 415-292-2583), is as sweet as a slice of pecan pie. Make reservations on the weekends and bring the kids if you have some — it's an all-ages club.

The Best for *Dancing with the Stars* Fans: Friday and Saturday nights at the **Top of the Mark** in the Mark Hopkins Hotel, 1 Nob Hill (☎ 415-616-6916), features the Black Market Jazz Orchestra for your dancing pleasure. Dress up and practice your dipping technique.

Chapter 2

Digging Deeper into San Francisco

*U*nlike most American cities that have evolved in a more measured fashion, San Francisco has been molded politically, socially, and physically by a variety of (literally) earth-shaking events. In this chapter, I give you a little rundown on the history of the City by the Bay along with some other useful background on local views and customs that give an insight into the city and its inhabitants.

History 101: The Main Events

As late (relatively speaking) as 1846, San Francisco was a sparsely populated town, described by the writer and California historian Robert Ernest Cowan as "the squalid little village." A mere two years later, this sleepy collection of shacks and saloons multiplied almost overnight into a thriving, lawless, still squalid, but much larger burg and nothing — not rampant corruption, numerous fires, or hordes of unsuccessful miners — could keep endless waves of people from arriving here by ship or other means to seek their fortunes.

But first a little background: The coastline of the Bay Area was navigated by Portuguese sailors as early as 1542, and although the area was an object of speculation among European explorers, it remained the unmolested province of the Ohlone Indian tribes until the late 18th century. San Francisco Bay itself wasn't discovered until 1769, when Sergeant Jose Francisco de Ortega, on a scouting mission for Gaspar de Portola, found the mouth of the port. Seven years later, a contingent of Spanish Catholics arrived, establishing a fort on the site of today's Presidio and one of many Franciscan missions, *Nuestra Sénora de Dolores*, a mile away in what is now the Mission District. The first service was held five days

San Francisco timeline, 1776–2006

1776 The first colonizing party, headed by Spaniard Captain Juan Bautista de Anza, arrives and establishes the Presidio of San Francisco and Mission Dolores, effectively founding San Francisco.

1835 The settlement of *Yerba Buena* develops around the port, now under the rule of Mexico.

1847 The United States annexes *Yerba Buena* and renames it San Francisco in honor of St. Francis of Assisi.

1847 James Marshall discovers gold at Sutter's Mill, near Sacramento; by the following year, San Francisco's population booms from around 800 to 26,000 residents.

1849 Isadore Boudin, an experienced French baker, introduces the ordinary sourdough yeast used by miners to a French-style loaf of bread and creates San Francisco sourdough bread.

1850 On September 9, California becomes the 31st state in the Union.

1868 The *Daily Morning Chronicle,* later the *San Francisco Chronicle,* begins publishing.

1869 The transcontinental railroad reaches San Francisco.

1873 Andrew Hallidie, inspired by an accident he witnesses when a team of horses slips on a rainy San Francisco hill, invents the cable car.

1887 George Hearst purchases a small daily newspaper, the *San Francisco Examiner,* to promote his race for the U.S. Senate. His son, William Randolph Hearst, turns it into a very successful tabloid.

1906 On April 18 at 5:13 a.m., a major earthquake rocks San Francisco and starts more than 50 fires, which burn uncontrollably for four days. Two-thirds of the city is destroyed, 250,000 people are left homeless, and more than 3,000 are dead or missing.

1915 The Panama-Pacific International Exposition celebrates the city's restoration and the completion of the Panama Canal.

1933 Alcatraz becomes a federal prison.

1936 The San Francisco–Oakland Bay Bridge opens on November 12. It remains one of the largest bridges in the world and carries over 270,000 vehicles each day — more traffic than any other toll bridge.

1937 The Golden Gate Bridge opens to pedestrian traffic on May 26 and to automobile traffic on May 27.

1945 The United Nations Charter is drafted in the War Memorial Veteran's Building in San Francisco's Civic Center and signed by the representatives of 50 countries in the Opera House.

1950	The Beat generation moves into the bars and cafes of North Beach.
1965	Jefferson Airplane opens at the Matrix on Fillmore.
1978	Supervisor Harvey Milk, America's first openly gay politician, and Mayor George Moscone are assassinated in City Hall by former supervisor Dan White.
1978	PIER 39 opens. One of San Francisco's most popular attractions, an estimated 10.5 million people visit it each year.
1989	On October 17 at 5:04 p.m., right before the start of Game 3 of the World Series between the Oakland A's and the San Francisco Giants, a 7.1-magnitude earthquake hits the Bay Area. Sixty-three people die, including one person at Candlestick Park from a heart attack.
1995	The new San Francisco Museum of Modern Arts opens.
1996	Former Assembly Speaker Willie Brown is elected mayor of San Francisco for the first of two terms.
2000	Pacific Bell Park (now SBC Park), the new home to the San Francisco Giants, opens.
2002	The San Francisco Giants make it to the World Series but lose to the Anaheim Angels in Game 7.
2004	Thirty-six-year-old supervisor Gavin Newsom becomes the city's 42nd mayor and quickly makes headlines by authorizing city hall to issue marriage licenses to same-sex couples. Six months later, the state supreme court invalidates 3,955 gay marriages.
2005	The new, seismically correct $202-million de Young museum opens in Golden Gate Park.
2006	San Francisco's Japantown neighborhood celebrates its 100th anniversary.

before the Declaration of Independence was signed in 1776. (Mission Dolores, the oldest building in the city and one of the few to survive earthquakes and fire, is Registered Landmark Number 1 of the City and County of San Francisco.) After this flurry of excitement, there wasn't much to report until Mexico severed ties with Spain in 1821 and became sovereign over California. American ships from Boston then began a vigorous trade with the settlement for otter and beaver skins, and later for goods such as *tallow* (rendered animal fat used for soap and candles). A slow migration into the area by hunters and trappers from the eastern seaboard, and the occasional AWOL sailors from merchant ships, helped increase the local population to around 250 people by 1833. In January 1847, now officially under American rule, *Yerba Buena* (Spanish for "good herb") was renamed San Francisco.

The discovery of gold in the American River near Sutter's Mill at the end of 1847 was the mighty force that propelled San Francisco into the big leagues. When word got out in the latter half of 1848, San Francisco's population of 812 quickly contracted as every able-bodied man and boy took off for the Sierra Nevada. However, by 1849, immigrants were arriving in San Francisco at the rate of 1,000 per week. The smart money stayed in the city and started businesses to take advantage of the newly rich and those hoping to join them — drinking establishments, gambling dens, and houses of prostitution most prominent among the enterprises. Naturally, crime and corruption were rife. By 1851, vigilante groups formed to do what police and politicians were bribed not to do, and with a few well-placed hangings, things slowly began to calm down.

By 1870, barely 23 years old, San Francisco was already the tenth largest city in the United States. In this time, it had survived a remarkable migration, a half-dozen fires, inflation, vice, graft, torrential rains, and an earthquake in 1865. The transcontinental railroad newly linked the East and West coasts, while the thousands of Chinese laborers who laid the rail were now the objects of vilification by underemployed whites who appeared to forget that they were immigrants, too.

Still, San Francisco thrived — not even Mother Nature it seems, could stop the momentum. Certainly, the great earthquake of April 18, 1906, was a momentous catastrophe; fires raged for four days and it is now believed that over 3,000 people (of a population of 400,000) died in collapsed and burning buildings or from related ills. Two-thirds of the city was destroyed, and thousands of newly homeless went to live in Golden Gate Park until housing could be constructed. But rebuilding began immediately, and in 1915, San Francisco reintroduced herself to the world by hosting the Panama-Pacific International Exposition.

The Gold Rush was responsible for the first mass influx of people into San Francisco, and World War II started the second, as workers from the south of the country flocked to the city's shipyards. Postwar prosperity combined with an anything-goes reputation attracted nonconformists, artists, writers, and freethinkers, paving the way for the Beats, and later the hippie movement, to influence an entire nation. The latter half of the 20th century found San Francisco grappling with the murders of its mayor, George Moscone, and the country's first openly gay politician, Supervisor Harvey Milk, in 1978. Dan White, a homophobic former city supervisor was convicted of manslaughter in the killings. California Senator Dianne Feinstein, at that time the president of San Francisco's Board of Supervisors, became mayor.

San Francisco's last big earthquake, an attention-getting 7.1 on the Richter scale, hit in the afternoon on October 17, 1989, as the Giants were preparing to play Game 3 of the World Series. In those days, before cellphones and wireless Internet, the city came to a halt. With buses and streetcars unable to operate, sections of the Bay Bridge damaged, and fires and collapsed buildings in the Marina neighborhood, the city felt strangely vulnerable. Miraculously, only 63 people died.

The 1990s will be remembered as the dot.com boom-and-bust years. San Francisco may not have been as obviously wild as it was during the aftermath of the Gold Rush, but it isn't a stretch to draw a few comparisons. Millionaires were created overnight in the frenzy to take rather specious companies public, while investors threw money at young entrepreneurs who turned out to have less-than-feasible business plans. Real-estate prices went mad, and even sensible people went looking for a technology start-up to join.

And then, it was over. The 21st century had barely introduced itself before the terrorist attacks of September 11, 2001, devastated the country. With the stock market on its downward spiral, and the economy reeling, a town that relies on tourism and business travel would no doubt feel the effects. Yet, entering the second half of the decade, San Francisco is not only in recovery mode, it has never looked better.

Taste of San Francisco: Local Cuisine

San Francisco's reputation as a food-lover's paradise is well deserved and tested on a daily basis. You can find thousands of restaurants around town, from dives to divas, all with their loyal followings and all under constant scrutiny by critics and self-proclaimed gourmands. Between the competition and the narrowed eyes of the food patrol, a restaurateur has to stay sharp, or at least hire a crackerjack public-relations firm, to make it through the first year in business. The constant buzz and change in the food scene can be a little nerve-racking to track, but it serves to make dining an event for locals and tourists alike. In the end, fortunately, it all comes down to ingredients. And where else but in San Francisco do you find the freshest, most beautiful, and even most politically correct fruits, veggies, fish, and organically raised meats? Well, Berkeley, maybe, but certainly nowhere else.

Background Check: Recommended Books and Movies

Getting acquainted with San Francisco through the work of authors and filmmakers will provide an extra dimension to your trip and perhaps some added excitement when you happen upon a location you recognize from a favorite cinematic moment or literary passage. San Francisco's own Chronicle Books publishes a great variety of material on the city, for children, cooks, art and architecture students, and readers of memoir and fiction. One of Chronicle's best books to stimulate your interest and curiosity is *San Francisco Stories: Great Writers on the City,* edited by John Miller. This collection of short pieces covers the personal and the political as recalled by acclaimed authors including Mark Twain, Jack Kerouac, Tom Wolfe, and Amy Tan. To find out about a smaller, more intimate city, check out *Good Life in Hard Times: San Francisco in the '20s and '30s,* by former journalist and San Francisco native Jerry Flamm (published by Chronicle Books).

One of the more famous and beloved pieces of modern fiction based in San Francisco is Armistead Maupin's *Tales of the City* (published by Perennial). If you've seen the miniseries, and especially if you haven't, this is a "must read" for a leisurely afternoon — or bring it with you on the plane. Maupin's 1970s soap opera covers the residents of 28 Barbary Lane (Macondry Lane on Russian Hill was the inspiration), melding sex, drugs, and growing self-awareness with enormous warmth and humor.

A work of fiction featuring San Francisco during the Gold Rush is *Daughter of Fortune,* by acclaimed novelist and Marin County resident Isabel Allende (published by HarperTorch). Allende's depiction of life in California during the mid–19th century is vividly described and is one of the novel's strengths.

As one of the loveliest spots on the planet, San Francisco has been a favorite of location scouts since the beginning of the film industry. Hundreds of movies and television shows have been shot or placed in San Francisco, making the hills and bridges among the most recognized of backgrounds. It may be difficult to locate at your local video store, but the 1936 Clark Gable/Jeanette MacDonald romance, *San Francisco,* is lauded for its dramatic reenactment of the 1906 earthquake and for MacDonald's rendition of the song of the same name. *The Maltese Falcon* (1941), Dashiell Hammett's classic detective story, with Humphrey Bogart starring as Sam Spade, includes shots of the Bay Bridge, the Ferry Building, and Burrit Alley (above the Stockton Tunnel). **John's Grill,** mentioned in the novel, continues to flog its association with Hammett's hero from its location at 63 Ellis St. (between Stockton and Powell streets).

Alfred Hitchcock's *Vertigo* (1958), starring James Stewart and Kim Novak, is admittedly an obvious choice on the list of great San Francisco films, but it's always worth viewing. Stewart plays a former detective hired to tail the wife of an old college friend, but the woman's identity is less than clear-cut. In the meantime, Stewart becomes obsessed with his prey as they make their way around the **Palace of the Legion of Honor, Fort Point, Mission Dolores,** and the detective's apartment at **900 Lombard St.** The city also fared well in the 1968 thriller *Bullitt,* starring a young Steve McQueen. Along with the hair-raising car chase over many hills, you'll see the Bay Bridge from a recognizable point on the **Embarcadero, Mason Street** heading north next to the **Fairmont Hotel,** the front of the **Mark Hopkins Hotel, Grace Cathedral,** and the fairly unchanged **Enrico's Sidewalk Café.**

For a change of pace and no tragic law-enforcement characters, screen the romantic comedy *What's Up Doc?* (1972) with Barbra Streisand and Ryan O'Neal. Along with being a very funny film, there's another car chase scene that includes **Lombard Street** and **Chinatown** and ends at **Alta Plaza Park** in **Pacific Heights.** If you have kids to rev up, the 1993 comedy *Mrs. Doubtfire,* starring Sally Field and the city's favorite son, Robin Williams, shows San Francisco under blue skies and cable cars with plenty of room. The house where the character's estranged wife and children live is located at **2640 Steiner St.** (at Broadway), in case you care to gawk. Finally, *24 Hours on Craigslist* (see Chapter 11) is a documentary that covers a day in the life of this Internet community bulletin-board phenom. The filmmaker posted an ad on Craigslist, followed up with a handful of volunteers — an Ethel Merman impersonator seeking a Led Zeppelin cover band; a couple looking for others to join a support group for diabetic cats; a single, older woman needing a sperm donor — and sent film crews to cover their stories. Unlike other films that show the physical splendors of San Francisco, *24 Hours on Craigslist* will give you a sense of the city's psyche, or at least offer an explanation of why non–San Franciscans think the place is populated with . . . uh . . . unusual types.

Chapter 3

Deciding When to Go

*Y*ou may not have much choice when it comes to scheduling your trip, especially if you have to plan around school vacations and holidays. But in case you do have some leeway, in this chapter I outline what's going on in San Francisco at different times of the year in terms of weather, crowds, and special events. We locals long for days of balmy temperatures and clear skies. I can only hope you find this kind of weather, but just in case, bring a warm jacket and maybe a hat no matter when you're visiting. And remember, a little fog never hurt anybody.

Revealing the Secret of the Seasons

Because of its temperate Northern California address, San Francisco beckons to tourists and business travelers year-round. However, San Francisco is most crowded between June and October. If you visit during this time of the year, I'd recommend that you make hotel and car reservations *at least* six weeks in advance, reserve a table at the more well-known restaurants three to four weeks in advance, and purchase your tickets to Alcatraz (see Chapter 11) shortly after you commit to this trip. Don't arrive in the city with just a suitcase, a camera around your neck, and a smile. You don't want to waste your time and energy searching for accommodations, or squabbling with your traveling companion because Slanted Door (see Chapter 10) couldn't seat you.

Something to remember about the San Francisco "summer" is that it may not be the summer you're expecting. Temperatures rarely top 70 degrees and are often quite cool. Bring a sweater and be prepared for morning fog — at any time of year.

The city is at its warmest and most glorious in September and October. In an average year, these months are also the busiest. It's when Fisherman's Wharf is packed to the gills, every cable car overflows with bodies, and there's not an available hotel room in sight. Unless something unusual is keeping the tourists home, don't even think about trying to get a discount on accommodations during this time.

School vacation schedules will probably dictate your travel dates if you're bringing the kids. Normally, the days start out with heavy fog in July and August but eventually clear up enough for you to lose the jacket or sweatshirt. Prepare for crowds, especially at the most popular tourist destinations. Fortunately, a little imaginative planning can help you entertain your children while avoiding some (though not all) of the masses. (See Chapter 11 for some offbeat sightseeing ideas.)

During the winter, the crowds do thin out considerably. (Those seeking a tan at this time of year should try Florida or maybe Singapore.) November through March, when the weather can be damp and chilly, is considered downtime for tourists in San Francisco. But if you don't mind sightseeing with an umbrella, or bundled up in a sweater and a hat, you can get a terrific deal at a nice hotel during these months. You may even be pleasantly surprised by blue skies and low 60s temperatures in the middle of February (and no fog!). In general, room rates are lower between November and mid-April, unless a big convention is in town (check with the **San Francisco Convention & Visitors Bureau** at ☎ **415-391-2000;** www.onlyinsanfrancisco.com). A few attractions even reduce their entrance fees at this time of year.

Wintertime can be a great time to see San Francisco, in spite of the weather, which will still be an improvement over much of the United States. A good number of the larger hotels offer packages, and some have special events for kids. The Ritz-Carlton hosts a Teddy Bear Tea throughout December, a popular affair that sells out early in the season. Along with sightseeing, you can admire the Christmas windows decorating Union Square, skate around the Embarcadero Center's outdoor ice rink, and take in one of many *Nutcracker* ballet or music performances.

In the following sections, I fill you in on the pros and cons of each season. For information on average temperatures and rainfall, take a look at Table 3-1.

Table 3-1		San Francisco's Average Temperatures and Rainfall										
	Jan	**Feb**	**Mar**	**Apr**	**May**	**June**	**July**	**Aug**	**Sep**	**Oct**	**Nov**	**Dec**
High (°F/°C)	56/13	59/15	60/16	61/16	63/17	64/18	64/18	65/18	69/21	68/20	63/17	57/14
Low (°F/°C)	46/8	48/9	49/9	49/9	51/11	53/12	53/12	54/12	56/13	55/13	52/11	47/8
Rain (in./cm)	4.5/11.5	2.8/7	2.6/6.5	1.5/4	0.4/1	0.2/0.5	0.1/0.3	0.1/0.3	0.2/0.5	1.1/3	2.5/6.5	3.5/9

Winter

You're unlikely to see snow unless you drive to Tahoe, but the weather won't exactly be balmy either. Still, a winter visit to San Francisco has its advantages, including the following:

- ✔ Hotel prices are lower, especially on weekends.
- ✔ Cable cars aren't jam-packed.
- ✔ Store windows are decorated for the holidays.
- ✔ The January sales linger into February.
- ✔ Restaurants won't be as busy.

But consider the following wintertime pitfall:

- ✔ The skies may be gray and/or rainy.

Spring

Spring is a popular time for travel, but in San Francisco, it's also a popular time for conventions. Here's are some of the advantages to expect if you're considering a springtime visit:

- ✔ Flowers are in bloom in the parks.
- ✔ The weather can be glorious.
- ✔ The major sites will be less crowded than in summer.

But there is a springtime drawback:

- ✔ Convention season starts, bringing hotel costs up and making it even harder to get reservations at the most popular eateries.

Summer

Many travelers are surprised at how cool and foggy San Francisco summers are. Here are some of the advantages to visiting in the summer months:

- ✔ Mimes are out in full force.
- ✔ Longer days make the evening tours of Alcatraz more attractive.
- ✔ The city sponsors free weekend concerts at Golden Gate Park and Stern Grove.
- ✔ The fruit and vegetable bounty available at the Ferry Building Farmer's Market is mouthwateringly spectacular.

But here are some negatives about visiting in the summertime:

- ✔ Mimes are out in full force.
- ✔ PIER 39 and Fisherman's Wharf are madhouses.
- ✔ Hotels are packed.
- ✔ Foggy mornings are downers.

Fall

If reliably warm, sunny days are a top priority for you, fall is the best time to visit. Here are some other advantages to planning your trip for the autumn months:

- ✔ It's the finest weather available all year on average.
- ✔ The cultural season begins.

But keep in mind the following drawbacks:

- ✔ Napa Valley is solidly booked on the weekends.
- U The heavy events calendar lures additional crowds.

Marking Your Calendar

I list San Francisco's most popular or unusual special events and festivals in the following sections. However, tons of other street fairs and happenings are scheduled during the year that I don't have room to mention. For more events, check out the *Bay Guardian* Web site (www. sfbg.com), the *San Francisco Chronicle* Web site (www.sfgate.com), or the Citysearch Web site (www.sanfrancisco.citysearch.com), or send $3 to the Convention and Visitors Bureau for its Festivals and Special Events calendar (see the appendix). Call the phone numbers included with each event for exact dates, locations, and ticket prices (if any).

You pay no entry charge for street fairs and holiday festivals, but bring along some cash for the crafts booths and food.

How do you keep a festival festive? Don't drive. Parking is always impossible, and you'll just get frustrated driving around in circles. Walk, take public transportation, or, if all else fails, take a cab — it's well worth the expense.

January/February

An important, well-attended, two-week event in San Francisco's Chinatown is **Chinese New Year** (☎ **415-391-9680;** www.chinese parade.com). Included in the event are lots of free entertainment, an exciting parade, and colorful sights. Dates vary.

March

A fair number of Irish expats live in San Francisco, making St. Patrick's Day a big excuse for a party. The **St. Patrick's Day Parade** (☎ 415-675-9885; www.sfstpatricksdayparade.com), along Market Street from Second Street to the Civic Center, features marching bands from around the bay and is one of San Francisco's largest. Sunday closest to March 17.

Indie music fans and the bands who love them converge for **Noise Pop** (☎ 415-358-6558; www.noisepop.com), a week of concerts held at all the coolest clubs around the end of the month. Past bands have included the White Stripes and Flaming Lips; the festival has grown to include film, alternative comedy, and even workshops on how to get your band noticed. For exact dates and how to score tickets keep abreast of the Web site.

April

The **San Francisco International Film Festival** (☎ 415-561-5000; www.sffs.org) is one of the oldest in the United States. It features more than 200 films and videos from over 30 countries, shown at the Castro Theatre on Castro Street, the Palace of Fine Arts in the Marina, and AMC Kabuki 8 Theatres at Fillmore and Post streets. Call for a schedule. April through early May.

Celebrate Japanese culture at the **Cherry Blossom Festival** (☎ 415-563-2313; www.nccbf.org) in San Francisco's Japantown. In this event, spanning two weekends, you'll find flower arranging, sumo wrestling, traditional drumming, and a parade that begins in Civic Center and ends in Japantown. Mid- to late April.

Men wear chaps outside the Castro for several reasons and these are revealed during the steer-wrestling, bull-riding, and bareback-riding competitions at the **Grand National Rodeo, Horse, and Stock Show** (☎ 415-404-4111; www.grandnationalrodeo.com) at the Cow Palace. The ten-day event also features horse shows and country-music concerts. Check the Web site for exact dates.

May

Whether you're commemorating Mexico's victory over the French in 1862 at the Battle of Puebla or just looking for some good food and music, you can find it at the **Cinco de Mayo Celebration** (☎ 415-206-0577; www.cincodemayosf.com and www.latinbayarea.com) in the Mission District around 23rd and Folsom streets. Festivities include Mexican and Central American music, crafts, and food. First Sunday in May.

If you like crowds and scantily dressed samba dancers, **Carnival** (☎ 415-920-0122; www.carnavalsf.com) in the Mission District (on Harison between 16th and 23rd streets) is a must-see. More than a half-million revelers turn out for this two-day celebration culminating in a Sunday morning parade. Memorial Day weekend.

June

The **Lesbian/Gay/Bisexual/Transgender Pride Celebration Parade** (☎ 415-864-FREE; www.sfpride.org), which runs from the Embarcadero to the two large plazas of the city's Civic Center, is a major happening. Held on Sunday morning, the parade is quite entertaining and often quite moving. Last weekend in June.

Enjoy three weekends of world dance and music performances in the **Ethnic Dance Festival** (☎ 415-474-3914; www.worldartswest.org), held at the Palace of Fine Arts Theater, next to the Exploratorium. Last three weekends of June.

Music and entertainment, food and drink, arts and crafts, yuppies — the **Union Street Arts Festival** (☎ 800-310-6563; www.unionstreet festival.com), on Union from Gough to Steiner streets, has it all. First weekend in June.

Go to the **North Beach Festival** (☎ 415-989-2220; www.sfnorthbeach. org), on Washington Square Park, Grant Avenue in North Beach, for the music, the arts and crafts, and the people-watching. Organizers claim that this festival is the oldest urban street fair in the country. Around the third weekend in June.

July

Fourth of July Waterfront Festival, Fisherman's Wharf (☎ 415-705-5500; www.pier39.com) is a daylong party at PIER 39, with live music and lots of activities, culminating in fireworks. July 4.

Yes, it's another street fair, but the **Fillmore Street Jazz Festival** (☎ 800-731-0003; www.fillmorejazzfestival.com), between Jackson and Eddy streets, has three stages with live music as well as everything you need to eat, drink, or display on your credenza. First weekend in July.

August

The **ACC Craft Show** (☎ 800-836-3470; www.craftcouncil.org) at Fort Mason Center is an exhibition and sale featuring juried crafts from some of the most gifted artists in the country. It's a treat for fans and a revelation to everyone else. Early August.

September

The **Autumn Moon Festival** (☎ 415-982-6306; www.moonfestival.org), on Grant Street between California and Pacific streets in Chinatown, features *moon cakes* (round pastries with embedded eggs), children's activities, and traditional dances. Dates vary.

Both national and local musicians perform on the Great Meadow at Fort Mason in the **San Francisco Blues Festival** (☎ 415-979-5588;

www.sfblues.com), the biggest outdoor blues event on the West Coast. Bring a blanket. Late September.

The adult-oriented arts-and-crafts **Folsom Street Fair** (☎ 415-861-3247; www.folsomstreetfair.com), on Folsom Street between 7th and 12th streets, attracts the black-leather and dog-collar crowd. Usually the last Sunday in September.

The **San Francisco Fringe Festival** (☎ 415-931-1094; www.sffringe. org) is a 12-day marathon of experimental theater and performance art held at the Exit Theater and various venues downtown. Starting the first weekend in September.

October

Comedy Celebration Day, Golden Gate Park (☎ 415-987-3663 or 415-665-8624; www.comedyday.com), offers four hours of free chuckles and guffaws in a comedy "concert" featuring nearly 30 of today's top performers. The event was founded 26 years ago by Bay Area comics to thank the audiences for nurturing their careers.

Hundreds of local artists invite the public into their studios every weekend throughout this month, as part of **Artspan/San Francisco Open Studios** (☎ 415-861-9838; www.sfopenstudios.com). Call for information, including how to obtain a studio map. Every weekend.

Community organizations and local merchants entertain a few hundred thousand people at the annual **Castro Street Fair** (☎ 415-841-1824; www.castrostreetfair.org), from Market to 19th streets between Noe and Collingwood streets in the Castro District. First Sunday in October.

Held in venues around the city, the eclectic two-week **San Francisco Jazz Festival** (☎ 800-850-7353 or 415-788-7353; www.sfjazz.org) sells out fast. Last week of October, beginning of November.

November

San Francisco International Automobile Show, Moscone Center (☎ 415-331-4406; www.sfautoshow.com), has cars, and lots of 'em, with all the newest models and special exhibits from American and international automakers. Admission is $8 for adults. Last week of November.

December

Starting after Thanksgiving and continuing through Christmas, the annual **Teddy Bear Tea** (☎ 415-773-6198) at the Ritz-Carlton fills up fast. Reservations open in August and are recommended, especially for weekends. Thanksgiving through Christmas.

Part II
Planning Your Trip to San Francisco

The 5th Wave   By Rich Tennant

In this part . . .

This part of the book covers the basics of trip planning. If you're an experienced traveler, you may skim the next four chapters for any pearls of brilliance that apply to you. If you're a travel novice, here you discover various options, including which airport to use. I thoroughly cover money — how much you need and what you're likely to spend it on. Then I move on to specific tips for families, seniors, disabled travelers, and gay or lesbian visitors to San Francisco. If you think you may need a car while you're in San Francisco, be sure to weigh the pros and cons on driving around the city in Chapter 7.

Chapter 4

Managing Your Money

- -

In This Chapter

▶ Figuring out the cost of things
▶ Knowing where to go for money
▶ Cutting your expenses down to size

- -

*V*acationing in San Francisco can be costly. Recent Convention and Visitors Bureau statistics show that the average daily per capita spending for all visitors, not including those who stay with relatives or friends, is a substantial $244.43. The major expenditure is for lodging, while food takes the next largest bite out of your pocketbook.

Money may or may not make the world go 'round, but nothing spoils a vacation faster than stressing over a higher-than-expected dinner tab or running out of dough altogether. This chapter covers everything from figuring the cost of your trip to the nitty-gritty of how to get your cash while you're in town.

Planning Your Budget

Creating a travel budget is easy, but sticking to it can be difficult, especially in a city that provides so many enticements to open your wallet. The Bay Area is not a cheap date. You'll likely spend the largest proportion of your funds on airfare (if you're flying) and lodging. You can spend as lavishly as you like on food, but you can also eat well inexpensively. I don't recommend that you rent a car (see Chapter 7 for my reasons), and that will save a bundle just on parking alone. Other expenses to consider include transportation around the city, snacks and beverages, attractions, shopping, entertainment, and incidentals such as telephone calls. After you figure your expenses, follow my general rule and add an extra 15 percent. (Unless you're unusually disciplined, you won't come in under budget.)

Transportation

Most people arriving in San Francisco do so by plane or car. If you're driving, be aware that gas prices in Northern California are among the highest in the country.

The cost of things to come

Knowing what to expect is always comforting, especially when it comes to counting the cost. Here are some average prices for goods and services in San Francisco:

- ✔ Lemonade: $1.95
- ✔ Latte in North Beach: $3
- ✔ An Anchor Steam beer at Johnny Foley's: $4.75
- ✔ Lunch for one at at the Cliff House Bistro (moderate): $20
- ✔ Lunch for one at Cafe Asia (inexpensive): $8.50
- ✔ Three-course dinner for one (excluding tax and tip) at The Blue Plate (moderate): $35
- ✔ Three-course dinner for one at Home (inexpensive): $23
- ✔ Super Shuttle from airport to hotel (excluding tip): $15
- ✔ Taxi from airport to city center (excluding tip): $30 to $45
- ✔ One-way Muni/bus fare to any destination within the city (adult): $1.50
- ✔ One-way Muni/bus fare anywhere within the city (senior/child 5–17): 50¢
- ✔ Movie ticket at the Metreon for an adult: $10
- ✔ Ticket to *Beach Blanket Babylon*: $33 to $77

Airline ticket prices depend on so many variables that I would be foolish to suggest what you'll pay to fly. See Chapter 5 for tips on how to get the best deal. Always contact low-cost carriers, such as **Southwest Airlines** or **JetBlue,** that don't show up on most travel Web sites. As of this writing, a round-trip flight in July from New York's JFK to Oakland on JetBlue was $430. Checking on Expedia.com, American had round-trip flights from JFK to San Francisco starting at $408. Of course, the more convenient flight times cost considerably more, and fuel surcharges may add to the cost.

Lodging

Chapter 9 discusses everything you need to know about hotels, but to summarize, prices depend on occupancy rates, and occupancy rates depend on variables such as the economy and the time of year. I've included a range of rooms to suit pocketbooks large and small, but keep in mind that bargains are relative. I've seen $79 rooms that would ruin some vacations. *Remember:* You get what you pay for.

Dining

Dining out is a big deal in the Bay Area. If your hometown is bereft of decent restaurants, budget for at least one splurge meal in San Francisco. Study Chapter 10 for ideas on where to eat well on the cheap.

Sightseeing

Many of San Francisco's enduring attractions are free — like the Golden Gate Bridge, the parks, the hidden staircases, and neighborhood walks — and others, such as the cable cars, are inexpensive. Part IV includes lots of ways to see the city without bruising your bank account.

Shopping

Souvenirs both annoy and inspire me. I fondly recall a small replica of the Eiffel Tower on a bookcase in my childhood home left by an older brother, but still I cluck disparagingly over the useless trinkets my family brings home from trips (and vice versa). My best suggestion is to give any kids in your party a sum of money to spend and gentle reminders that when it's gone, it's gone. Adults should pat themselves on the back for contributing to the local economy, which is much appreciated, I'm sure.

On the other hand, if you consider giving your credit card a workout a necessary part of vacation, you've come to the right place. Plenty of upscale chains and boutiques exist in San Francisco that you may not find back home. Chapter 12 discusses where to shop, no matter what your budget, and gives a few suggestions for finding low-cost gifts.

Nightlife

You can live large with seats for the ballet or nurse a beer in a Mission District music club for under ten bucks — it just depends on your predilections (and your budget). Chapters 15 and 16 cover some of the entertainment options and tell you where to find all the local listings.

Taxing your wallet

Along with the more obvious expenses, such as souvenir bridges and *Escape from Alcatraz* T-shirts, you have those little extras called taxes that add up. In our fair city, a sales tax of 8.5 percent is added to just about everything but snacks and take-out food. Additionally, a hotel tax of 14 percent is added to the cost of your room and an additional 14 percent is now added to the valet parking fees charged by hotels. The good news is that most of it goes to fund local arts organizations, which makes it a bit more palatable, I hope.

Cutting Costs — but Not the Fun

San Francisco can be expensive, but you can save money by following some of these tips:

✔ **Go off season.** You can save big-time on airfare and hotel costs if you travel during the off season — winter or early spring. Yes, it may be cold and/or wet, but you may also luck out. *Remember:* We're talking California — if global warming doesn't alter the weather patterns, maybe we'll have a drought.

✔ **Travel midweek.** If you can travel on a Tuesday, Wednesday, or Thursday, you may find cheaper flights to your destination. When you ask about airfares, see if you can get a cheaper rate by flying on a different day. For more tips on getting a good fare, see Chapter 5.

✔ **Always ask for discount rates.** Membership in AAA, frequent-flier plans, trade unions, AARP, or other groups may qualify you for savings on car rentals, plane tickets, hotel rooms, and even meals. Ask about everything; you may be pleasantly surprised.

✔ **Try a package tour.** For many destinations, including San Francisco, you can book airfare, hotel, ground transportation, and even some sightseeing just by making one call to a travel agent or packager — and for a lot less money than if you tried to put the trip together yourself. (See Chapter 5 for specific suggestions of companies to contact.)

✔ **Get out of town.** In many places, big savings are just a short drive or taxi ride away. Hotels just outside the city, across the bay, or less conveniently located can be great bargains. Outlying motels often have free parking, with lower rates than downtown hotels offering amenities that you may never use. Sure, at a motel you'll be carrying your own bags, but the rooms are often just as comfortable and a lot cheaper. See Chapter 9 for more on hotels.

✔ **Reserve a hotel room with a kitchenette and use it.** You may not feel like you're on vacation if you have to do your own cooking, but you can save a lot of money by not eating out three times a day. Even if you only make breakfast and an occasional lunch in your room, you'll still save. And you won't have to worry about any unexpected room-service bills.

✔ **Ask whether kids stay free.** A room with two double beds usually doesn't cost any more than a room with a queen-size bed. And many hotels won't charge you the additional-person rate if the additional person is pint-sized and related to you. Even if you have to pay $10 or $15 for a rollaway bed, you can save hundreds of dollars by taking one rather than two rooms.

✔ **Find out which days attractions offer free admission.** Take advantage of free museum days and other free admission days.

✔ **Skip the souvenirs.** Your photographs and memories should be the best mementos of your trip. Forgo the T-shirts, key chains, salt-and-pepper shakers, and other trinkets, and save a bundle.

✔ **Don't rent a gas guzzler.** If you decide you need a car, renting a smaller car is cheaper, and you save on gas to boot. Unless you're

Unearthing those hidden expenses

My credit-card bill never ceases to amaze me. I often wonder where half those charges came from and then reminisce fondly about the recent past as I dig through the statement. You may not want to be reminded of your vacation in such a potentially harsh manner — better to stick with photographs — but that means paying attention to expenses that are less obvious than shelter and sustenance. For example, remember that the cost of your hotel is more than the stated room rate. A hotel tax of 14 percent is added on, plus any minibar, telephone, bar, and room-service charges. Parking in San Francisco can bankrupt you. Remember, too, minor items such as film and developing; bridge tolls; San Francisco sweatshirts times the number of people in your family who forgot to pack a jacket; and tips for the bellmen, waiters, and tour bus drivers (they add up quickly). Do you have to kennel your dog? May as well include that on the list.

traveling with kids and need lots of space, don't go beyond the economy size. For more on car rentals, see Chapter 7.

✔ **Don't rent a car.** The city is easily navigable on foot or by public transit. You save as much as $50 a day on hotel parking by not having a car, too.

✔ **Ride public transportation, such as Muni or BART.** Purchase a Muni Passport and use it often (see Chapter 8).

✔ **Walk a lot.** A good pair of walking shoes can save lots of money in taxis and other local transport. As a bonus, you'll get to know your destination more intimately, as you explore at a slower pace.

✔ **Dine out at expensive restaurants for lunch instead of dinner.** Lunch tabs are usually a fraction of what a dinner costs at most top-notch restaurants, and the menu often boasts many of the same specialties.

✔ **Don't drink a lot of alcohol at meals.** A restaurant's wine and spirits list is a tidy profit center. Buying some wine or liquor and having a pre-dinner cocktail in your hotel room is a lot cheaper.

Handling Money

You're the best judge of how much cash you feel comfortable carrying or what alternative form of currency is your favorite. That's not going to change much on your vacation. True, you'll probably be moving around more and incurring more expenses than you generally do (unless you happen to eat out every meal when you're at home), and you may let your mind slip into vacation gear and not be as vigilant about your safety as when you're in work mode. But, those factors aside, the only type of payment that isn't as easy to use when you're away from home is your personal checkbook.

Using ATMs and carrying cash

The easiest and best way to get cash away from home is from an automated teller machine (ATM). The **Cirrus** (☎ 800-424-7787; www.master card.com) and **PLUS** (☎ 800-843-7587; www.visa.com) networks span the globe. Look at the back of your bank card to see which network you're on, and then call or check online for ATM locations at your destination. Be sure you know your personal identification number (PIN) and be sure to find out your daily withdrawal limit. Also keep in mind that many banks impose a fee every time your card is used at a different bank's ATM. On top of this, the bank from which you withdraw cash may charge its own fee. To compare banks' ATM fees in the United States, use www.bankrate.com.

Charging ahead with credit cards

Credit cards are a safe way to carry money. They also provide a convenient record of all your expenses, and you can withdraw cash advances from your credit cards at banks or ATMs as long as you know your PIN (although this is an expensive way to acquire what's essentially a loan). If you've forgotten yours, or didn't even know you had one, call the number on the back of your credit card and ask the bank to send it to you. It usually takes five to seven business days, though some banks will provide the number over the phone if you tell them your mother's maiden name or some other personal information.

Toting traveler's checks

These days, traveler's checks are less necessary because most cities have 24-hour ATMs that allow you to withdraw cash as needed. However, keep in mind that you'll likely be charged an ATM fee if the bank isn't your own. If you're withdrawing money every day, you may be better off with traveler's checks — as long as you don't mind showing identification every time you want to cash one.

You can get traveler's checks at almost any bank. **American Express** offers denominations of $20, $50, $100, $500, and (for cardholders only) $1,000. You'll pay a service charge ranging from 1 to 4 percent. You can also get American Express traveler's checks over the phone by calling ☎ 800-221-7282; American Express Gold and Platinum cardholders who use this number are exempt from the 1 percent fee.

Visa offers traveler's checks at Citibank locations nationwide, as well as at several other banks. The service charge ranges between 1.5 and 2 percent; checks come in denominations of $20, $50, $100, $500, and $1,000. Call ☎ 800-732-1322 for information. AAA members can obtain Visa checks without a fee at most AAA offices or by calling ☎ 866-339-3378. **MasterCard** also offers traveler's checks. Call ☎ 800-223-9920 for a location near you.

If you choose to carry traveler's checks, be sure to keep a record of their serial numbers separate from your checks, in case they're stolen or lost. You'll get a refund faster if you know the numbers.

Dealing with a Lost or Stolen Wallet

Although it's unlikely that you'll be the victim of a crime while on vacation, some talented pickpockets do roam the streets of San Francisco. And I can tell you from personal experience that discovering your wallet has magically disappeared, leaving you with only the change that's fallen to the bottom of your purse, is not amusing.

 If you carry a handbag, hold it in front of you, not dangling from your shoulder, and keep it zipped up. Never leave your pocketbook or backpack unattended. Carry your wallet in an inside pocket. Carry only as much cash as you need in a day and consider keeping your ATM card, credit cards, and driver's license in an inside pocket.

Be sure to contact all your credit-card companies the minute you discover your wallet has been lost or stolen and file a report at the nearest police precinct. Your credit-card company or insurer may require a police-report number or record of the loss. Most credit-card companies have a toll-free number to call if your card is lost or stolen; they may be able to wire you a cash advance or deliver a replacement card in a day or two. Call the following emergency numbers in the United States:

- ✔ **American Express:** ☎ **800-221-7282** (for cardholders and traveler's check holders)
- ✔ **MasterCard:** ☎ **800-307-7309** or 636-722-7111
- ✔ **Visa:** ☎ **800-847-2911** or 410-581-9994

For other credit cards, call the directory at ☎ **800-555-1212.**

If you need emergency cash when the banks and American Express offices are closed, you can have money wired to you via **Western Union** (☎ **800-325-6000;** www.westernunion.com).

Identity theft and fraud are potential complications of losing your wallet, especially if you've lost your driver's license along with your cash and credit cards. Notify the major credit-reporting bureaus immediately; placing a fraud alert on your records may protect you against liability for criminal activity. The three major U.S. credit-reporting agencies are **Equifax** (☎ **800-766-0008;** www.equifax.com), **Experian** (☎ **888-397-3742;** www.experian.com), and **TransUnion** (☎ **800-680-7289;** www.transunion.com). Finally, if you've lost all forms of photo ID, call your airline and explain the situation; it may allow you to board the plane if you have a copy of your passport or birth certificate and a copy of the police report you've filed.

Chapter 5

Getting to San Francisco

*T*he Internet has made it possible for anyone to play travel agent. You want to compare flight schedules and ticket prices? You want to take a virtual tour of a hotel? You want to purchase theater tickets online? It's getting easier by the day. Or would you rather let your local travel agent make the calls? If you do use a travel agent, make sure the agent has in-depth knowledge of the destination and isn't just reserving the hotel that will give him the largest commission. In-laws of mine (who shall remain nameless) let their travel agent recommend the hotel on their last trip to San Francisco, and it turned out to be a dump because the agent hadn't done her homework. The pitiful looks on their faces made me want to hit them over their heads — with *San Francisco For Dummies,* of course.

Flying to San Francisco

The most convenient airports to San Francisco are **San Francisco International** (SFO), which is 14 miles south of downtown, and **Oakland International Airport,** which is across the Bay Bridge off Interstate 880. SFO is closer, and more airlines fly into this major hub. Oakland is smaller and easier to get in and out of, but you'll pay about 10 percent more for cab fares and 50 percent more for shuttles.

You can sometimes get a lower fare or a more convenient flight flying into Oakland, so always compare prices and travel times for each airport. Oakland also generally enjoys better weather than San Francisco. Flights into SFO are frequently delayed due to foggy conditions, a fact worth remembering as you mull over just how much reading material to bring with you on the plane.

International travelers flying directly to the Bay Area don't have a choice of airports — it's SFO or nothing. But the spacious new International Terminal has lots of good dining and shopping choices, plus convenient connections to BART and car-rental desks.

Finding out which airlines fly to San Francisco

Airlines that fly into SFO include:

- ✔ **Air Canada** (☎ 888-247-2262; www.aircanada.ca)

- ✔ **Alaska Airlines** (☎ 800-252-7522; www.alaskaair.com)

- ✔ **American Airlines** (☎ 800-443-7300; www.aa.com)

- ✔ **America West Airlines** (☎ 800-235-9292 in the U.S. or Canada, 001-800-235-9292 in Mexico; www.americawest.com)

- ✔ **British Airways** (☎ 800-247-9297; www.british-airways.com)

- ✔ **Continental Airlines** (☎ 800-523-3273; www.continental.com)

- ✔ **Delta Air Lines** (☎ 800-221-1212 or 404-765-5000; www.delta.com)

- ✔ **Northwest Airlines** (☎ 800-225-2525; www.nwa.com)

- ✔ **United Air Lines** (☎ 800-864-8331; www.united.com)

- ✔ **US Airways** (☎ 800-288-2118; www.usairways.com)

- ✔ **Virgin Atlantic Airways** (☎ 800-821-5438; www.virgin-atlantic.com)

Airlines that fly into Oakland International Airport include many of the preceding, plus **JetBlue** (☎ 800-538-2583; www.jetblue.com) and **Southwest Airlines** (☎ 800-435-9792; www.southwest.com).

Getting the best deal on your airfare

Competition among the major U.S. airlines is unlike that of any other industry. Every airline offers virtually the same product (basically, a coach seat is a coach seat is a. . .), yet prices can vary by hundreds of dollars.

Business travelers who need the flexibility to buy their tickets at the last minute and change their itineraries at a moment's notice — and who want to get home before the weekend — pay (or at least their companies pay) the premium rate, known as the *full fare*. But if you can book your ticket far in advance, can stay over Saturday night, and are willing to travel midweek (Tues, Wed, or Thurs), you can qualify for the least expensive price — usually a fraction of the full fare. On most flights, even the shortest hops within the United States, the full fare is close to $1,000 or more, but a 7- or 14-day advance-purchase ticket may cost less than half of that amount. Obviously, planning ahead pays.

The airlines also periodically hold sales, in which they lower the prices on their most popular routes. These fares have advance-purchase requirements and date-of-travel restrictions, but you can't beat the prices. As you plan your vacation, keep your eyes open for these sales, which tend to take place in seasons of low travel volume — generally November through March. You almost never see a sale around the peak summer-vacation months of July and August, or around Thanksgiving or Christmas, when many people fly.

Consolidators, also known as *bucket shops,* are another source for tickets, although they usually can't beat the Internet on fares within North America. Start by looking in Sunday newspaper travel sections.

Bucket-shop tickets are usually nonrefundable or have stiff cancellation penalties, often as high as 50 to 75 percent of the ticket price, and some put you on charter airlines with questionable safety records.

Several reliable consolidators are available on the Internet. **STA Travel** (☎ 08701-630-026; www.statravel.com), the world's leader in student travel, offers good fares for travelers of all ages. **Flights.com** (☎ 312-332-0090; www.flights.com) also has "local" Web sites in 12 countries. **LowestFare** (☎ 800-678-0998; www.lowestfare.com) is owned by package-holiday megalith MyTravel and so has especially good access to fares for sunny destinations. **Air Tickets Direct** (☎ 888-858-8884; www.airtickets direct.com) is based in Montreal and leverages the currently weak Canadian dollar for low fares.

Booking your flight online

The "big three" online travel agencies, **Expedia** (www.expedia.com), **Travelocity** (www.travelocity.com), and **Orbitz** (www.orbitz.com) sell most of the air tickets bought on the Internet. (Canadian travelers should try www.expedia.ca and www.travelocity.ca; U.K. residents can go for expedia.co.uk and opodo.co.uk.) Each has different business deals with the airlines and may offer different fares on the same flights, so shopping around is wise. Expedia and Travelocity will also send you an e-mail notification when a cheap fare becomes available to your favorite destination. Of the smaller travel agency Web sites, **SideStep** (www.sidestep.com) receives good reviews from users. It's a browser add-on that purports to "search 140 sites at once," but in reality only beats competitors' fares as often as other sites do.

Great last-minute deals are available through free weekly e-mail services provided by the airlines. Most of these deals are announced on Tuesday or Wednesday and must be purchased online. Most are only valid for travel that weekend, but some (such as Southwest's) can be booked weeks or months in advance. Sign up for weekly e-mail alerts at airline Web sites or check mega-sites that compile lists of last-minute specials, such as **Smarter Travel** (www.smartertravel.com). For last-minute trips, www.site59.com in the United States and www.lastminute.com in Europe often have better deals than the major-label sites.

If you're willing to give up some control over your flight details, use an opaque-fare service like **Priceline** (www.priceline.com) or **Hotwire** (www.hotwire.com). Both offer rock-bottom prices in exchange for travel on a "mystery airline" at a mysterious time of day, often with a mysterious change of planes en route. The mystery airlines are all major, well-known carriers — and the possibility of being sent from Philadelphia to Chicago via Tampa is remote. But your chances of getting a 6 a.m. or 11 p.m. flight are pretty high. Hotwire tells you flight prices before you buy; Priceline usually has better deals than Hotwire, but you have to play their "name our price" game. *Note:* In 2004 Priceline added non-opaque service to its roster. You now have the option to pick exact flights, times, and airlines from a list of offers — or bid on opaque fares as before.

Driving to San Francisco

You can get to San Francisco by driving along three major highways. **Interstate 5** runs through the center of the state. If you drive this route, you'll intersect **Interstate 80,** which goes over the Bay Bridge into the city. Getting to San Francisco from Los Angeles along Interstate 5 takes about six hours. The other major route you can take is **Highway 101,** which heads up from Los Angeles through San Francisco (about seven hours) to Marin County, Napa/Sonoma, and other points north. **Highway 1** is the more scenic coastal route that takes you closer to Monterey and Santa Cruz. It's really lovely, but the trip up from Los Angeles will take a lot longer — approximately eight to ten hours.

Arriving by Other Means

Amtrak (☎ **800-872-7245** or 800-USA-RAIL; www.amtrak.com) doesn't stop in San Francisco proper, but it does stop in Emeryville, a small town just south of Berkeley. Passengers then ride an Amtrak bus (which departs shortly after each train arrives) from Emeryville to the Ferry Building or the Caltrain station in downtown San Francisco. (The Ferry Building is more convenient to the hotels recommended in this book.)

Traveling by train may seem romantic, but don't assume it's cheaper than flying. At this writing, the lowest round-trip train fare from Los Angeles to San Francisco is $94, which is still more expensive than a 14-day advance-purchase ticket from one of the airlines serving the Los Angeles–San Francisco corridor. The trip from Chicago takes two days and costs from $135 one way. But consider taking the train for the experience of chugging across the country, if you have the time, or if you're like my mother-in-law, who flunked a workshop on getting over one's fear of flying. (She skipped the graduation flight.)

Joining an Escorted Tour

You may be one of the many people who love escorted tours. The tour company takes care of all the details and tells you what to expect at each leg of your journey. You know your costs up front and, in the case of the tame ones, you don't get many surprises. Escorted tours can take you to the maximum number of sights in the minimum amount of time with the least amount of hassle.

If you decide to go with an escorted tour, I strongly recommend purchasing travel insurance, especially if the tour operator asks to you pay up front. But don't buy insurance from the tour operator! If the tour operator doesn't fulfill its obligation to provide you with the vacation you paid for, there's no reason to think that it'll fulfill its insurance obligations either. Get travel insurance through an independent agency. (I tell you more about the ins and outs of travel insurance in Chapter 7.)

When choosing an escorted tour, along with finding out whether you have to put down a deposit and when final payment is due, ask a few simple questions before you buy:

✔ **What is the cancellation policy?** Can they cancel the trip if they don't get enough people? How late can you cancel if you're unable to go? Do you get a refund if you cancel? If they cancel?

✔ **How jam-packed is the schedule?** Does the tour schedule try to fit 25 hours into a 24-hour day, or does it give you ample time to relax by the pool or shop? If getting up at 7 a.m. every day and not returning to your hotel until 6 or 7 p.m. at night sounds like a grind, certain escorted tours may not be for you.

✔ **How large is the group?** The smaller the group, the less time you spend waiting for people to get on and off the bus. Tour operators may be evasive about this, because they may not know the exact size of the group until everybody has made reservations, but they should be able to give you a rough estimate.

✔ **Is there a minimum group size?** Some tours have a minimum group size and may cancel the tour if they don't book enough people. If a quota exists, find out what it is and how close they are to reaching it. Again, tour operators may be evasive in their answers, but the information may help you select a tour that's sure to happen.

✔ **What exactly is included?** Don't assume anything. You may have to pay to get yourself to and from the airport. A box lunch may be included in an excursion, but drinks may be extra. Beer may be included but not wine. How much flexibility do you have? Can you opt out of certain activities, or does the bus leave once a day, with no exceptions? Are all your meals planned in advance? Can you choose your entree at dinner, or does everybody get the same chicken cutlet?

Depending on your recreational passions, I recommend one of the following tour companies: **Globus** (☎ 866-755-8581; www.globusjourneys.com) or **Freedom Tours** (☎ 212-202-5130; www.freedom-tour.com). Escorted tours almost always encompass more than one city and, in the case of these operators, take in California highlights.

Choosing a Package Tour

For lots of destinations, package tours can be a smart way to go. In many cases, a package tour that includes airfare, hotel, and transportation to and from the airport costs less than the hotel alone on a tour you book yourself. That's because packages are sold in bulk to tour operators, who resell them to the public. It's kind of like buying your vacation at a buy-in-bulk store — except the tour operator is the one who buys the 1,000-count box of garbage bags and resells them 10 at a time at a cost that undercuts the local supermarket.

Package tours can vary as much as those garbage bags, too. Some offer a better class of hotels than others; others provide the same hotels for lower prices. Some book flights on scheduled airlines; others sell charters. In some packages, your choice of accommodations and travel days may be limited. Some let you choose between escorted vacations and independent vacations; others allow you to add on just a few excursions or escorted day trips (also at discounted prices) without booking an entirely escorted tour.

To find package tours, check out the travel section of your local Sunday newspaper or the ads in the back of national travel magazines such as *Travel + Leisure, National Geographic Traveler,* and *Condé Nast Traveler.* **Liberty Travel** (call ☎ 888-271-1584 to find the store nearest you; www.libertytravel.com) is one of the biggest packagers in the Northeast, and usually boasts a full-page ad in Sunday papers.

Another good source of package deals is the airlines themselves. Most major airlines — including **American Airlines Vacations** (☎ 800-321-2121; www.aav7.aavacations.com), **Delta Vacations** (☎ 800-654-6559; www.deltavacations.com), **Continental Airlines Vacations** (☎ 800-301-3800; www.covacations.com), and **United Vacations** (☎ 888-854-3899; www.unitedvacations.com) — offer air/land packages. Several big **online travel agencies** — Expedia, Travelocity, Orbitz, Site59, and Lastminute.com — also do a brisk business in packages. If you're unsure about the pedigree of a smaller packager, check with the Better Business Bureau in the city where the company is based, or go online to www.bbb.org. If a packager won't tell you where it's based, don't fly with that packager.

American Airlines, in particular, tends to have good packages to San Francisco, because it's one of the airline's hubs. British travelers should check into **Travel Bag** (☎ 0870-607-0620; www.travelbag.co.uk).

The biggest hotel chains also offer packages. If you already know where you want to stay, call the hotel itself and ask if it offers land/air packages.

Chapter 6

Catering to Special Travel Needs or Interests

In This Chapter

▶ Getting ready for a trip with the kids, San Francisco–style
▶ Going for high adventure for the disabled or senior traveler
▶ Checking out the scene for gay and lesbian travelers

*A*h, don't you long for the good old days when you could grab a backpack, throw in a pair of jeans, and venture out into the world? Now there's the family to consider, with Junior needing to run around and drain his batteries every few hours, your teenage daughter determined to track down the perfect pair of jeans, and your spouse needing a break and maybe a beer. Or perhaps you have a physical limitation that makes traveling a challenge. Or maybe you want to take advantage of your status as an elder statesperson. Read on, friend! I like nothing better than to dispense advice.

San Francisco, already celebrated as a haven for gay and lesbian visitors, pretty much holds hajjlike status under the leadership of Mayor Gavin Newsome. If you're gay or lesbian, the resources I list in this chapter will help you find areas of the city and entertainment venues that will be of special interest to you.

Focusing on the Family

Babes in backpacks and strollers are a common sight on the streets of San Francisco, so you can be assured that munchkins are welcome here. But taking a vacation with your kids can sometimes mean *you're* not exactly on vacation, at least in my experience. Here are some tried-and-true ways to make your trip as relaxed and enjoyable as possible.

Looking at the trip from a kid's point of view

Before you board the plane or pack up the car, sit down with your family and this book and go over the sights and activities listed in Chapter 11. Let your kids choose three to six things to see and do (based on the number of days you plan to stay in San Francisco), and then have them rate their choices in order of preference. You do the same for the places you want to visit. Next, fill a calendar with the days or times you plan to do a kid activity and the times you plan to do something more adult-oriented, such as enjoying the Museum of Modern Art or joining a walking tour (see Chapter 11). Remember to block out time for eating, snacking, resting, and dropping by neighborhood parks.

Family trips are supposed to be fun, but kids turn cranky when exhaustion sets in (doesn't everybody?), so don't pull them in a hundred different directions. Neither you nor they need to see everything in one day. A long afternoon in Golden Gate Park watching the squirrels may be more memorable than dashing from Coit Tower to Alcatraz. Bring along books, paper, crayons and pencils, perhaps an inexpensive camera, a Walkman, or any other unobtrusive, portable toys and games your children can easily carry in their backpacks. Give kids their own copy of the itinerary that your family worked out together to remind them that their time will come.

Finding kid-friendly sleeps, eats, and entertainment

Most hotels are more than happy to accommodate your entire clan. Chapter 9 offers tips for figuring out what kind of accommodations are right for you and yours.

Chapter 11 describes various places to go and things to do with young kids as well as teenagers. But if you'd still like more direction, consider the itinerary in Chapter 13 or look for the Frommer's guide *San Francisco with Kids* (published by Wiley Publishing). And don't forget to look out for the Kid Friendly icon to point you toward hotels, restaurants, and attractions that may especially appeal to the children. You'll have no trouble planning the perfect trip for tots, teens, and in-betweens.

Locating a baby sitter

You and your spouse or a friend may want to go out on the town without the little, or not-so-little, ones in tow. Many hotels (particularly the pricey ones) recommend baby-sitting services for their guests, although, for liability reasons, you'll have to make the arrangements. Rates vary, as do add-ons, such as transportation and agency fees, but you can expect to pay from $16 to $25 per hour with a four-hour minimum. Town and Country Resources (☎ 800-457-8222; www.tandcr.com) and Bay Area 2nd Mom (☎ 888-926-3666; www.2ndmom.com) are two good companies used by many of the downtown hotels. Call at least a day or two in advance.

You can find good family-oriented vacation advice on the Internet from sites like the **Family Travel Forum** (www.familytravelforum.com), a comprehensive site that offers customized trip planning; **Family Travel Network** (www.familytravelnetwork.com), an award-winning site that offers travel features, deals, and tips; **Traveling Internationally with**

Your Kids (www.travelwithyourkids.com), a comprehensive site that offers customized trip planning; and **Family Travel Files** (www.the familytravelfiles.com), which offers an online magazine and a directory of off-the-beaten-path tours and tour operators for families.

Seeing San Francisco as a Senior

Mention the fact that you're a senior citizen when you make your travel reservations. Although all the major U.S. airlines except America West have cancelled their senior discount and coupon-book programs, many hotels still offer discounts for seniors. In most cities, people over the age of 62 qualify for reduced admission to theaters, museums, and other attractions, as well as discounted fares on public transportation.

Members of **AARP** (formerly known as the American Association of Retired Persons), 601 E St. NW, Washington, DC 20049 (☎ **888-687-2277** or 202-434-2277; www.aarp.org), get discounts on hotels, airfares, and car rentals. AARP offers members a wide range of benefits, including *AARP: The Magazine* and a monthly newsletter. Anyone over 50 can join.

Another reason to celebrate reaching, or passing, 55 years is **Elderhostel** (☎ **877-426-8056;** www.elderhostel.org). This organization provides amazing travel/learning opportunities all over the world that may encompass a weekend of art lectures and museum viewings or multiple weeks on safari with the grandkids. Prices are reasonable and include hotels, excursions, and most meals. San Francisco–based programs include a six-day wine and food extravaganza with day trips to the Napa Valley. **ElderTreks** (☎ **800-741-7956;** www.eldertreks.com) offers small-group tours to off-the-beaten-path or adventure-travel locations, restricted to travelers 50 and older. **INTRAV** (☎ **800-456-8100;** www.intrav.com) is a high-end tour operator that caters to the mature, discerning traveler, not specifically seniors, with trips around the world that include guided safaris, polar expeditions, private-jet adventures, and small-boat cruises down jungle rivers.

Recommended publications offering travel resources and discounts for seniors include: the quarterly magazine *Travel 50 & Beyond* (www.travel50andbeyond.com); *Travel Unlimited: Uncommon Adventures for the Mature Traveler* (Avalon); and *101 Tips for Mature Travelers,* available from Grand Circle Travel (☎ **800-221-2610** or 617-350-7500).

Seniors 65 and older get automatic discounts on public transportation fares in San Francisco. Just present identification showing your age for reduced admission at movies, museums, and many other attractions. Many tour companies also offer a discount for those over 62.

Accessing San Francisco: Advice for Travelers with Disabilities

Traveling is a challenge when you're physically disabled, but don't let that stop you from seeing the world. More resources are out there than ever before. An especially helpful guide is *A World of Options,* a 658-page book detailing options for travelers with disabilities. For $45 you can find out about adventures from biking trips to scuba outfitters. Order it from Mobility International USA, P.O. Box 10767, Eugene, OR 97440 (☎ **541-343-1284,** voice and TTY; www.miusa.org). For more personal assistance, call the **Travel Information Service** at ☎ **215-456-9603** or 215-456-9602 (for TTY).

The U.S. National Park Service offers a **Golden Access Passport** that gives free lifetime entrance to all properties administered by the National Park Service (NPS) — national parks, monuments, historic sites, recreation areas, and national wildlife refuges — for persons who are visually impaired or permanently disabled, regardless of age. You may pick up a Golden Access Passport at any NPS entrance fee area by showing proof of medically determined disability and eligibility for receiving benefits under federal law. Besides free entry, the Golden Access Passport also offers a 50 percent discount on federal-use fees charged for such facilities as camping, swimming, parking, boat launching, and tours. For more information, go to www.nps.gov/fees_passes.htm or call ☎ **888-467-2757.**

Many travel agencies offer customized tours and itineraries for travelers with disabilities. **Flying Wheels Travel** (☎ **507-451-5005;** www.flyingwheelstravel.com) offers escorted tours and cruises that emphasize sports and private tours in minivans with lifts. **Access-Able Travel Source** (☎ **303-232-2979;** www.access-able.com) offers extensive access information and advice for traveling around the world with disabilities. **Accessible Journeys** (☎ **800-846-4537** or 610-521-0339; www.accessiblejourneys.com) is an organization that provides travel planning resources and information for wheelchair travelers and their families and friends.

Avis Rent A Car has an "Avis Access" program that offers such services as a dedicated 24-hour toll-free number (☎ **888-879-4273**) for customers with special travel needs; car features such as swivel seats, spinner knobs, and hand controls; and accessible bus service.

Organizations that offer assistance to disabled travelers include **MossRehab** (www.mossresourcenet.org), which provides a library of accessible-travel resources online; **Society for Accessible Travel and Hospitality** (SATH; ☎ **212-447-7284;** www.sath.org; annual membership fees: $45 adults, $30 seniors and students), which offers a wealth of travel resources for all types of disabilities and informed recommendations on destinations, access guides, travel agents, tour operators, vehicle rentals, and companion services; and the **American Foundation for** the Blind (AFB; ☎ 800-232-5463; www.afb.org), a referral resource for the blind or visually impaired that includes information on traveling with Seeing Eye dogs.

For more information specifically targeted to travelers with disabilities, the community Web site **iCan** (www.icanonline.net/channels/travel/index.cfm) has destination guides and several regular columns on accessible travel. Also check out the quarterly magazine *Emerging Horizons* ($14.95 per year, $19.95 outside the United States; www.emerginghorizons.com); **Twin Peaks Press** (☎ 360-694-2462; http://disabilitybookshop.virtualave.net/blist84.htm), offering travel-related books for travelers with special needs; and *Open World Magazine,* published by SATH (subscription: $13 per year, $21 outside the United States).

The Bay Area–based Center for Independent Living publishes a 25-page booklet called *San Francisco Access,* covering hotels, transportation options, and other information helpful to disabled travelers. You can obtain a copy for free by contacting the San Francisco Convention & Visitors Bureau (☎ 415-391-2000; www.onlyinsanfrancisco.com). The organization also has a fine Web site, www.accessnca.com, with detailed information on traveling all around Northern California.

Touring on wheels

If you're a wheelchair user, you'll find San Francisco's public areas quite accessible. All sidewalks have curb cuts, and ramps for easy on/off access have been erected throughout the municipal railway system (Muni). You can find some buses equipped with wheelchair lifts as well. For information on public transportation accessibility, request a free copy of the **Muni Access Guide** from Muni's Accessible Services Program by phoning ☎ 415-923-6142 or writing the program at 949 Presidio Ave., San Francisco, CA 94115. If you need a ramped taxi, phone **Yellow Cab** at ☎ 415-626-2345 — there's no extra charge.

Many of the major car-rental companies now offer hand-controlled cars for drivers with disabilities. Avis can provide such a vehicle at any of its locations in the United States with 48-hour advance notice; Hertz requires notice between 24 and 72 hours in advance at most of its locations. **Wheelchair Getaways** (☎ 800-642-2042; www.wheelchairgetaways.com) rents specialized vans with wheelchair lifts and other features for travelers with disabilities in more than 100 cities across the United States.

Staying accessible

The Americans with Disabilities Act requires hotels built within the past 17 years to be much more handicapped-friendly. However, lodgings that are housed in old buildings may have entry stairs, tiny elevators, narrow hallways, and minuscule bathrooms, making them unsuitable for anyone having to maneuver in a wheelchair.

You can enjoy the **Tuscan Inn** near Fisherman's Wharf or **The Orchard Hotel** near Union Square (see Chapter 9), which are somewhat newer properties that are fully accessible. Also, look for the chain hotels, such as the **Embarcadero Hyatt Regency** (see Chapter 9), that are equipped to provide certain services such as TTY phones.

 When making reservations, advise the reservation clerk at your hotel of your needs — be it TTY phones or grip bars — to make your stay more comfortable.

All newly built or restored restaurants are also up to date when it comes to meeting requirements for accessible bathrooms and entrances. If you have any doubts about access, ask when you call for a table.

Getting to the sights

You won't have any problem accessing the main attractions in San Francisco. **Golden Gate Park** is completely accommodating, as are the museums, the **Exploratorium,** and many other sites. Some areas are not very accessible, though (for example, places that have a series of stairs, such as the **Filbert Street Steps**). **Fort Point** has a wheelchair ramp, and its first floor is easily maneuverable; a walk or roll above **Fort Funston** is also accessible for travelers with disabilities.

Anyone who would prefer to admire the hills without actually trekking over them will appreciate the easy, flat walks that shun both stairs and vertical climbs detailed by **"On the Level San Francisco Excursions."** The company publishes 20-page color booklets of self-guided walking tours in various neighborhoods and parks, with historical highlights and helpful hints on parking and obstacles. Each booklet is $3.95 and can be purchased online at www.onthelevelsf.com. Guided walks are also available for $18 per person. Call ☎ 415-921-1382 or check the Web site for information on locations and schedules.

Traveling Tips for Gay and Lesbian Visitors

San Francisco remains an important and historic destination for gay travelers. You'll find the majority of gay bars and inns in the **Castro District,** the heart of San Francisco's gay community. The lesbian community resides mostly in portions of **Noe Valley** and the **Mission District** (with Valencia Street as the main drag).

Check out these great Web sites for your trip planning: **Gay.com** (www.gay.com) and **Citysearch** (www.sanfrancisco.citysearch.com), which has a complete section devoted to gay and lesbian nightlife and an interesting history of the Castro. Also take a look at the handy print guide *Betty and Pansy's Severe Queer Review of San Francisco.* You can order this book through **A Different Light** bookstore, 489 Castro St., San Francisco, CA 94114 (☎ 415-431-0891; www.adlbooks.com). When you get to the city, pick up a copy of the *Bay Area Reporter* for comprehensive entertainment listings. It's free and available in coffee-houses, in bookstores, and around the Castro.

For information on specific hotels that cater to gay visitors, check out *Frommer's San Francisco* (Wiley Publishing). But there aren't any compelling reasons to plunk yourself down in such a hotel unless you don't intend to leave the Castro. And if that's the case, you'll be missing out on the alternative gay scene **South of Market** (see Chapter 16).

The International Gay and Lesbian Travel Association (IGLTA; ☎ 800-448-8550 or 954-776-2626; www.iglta.org) is the trade association for the gay and lesbian travel industry and offers an online directory of gay- and lesbian-friendly travel businesses; go to its Web site and click on "Members."

Many agencies offer tours and travel itineraries specifically for gay and lesbian travelers. **Above and Beyond Tours (☎ 800-397-2681** or 760-325-0702; www.abovebeyondtours.com) is the exclusive gay and lesbian tour operator for United Airlines. **Now, Voyager (☎ 800-255-6951** or 415-626-1169; www.nowvoyager.com) is a well-known San Francisco–based gay-owned and -operated travel service.

The following travel guides are available at many newsstands, most travel bookstores, and gay and lesbian bookstores: *Out and About* (**☎ 415-834-6500;** www.outandabout.com), which offers guidebooks and a newsletter ($20 per year; ten issues) packed with solid information on the global gay and lesbian scene; *Spartacus International Gay Guide* (Bruno Gmünder Verlag; www.spartacusworld.com/gayguide) and *Odysseus,* both good, annual English-language guidebooks focused on gay men; the *Damron* guides (**☎ 800-462-6654** or 415-255-0404; www.damron.com), with separate, annual books for gay men and lesbians; and *Gay Travel A to Z: The World of Gay & Lesbian Travel Options at Your Fingertips* by Marianne Ferrari (Ferrari International; Box 35575, Phoenix, AZ 85069), a very good gay and lesbian guidebook series.

Chapter 7

Taking Care of the Remaining Details

In This Chapter

▶ Buying travel insurance — or not

▶ Dealing with illness away from home

▶ Deciding whether to drive

*I*n case you need something to worry about, this chapter covers 21st-century issues such as whether or not you need travel insurance, what to do if you fall ill, and how to deal with all those people staring at your shoes in the airport security lines. I also flog my opinion about driving in San Francisco — but whether you decide to get behind the wheel or eschew driving in the city, you don't want to miss my parking tips.

Renting a Car (Or Six Reasons Why You Shouldn't!)

If lots of traffic, steep hills, no parking spaces, one-way streets, crazy bike messengers, and the occasional threat of a tow are your idea of fun, then get yourself a car. If you'd rather not deal with those sorts of hassles (and did I mention overly enthusiastic parking enforcement agents?), plenty of taxis are available to cart you all over the city.

San Francisco doesn't have one of those enviable public-transportation systems found in other cities; a bus can take you just about anywhere, slowly, but San Francisco's municipal railway system (Muni Metro) is fairly limited. The Muni streetcars can get you close to where you want to go, but often you'll still need to catch a bus or cab or walk to get to many places. However, because San Francisco neighborhoods are small and distinct, and because you'll find beautiful or bizarre happenings around every corner, walking around is delightful.

Day-tripping: The one reason you should rent a car

If you plan on any out-of-city excursions, like wine tasting (if you don't like escorted tours, that is), you may want to rent a car. To avoid parking fees, wait until the day of your trip to pick up your auto. Most companies, including **Enterprise Rent-A-Car** (☎ **800-261-7331;** www.enterprise. com) can pick you up and drop you off at your hotel.

If you must rent: Getting the best rate

As much as airline fares vary, car-rental rates vary even more. How much you pay is determined by the car size, how long you keep it, where you drive it, and tons of other factors.

One tip that could save you some cold, hard cash is to ask a few key questions, including the following:

- ✔ **Are weekend rates lower than weekday rates?** For example, ask whether picking up the car Friday morning is cheaper than picking it up Thursday night.

- ✔ **Can I get the weekly rate if I'm keeping the car five or more days?**

- ✔ **Will I be charged a fee for not returning the car to the same renting location?** Some companies assess a drop-off charge in this instance; others, such as National, do not.

- ✔ **Is it cheaper to pick up the car at the airport or at a location in town?** Remember to include garage charges if you must park at your hotel.

- ✔ **Are any specials running right now?** If you see an advertised price in your local newspaper, be sure to ask for that specific rate; otherwise, you may be charged the standard rate.

 When making your rental reservations, don't forget to mention membership in AAA, AARP, frequent-flier programs, and trade unions. These usually entitle you to discounts ranging from 5 to 30 percent. Ask your travel agent to check any and all of these rates. And check to see whether your rental earns you points on your frequent-flier account — most rentals are worth at least 500 miles.

Comparing rates on the Web

As with other aspects of planning your trip, using the Internet can make comparison-shopping for a car rental much easier. All the major booking sites — **Travelocity** (www.travelocity.com), **Expedia** (www.expedia. com), **Yahoo! Travel** (www.travel.yahoo.com), and **Cheap Tickets** (www.cheaptickets.com), for example — have search engines that can dig up discounted car-rental rates. Just enter the size of the car you want, the pickup and return dates, and the city where you want to rent, and the server returns a price. You can even make the reservation through these sites.

Taking care of insurance, gas, and other charges

In addition to the rental prices, other optional charges can raise the cost of your car rentals. For example, if you choose to add the Collision Damage Waiver (CDW), you may pay an added fee of as much as $10 per day! Many credit-card companies already offer this insurance option when you charge the car rental to that credit card, so call your credit-card company to inquire about this before you leave home.

Another optional charge is additional *liability insurance* (which covers you if you're in an accident where others are injured), *personal accident insurance* (if you or your passengers are injured), and *personal effects insurance* (if someone steals your luggage from your car). The insurance on your car at home probably covers you for most of these. If your own insurance doesn't cover you for rentals, or if you don't have auto insurance, consider getting the additional coverage. Car-rental companies are liable for certain amounts, varying from state to state.

As for putting gas in your car, you have the option of paying for a full tank of gas up front. In this package, the gas price is average compared with local prices, but you don't get reimbursed for gas you leave in the tank after your trip. Your other option is to pay only for the gas you use, but you have to return the car with a full tank of gas or the company will charge you $3 to $4 a gallon for the deficiency. If you don't want to bother filling up the tank at the last minute, then go with the package deal. If you know you won't be rushed, then don't bother.

Playing It Safe with Travel and Medical Insurance

Three kinds of travel insurance are available: trip-cancellation insurance, medical insurance, and lost-luggage insurance. The cost of travel insurance varies widely, depending on the cost and length of your trip, your age and health, and the type of trip you're taking, but expect to pay between 5 and 8 percent of the vacation itself. In the following sections, I offer my advice on all three.

For more information, contact one of the following recommended insurers: **Access America** (☎ 866-807-3982; www.accessamerica.com); **Travel Guard International** (☎ 800-826-4919; www.travelguard.com); **Travel Insured International** (☎ 800-243-3174; www.travelinsured.com); and **Travelex Insurance Services** (☎ 888-457-4602; www.travelex-insurance.com).

Trip-cancellation insurance

Trip-cancellation insurance helps you get your money back if you have to back out of a trip, if you have to go home early, or if your travel supplier goes bankrupt. Allowed reasons for cancellation can range from sickness to natural disasters to the State Department declaring your destination unsafe for travel. (Insurers usually won't cover vague fears, though, as many travelers who tried to cancel their trips in Oct 2001 because they were wary of flying discovered.)

A good resource is **"Travel Guard Alerts,"** a list of companies considered high-risk by Travel Insured International (www.travelinsured. com). Protect yourself further by paying for the insurance with a credit card — by law, consumers can get their money back on goods and services not received if they report the loss within 60 days after the charge is listed on their credit-card statement.

Medical insurance

For domestic travel, buying medical insurance doesn't make sense for most travelers. Most existing health policies cover you if you get sick away from home — but check before you go, particularly if you're insured by an HMO.

Lost-luggage insurance

Lost-luggage insurance is not necessary for most travelers. On domestic flights, checked baggage is covered up to $2,500 per ticketed passenger. If you plan to check items more valuable than the standard liability, see if your valuables are covered by your homeowner's policy, get baggage insurance as part of your travel-insurance package, or buy Travel Guard's "BagTrak" product. Don't buy insurance at the airport — it's usually overpriced. Be sure to take any valuables or irreplaceable items with you in your carry-on luggage, because many valuables (including books, money, and electronics) aren't covered by airline policies.

If your luggage is lost, immediately file a lost-luggage claim at the airport, detailing the luggage contents. For most airlines, you must report delayed, damaged, or lost baggage within four hours of arrival. The airlines are required to deliver luggage, once found, directly to your house or destination free of charge.

Staying Healthy When You Travel

Getting sick will ruin your vacation, so I *strongly* advise against it (of course, last time I checked, the bugs weren't listening to me any more than they probably listen to you).

For domestic trips, most reliable health-care plans provide coverage if you get sick away from home. Talk to your doctor before leaving on a trip if you have a serious and/or chronic illness. For conditions such as epilepsy, diabetes, and heart problems, wear a **MedicAlert identification tag** (☎ 888-633-4298; www.medicalert.org), which immediately alerts doctors to your condition and gives them access to your records through MedicAlert's 24-hour hot line. The United States **Centers for**

Avoiding "economy-class syndrome"

Deep vein thrombosis, or as it's known in the world of flying, "economy-class syndrome," is a blood clot that develops in a deep vein. It's a potentially deadly condition that can be caused by sitting in cramped conditions — such as an airplane cabin — for too long. During a flight (especially a long-haul flight), get up, walk around, and stretch your legs every 60 to 90 minutes. Other preventative measures include frequent flexing of the legs while sitting, drinking lots of water, and avoiding alcohol and sleeping pills. If you have a history of deep vein thrombosis, heart disease, or another condition that puts you at high risk, some experts recommend wearing compression stockings or taking anticoagulants when you fly; always ask your physician about the best course for you. Symptoms of deep vein thrombosis include leg pain or swelling, or even shortness of breath.

Disease Control and Prevention (☎ **800-311-3435;** www.cdc.gov) provides up-to-date information on health hazards by region or country and offers tips on food safety.

Staying Connected by Cellphone or E-Mail

These days, even if you're across the country, you can still be in instant contact with the folks back home via your cellphone, personal digital assistant (PDA), or laptop computer.

Using a cellphone across the United States

Just because your cellphone works at home doesn't mean it'll work elsewhere in the country (thanks to the United States' fragmented cellphone system). It's a good bet that your phone will work in major cities. But take a look at your wireless company's coverage map on its Web site before heading out — T-Mobile, Sprint, and Nextel are particularly weak in rural areas. If you need to stay in touch at a destination where you know your phone won't work, rent a phone that does from **InTouch USA** (☎ **800-872-7626;** www.intouchglobal.com) or a rental-car location, but beware that you'll pay $1 a minute or more for airtime.

If you're not from the United States, you'll be appalled at the poor reach of our **GSM wireless network,** which is used by much of the rest of the world. Your phone will probably work in most major U.S. cities; it definitely won't work in many rural areas. And you may or may not be able to send SMS (text messaging) home. (International budget travelers like to send text messages home because doing so is much cheaper than making international calls.) Assume nothing — call your wireless provider and get the full scoop. In a worst-case scenario, you can always rent a phone; InTouch USA delivers to hotels.

Accessing the Internet away from home

Travelers have any number of ways to check their e-mail and access the Internet on the road. Of course, using your own laptop — or even a personal digital assistant (PDA) or electronic organizer with a modem — gives you the most flexibility. But even if you don't have a computer, you can still access your e-mail and even your office computer from cybercafes.

Finding a city that *doesn't* have a few cybercafes is difficult nowadays. Although no definitive directory for cybercafes exists — these are independent businesses, after all — two places to start looking are at **The Cybercafe Search Engine** (www.cybercaptive.com) and **Cybercafes.com** (www.cybercafe.com).

Aside from cybercafes, most **youth hostels** nowadays have at least one computer you can use to get on the Internet. And most **public libraries** offer Internet access free or for a small charge. Avoid **hotel business centers** unless you're willing to pay exorbitant rates.

Most major airports now have **Internet kiosks** scattered throughout. These kiosks, which you'll also see in malls, hotel lobbies, and tourist information offices, give you basic Web access for a per-minute fee that's usually higher than cybercafe prices. The kiosks' clunkiness and high prices mean they should be avoided whenever possible.

To retrieve your e-mail, ask your **Internet service provider (ISP)** if it has a Web-based interface tied to your existing e-mail account. If your ISP doesn't have such an interface, you can use the free **mail2web** service (www.mail2web.com) to view and reply to your home e-mail. For more flexibility, you may want to open a free, Web-based e-mail account with **Yahoo! Mail** (http://mail.yahoo.com). (Microsoft's Hotmail is another popular option, but Hotmail has severe spam problems.) Your home ISP may be able to forward your e-mail to the Web-based account automatically.

If you need to access files on your office computer, look into a service called **GoToMyPC** (www.gotomypc.com). The service provides a Web-based interface for you to access and manipulate a distant PC from anywhere — even a cybercafe — provided your "target" PC is on and has an always-on connection to the Internet (such as with Road Runner cable). The service offers top-quality security, but if you're worried about hackers, use your own laptop rather than a cybercafe computer to access the GoToMyPC system.

If you're bringing your own computer, the buzzword in computer access to familiarize yourself with is Wi-Fi (wireless fidelity), and more and more hotels, cafes, and retailers offer wireless *hotspots* from where you can get high-speed connection without cable wires, networking hardware, or a phone line. You can get Wi-Fi connection one of several ways. Many laptops sold in the last year have built-in Wi-Fi capability (an

802.11b wireless Ethernet connection). Mac owners have their own networking technology, Apple AirPort. For those with older computers, an 802.11b/**Wi-Fi card** (around $50) can be plugged into your laptop. You sign up for wireless access service much as you do cellphone service, through a plan offered by one of several companies that have made wireless service available in airports, hotel lobbies, and coffee shops. **T-Mobile Hotspot** (www.t-mobile.com/hotspot) serves up wireless connections at more than 1,000 Starbucks coffee shops nationwide. **Boingo** (www.boingo.com) and **Wayport** (www.wayport.com) have set up networks in airports and high-class hotel lobbies. iPass providers also give you access to a few hundred wireless hotel lobby setups. Best of all, you don't need to be staying at the Four Seasons to use the hotel's network; just set yourself up on a nice couch in the lobby. The companies' pricing policies can be Byzantine, with a variety of monthly, per-connection, and per-minute plans, but in general you pay around $30 a month for limited access — and as more and more companies jump on the wireless bandwagon, prices are likely to get even more competitive.

Several places provide **free wireless networks** in cities around the world. To locate these free hotspots, go to www.personaltelco.net/index.cgi/WirelessCommunities.

If Wi-Fi is not available at your destination, most business-class hotels offer dataports for laptop modems, and many hotels now offer free high-speed Internet access using an Ethernet network cable. You can bring your own cables, but most hotels rent them for around $10. Call your hotel in advance to see what your options are.

In addition, major Internet service providers (ISPs) have local access numbers, allowing you to go online with a local call. Check your ISP's Web site or call its toll-free number and ask how you can use your current account away from home, and how much it will cost. If you're traveling outside the reach of your ISP, the **iPass** network has dial-up numbers in most countries. You'll have to sign up with an iPass provider, who will then tell you how to set up your computer for your destination(s). For a list of iPass providers, go to www.ipass.com and click on "Individual Purchase." One solid provider is **i2roam** (☎ 866-811-6209 or 920-235-0475; www.i2roam.com).

Wherever you go, bring a connection kit of the right power and phone adapters, a spare phone cord, and a spare Ethernet network cable, or find out whether your hotel supplies them to guests.

Keeping Up with Airline Security Measures

With the federalization of airport security, security procedures at U.S. airports are more stable and consistent than ever. Generally, you'll be fine if you arrive at the airport one hour before a domestic flight and two hours before an international flight; if you show up late, tell an airline employee and she'll probably whisk you to the front of the line.

Bring a **current, government-issued photo ID** such as a driver's license or passport. Keep your ID ready to show at check-in, the security checkpoint, and sometimes even the gate. (Children under 18 do not need government-issued photo IDs for domestic flights, but they do for international flights to most countries.)

In 2003, the Transportation Security Administration (TSA) phased out gate check-in at all U.S. airports. And E-tickets have made paper tickets nearly obsolete. Passengers with E-tickets can beat the ticket-counter lines by using airport electronic kiosks or even online check-in from home. Online check-in involves logging on to your airline's Web site, accessing your reservation, and printing out your boarding pass — which may even get you bonus miles! If you're using a kiosk at the airport, bring the credit card you used to book the ticket or your frequent-flier card. Print out your boarding pass from the kiosk and proceed to the security checkpoint with your pass and a photo ID. If you're checking bags or want an exit-row seat, you'll be able to do so using most kiosks. Even the smaller airlines are employing the kiosk system, but always call your airline to make sure these alternatives are available. Curbside check-in is also a good way to avoid lines, although a few airlines still ban curbside check-in; call before you go.

Security checkpoint lines are getting shorter than they were, but some doozies remain. If you have trouble standing for long periods of time, tell an airline employee; the airline will provide a wheelchair. Speed up security by not wearing metal objects such as big belt buckles. If you have metallic body parts, a note from your doctor can prevent a long chat with the security screeners. Keep in mind that only ticketed passengers are allowed past security, except for folks escorting disabled passengers or children.

Federalization has stabilized what you can carry on and what you can't. The general rule is that sharp things are out, nail clippers are okay, and food and beverages must be passed through the X-ray machine — but security screeners can't make you drink from your coffee cup. Bring food in your carry-on luggage rather than checking it, because explosive-detection machines have been known to mistake food (especially chocolate, for some reason) for bombs. Travelers in the United States are allowed one carry-on bag plus a *personal item* such as a purse, briefcase, or laptop bag. Carry-on hoarders can stuff all sorts of things into a laptop bag; as long as it has a laptop in it, it's still considered a personal item. The TSA has issued a list of restricted items; check its Web site (www. tsa.gov/public/index.jsp) for details.

Airport screeners may decide that your checked luggage needs to be searched by hand. You can now purchase luggage locks that allow screeners to open and relock a checked bag. Look for Travel Sentry certified locks at luggage or travel shops and Brookstone stores (www.brookstone.com). These locks, approved by the TSA, can be opened by luggage inspectors with a special code or key. For more information on the locks, visit www.travelsentry.org. If you use something other than TSA-approved locks, your lock will be cut off if a TSA agent needs to hand-search your luggage.

Part III

Settling Into San Francisco

By Rich Tennant

SAN FRANCISCO'S AMAZING CABLE CARS

Travelers can ride from Market Street to the Financial District, through the Rocky Mountains and on to Denver, all for the price of one Muni Passport.

In this part . . .

*B*ack in his student days, my husband was the kind of traveler who would blithely arrive in some distant destination without any notion of where he would eat or sleep, expecting that these things would somehow manage themselves. I, however, have always preferred the security of knowing a pillow, an airplane, or a theater seat has my name on it — so go ahead and guess which one of us does the travel planning.

The hard truth, especially for people like my spouse who aren't, shall we say, detail-oriented, is that you have a better trip when you solidify your plans prior to setting foot on the airplane or the gas pedal. (Spontaneity is also a virtue, but usually after your suitcase is unpacked and you have a vague idea of where you are.) This part takes you from the airport to the city, introduces you to the neighborhoods, and explains how to use San Francisco's public-transportation system. If you're driving, you can flip directly to the tips for upping your parking karma quotient — you need it around San Francisco! I also prod you to think about what you require in accommodations so you can make a good match with a hotel or motel. This part is where you can get some recommendations on where to go for a great meal at any time of the day.

Chapter 8

Arriving and Getting Oriented

* *

In This Chapter

▶ Figuring out how to get where you want to go
▶ Exploring the neighborhoods
▶ Gathering information

* *

*Y*ou can't really glean much about a place from its airports and highways. But as you head toward San Francisco, the industrial sites
and parking lots you pass gradually become the neighborhoods and
landmarks you may have seen in films and photographs or heard about
from fellow travelers. Even those of us who know the city as well as we
know our best friends can't help but let out a sigh of delight when the
Golden Gate Bridge or the downtown skyline comes into view. Welcome
to San Francisco!

The Ins, but Especially the Outs, of Bay Area Airports

San Francisco International Airport (SFO) consists of four main terminals: North (Terminal 3), South (Terminal 1), Central (Terminal 2), and
International. The baggage level of each terminal also houses information booths. Bank of America operates a branch on the mezzanine level
of the North terminal, and you can find ATMs on the upper level of all
terminals. International visitors will find Travelex currency exchange
offices throughout the International terminal.

You can call the airport (☎ **650-821-8211**) for recorded information, or
try ☎ 650-817-1717 for transit information. The information desk in each
of the terminals can also give you information on how to reach your destination. Or go to the SFO Web site at www.flysfo.com for more about
the airport and ground transportation.

To reach your destination by taxi or shuttle, here are the specifics:

✔ Taxis line up for passengers at the center island outside the lower level of the airport. The 14-mile trip to Union Square takes 20 to 30 minutes or so, depending on traffic, and should cost around $33 to $40 plus tip.

✔ If you're patient enough to wait 10 to 20 minutes for the one heading to your neighborhood, shuttle vans offer door-to-door service from the airport. However, the shuttle may make up to three stops before it's your turn to exit. You can find the shuttles by leaving the airport from the upper level and heading to the center island outside the ticket counter nearest you. A guide will direct you. Look for exact shuttle fares posted throughout the terminals; most charge around $15. **Super Shuttle** (☎ 415-558-8500; www.supershuttle.com) is my personal favorite. You don't need to make advance reservations.

✔ **Bay Area Rapid Transit,** known as BART, now connects travelers from the airport to San Francisco, the East Bay, and the Millbrae Caltrain Station, a few miles south of the airport. BART fares into San Francisco are $5.15. At Millbrae, you can board Caltrain and ride to the depot at Fourth and King streets in San Francisco. The fare is a bargain at $3.75 for adults and $1.75 for children and seniors, and the ride takes under 30 minutes. For the train schedule, go to www.caltrain.com or call ☎ 510-817-1717. BART airport stations are located on level 3 of the International terminal, or you can take the automated AirTrain to the Garage G/BART Station stop from the domestic terminals.

✔ If you're renting a car, the free AirTrain will transport you to the building where all the counters and cars are located. Catch the AirTrain on level 5 in any of the domestic terminal garages.

To drive yourself into town, follow the airport signs to Highway 101 North and Highway 280. Stay toward the left, so you don't end up on 280. If you want to go to Union Square, exit 101 North at Fourth Street. Traffic is manageable until rush hour, from 3 to 7 p.m.

At **Oakland International** (☎ 510-563-3300), all ground transportation is on one level. A shuttle service called **Bayporter Express** (☎ 415-467-1800; www.bayporter.com) picks up passengers from Terminal 1 at the center island and from Terminal 2 around the corner from baggage claim. The fare to San Francisco is $26 for one person, $38 for two people in the same party, and $7 for kids under 12. You'll have an easier time if you make reservations for the 45- to 60-minute ride. To take a cab downtown, expect to pay around $45; the trip takes 30 to 40 minutes, depending on traffic. If you need cash, you can find ATMs in the airport.

BART (☎ 510-465-2278; www.bart.gov) also runs from Oakland into the city. You can catch the **AirBART** shuttle (☎ 510-430-9440), which runs every 20 minutes, in front of Terminal 1 or 2. The fare is $2 for adults, 50¢ for children and seniors for the 15-to-30-minute ride to the Oakland Coliseum BART station. From there, transfer to a BART train into San Francisco; the fare is about $3.35. Purchase your ticket from kiosks inside the airport or at the BART station. If you're staying around Union Square, exit BART on Powell Street; the trip takes about 25 minutes.

All the major rental-car counters are inside the terminals. If you're driving into San Francisco, exit the airport on Hegenberger Road. Follow it north to Highway 880 toward San Francisco. From there, follow the signs to Highway 80 to San Francisco. When you reach the Bay Bridge, you'll have to pay $3 at the tollbooths to cross. On the other side, exit on Fifth Street to reach Union Square.

Arriving by Train or Car

Taking the train to San Francisco can be fun and romantic (as well as convenient), and although I hope you'll pay attention to my advice not to drive in San Francisco, there's no reason you shouldn't drive there and put the car away when you arrive.

By train

Amtrak trains arrive in Emeryville, just south of Berkeley. From there, an Amtrak bus will take you to downtown San Francisco. The buses stop at the Caltrain station, where there's a Muni streetcar line to the Embarcadero (and thus, into downtown), and at the Ferry Building. The Ferry Building is more convenient to the hotels in this book, and from there you can take a taxi or streetcar to Union Square or wherever.

By automobile

Drivers arriving from east of town will cross the Bay Bridge into downtown. Cars coming from the south on Highway 101 will discover the same view a few miles past 3Com (or Candlestick) Park. Anyone making the journey along Highway 101 from the north will enter San Francisco from the Golden Gate Bridge. After you pass the tollbooth (it's $5 coming into the city), exit along the bay to Van Ness Avenue.

Figuring Out the Neighborhoods

San Francisco is at the end of a 32-mile-long peninsula between the Pacific Ocean and the San Francisco Bay. The city covers just 7 square miles. Streets are laid out in a grid pattern, except for two major diagonal arteries, **Market Street** and **Columbus Avenue.** Market cuts through town from the Embarcadero up toward Twin Peaks. Columbus runs at an angle through North Beach, beginning near the Transamerica Pyramid in the Financial District and ending near the Hyde Street Pier. You'll find numbered *streets* downtown, and numbered *avenues* in the Richmond and Sunset districts southwest of downtown.

San Francisco Neighborhoods

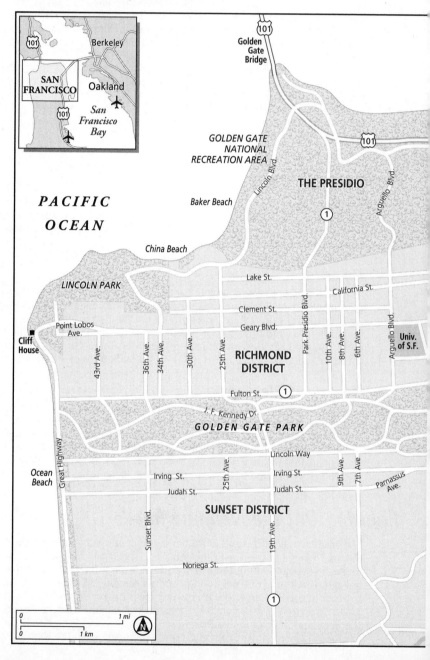

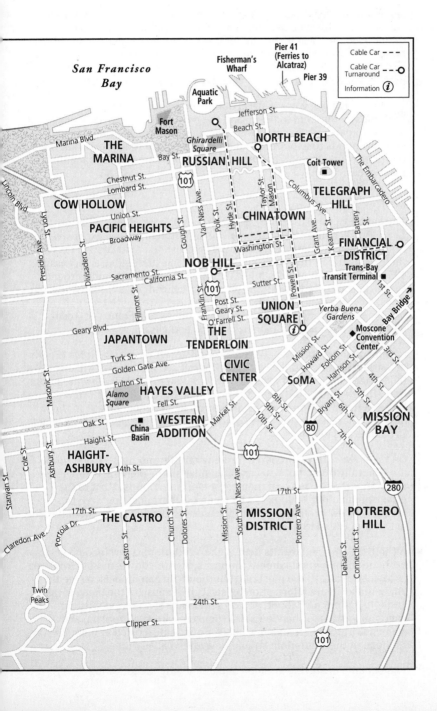

San Francisco neighborhoods are a diverse and interesting group. Of course, you'll have no trouble distinguishing Union Square from Chinatown, but even if you amble through largely residential neighborhoods, you'll notice distinct differences in the makeup of the residents and the commercial establishments. The best way to immerse yourself in the local culture is to pick a neighborhood and take a stroll.

This section gives you a general outline of the six most popular neighborhoods to tour and lodge in, and the advantages and disadvantages of staying in each. I follow that with brief descriptions of other worthy neighborhoods to explore. See the "San Francisco Neighborhoods" map to orient yourself, and Chapter 11 for more on the major attractions in these areas.

Union Square

The center of tourist activity, Union Square is tucked inside Sutter, Grant, Market, and Mason streets. Big department stores, expensive boutiques, theaters, restaurants, and the greatest concentration of hotels in the city surround the actual square, which has undergone a successful $25-million facelift in 2002. It lies on top of the very first underground garage in the United States and features a central plaza outlined in palm trees, a good cafe, outdoor tables, the TIX Bay Area outlet for half-price tickets, a See's Candy outlet, and a shop selling San Francisco–related necessities such as sweatshirts, posters, and gifts.

Union Square is about as convenient as it gets. Chinatown, SoMa (South of Market Street), and the Financial District are within easy walking distance, and public transportation can take you just about anywhere from here. Buses, Muni, BART, and the Powell Street cable cars all run through the area. You can even hail a cab from street corners in Union Square, whereas in other parts of town you usually need to call for one. Urbanites will love it.

On the downside, be prepared for heavy traffic and noise. Hotel rooms are generally quiet, but you can often hear sirens piercing through the walls or garbage trucks on their early morning rounds. Most of the hotels are in older buildings, which can be charming; however, this means that the rooms and baths often are somewhat small. Valet parking in the area runs $18 to $45 a day.

 Although Union Square sits next to the Tenderloin, a low-income neighborhood of immigrant families, druggies, and the down-and-out, the area is basically safe, as are most neighborhoods in San Francisco (see the appendix for more information on safety). Because of the many locals and tourists out and about, you do see plenty of street people and vagrants looking for handouts. Pickpockets can be a problem, and women are advised to avoid walking around unescorted at night. Certain sections of the Tenderloin should be avoided at any time.

The benefits of staying in Union Square include the following:

- ✔ Chinatown is around the corner.
- ✔ You have dining, shopping, and nightlife all in one place.
- ✔ Public transportation is excellent.

But here are the drawbacks:

- ✔ You're right near the Tenderloin.
- ✔ The traffic is relentless during the day.
- ✔ The panhandling can get on your nerves.

Nob Hill

Just above Union Square is Nob Hill, one of the oldest and most fashion-able addresses in town. Enveloping California Street from Leavenworth to Stockton and overlooking the Financial District, the area boasts beau-tiful, upper-crust residential apartments and the majestic Grace Cathedral. You can find the swanky Pacific Heights neighborhood (home to the Gettys and author Danielle Steel) to the west. A small selection of plush hotels cascades down the hill toward the Financial District, along with the California Street cable-car line.

Nob Hill accommodations are pricey, with good reason. They offer a quiet, sophisticated, residential atmosphere that contrasts with the hustle and bustle of Union Square and Fisherman's Wharf. Here you see well-dressed business travelers and tourists going about their business, in contrast to the panhandlers and down-and-outers hanging around Market Street. Nob Hill is also quite safe, even at night. Although you may be walking up and down very steep grades, Nob Hill is really just a short stroll from Union Square. Muni buses and the California Street cable car provide any needed public transportation connections. And access to some of the city's finest bars and restaurants is often just an elevator ride away. Nob Hill streets also offer breathtaking views of downtown.

The benefits of staying in Nob Hill include the following:

- ✔ The area is very safe.
- ✔ It's more peaceful and residential than Union Square.

But here are the drawbacks:

- ✔ You need to be in good condition to walk up and down the hills.
- ✔ It's expensive.
- ✔ Fewer shops and restaurants are nearby.

SoMa

South of Market Street (or SoMa for short) between Tenth, King, and Steuart streets has exploded in the past 15 years, particularly along

Mission Street between Second and Fifth. The George Moscone Convention Center, on Howard Street between Third and Fourth, pioneered the renaissance of this section of downtown, and was followed by the **San Francisco Museum of Modern Art,** the **Cartoon Art Museum, Yerba Buena Gardens,** and the kid-magnet **Metreon** (see Chapter 11). Clubs have multiplied around Harrison Street; restaurants and bars are thick from Howard Street down to the tiny South Park enclave.

Still, vestiges of the old neighborhood remain. Nearby Sixth Street is the purview of seedy residential hotels and corner stores specializing in cheap wine. Market Street itself is depressing west of Sixth Street — a combination of low-rent tourist shops, peep shows, and check-cashing counters, with a few legitimate theaters. The farther south you venture toward I-80, the more industrial things get. And you're competing for space in hotels with thousands of guys wearing plastic nametags and rushing to Moscone for that panel discussion on skeletal malocclusions.

The benefits of staying in SoMa include the following:

✔ It's the center for cutting-edge art and performance.

✔ You can find lots of worthy ways to spend time.

✔ Some great restaurants and clubs are located in the area.

But here are the drawbacks:

✔ It still has a fringe element about it.

✔ The hotel choices are more limited than around Union Square.

✔ You get lots of convention traffic.

The Embarcadero

Liberated from the pylons and cement of the Embarcadero Freeway, which was damaged by the 1989 Loma Prieta earthquake and subsequently torn down, the Embarcadero now glows in the light reflected off the waters of the bay. Paralleling the eastern edge of Fisherman's Wharf to the beginning of China Basin, the views along the lovely stretch of road that wraps around the northeast side of the city are some of the most sigh-inducing — the Bay Bridge soars above you, Alcatraz seems a mere stone's throw away, and on sunny weekends sailboats blissfully glide around the bay. The newly remodeled Ferry Building, a fitting centerpiece at the end of Market Street, contains the best of the best food purveyors.

This is a very safe area and is generally quiet in the evenings, except during rush hour, when it's a major thoroughfare for bridge traffic. The most popular activities at the Embarcadero consist of promenading slowly down Herb Caen Way (a stretch of sidewalk near the Ferry Building named for the *San Francisco Chronicle*'s legendary columnist), jogging, biking, skateboarding, and now shopping. With the Ferry

Building drawing out the locals, sections of the Embarcadero are as lively as Union Square. Some of the hottest kitchens are based here, too, and you can find music and nightlife in unexpected venues.

Locals also trek to the Embarcadero Center, a collection of five multiuse office buildings connected by bridges and walkways, to check out the upscale chain stores and movie theaters. You can catch BART and Muni streetcars from the Embarcadero underground station to just about anywhere. A Muni extension from the Embarcadero to the Caltrain station rolls down past the magnificent downtown ballpark, and charming old streetcars breeze all the way down Market Street to Fisherman's Wharf and back. As for accommodations, the hotels are expensive. The neighborhood's popularity is apparent in the amount of building and remodeling completed around the waterfront.

The benefits of staying in the Embarcadero include the following:

- ✔ It has beautiful bay views.
- ✔ It's a great location for strollers and joggers.
- ✔ Public transportation options are excellent.
- ✔ It's convenient to shopping and dining.

 But here are the drawbacks:

- ✔ Rush-hour traffic is heavy.
- ✔ Hotel choices are limited (and expensive).
- ✔ Walks to other neighborhoods are relatively long.

North Beach/Fisherman's Wharf

Although just a few blocks separate North Beach from Fisherman's Wharf, the two neighborhoods are as different as focaccia is from sourdough. North Beach isn't an actual beach of course — it's the old Italian neighborhood next to Chinatown. Head here to sit in cafes, to browse in City Lights bookstore, and to sample the selections at the various delis and pastry shops. Columbus Avenue is the main street, but you can find family-style restaurants and crowded bars from Washington to Grant. XXX-rated clubs stick together on Broadway; Telegraph Hill is to the east, behind Coit Tower and the Filbert steps.

North Beach is the most European of any neighborhood in town, and the one in which I'd most like to wake up. Ducking into a cafe for a latte, choosing a pastry from any number of Italian bakeries, watching Chinese senior citizens practicing tai chi in Washington Square Park — what a heavenly way to pass the morning. Stores sell goods you haven't already seen a thousand times over, and the food is divine and diverse.

And then there's Fisherman's Wharf. I suppose 15.7 million tourists can't all be wrong, but just between you and me, I don't get it. Located on Bay

Street between Powell and Polk streets, the former working piers were the center of the city's harbor and fishing industries. Now, waterfront life is limited to a few sport-fishing boats for tourist attractions, and the sounds of cash registers have usurped the old-timers.

A group of chain hotels huddles around North Point Street, about 2 blocks off the Hyde Street cable-car turnaround. A walk west along the waterfront, through the most tourist-oriented section, ends at the delightful Aquatic Park, but along the way, you pass a gauntlet of T-shirt emporiums, fast-food eateries, knick-knack shops, and beggars, one of whom camouflages himself with branches and jumps out at unsuspecting pedestrians — I kid you not.

As you may guess, prices are slightly lower off-season in North Beach and Fisherman's Wharf, but so is the safety factor. Watch your wallet, particularly around PIER 39. Auto break-ins are also a problem. Depending on the weather, North Beach can be raucous during the evenings, and blocks of Broadway pulsate with bars and girlie clubs. Parking in either district is impossible unless you head for the nearest garage, which can get expensive.

The benefits of staying in Fisherman's Wharf/North Beach include the following:

✔ You can navigate your way through either location on foot.

✔ You can find plenty of great meals in North Beach.

✔ You have access to convenient public transportation.

But here are the drawbacks:

✔ You're surrounded by tourists on Fisherman's Wharf.

✔ The parking is a nightmare.

✔ Hotel choices are limited.

The Marina/Cow Hollow

Between Van Ness Avenue, Broadway Street, Lyon Street, and Marina Boulevard is the Marina/Cow Hollow neighborhood, a residential utopia for singles of all ages. You'll find famous Union Street, and 4 blocks farther north, Chestnut Street, in these parts, both popular for their trendy cloister of shops, restaurants, and young urban professionals. Architecture and history fans can get a close look at the **Octagon House** (circa 1861) at 2645 Gough St. (at Union).

If you're driving to San Francisco or renting a car while you're here, this neighborhood has its advantages. Outdoorsy types love the location, which is close to the Presidio and Crissy Field. Most, but not all, of the accommodations here include free parking. You can walk to several great sights from the Marina/Cow Hollow area, including the Exploratorium, the Palace of Fine Arts, Fort Mason, and the Golden Gate Bridge. This is a good neighborhood for families, because the prices are more reasonable than in more tourist-oriented areas.

The downside of staying here is also the location. The majority of lodgings in the area are motels along Lombard Street, a four- to six-lane conduit to the Golden Gate Bridge and Van Ness Avenue and the busiest street in the city. Most visitors find the traffic horrendous in this area. A few hotels are located off the main drag (I review some in Chapter 9), but great places to stay are somewhat hard to find.

The benefits of sleeping in the Marina/Cow Hollow area include the following:

✔ It's near Chestnut and Union streets shopping.

✔ Hotel/motel parking is usually free.

✔ It's within walking distance of the Marina and the Golden Gate Bridge.

But here are the drawbacks:

✔ Accommodation choices are limited to motels and B&Bs.

✔ Traffic is heavy on Lombard Street.

✔ The immediate surroundings are less scenic.

Other 'hoods to discover

These districts are also where you may spend some time, including the one where Barry Bonds's homers wind up in the water!

The Castro

A historic and active gay community is the Castro's claim to fame. Visitors can admire the beautifully restored Victorian homes, visit the Castro Theatre, and try out a new image in the superb men's clothing stores. For shopping and people-watching, head to Castro Street, between Market and 18th streets.

China Basin/Mission Bay

This neighborhood is old, but before the Giants' baseball stadium relocated here visitors had no reason to explore the area. Boy, have things changed: The area is teeming with new offices and live/work developments. King Street from Third Street to the Embarcadero is the main drag; that's where you can find restaurants, bars, and the boys of summer. West of 3rd Street along the water is the new Mission Bay development, featuring UCSF's latest campus for research and teaching, condos galore, and an entirely new neighborhood to serve them.

Chinatown

The borders of Chinatown are always in a state of flux, but you can generally wander this densely packed area roughly between Broadway, Taylor, Bush, and Montgomery streets. It is every bit as vivid and fascinating as advertised. The **Dragon Gate** entrance on Grant Avenue leads to touristy shops, but you'll swear you're in another country after you wander up Stockton and through the abundant alleyways.

The Civic Center and Hayes Valley

If you're seeking the New Main Library; the fairly new Asian Art Museum; the Ballet, Symphony, and Opera buildings; or City Hall, then the Civic Center, bordered by Van Ness and Golden Gate avenues, and Franklin, Hyde, and Market streets, is where you want to be.

This neighborhood has a large homeless population and is dicey after dark. If you have plans in the area at night, I recommend taking a cab.

Hayes Valley, west of Civic Center, is bound by Franklin Street to the east, Webster Street to the west, Grove Street to the north, and Page Street to the south. Here you'll find hip places to shop and many quality restaurants.

Financial District

The Financial District encompasses prime bay real estate roughly between Montgomery Street and the Embarcadero, on either side of Market Street. The **Transamerica Pyramid,** at Montgomery and Clay streets, is a skyline landmark. Seek out **Belden Place,** an alley between Kearny, Bush, and Pine streets, for outdoor dining opportunities. Antiques hounds will like the hunting grounds around Jackson Square.

Haight-Ashbury

The Haight, or Haight-Ashbury, is surrounded by Stanyan Street to the east, Divisadero Street to the west, Fulton Street to the north, and Waller Street to the south. The area still hasn't fully recovered from what must have been a bummer to some of its residents — the demise of the '60s. You can find most of the action on Haight Street, which continues to hold a magical appeal over scruffy groups of youngsters campaigning for handouts. Used-clothing stores compete for space with all kinds of commercial endeavors, most of which are perfectly legit.

Japantown

Off Geary, between Webster and Laguna streets, is Japantown, which at first glance appears to consist of ugly indoor shopping centers. However, you can find some good, inexpensive noodle restaurants and some interesting shops housed in these dismal gray buildings. Check out the AMC-Kabuki movie theaters here, or have a soak at the Kabuki Hot Springs. Across Sutter Street (between Fillmore and Webster) look for Cottage Row, the last morsel left of the old Japantown.

The Mission District

Located from Cesar Chavez Street to Market Street between Dolores and Potrero streets, the Mission District is a busy, largely Hispanic community home to a growing number of artsy types seeking cheap (well, relatively cheap) rentals. Check out Mission Dolores, Dolores Park, and 24th Street, along with a plethora of affordable restaurants and eye-catching outdoor murals. There's a growing multitude of restaurants on Valencia and Guererro streets between 16th and 23rd streets, and on 16th Street between Mission and Guererro.

Pacific Heights

Pacific Heights, which is bordered by Broadway, Pine, Divisadero, and Franklin streets, is where the wealthy lounge around their extravagant but tasteful homes. You can visit the **Haas-Lilienthal House,** an 1886 Queen Anne Victorian at 2007 Franklin St., at Washington, and stare at *Mrs. Doubtfire*'s fictional digs at Broadway and Steiner. The closest shopping blocks are Fillmore Street between Jackson and Pine streets.

The Presidio

These 1,500 acres on the westernmost point of the city are part of the **Golden Gate National Recreation Area.** If you love to hike, go to the visitor center for maps and suggestions — the views and landscape are sensational. If you'd rather play tenpins, a great little bowling alley is also located here. A patch of Presidio land along the bay, named **Crissy Fields,** is the newest park in the city and features wetlands, picnic areas, bay views, and a drop-in center with weekend activities. That new collection of buildings facing the bay belongs to George *(Star Wars)* Lucas and is the Letterman Digital Arts Center campus.

The Richmond District

Stretching from **Golden Gate Park** at one edge to the Pacific Ocean at the other, **Lincoln Park, Land's End,** the **California Palace of the Legion of Honor museum,** and the newly remodeled **Cliff House** are all located in this large neighborhood. Clement Street is akin to Chinatown without the fun architecture or alleyways, and you can find authentic Russian food on Geary.

Russian Hill

Polk Street from Broadway up to around Greenwich Street has become *très* chic. This is a delightful area for shopping and snacking with some terrific little restaurants, bakeries, antiques shops, and boutiques. Just to the northwest, you'll find the wiggly part of Lombard Street and Macondry Lane, immortalized in Armistead Maupin's *Tales of the City.*

The Tenderloin

The blocks bounded by Sutter and Mason streets and Van Ness and Golden Gate avenues are a section of town currently home to immigrant families — largely from Southeast Asia — attempting to live their lives alongside flop houses, bars, massage parlors, and people subsiding on the fringes of society. A slim rectangle of space from roughly O'Farrell to Market streets between Larkin and Polk is dangerous at night and rough during the day. The only place worth visiting here is **Glide Memorial Church** for Sunday services, although the city is promoting the growing presence of Vietnamese restaurants.

The Western Addition

I mention this old neighborhood between Geary, Haight, Gough, and Divisadero streets because people studying their maps often believe it's an easy walk from Civic Center to Golden Gate Park by way of Oak or Fell streets. That's not entirely accurate. First, it's hilly. Second, it's not the safest section of town. And third, it's farther than it appears.

Finding Information After You Arrive

If you need more information about the city, ask your concierge or desk clerk, or stop by the **Convention and Visitors Bureau Information Center** on the lower level of Hallidie Plaza, 900 Market St. (at Powell), or call ☎ **800-220-5747** or 415-391-2000. The office is open Monday through Friday from 9 a.m. to 5 p.m., Saturday and Sunday from 9 a.m. to 3 p.m. during the summer. It's closed Thanksgiving, Christmas, New Year's Day, Easter Sunday, and Sundays from November to April.

Look for a free *Bay Guardian* or *SF Weekly* from sidewalk kiosks or coffeehouses for listings of city events and entertainment. The Convention and Visitors Bureau also operates a 24-hour events line at ☎ **415-391-2001.**

Getting Around San Francisco

As you may glean from earlier chapters, having a car in the city isn't advised and isn't necessary most of the time. San Francisco really caters to walkers, with benches appearing just when you need one and cafes at hand for a shot of caffeine when energy flags. Getting around on a bus or Muni metro streetcar is cheap if not perfect. In the rare instance that you do need a car, renting one downtown is easy and convenient.

This section contains everything you need to know about cruising around the city *sans* auto. It even includes some inside tips on parking should you decide to throw caution to the wind and join the legendary drivers — and I don't mean that in a good way — gracing our city's roads and highways.

The one-stop shopping number for traffic or public transit information is ☎ **415-817-1717.** This number connects you to whatever you need, whether BART and Muni routes or traffic conditions.

because the streets bump into Columbus Avenue, navigating the area can be confusing. On the weekends, Lombard Street and Van Ness Avenue take the brunt of all the cars inching their way toward the Golden Gate Bridge. Getting through Chinatown's narrow, crowded streets by car is basically impossible during waking hours. If you must cross town, I suggest taking California Street past the Financial District.

 For sanity's sake, avoid traveling north on the Golden Gate or Bay bridges between 3 and 7 p.m. weekdays. If you plan to drive to Point Reyes or the Wine Country (see Chapter 14), do *not* leave on a Friday after 2 p.m., if at all possible. Traffic across the Golden Gate Bridge is awful on weekends, especially if the weather is nice. Go before noon on a Friday, and avoid returning on a Sunday afternoon.

Driving by the rules

California law requires that both drivers and passengers wear seat belts. You may turn right at a red light (unless otherwise indicated) after yielding to traffic and pedestrians and after making a complete stop. Cable cars and streetcars always have the right-of-way, as do pedestrians, especially if they use intersections and crosswalks. On Market Street, one lane is exclusively for buses unless you're making a right turn. Heed the signs.

Being cautious with red lights

 San Francisco drivers have a tendency to run red lights, so pause to check oncoming traffic before entering an intersection just after the light turns green.

Parking the car

 I'm not going to take up space discussing the many parking laws; just take my advice: Park in a garage. They are expensive but could save you some money in the long run because parking tickets start at $40.

Legal street parking spaces are next to unpainted curbs. Yellow-, white-, green-, and red-painted curbs are all off-limits in general — the only exception being commercial zones (yellow curbs), which are okay to park in after delivery hours. Pay attention to the signs posted on the streets. Be aware of tow-away zones. You can't park on most streets downtown between 4 and 6 p.m. without running the risk of having your car towed. Otherwise, you'll find your rental at the **AutoReturn Lot** at 450 Seventh St., at Harrison Street (☎ **415-865-8200**), faster than you can say "Where'd I park the car?" If your wheels aren't where you thought you left them, call ☎ **415-553-1239** to find out whether your vehicle has been towed or merely stolen. If your car has been towed, you'll need to go to AutoReturn in person to pay the ticket and the storage charges (which vary depending on how long the car has been there). This misadventure will cost you at least $185, cash or credit card only.

Legal parking spots are hard to come by. If you're driving, park in a public garage or use the services of a valet. And if you do happen to find a legal space within walking distance of your destination, *grab it.*

Improving your parking karma

So, you want a parking space, huh? You'll have to be one step ahead of the crowd. Try these suggestions for a little edge:

- ✔ **Carry quarters.** Most parking meters accept nothing else; 25¢ buys six minutes in most parts of town.

- ✔ **Watch the clock.** Many crosstown downtown streets do not allow parking during rush hour, from 4 to 6 p.m. Get to the Financial District, Union Square, SoMa, or Nob Hill a few minutes before 6 p.m. to grab the great street parking space of your choice.

- ✔ **Spring for valet parking.** The extra money now may be worth avoiding the headache of finding a parking spot later.

- ✔ **Check out public parking garages.** Public parking garages are cheaper than private ones. In North Beach, park in the garage on Vallejo Street (between Kearny and Green). In Chinatown, park at the Portsmouth Square garage on Kearny Street.

- ✔ **Make note of street-sweeping times.** If you find street parking galore in some outlying neighborhood, check signs for sweeping hours and days. That's generally the real reason for your good luck. Don't park without checking the signs, unless you want to give the Department of Traffic a $35 donation. If your timing is right however, you'll pull up after the sweeper trucks have made their rounds, when it's perfectly okay to park.

- ✔ **Stop "runaway" car syndrome.** To keep your car from rolling away while you're parked on a hill, put the car in gear, apply the hand brake, and *curb your wheels* — turn your wheels toward the curb when facing downhill and away from the curb when facing uphill. It's the law! (This tip won't contribute to your finding a parking place, but it will help you keep the one you found.)

Chapter 9

Checking In at San Francisco's Best Hotels

. . . .

In This Chapter

▶ Choosing your chain or independent hotel

▶ Getting the best rates

▶ Using the Internet to uncover hotel deals

▶ Knowing the questions to ask to get the room you want

▶ Getting a room if you don't have reservations

▶ Discovering the perfect San Francisco hotel

. . . .

So, you're ready to make San Francisco your home — for a short period of time at least. You probably have an idea of how much you're willing to spend (if not, check out Chapter 4), and you may have an idea what neighborhood suits your fancy (see Chapter 8 for descriptions). Other features and amenities will be important to you, too. If you don't stay in hotels very often, you may not know what level of service or quality of room you really need to enjoy your stay. Consider, among other variables, whether you really care if your room resembles something out of *Condé Nast Traveler,* has a clear view of the bay, is vulnerable to street noise, or has a bathtub large enough for you and a close friend. Will you feel despondent if the hotel can't supply a cup of herbal tea at 10 p.m.? Will you behave badly all day if you can't hit the treadmill first thing in the morning? If you're traveling with your laptop, is Wi-Fi a necessity? If you're traveling with your lap dog, is the hotel Fido friendly? Avoid disappointment and surprises by discussing your requirements with the reservations staff.

The hotel selections in this chapter are, in my opinion, among the best in San Francisco — balancing comfort, location, character, and price. With few exceptions, each has a distinct, only-in-San-Francisco style I believe you'll find memorable and pleasing. For those traveling on frequent-flier miles (which you can sometimes redeem for rooms, or rack up additional miles for staying at a partner hotel), you won't find many of the big chain hotels listed here, but there are plenty: Turn to the appendix for toll-free numbers and Web sites. I also leave out the majority of hotels on less desirable blocks, many of the priciest palaces, as

San Francisco Hotels

The Andrews Hotel **25**
The Argent Hotel **40**
Argonaut Hotel **7**
Campton Place **39**
Castle Inn **6**
Chancellor Hotel **21**
Clift **32**
Commodore Hotel **26**
Cow Hollow Motor Inn & Suites **2**
Embarcadero Hyatt Regency **44**
The Fairmont Hotel **12**
Galleria Park Hotel **43**
Golden Gate Hotel **16**
Handlery Union Square Hotel **34**
Harbor Court Hotel **46**
Hayes Valley Inn **5**
Hotel Adagio **24**
Hotel Bijou **36**
Hotel Bohème **11**
Hotel Del Sol **4**
Hotel Griffon **46**
Hotel Milano **37**
Hotel Monaco **30**
Hotel Palomar **38**
Hotel Rex **17**
Hotel Triton **19**
Hotel Vitale **45**
The Huntington Hotel **14**
Inn at Union Square **22**
Kensington Park Hotel **23**
King George Hotel **33**
The Marina Courtyard Motel **1**
The Maxwell **28**
Monticello Inn **35**
Nob Hill Lambourne **13**
The Orchard Hotel **20**
St. Regis Hotel **41**
San Remo Hotel **9**
The Serrano Hotel **31**
Tuscan Inn **8**
Union Street Inn **3**
W San Francisco **42**
The Warwick Regis Hotel **27**
Washington Square Inn **10**
Westin St. Francis **29**
White Swan Inn **15**

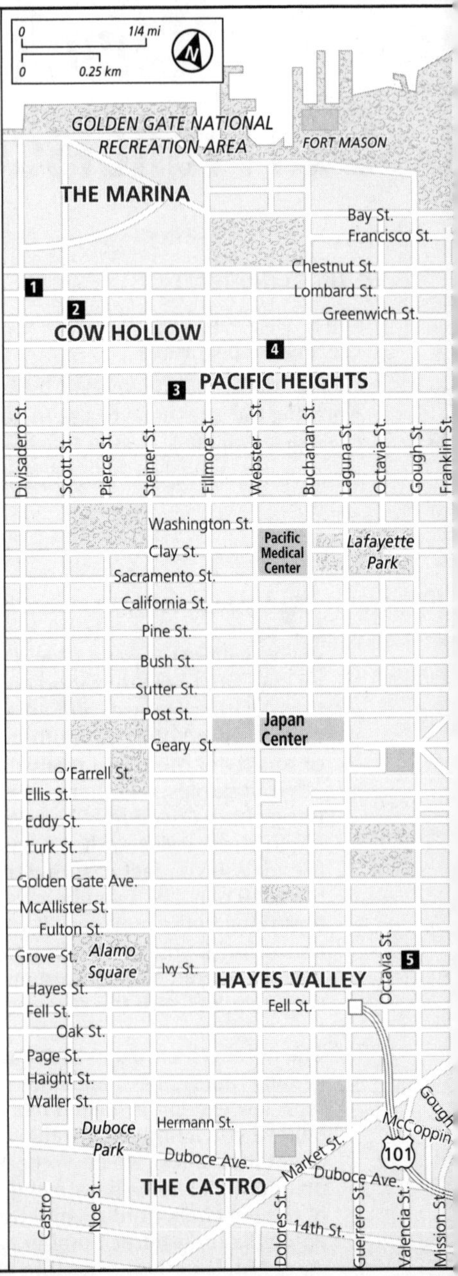

Map of San Francisco Hotels showing neighborhoods: Golden Gate National Recreation Area, Fort Mason, The Marina, Cow Hollow, Pacific Heights, Hayes Valley, The Castro, with Pacific Medical Center, Lafayette Park, Japan Center, Alamo Square, Duboce Park. Streets labeled include Bay St., Francisco St., Chestnut St., Lombard St., Greenwich St., Divisadero St., Scott St., Pierce St., Steiner St., Fillmore St., Webster St., Buchanan St., Laguna St., Octavia St., Gough St., Franklin St., Washington St., Clay St., Sacramento St., California St., Pine St., Bush St., Sutter St., Post St., Geary St., O'Farrell St., Ellis St., Eddy St., Turk St., Golden Gate Ave., McAllister St., Fulton St., Grove St., Hayes St., Fell St., Oak St., Page St., Haight St., Waller St., Hermann St., Duboce Ave., 14th St., Castro, Noe St., Dolores St., Guerrero St., Valencia St., Mission St.

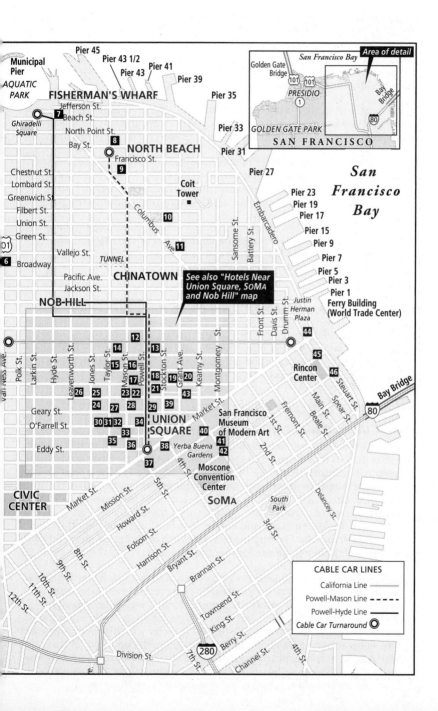

Area of detail

San Francisco Bay

Golden Gate Bridge

PRESIDIO

GOLDEN GATE PARK

SAN FRANCISCO

Bay Bridge

Municipal Pier

AQUATIC PARK

Pier 45
Pier 43 1/2
Pier 43
Pier 41
Pier 39
Pier 35
Pier 33
Pier 31
Pier 27
Pier 23
Pier 19
Pier 17
Pier 15
Pier 9
Pier 7
Pier 5
Pier 3
Pier 1

FISHERMAN'S WHARF

Jefferson St.
Beach St.
North Point St.
Bay St.
Francisco St.

Ghiradelli Square

Chestnut St.
Lombard St.
Greenwich St.
Filbert St.
Union St.
Green St.
Vallejo St.
Broadway

NORTH BEACH

Coit Tower

Columbus Ave.

TUNNEL

CHINATOWN

Pacific Ave.
Jackson St.

NOB HILL

See also "Hotels Near Union Square, SOMA and Nob Hill" map

Sansome St.
Battery St.
Embarcadero

San Francisco Bay

Front St.
Davis St.
Drumm St.

Justin Herman Plaza

Ferry Building (World Trade Center)

UNION SQUARE

Geary St.
O'Farrell St.
Eddy St.

Taylor St.
Mason St.
Powell St.
Stockton St.
Grant Ave.
Kearny St.
Montgomery St.
Market St.

Leavenworth St.
Jones St.
Polk St.
Larkin St.
Hyde St.
Van Ness Ave.

San Francisco Museum of Modern Art

Yerba Buena Gardens

Moscone Convention Center

SoMa

Rincon Center

Steuart St.
Main St.
Spear St.
Beale St.
Fremont St.
1st St.
2nd St.
South Park
Delancey St.
3rd St.

Bay Bridge

CIVIC CENTER

Market St.
Mission St.
Howard St.
Folsom St.
Harrison St.
Bryant St.
Brannan St.
Townsend St.
King St.
Berry St.
Channel St.
Division St.

4th St.
5th St.
7th St.

8th St.
9th St.
10th St.
11th St.
12th St.

CABLE CAR LINES

California Line
Powell-Mason Line
Powell-Hyde Line
Cable Car Turnaround

well as those a bit too far from the action. Finally, two very well known hotels are listed that I actually don't love, but I include them for reasons mentioned in the write-ups.

See the indexes at the end of this chapter for lists of recommended hotels organized by neighborhood and price.

No matter where you stay in San Francisco, you're no more than 20 minutes by cab from the major sites, shopping areas, and restaurants. The majority of the city's hotels are in a few of the central neighborhoods.

With guidance from Chapter 8, pick the neighborhood you want to stay in based on your interests and needs — for example, are you hoping to shop the major stores? Are you an enthusiastic museum-goer? Do you hope to find peace and quiet? Or do you want to be close to the bay?

Refer to *Frommer's San Francisco* (Wiley Publishing) for accommodations in neighborhoods outside the central part of the city that aren't covered here, or go to **Citysearch** (www.sanfrancisco.citysearch.com), where you can search for hotels by area and price.

Getting to Know Your Options

Hotels come in many shapes, sizes, and price ranges. You'll find chain hotels and motels, independent hotels, and hotels that serve business travelers rather than vacationers. So what are the differences between these various accommodations?

Choosing between chain hotels and independent hotels

Hotels affiliated with huge chains, such as Holiday Inn, Hilton, Sheraton, Marriott, and Hyatt, are often monolithic or merely architecturally homely structures that are a bit on the boring side and look pretty much the same wherever you travel. Even the rooms will have similar, if not identical, décor. But there's a comfort in that, and for travelers who like the assurance of a brand name, chains are a fine choice. In San Francisco, businesspeople and conventioneers often make up the clientele at these hotels. The appendix at the back of this book has a list of toll-free telephone numbers for the major chains.

Independent hotels (sometimes also called *boutique hotels*) are smaller in scope than the big-name properties. They target travelers who want a unique, individualized atmosphere with a local slant. Some appeal to older couples seeking quiet and cozy budget lodgings, while other independents seek to attract a sophisticated traveler with hip furnishings and wild color schemes. San Francisco is a leader in the boutique hotel scene, with a great assortment to choose from. If you want more-interesting surroundings, where your fellow guests may be movie fans, literati, musicians, or shopaholics, you may enjoy a stay in a boutique hotel.

Make sure you know what you're getting into, though — boutique hotels are not for everyone. The needs of a business traveler are not met at lower-end independent hotels, and staff members are not always immediately available to answer questions or provide services. Room service is also iffy unless a restaurant is connected to the property. However, San Francisco's boutique properties tend to provide good to amazing levels of service and amenities.

Do I really get breakfast in bed? Unpacking in a B&B

B&Bs, or bed-and-breakfast inns, can come in the form of an extra bedroom or two in a private home or a house renovated for the purpose of providing accommodations to visitors. Some B&Bs are lavishly decorated, with an owner who prides himself on serving gourmet breakfasts and afternoon sherry. Other owners put less effort into the business, keeping some food in the fridge and engaging in casual conversation with guests about the local sites, rather than providing any official tour guidance. Accommodations at a B&B usually come with a continental or full breakfast. You may have to share the bathroom with fellow guests. Rooms at B&Bs are usually more economical than hotel accommodations, but a few luxury B&Bs have equally high-end prices.

Some small hotels advertise as B&Bs. In general, these properties have a dozen or so bedrooms, include continental breakfast with the room, and often offer wine in the afternoon.

I recommend a few stellar B&Bs in this book, but plenty more are in the city. For more information on bed-and-breakfasts and lists of properties, the following resources can help:

- ✔ **Bed & Breakfast San Francisco** (☎ 415-899-0060; www.bbsf.com). This organization has information on small B&Bs.

- ✔ **California Association of Bed and Breakfast Inns,** 2715 Porter St., Soquel, CA 95073 (☎ 800-373-9251; www.cabbi.com). Their Web site has links to member inns.

- ✔ **Bed and Breakfast Inns of Napa Valley** (☎ 707-944-4444; www.napavalley.com/lodging). This organization is a great resource if you plan to take a side trip to Wine Country.

Family ties: Choosing a kid-friendly hotel

The younger generation loves San Francisco for its beauty, wealth of activities, great food, and those cable cars. Hotels are waking up to the fact that families appreciate attention paid to their children, but by and large, that's going to mean different things to different marketing departments. The Ritz-Carlton, for example, will send a bellhop to baby-proof your quarters and provide the nanny with some aspirin, while the desk clerk at Hotel Del Sol will dig out a beach ball for the kids. Few hotels have swimming pools, by the way. (For more on accommodations for families, take a look at *Frommer's San Francisco with Kids,* published by

Wiley Publishing.) If you're taking your darlings along on this trip, you have three choices for sleeping arrangements: Share a room with them, rent two rooms, or reserve a suite.

Sharing a room with your family means reserving a *double/double, queen/queen, or king/king* — one room with two double, queen, or king beds. Double/doubles are the least expensive option and work best for a family of four with kids too young to have a room of their own. If you come to terms with the fact that you won't be staying up late, you won't be sleeping in, and this trip will revolve around the kids' needs, you can have a calm holiday.

Renting two rooms connected by an interior door or across the hall from each other is a great option if you have a large family or are traveling with older, more independent kids. Although you end up spending twice the money, renting two rooms ensures that you can get some R & R from the rigors of parenting, if only for a few blissful hours.

Reserving a suite may seem like an extravagant way to give yourself a little space while keeping a close eye on the children, but it's really a clever way to enjoy a high-quality hotel experience. Look at it this way: $260 buys you two rooms at the Golden Gate Hotel on Union Square, but at the Lambourne, $299 sets the nuclear family up in a two-room suite complete with a stereo system, compact kitchenette, and continental breakfast in the tony environs of Nob Hill.

 Unlike in resort destinations, few hotels in San Francisco offer special kids' programs or amenities. The hotels that I designate as Kid Friendly are the ones that are a good choice for families because of room size, location, or their willingness, in my opinion, to accommodate a family's needs and make them feel welcome.

Finding the Best Room at the Best Rate

The *rack rate* is the maximum rate that a hotel charges for a room. If you walked in off the street and asked for a room, the rack rate is the amount you would be billed. The hotel usually posts the rate on the back of your door, along with the fire/emergency exit diagrams.

 Hotels will be delighted to charge you the rack rate, but you often don't have to pay it, especially if the hotel isn't full. The best way to avoid this is surprisingly simple: Just ask for a cheaper or discounted rate when you book. Things like special weekend rates or AAA and AARP discounts can add up to big savings, so don't be afraid to ask. If your timing is right and business is slow, you may be pleasantly surprised.

In all but the smallest accommodations, the rate you pay depends on many factors — chief among them how you make your reservation.

A travel agent may be able to negotiate a better price with certain hotels than you can get yourself. (That's because the hotel often gives the agent a discount in exchange for steering business toward that hotel.)

 Reserving a room through the hotel's toll-free number may also result in a lower rate than calling the hotel directly. On the other hand, the central reservations number may not know about discount rates at specific locations. For example, local franchises may offer a special group rate for a wedding or family reunion, but they may neglect to tell the central booking line. Your best bet is to call both the local number and the toll-free number and see which one gives you a better deal.

Room rates (even rack rates) change with the season, as occupancy rates rise and fall. But even within a given season, room prices are subject to change without notice, so the rates quoted in this book may be different from the actual rate you receive when you make your reservation. Be sure to mention membership in AAA, AARP, frequent-flier programs, any other corporate rewards programs you can think of — or your Uncle Joe's Elks lodge in which you're an honorary inductee, for that matter — when you call to book. You never know when the affiliation may be worth a few dollars off your room rate.

 The rack rates I give in the hotel listings do not include the 14 percent hotel tax. And those outrageous valet garage prices are *per day*. Many of these hotels offer weekend discounts and parking or breakfast packages. Before you book, always ask if any specials, packages, or promotions are going on that may get you a better deal.

 If you're driving, don't feel obliged to use the hotel's valet to park. The cost just keeps increasing. If you're planning to keep the car garaged, drop your luggage at the hotel and head to the nearest public parking structure. Around Union Square, you'll find the **Ellis-O'Farrell Garage,** 123 O'Farrell St. ($30 per day; ☎ **415-986-4800;** www.eofgarage.com); the **Sutter-Stockton Garage,** 444 Stockton St. ($26 per day; ☎ **415-982-7275**); and the **Union Square Garage,** 333 Post St. ($31 per day; ☎ **415-397-0631**). SoMa has the city's largest garage, the **Fifth and Mission Garage,** 833 Mission St. ($23 per day; ☎ **415-982-8522;** www.fifthand mission.com). Of course, you don't get in-and-out privileges, nor will anyone fetch the car for you, but one of the biggest complaints hotel guests have is how slow the valets are to bring the cars around. Save yourself time and money and self-park.

Getting the Best Room at the Best Rate

Obviously, you can get all the service and style you want if price is no object. But when it is, as is so often the case, here's a little advice for chatting up the reservations desk: Charm is useful; being completely clear about your expectations is just as important.

Finding the best rate

Make sure you cover all the bases when researching hotels. Sometimes you can get the best rate through the hotel's toll-free reservations number, but sometimes the local manager will run a discount or promotion that central reservations doesn't know about, and it's better to call the hotel directly. Also, most hotels are now likely to meet any price you can get on an Internet hotel reservation service. That way they still get your business without paying a commission to the service.

 If you reserve over the Internet, print out your booking transaction (including your confirmation number) and bring it with you. Hotels have been known to make mistakes on the final bill, such as charging for parking or breakfast when it was included in a package or promotion, and proof in hand will smooth negotiations.

 When budgeting for hotel rates, watch out for hidden fees and extra costs. Knowing things up front is better than getting stuck later. Traveling with man's best friend? Be sure to ask if there's a cleaning charge for pets on top of the room rate.

Figuring in taxes and extra expenses

A hotel room that costs $99 a night actually will end up closer to $114 because of the hotel tax. It's steep, but it's unavoidable. Room-service charges can also inflate your final room tab. Local phone calls, minibars in your room, enticing baskets of goodies on an end table — none of these are gratis (unless they're marked "complimentary").

 If you like to snack in bed, buy your favorite goodies at a nearby market or convenience store, and bring them up to your room.

Don't forget that most hotels tack on a fee for merely dialing out on the phone in your room. This starts at 75¢ and increases depending on what the market will bear. This is, of course, in addition to long-distance charges. For dinner reservations or event tickets, let your hotel concierge do the talking.

Bargain hunting in season

Officially, the low season in San Francisco is from November to March, but one highly experienced downtown concierge joked that the low season was the weekends (when business travelers leave town). Although more tourists do visit between spring and early fall, your actual concerns should center around convention and business travelers. The San Francisco Convention and Visitors Bureau keeps a calendar of major conventions, and I recommend checking with them before you finalize your plans (see the appendix). Hotels and restaurants around Union Square and SoMa are always packed when Moscone Center is booked.

Generally, you'll get your best rate in the winter, on weekends when the suits go home, and around holidays when you're actually supposed to be at Cousin Seymour's and not gallivanting around San Francisco. Don't let that discourage you from arriving whenever it's convenient for you, of course. Just make your reservations far in advance.

As room rates fluctuate with the season (and the economy), occupancy rates also rise and fall. A hotel is less likely to extend discount rates if it is close to full, but most (the Ritz-Carlton being an exception) will negotiate if they're close to empty. Tourist-oriented hotels usually offer discounted rates for midweek stays because they're usually most crowded on weekends. The reverse is true for business hotels downtown. Wine Country hotels tend to charge the most in the fall, around harvest time, and on weekends during the summer. Rates listed in this book are probably different from the rate you'll be quoted when you make your reservation, because room prices are subject to change without notice. In addition, discounts for membership in AAA, AARP, frequent-flier programs, and other programs can change room rates significantly, regardless of the season. The word on the street is that hotel room prices are on the increase as are occupancy rates.

Surfing the Web for hotel deals

You can sometimes get a good deal by booking through a lodging Web site. Although the major travel Web sites (such as Travelocity, Expedia, Yahoo! Travel, and Cheap Tickets) offer hotel booking, you're often better off using a site devoted primarily to lodging, because you may find properties that aren't listed with more general online travel agencies. Some lodging sites specialize in a particular type of accommodation, such as bed-and-breakfasts, which you won't find on the more mainstream booking services. Others, such as Travelweb (see the following list), offer weekend deals on major chain properties, which cater to business travelers and have more empty rooms on weekends. (However, national chains now offer the same prices on their own sites as you'll find on travel Web sites.)

 Don't assume that the hotels offered on the sites are all in handy, safe neighborhoods or offer the amenities you want. These sites merely list the properties; they don't judge them.

Check out these hotel-lodging sites on the Web:

- ✔ The name **All Hotels on the Web** (www.all-hotels.com) is something of a misnomer, but the site *does* have tens of thousands of listings throughout the world. Bear in mind that each hotel has paid a small fee (of $25 and up) to be listed, so it's less an objective list and more like a book of online brochures.

- ✔ **TravelNow** (www.travelnow.com) lists bargain rates at hotels in more than 50 cities. The cool thing is that TravelNow prebooks blocks of rooms in advance, so sometimes it has rooms — at discount rates — at hotels that are "sold out." Select a city, enter your dates, and you get a list of best prices for a selection of hotels. This site is notable for delivering deep discounts in cities where hotel rooms are expensive, but don't assume all their listings are for hotels you'd feel comfortable in. The toll-free number (☎ **800-511-5741**) is printed all over this site; call it if you want more options than are listed online.

✔ **InnSite** (www.innsite.com) has B&B listings in all 50 U.S. states. You can find an inn at your destination, see pictures of the rooms, and check prices and availability. This extensive directory of bed-and-breakfasts only includes listings if the proprietor submitted one (getting an inn listed is free). The descriptions are written by the innkeepers, and many listings link to the inns' own Web sites. Try also the **Bed and Breakfast Channel** (www.bedandbreakfast.com).

✔ **Places to Stay** (☎ **800-390-4687**; www.placestostay.com) lists one-of-a-kind places in the United States and abroad that you may not find in other directories, with a focus on resort accommodations. Again, listing is selective — this isn't a comprehensive directory, but it can give you a sense of what's available at different destinations.

✔ **Travelweb** (www.travelweb.com) lists more than 26,000 hotels, focusing on major chains, and you can book almost 90 percent of these online. Travelweb's Click-It Weekends, updated each Monday, offers weekend deals at many leading hotel chains.

✔ **HotelRes** (www.hotelres.com) lists over 245 hotels in and around San Francisco, including most of those mentioned in this book. The site is easy to navigate and clearly lists amenities, driving directions, and room availability/prices for specific dates. It's one of the best San Francisco–centric hotel sites I've checked.

Finally, *always* examine the hotel's own Web pages. I found a terrific deal on the site of one of my favorite hotels, and the price was $40 a night less than what the reservations clerk offered me over the phone.

Of the "big three" sites, **Expedia** (☎ **800-EXPEDIA**; www.expedia.com) offers a long list of special deals and virtual tours or photos of available rooms so you can see what you're paying for (a feature that helps counter the claims that the best rooms are often held back from bargain booking Web sites). **Travelocity** (☎ **888-872-8356**; www.travelocity.com) posts unvarnished customer reviews and ranks its properties according to the AAA rating system.

Also reliable are **Hotels.com** (☎ **800-246-8357**; www.hotels.com) and **Quikbook.com** (☎ **800-789-9887**; www.quikbook.com). An excellent free program, **TravelAxe** (www.travelaxe.net), can help you search multiple hotel sites at once, even ones you may never have heard of — and conveniently lists the total price of the room, including the taxes and service charges. **Travelweb** (www.travelweb.com), which I discuss earlier, is partly owned by the hotels it represents (including the Hilton, Hyatt, and Starwood chains) and is, therefore, plugged directly into the hotels' reservations systems — unlike independent agencies, which have to fax or e-mail reservation requests to the hotel, a good portion of which get misplaced. More than once, travelers have arrived at the hotel, only to be told that they have no reservation. To be fair, many of the major sites are undergoing improvements in service and ease of use, and Expedia will soon be able to plug directly into the reservations systems of many hotel chains — none of which can be bad news for consumers.

In the meantime, get a confirmation number and make a printout of any online booking transaction.

In the opaque Web site category, **Priceline** (www.priceline.com) and **Hotwire** (www.hotwire.com) are even better for hotels than for airfares; with both, you're allowed to pick the neighborhood and quality level of your hotel before offering up your money. On the downside, many hotels stick Priceline guests in their least desirable rooms. Be sure to go to the **BiddingForTravel** Web site (www.biddingfortravel.com) before bidding on a hotel room on Priceline; it features a fairly up-to-date list of hotels that Priceline uses in major cities. For both Priceline and Hotwire, you pay up front, and the fee is nonrefundable. *Note:* Some hotels don't provide loyalty-program credits or other frequent-guest amenities when you book a room through opaque online services.

The Web can be a good resource for hotel deals, but in my humble opinion, you usually get the most accurate information by calling the hotel directly. No matter what assurances you receive from online agencies, travel agency Web sites *cannot* guarantee specific rooms (unless, perhaps, you requested the bridal or presidential suite), and they know very little about the hotel they're selling. In many cases, the "reviews" you read online are provided and paid for by the hotels and, therefore, are likely to be promotional rather than critical.

Another problem recently brought to my attention is the difficulty in getting a refund from some of these reservation services if you have to cancel your stay. It's the service, not the hotel, that has your money until it settles with the hotel after you've checked out. Finally, there may be a difference between the amount of dough you pay the agency for your room and the amount the agency pays the hotel (that's the profit motive for you). If you don't like the place, again, you're stuck negotiating for a refund from the online agency rather than the hotel itself.

Reserving the best room

After you've made your reservation, asking one or two pointed questions can go a long way toward making sure you have the best room in the house:

✔ **Is there a corner on the market?** Ask for a corner room. They're usually larger, quieter, closer to the elevator, and have more windows and light than standard rooms, and they don't always cost any more.

✔ **What's that noise?** Inquire about the location of the restaurants, bars, and discos in the hotel — these could all be a source of irritating noise. The quietest rooms tend to be on the highest floors, facing away from the street.

✔ **Are you renovating?** If the hotel is renovating, request a room away from the jackhammers. And try to get a room on the most recently renovated floor — the furnishings and décor will be newer and nicer.

✔ **Does this room come in another color?** If you aren't happy with your room, talk to the front-desk manager. If he has another room available, he should be happy to accommodate you, within reason.

✔ **What size beds do you offer?** If having a queen- or king-size bed is important to you, be sure to ask for it when booking.

✔ **Mind if I smoke?** You can smoke outside in San Francisco to your heart's content, but be aware that the city has stringent antismoking laws inside public buildings, restaurants, and even bars. A sizable number of hotels, especially the smaller ones, are smoke-free. Other hotels only have smoking rooms on designated floors. Common courtesy in San Francisco is to ask before lighting up; you'd be surprised at the number of people who are allergic to smoke. If a smoking (or nonsmoking) room is important to you, let the reservations desk know when you call.

Arriving without Reservations

I am amazed at how many people come to San Francisco without hotel reservations, believing that a fabulous $30-a-night room is awaiting them in a fancy hotel. They usually end up sleeping in the "No-Tell Motel" in a dicey neighborhood because that's all that was available. Or they spend the better part of a day looking for accommodations, wasting valuable vacation time searching for a bargain, or finally, just a room, when there are none to be had. Don't be one of them. Reserve your vacation lodgings ahead of time.

However, if you're reading this book in the airport while waiting to board your flight to our fair city, you can try the following suggestions if you don't have a place to stay already:

✔ Call a free reservation service such as **San Francisco Reservations** (☎ **800-677-1500** or 510-628-4450 outside of North America) or **California Reservations** (☎ **415-252-1107**).

✔ Make your way to a boutique hotel and hope the desk clerk takes pity on you. Most of the boutique properties in town are part of small, independent companies, and a good-hearted staff person may be willing to make some calls to sister hotels to help you secure a room.

✔ Find a friendly concierge you can leave your luggage with so you can look for a room in the neighborhood unencumbered. If the town appears to be booked solid (ask the desk clerk's opinion), don't be picky or cheap. You can always move the next day if something better opens up.

Getting the Most for Your Money

Every accommodation that I recommend in this book is marked with one to four dollar signs. Here's a quick breakdown of the price categories, and what amenities and services you should expect in each range. All rates are for a standard double-occupancy room, excluding taxes.

✔ **$ ($125 or less):** Accommodations in this category are often in older buildings that may show their age. Room service, laundry or dry cleaning, valet parking, and porters do not come with the package, but the rooms are carefully tended, and the properties themselves exhibit some charm. The least expensive rooms may not have their own bathrooms.

The rooms I recommend in this price category tend to be on the "cozy" side and are typically furnished with inexpensive bedspreads, towels, and curtains. You won't find irons, little toiletries, or robes in the closet. Air-conditioning is also considered a luxury, although you rarely need it in San Francisco. A concierge won't be at the ready to cater to your every whim, but most desk clerks are delighted to help you arrange tours, tickets for shows, and dinner reservations. Many of the budget hotels recommended here offer a free continental breakfast, making them especially good deals.

✔ **$$ ($126–$175):** In this price category, I recommend some wonderful, charming places with stylish (but still small) rooms, handsome lobbies, and good to great service. Antique armoires and marble-tiled bathrooms are standard-issue in a few picks, but in general, these properties are for leisure travelers with minimal demands beyond comfort and an appealing décor. A separate concierge desk is not always available, but the front desk staff is usually willing to make reservations and book tours. Parking is sometimes valet, but more often it's self-parking at lots up to 3 blocks away. Room service is usually nonexistent, although you will probably find a cafe or restaurant attached to the property. Make sure to inquire about extras such as bathrobes and modem lines if these things are important to you. Often the more expensive suites are well equipped, but the low-end rooms won't have that all-important hair dryer unless you ask for it.

✔ **$$$ ($176–$300):** At this price, expect attentive service — usually including valet parking and porters — and larger rooms with finer fabrics and décor. Many properties in this range also have on-site StairMasters, and at least one has a pool. Although at the low end of this scale you may not find hand-milled soaps in the bathroom, at the high end, you'll feel pretty pampered.

When you're willing to pay this kind of money for a hotel, you probably have certain expectations. Make them known when you make your reservation. Don't wait until check-in to ask if you can receive faxes or if valet parking actually means a bellhop is going to fetch your car for you at 6 a.m.

✔ **$$$$ ($301 or more):** Your big bucks buy views, personal service, and sheets with high thread counts. Be prepared to be royally pampered by the well-trained staff. Large rooms usually feature fancy products and thick terry robes in the mirrored bathroom, an iron in the closet, art on the walls, and in some cases, umbrellas and flowers. Honor bars and baskets of overpriced goodies are also standard. For this much money, it would be a shame if you didn't spend some quality time in the hotel, fingering the drapes and calling down to the concierge desk for a weather report. Again, room rates are tied to location, with Nob Hill and the Embarcadero charging whatever the market will bear.

San Francisco's Best Hotels

Andrews Hotel
$–$$ Union Square

The services and location make this 48-room 1905 Victorian hotel a deal for couples on a budget, although the rooms and baths are pretty small, even by local standards. You do get a continental breakfast buffet provided on each floor and evening wine *gratis,* and an attractive, homey, wood-trimmed décor. Amiable receptionists serve double duty as concierge staff. You won't have air-conditioning or a tub in which to soak (most rooms only have showers), but you can open the windows. Since joining the Joie de Vivre Hospitality Group, the Andrews has upgraded its amenities and now provides fresh flowers and in-room VCRs. Complimentary videos are available from the reception desk. Consider spending the extra $20 per night on a sunny Bay King room like #403. Avoid the dark tiny rooms ending in 08. If street noise keeps you awake, request a room in the rear of the building.

See map p. 98. 624 Post St., between Taylor and Jones streets, 2 blocks west of Union Square. ☎ ***800-926-3739*** *or 415-563-6877. Fax: 415-928-6919.* www.andrews hotel.com. *Parking: $26. Rack rates: $109–$179. Ask about AARP and extended-stay discounts. AE, MC, V.*

 ### Argonaut Hotel
$$$–$$$$ Fisherman's Wharf

In an enviable position on the western side of the Cannery, this perky boutique hotel makes the innumerable chains around Fisherman's Wharf blush in comparison. Many of the heavily nautical-themed rooms have a view of either Alcatraz or the Golden Gate Bridge, while the lesser-priced interior rooms are touted as being quieter. Designers kept the 1907 brick walls and wooden beams in place, where possible, adding plantation shutters and using a palette of primary colors, which makes the place fun and attractive to families and visitors who want quality lodgings in this admittedly touristy area. Bedrooms are fairly spacious, but I was surprised at the ordinary-looking bathrooms with shallow tubs. Amenities are generous, including Aveda products, flat-panel TVs, DVD players, robes, well-stocked minibars, and coffeemakers. The hotel's restaurant, **Blue Mermaid,** serves all day and is better than average for wharf food.

See map p. 84. 495 Jefferson St., at Hyde Street. ☎ *866-415-0704 or 415-563-0800. Fax: 415-563-2800.* www.argonauthotel.com. *Parking: $36. Rack rates: $179–$299. Check Web site for special rates. AE, DC, DISC, MC, V.*

Campton Place
$$$$ Union Square

The soothing music piped into Campton Place's classically decorated lobby tells you right away that this is one genteel hotel. The atmosphere is intimate, clubby, and reserved — you'll want to use your company manners as the valet unpacks your bags and shows off the many luxury amenities (a Bose sound system, for one). You can even bring your dog (if he's well-behaved). Although the standard guest rooms are smaller than you may expect, they're elegantly appointed and bathrooms are above average in size and comfort. The restaurant has been the recipient of many awards and kudos — you may want to eat here even if you stay elsewhere. The property was acquired by the Kor Hotel Group in late 2005, and standards remain high — *Travel + Leisure* included Campton Place in its 2006 list of the World's Best Hotels.

See map p. 98. 340 Stockton St., at Post Street. ☎ *800-235-4300 or 415-781-5555. Fax: 415-955-5536.* www.camptonplacesanfrancisco.com. *Parking: $45. Rack rates: $385–$525. AE, DC, DISC, JCB, MC, V.*

Castle Inn
$–$$ Russian Hill

The Castle Inn is a good choice away from Union Square and the worst traffic on Van Ness Avenue. Units at this clean, convenient, friendly motel have been upgraded with maple furniture and new carpeting. They include in-room VCRs, microwave ovens, small refrigerators, continental breakfast, and even complimentary Wi-Fi. Guests are within walking distance of Polk Street's bars and restaurants and Fisherman's Wharf. If you have a car to park and want to avoid the exorbitant garage fees in Union Square and around Fisherman's Wharf, the Castle Inn is a smart pick but not so great if you want to be closer to shops and theater.

See map p. 84. 1565 Broadway, at Van Ness Avenue. ☎ *800-822-7853 or 415-441-1155. Fax: 415-775-2237.* www.castleinnsf.com. *Free parking. Rack rates: $85–$145. AE, CB, DC, DISC, MC, V.*

Hotels near Union Square, SoMa, and Nob Hill

San Francisco Bay

Golden Gate Bridge

PRESIDIO

Area of Detail

GOLDEN GATE PARK

SAN FRANCISCO

California St.

† Grace Cathedral

HUNTINGTON PARK

Nob Hill Masonic Center

Pine St.

NOB HILL

Bush St.

Sutter St.

Post St.

Cosmo

Geary St.

O'Farrell St.

Ellis St.

Eddy St.

Turk St.

Taylor St.

Shannon

Leavenworth St.

Jones St.

Andrews Hotel **2**
The Argent Hotel **33**
Campton Place **24**
The Cartwright Hotel **14**
Chancellor Hotel **21**
Clift **6**
Commodore International **1**
The Fairmont Hotel **10**
Galleria Park Hotel **19**
Golden Gate Hotel **12**
Handlery Union Square Hotel **26**
Hotel Adagio **3**
Hotel Bijou **30**
Hotel Milano **31**
Hotel Monaco **4**
Hotel Palomar **32**
Hotel Rex **13**
Hotel Triton **20**
The Huntington Hotel **9**
Inn at Union Square **22**
Kensington Park Hotel **23**
King George Hotel **28**
The Maxwell **27**
Monticello Inn **29**
Nob Hill Lambourne **16**
The Orchard Garden **18**
The Orchard Hotel **15**
Petite Auberge **8**
Ritz-Carlton **17**
St. Regis Hotel **34**
The Serrano Hotel **5**
W San Francisco **35**
The Warwick Regis Hotel **7**
Westin St. Francis **25**
White Swan Inn **11**

CABLE CAR LINES
California Line
Powell-Mason Line
Powell-Hyde Line
Cable Car Turnaround ⭕

Information ⓘ

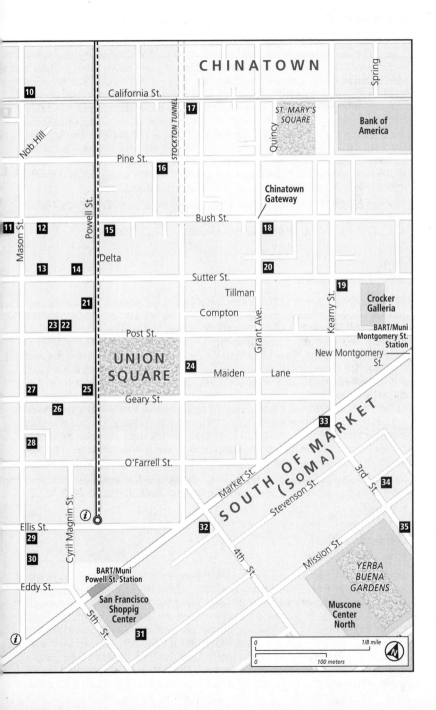

CHINATOWN

10

California St.

17

ST. MARY'S SQUARE

Bank of America

STOCKTON TUNNEL

Spring

Quincy

Nob Hill

Pine St.

16

Chinatown Gateway

Powell St.

Bush St.

18

11 12 15

Mason St.

Delta

20

13 14

Sutter St.

Tillman

19

Compton

Crocker Galleria

21

Grant Ave.

Kearny St.

BART/Muni Montgomery St. Station

23 22

Post St.

New Montgomery St.

UNION SQUARE

24

Maiden   Lane

27 25

26

Geary St.

SOUTH OF MARKET (SoMa)

33

O'Farrell St.

28

Market St.

Stevenson St.

3rd St.

34

Cyril Magnin St.

ⓘ

Ellis St.

32

35

29

Mission St.

30

4th St.

YERBA BUENA GARDENS

Eddy St.

BART/Muni Powell St. Station

Muscone Center North

San Francisco Shoppig Center

5th St.

31

ⓘ

0   1/8 mile

0   100 meters

N

Chancellor Hotel
$$ Union Square

The 137-room Chancellor has been owned and managed by the same family since 1917 and offers a level of intimacy and value you just won't find in many other comparable inns. It's right on the Powell Street cable-car line, a handbag's throw from Saks Fifth Avenue. The little bathrooms are well stocked; the petite bedrooms, brightly decorated and comfortably furnished; and you get a choice of pillows. For views, request front rooms ending in 00 to 05, but aim for the higher floors — the garbage trucks start their rounds at 5 a.m. and you don't want to be near the street. Amenities include ceiling fans (instead of air-conditioning), and coffee and cookies at the front desk. The hotel has a restaurant open for breakfast and lunch; it provides room service as well. Smoking is prohibited.

See map p. 98. 433 Powell St., between Post and Sutter streets. ☎ **800-428-4748** *or 415-362-2004. Fax: 415-362-1403.* www.chancellorhotel.com. *Parking: $30. Rack rates: $155–$185. AAA, AARP discounts available. AE, DC, DISC, MC, V.*

Clift
$$$$ Union Square

This is not your father's Clift Hotel, and if you're old enough to have memories of this landmark in its heyday, you're in for a shock. An Ian Schrager/Phillippe Starcke renovation in 2000 kicked the venerated Clift into the 21st century, cleaning up the fusty interior (which badly needed it) but stripping the hotel of its soul. Once known for fabulous service and a classy, San Francisco aura, the new Clift employs helpful staff, but we can argue the second point. The postmodern guestrooms lack warmth (and at these prices deserve roomier baths) and, strangely enough, the focal points of the white interiors are orange Lucite nightstands. You'll find a few amusing details in the lobby and bar, but the once-venerated Redwood Room is a pale imitation, with sulky 20-somethings crowding the bar. Schrager hotels are as much stage settings as places to sleep, which can be great fun if you're in the mood. Just be advised that style has usurped substance.

See map p. 98. 495 Geary St., at Taylor Street. ☎ **800-697-1791** *or 415-775-4700. Fax: 415-447-6580.* www.clifthotel.com. *Parking: $45. Rack rates: $365–$900. AE, CB, DC, MC, V.*

Commodore Hotel
$–$$ Union Square

Colorful but diminutive rooms and bathrooms (that could use some insulation to deter noise) provide a lively backdrop to an older building that shows some signs of wear. And this section of Sutter Street is close enough to the Tenderloin to put me on alert for drug dealers and prostitutes. Still, the location doesn't discourage European tourists, who appreciate the value and relaxed vibe. It's 3 flat blocks from Union Square, so food and entertainment are near at hand. Dennis Leary's diner, Canteen (see review in Chapter 10), is on one side of the lobby, and the fun, trendy Red Room bar is on the other. The hotel has no air-conditioning. If you can get a good deal here (under $100) and a room high up, you won't be unhappy. Otherwise, the Maxwell offers similar rates and is a step up in location and décor.

See map p. 98. 825 Sutter St., near Jones Street. ☎ *800-338-6848 or 415-923-6800. Fax: 415-923-6804.* www.jdvhospitality.com. *Parking: $28. Rack rates: $109–$149. AAA, AARP discounts available. AE, CB, DC, DISC, MC, V.*

Cow Hollow Motor Inn & Suites
$–$$$ The Marina/Cow Hollow

These serviceable, nonsmoking motel rooms, unfortunately accessed by elevators inside the parking garage, are clean and quiet, thanks to a diligent staff and double-paned windows, respectively. The early Sears Roebuck furnishings may not yet have made a style comeback, but you'll appreciate the in-room coffeemaker, hair dryer, and relatively spacious baths. What makes the Cow Hollow Inn of particular interest, besides free parking, free Wi-Fi, and low rates, is that it's around the corner from the best blocks of Chestnut Street, where the shopping and dining set a high standard. Families can settle into one of six suites with kitchens and a separate entrance right on Chestnut Street. Try to avoid rooms ending in 28, which are next to noisy ice machines.

See map p. 84. 2190 Lombard St. ☎ *415-921-5800. Fax: 415-922-8515.* www.cow hollowmotorinn.com. *Free parking. Rack rates: $72–$125 double; $225–$275 suite. AE, MC, V.*

Embarcadero Hyatt Regency
$$$–$$$$ The Embarcadero

This enormous (you're likely to get lost looking for your room) corporate hotel at the foot of Market Street gets the thumbs up for its location (but for the money, I'd stay at the Harbor Court or Vitale). Rooms are well equipped and spacious (some also have beautiful views), plus there are two restaurants and a few shops in the atrium lobby, as well as an on-site fitness center. This is probably your best bet for a hotel in the Embarcadero area if you're traveling with kids, who will love the indoor glass elevators. And the hotel's revolving **Equinox Bar and Restaurant** is irresistible to out-of-towners, who line up for a ride to the view. If you won't be needing the car, self-park it in an Embarcadero Center lot for $29 per day.

See map p. 84. 5 Embarcadero Center, at Market Street. ☎ *800-233-1234 or 415-788-1234. Fax: 415-398-2567.* www.sanfrancisco.regency.hyatt.com. *Parking: $43. Rack rates: $169–$329. Corporate discounts available. AE, CB, DC, DISC, MC, V; personal checks from U.S. banks. Dogs welcome.*

The Fairmont Hotel
$$$$ Nob Hill

I've always had a soft spot for the regal Fairmont because it's the first hotel I remember staying in when I was a child. I'm still bowled over when I stroll into the pillared and golden-colored lobby, which is usually humming with businesspeople and older leisure travelers. Depending on the time of year, you can get pretty decent rates (under $200) albeit in one of the "cozy" queens located in the main building. These are as spacious as guest rooms in the Tower building but don't have views and are priced accordingly. Tower rooms also have gorgeous marble baths with separate showers; all bedrooms are filled with amenities. Make sure to have a drink in the kitschy **Tonga Room** and marvel at the regularly scheduled storms. If you have kids along, take advantage of the 5 to 7 p.m. happy hour featuring a $7 all-you-can-eat Asian-inspired buffet — lots of young locals do. Should you be interested in a real San Francisco treat, you'll find it at the Fairmont, but if it's five-star treatment you're after, head for the Ritz or the St. Regis.

See map p. 98. 950 Mason St., at California Street. ☎ *800-441-1414 or 415-772-5000.* www.fairmont.com. *Parking: $43. Rates: $259–$750 double. AE, CB, DC, DISC, MC, V.*

Golden Gate Hotel
$ **Union Square**

If you're flexible (or broke) enough to share a bathroom, this cheerful, charming, 23-room Edwardian hotel with the feel of a B&B is a fabulous deal, in a great location for cable-car lovers and walkers. Traveling with older children? Take two of the small, pretty rooms, and buy yourself some privacy. A complimentary continental breakfast and afternoon tea are served, which adds to the feeling that the Golden Gate is run for love rather than money. There's a hotel cat and a dog, so if you're allergic, this unfortunately isn't the spot for you. The hotel has no air-conditioning.

See map p. 98. 775 Bush St., between Powell and Mason streets, 2 blocks from the Chinatown gate. ☎ *800-835-1118 or 415-392-3702. Fax: 415-392-6202.* www.golden gatehotel.com. *Self-parking: A relative bargain at $18. Rates: $85–$95 (shared bath) or $115–$130 (private bath) double. DC, MC, V.*

Handlery Union Square Hotel
$$$ **Union Square**

This favorite with tour packagers happens to be one of the better family hotels downtown because it features a small, heated outdoor pool — a rarity in San Francisco — as well as Nintendo, if you consider that a positive. (And kids under 15 stay free!) The regular doubles with smallish bathrooms have been renovated as has the lobby, but splash out on one of the larger Club Rooms located in an adjacent building. These feature a dressing area, cozy robes, the morning paper, and extra space. The hotel's two-bedroom suites are also a good value, and refrigerators are provided on request. Rooms by the pool are quietest.

See map p. 98. 351 Geary St., between Powell and Mason streets, ½ block from Union Square. ☎ *800-843-4343 or 415-781-7800. Fax: 415-781-0269.* www.handlery. com. *Parking: $36. Rack rates: $149–$269. Ask about AAA discount; corporate, federal government, and senior citizen rates; and Internet specials. AE, CB, DC, JCB, MC, V.*

Harbor Court Hotel
$$$ The Embarcadero

Located just steps from the bay and now under Kimpton Hotel manage-ment, this is an especially romantic and sophisticated property, lower key than the Hotel Vitale but equally as stylish. Rooms were all remodeled in 2005 and while they are pretty small, they're so warmly decorated and comfy I can imagine moving in for a long weekend, only stirring to watch the Yoga channel on the flat screen TV. Reserve or upgrade to a queen or king bay room, which features dramatic views of the water and Bay Bridge. Guests have free access to the state-of-the-art Embarcadero YMCA pool and health club right next door. A complimentary wine reception is held each evening, and after a glass you can step into trendy **Ozumo** (see review in Chapter 10), which is accessible from the lobby.

See map p. 84. 165 Steuart St., between Mission and Howard streets. ☎ **866-792-6283** *or 415-882-1300. Fax: 415-882-1313.* www.harborcourthotel.com. *Parking: $38. Rack rates: $159–$259. AE, CB, DC, DISC, MC, V.*

Hayes Valley Inn
$ Hayes Valley/Civic Center

In the not-so-distant past, I'd never have recommended lodging in this neighborhood, but the upscale shopping and dining opportunities have developed to such an extent that it overrides any other concerns (such as panhandlers). Hotel choices are limited, but for budget travelers — or anyone who would prefer to spend their dough on good meals or local designers — this 28-room Edwardian B&B is a find. Yes, you'll have to share the very clean toilets and showers, but you can brush your teeth at the sink/vanity in your sweetly decorated room. Expect to meet European tourists over cereal, bagels, orange juice, and coffee (included in the rates). Street-side rooms are larger, but noisier. The Van Ness Muni station or F-Market streetcars are a few minutes walk east. The Asian Art Museum, opera, ballet, and symphony are a few minutes walk north.

See map p. 84. 417 Gough St., near Hayes Street. ☎ **800-930-7999** *or 415-431-9131. Fax: 415-431-2585.* www.hayesvalleyinn.com. *Parking: Self-park in nearby lots. Rack rates: $84–$105 double. MC, V.*

Hotel Adagio
$$ Union Square

In a previous incarnation, this 1929 Colonial Revival building housed the tired Shannon Court Hotel, but a total face-lift in 2003 has turned Joan Crawford into Cindy Crawford. The Adagio's modern bedrooms and clean, masculine lines won't appeal to frill-seekers, but the hotel is closer in spirit to the W and the Clift (which is just down the block) — albeit more com-petitively priced. Sleek young things already jostle for space in the bar and a table in the *mucho caldo* **Cortez** restaurant (see Chapter 10). Because this is an older building, air-conditioning consists of ceiling fans and win-dows that open. A nicely fitted fitness center, high-speed and wireless Internet access, high-end bath products, complimentary afternoon tea, and Executive-level guest rooms that come with views and a continental breakfast bring the hotel squarely into the here and now.

See map p. 98. 550 Geary St., between Taylor and Jones streets. ☎ *800-228-8830 or 415-775-5000. Fax: 415-775-9388.* www.jdvhospitality.com. *Parking: $33. Rack rates: $129–$299. AE, CB, DC, DISC, MC, V.*

Hotel Bijou
$–$$ Union Square

Film buffs will get a kick out of this cinema-themed inn. In the evening, it shows San Francisco–based videos in a ten-seat screening room off the lobby, and there's even a candy counter. Freshly decorated rooms and baths (some with shower only) are tight and amenities few, but the staff is professional and service oriented. Continental breakfast is included in the rates. Be warned: This hotel shares the block with a sleazy strip club; if you think that may bother you, book elsewhere.

See map p. 98. 111 Mason St., at Eddy Street, around the corner from Hallidie Plaza. ☎ *800-771-1022 or 415-771-1200. Fax: 415-346-3196.* www.hotelbijou.com. *Parking: Shockingly reasonable at $27. Rack rates: $89–$149. AE, DC, MC, V.*

Hotel Bohème
$$–$$$ North Beach/Fisherman's Wharf

Set in the heart of North Beach, this charming, intimate hotel echoes the old Bohemian feel of the area. Fifteen small but romantic, beautiful (and recently refreshed) rooms are vividly painted and arrayed with iron beds and generous in-room amenities. Teensy bathrooms have showers only, no tubs. The accommodating staff is happy to assist with tours, rental cars, and restaurant reservations; you'll have to schlep your own luggage up the narrow stairs, though. The hotel has no air-conditioning, but the windows open. You're likely to find a younger, less conservative crowd staying here than at the Washington Square Inn, another small hotel in this neighborhood and price range.

See map p. 84. 444 Columbus Ave., between Vallejo and Green streets. ☎ *415-433-9111. Fax: 415-362-6292.* www.hotelboheme.com. *Self-parking: $31 in a garage 1½ blocks away. Rack rates: $159–$179. AE, CB, DC, DISC, JCB, MC, V.*

Hotel Del Sol
$$ Marina/Cow Hollow

Paint, mosaic tiles, and imagination can do a lot to reinvent a motel, and there's no better example than the Del Sol. You'll think you're in Southern California (after the fog lifts), but it's lots better here, because you can walk around the neighborhood without getting startled looks from drivers. The heated pool and a hammock suspended between palm trees complete the hallucination. Multicolored, fun, reasonably sized guest rooms and suites could have stepped out of a '90s Habitat catalog, and one is configured especially for families, with games and bunk beds. The best part: Parking is free and you're not on busy Lombard Street.

See map p. 84. 3100 Webster St., at Filbert Street. ☎ **877-433-5765** *or 415-921-5520. Fax: 415-931-4137.* www.thehoteldelsol.com. *Free parking. Rack rates: $109–$179. AE, DC, DISC, MC, V.*

Hotel Griffon
$$$ The Embarcadero

Of the Embarcadero hotels, the Griffon has decent concierge services, and six end rooms plus three suites that offer unsurpassed bay views. Sadly, the small rooms don't sing style — vintage white-brick walls and a lack of artwork equal a drab appearance. In some, sink/vanity combos sit just a few feet from the bed — an arrangement I find unsettling. Despite this, the hotel still has more personality than the Embarcadero Hyatt, and I like the location — very close to the water. A well-equipped YMCA (free for guests) is next door, and a good restaurant is off the lobby. Continental breakfast is included in the rates. This is a nonsmoking hotel.

See map p. 84. 155 Steuart St., between Mission and Howard streets. ☎ **800-321-2201** *or 415-495-2100. Fax: 415-495-3522.* www.hotelgriffon.com. *Self-parking: $24. Rack rates: $220–$285. AE, DC, DISC, MC, V.*

Hotel Milano
$–$$$ SoMa

This well-designed and well-maintained Italian-themed boutique hotel isn't flashy or hip, but you won't find a better value in SoMa. Amenities include a spacious on-site fitness room, a bar, and more floor space in your room than you'll find in other hotels in this price range. The multistory San Francisco Shopping Centre is a few feet away, and Yerba Buena Gardens is just around the corner, so you won't lack for things to do. Personally, I prefer the intimacy of this hotel to The Argent (also in this neighborhood and price range), but if you're looking for a room with a view, The Argent is a better bet.

See map p. 98. 55 Fifth St., between Market and Mission streets. ☎ **800-398-7555** *or 415-543-8555. Fax: 415-543-5885.* www.hotelmilanosf.com. *Parking: $30. Rack rates: $109–$199. AE, DC, DISC, MC, V.*

Hotel Monaco
$$$ Union Square

You'll wish you'd brought your fox-tail-trimmed scarf and vintage Vuitton steamer trunk when you sashay into the Art Deco–inspired Monaco. The medium-sized rooms are lushly decorated with patterned wallpaper, floral prints, and canopied beds. All the amenities — like room service and a spa and fitness center — are available, plus it's a pet-friendly hotel. The aptly named **Grand Cafe** restaurant (reviewed in Chapter 10) is next door. And if you're feeling lonely, they'll deliver a bowl of goldfish to your room. If you're carting along the children, tell the desk staff — they provide milk and cookies for munchkins.

See map p. 98. 501 Geary St., at Taylor Street. ☎ **866-622-5284** *or 415-292-0100. Fax: 415-292-0111.* www.hotelmonaco.com. *Parking: $39. Rack rates: $219–$599. AE, CB, DC, DISC, MC, V.*

Hotel Palomar
$$$$ SoMa

This newish, extremely grown-up hotel sits above a busy corner close to Union Square and the attractions South of Market. The hotel was designed for sophisticated business and leisure travelers; you can expect a high-quality experience (at high-quality prices) in luxuriously sedate surroundings. The ample guest rooms are fitted for work and play with multiline phones, fax machines, CD players, spa tubs, and Aveda products. There's room service, a fitness center, and **The Fifth Floor,** one of the more glamorous restaurants in town. Palomar guests, of course, don't have to wait four weeks for a table. Hotel Palomar compares in price to its neighbor, the W. So what's the difference between the two hotels? The Palomar is what the W will be when it's all grown up. But the W is convinced it's having more fun.

See map p. 98. 12 Fourth St., at Market Street. ☎ **866-373-4941** *or 415-348-1111. Fax: 415-348-0302.* www.hotelpalomar.com. *Parking: $42. Rack rates: $309–$409. Rates include morning paper and shoeshine. AE, DC, DISC, MC, V.*

Hotel Rex
$$–$$$ Union Square

Dorothy Parker fans will appreciate this 94-room delight, which, despite its artsy leanings, is warm and unpretentious. Listen to the cable cars clank by or peruse a book from the lobby library while drinking complimentary wine. The rooms are all smartly designed and decorated; sizes vary from smallish doubles to executive kings with more ample space. Enjoy full service here, including amenities such as CD players and the new **Café Andrée** serving three squares and Sunday brunch. The hotel hosts live jazz music on Friday nights.

See map p. 98. 562 Sutter St., between Powell and Mason streets. ☎ **800-433-4434** *or 415-433-4434. Fax: 415-433-3695.* www.thehotelrex.com. *Parking: $34. Rack rates: $129–$269. Rates include evening wine. AE, DC, DISC, MC, V.*

Hotel Triton
$$$ Union Square

The music of the Grateful Dead and/or their close personal friends blares from lobby speakers in this hip 'n happening ode to rock 'n' roll. Doubles are bite-size here, but, oh baby, are they funky. This wacky place is heavy on a playful style but also provides plenty of amenities, including Nintendo and happy hour with free wine and beer. To pay homage to the ab gods, there's a small on-site fitness room. The fabulous location, across from Chinatown's Dragon Gate, makes standing outside on the sidewalk an exotic experience. Rooms ending in 07 are especially compact, so you probably want to avoid them.

See map p. 98. 342 Grant Ave., at Sutter Street, across from the Dragon Gate. ☎ *888-364-2622 or 415-394-0500. Fax: 415-394-0555.* www.hotel-tritonsf.com. *Parking: $38. Rack rates: $219–$279. AE, CB, DC, DISC, MC, V. Well-behaved dogs welcome.*

Hotel Vitale
$$$–$$$$ The Embarcadero

If you consider yourself urbane yet earthy, practical yet appreciative of the better things in life, the Hotel Vitale has a room with your name on it. Expensive but not over-the-top extravagant, this new property claims the most coveted patch of earth in town — right across the boulevard from the Ferry Building. Spoiled by delicious views, an F-Market streetcar stop behind the building, and within walking distance to well-regarded restaurants, the hotel is well situated. Inside, it is a delight as well. You'll notice first how good the place smells (small vials with dried lavender grace the hallways), and attention to detail continues inside the guestrooms. Deluxe waterfront sanctuaries feature a sexy walk-in shower rather than skimpy bathtub/shower combos in the still-spacious, but viewless interior rooms. A spa with two outdoor soaking tubs, and a daily yoga class will provide any centering one requires. It's contemporary, chic, and full of vitality.

See map p. 84. 8 Mission St., at Steuart Street. ☎ *888-890-8688 or 415-278-3700. Fax: 415-278-3750.* www.hotelvitale.com. *Parking: $42. Rack rates: $309–$699. AE, CB, DC, DISC, MC, V.*

The Huntington Hotel
$$$$ Nob Hill

The Boston Brahmin in you will adore this refined, quiet oasis with its subtle elegance, impeccable service, and a gorgeous spa. The 1924 building originally housed apartments, so guest rooms and baths are larger than average; most are labeled suites. Rooms above the eighth floor have views; the ones below are extra spacious, and by the end of 2007 every guest room will have been updated. Children are welcome in the hotel (but not in the spa), and manicured Huntington Park, complete with a playground, is across the street. The staff, concierge included, will anticipate your every need. If you can afford to lay down the cash for a room here, you could also choose to stay at the Fairmont or Ritz-Carlton, the Huntington's Nob Hill neighbors, but I love the old-fashioned San Franciscan feel of the Huntington. If you want the total San Francisco experience, this is it. You'll certainly get pampered here, but if you're looking for something more glamorous, go with the Ritz.

See map p. 98. 1075 California St., at Taylor Street. ☎ *800-227-4683 or 415-474-5400. Fax: 415-474-6227.* www.huntingtonhotel.com. *Parking: $29. Rack rates: $350– $500 double; $600–$1,350 suites. AE, DC, DISC, MC, V.*

Inn at Union Square
$$–$$$ **Union Square**

This small, very discreet hotel is just the ticket if you desire a bit of luxury but don't care to make a scene. You get those little extras — continental breakfast, newspapers, bathrobes, wine and cheese in the early evening, nice linens, 24-hour concierge, health-club access — combined with very reasonable rates that make it a pleasure to part with some, but not too much, of your money. Tasteful rooms range from small to very large, and all have benefited from last year's tidying with new furniture, fabrics, and wallpaper. The hotel has no air-conditioning and it's non-smoking.

See map p. 98 440 Post St., near Powell Street. ☎ *800-288-4346 or 415-397-3510. Fax: 415-989-0529.* www.unionsquare.com. *Parking: $40. Rack rates: $209–$265. AE, CB, DC, DISC, MC, V.*

The Marina Courtyard Motel
$–$$ **The Marina/Cow Hollow**

Because this was originally an apartment building, 15 of the rentals in this funky, flower-bedecked, courtyard-style budget motel feature fully equipped kitchens. A granddaughter of the original owner redecorated the medium-sized studios with Italian bathroom tiles, Mission-style furniture, and pretty quilts, making this one of the few places on Lombard Street with even a hint of charm. Families can reserve two connecting rooms with a shared bath. Surprisingly, considering the location, rooms off the street are remarkably quiet. The front desk clerk will arrange tours or rental cars at your request. It is the definition of cheap and cheerful.

See map p. 84. 2576 Lombard St., near Divisadero Street. ☎ *800-346-6118 or 415-921-9406. Fax: 415-921-0364.* www.marinamotel.com. *Free parking in little garages on the premises. Rack rates: $85–$135; family room $99–$135. AE, MC, V. Dogs welcome.*

The Maxwell
$–$$$ **Union Square**

If you're a serious shopper, you'll like this attractive, deservedly popular hotel's supportive resources, such as its *Shopologist* newsletter. The guest rooms, which are either spacious and Art Deco chic or dark and small depending on your pocketbook or the kindness of the desk clerk, lie off an intimate, theatrical lobby. (The difference in price between a deluxe king and an executive queen or king may be as little as $10, so I suggest you pony up and buy yourself more space.) During the last remodel, designers thoughtfully didn't alter the original bathroom tile or the deep bathtubs. Max's on the Square provides room service. Be sure to check prices on their junior suites, especially off season. They can be quite a good deal.

See map p. 98. 386 Geary St., at Mason Street. ☎ *888-734-6299 or 415-986-2000. Fax: 415-397-2447.* www.maxwellhotel.com. *Parking: $32 valet, $26 at a nearby garage. Rack rates: $109–$229. Ask about corporate discounts and special packages. AE, DC, DISC, MC, V.*

Monticello Inn
$$ Union Square

With easy access to the Powell Street BART station, Union Square, and the greatly expanded shopping opportunities on Market and 5th streets (a new Bloomingdale's anchoring a new Westfield mall), the Colonial-themed and quite delightful Monticello is sitting pretty. You'll find spacious rooms with Chippendale reproductions (the designer, not the dancers), a lending library, weekly book signings, complimentary wine in the evening, and lots of value-minded packages to lure you away from more chic lodgings. The hotel restaurant is Puccini and Panetti, and it caters to families, unlike most Union Square eateries. The king/king rooms are another good choice for child-toting travelers. The noise-sensitive should request rooms facing the inside courtyard. As at all Kimpton hotels, your pets are invited to join the fun.

See map p. 98. 127 Ellis St., between Powell and Mason streets. ☎ *800-669-7777 or 415-392-8800. Fax: 415-398-2650.* www.monticelloinn.com. *Parking: $33. Rack rates: $139–$199 double. AE, DC, DISC, MC, V. Pets welcome.*

Nob Hill Lambourne
$$$–$$$$ Nob Hill

An intimate 20-room hotel, the relaxed and soothing Lambourne has spacious rooms with compact kitchenettes and many amenities. Suites are available for vacationing families — and they're beauties. Massages and other on-site spa treatments can be scheduled by the front-desk staff, and nightly turndown service substitutes vitamins for chocolates on your buckwheat-hull-filled pillow. Continental breakfast is included in the rates, and a fresh fruit basket is in the hallway for your pleasure. You won't find a better deal on Nob Hill, and you'll feel like management has your best interests at heart. Smoking is not allowed.

See map p. 98. 725 Pine St., at Stockton Street. ☎ *800-274-8466 or 415-433-2287. Fax: 415-433-0975.* www.nobhilllambourne.com. *Parking: $32. Rack rates: $139–$209 including continental breakfast and evening wine reception. AE, CB, DC, DISC, MC, V.*

The Orchard Hotel
$$$ Union Square

Opened in 2001, the sedate 105-room Orchard was built from scratch and boasts some of the largest bedrooms and most luxurious baths in the neighborhood. It may have less va-va-voom than older, true boutique hotels such as Hotel Rex or the Maxwell (yet oceans more than your Hiltons or Sheratons), but for sheer comfort, this is probably your best bet in this price range around Union Square. The conservatively decorated guest rooms will gratify business as well as vacation travelers and include CD/DVD players, high-speed Internet access, and top amenities, including room service, provided by the well-mannered and charming staff. Cable cars stop just around the corner. A sister hotel, **The Orchard Garden,** hadn't yet opened before this book went to press, but put it on your list. If it's managed as well as the Orchard, it's bound to be a terrific place. Plus, this is California's first sustainable, energy-efficient, healthy hotel, designed and built to receive certification from the U.S. Green Building Council.

See map p. 98 665 Bush St., between Stockton and Powell streets. ☎ **888-717-2881** *or 415-362-8878. Fax: 415-362-8088.* www.theorchardhotel.com. *Parking: $34. Rack rates: $229–$299. Rates include continental breakfast. AE, DC, MC, V.*

The Orchard Garden. 466 Bush St. next to the Chinatown Gate. ☎ **415-399-9807.** www.theorchardgardenhotel.com. *See Web site for rack rates. AE, DC, MC, V.*

Petite Auberge
$$–$$$ Union Square

Romantics will find happiness here among the florals and French country effects. The high-end rooms are enormous, the less expensive rooms are cozy and have showers only — but all are comfortable. Along with a full breakfast served downstairs in the homey dining room, complimentary tea, wine, and hors d'oeuvres are served in the afternoon. Petite Auberge is well known and exceedingly popular, so if you want to experience the charms of a Provençal inn in the city, book well in advance.

See map p. 98. 863 Bush St., between Mason and Taylor streets. ☎ **800-365-3004** *or 415-928-6000. Fax: 415-673-7214.* www.foursisters.com. *Parking: $32. Rack rates: $99–$209. AE, DC, MC, V.*

Ritz-Carlton
$$$$ Nob Hill

Okay, big spenders, here's your hotel. The Ritz takes posh to the extreme, and those who want to be treated like landed gentry will feel their money was well spent. After you settle into your beautiful, spacious, and recently remodeled nest (a $12.5-million upgrade added Wi-Fi, flat-panel TVs, fancy showerheads, and 400-thread-count sheets, in case you were counting), you can swim in the indoor pool, exercise in the fitness center, shop for antiques, and eat in a nationally renowned restaurant, all without ever leaving the cushy confines. And how can you not love a hotel where the mantra is "Instant guest pacification will be ensured by all"?

See map p. 98. 600 Stockton St., between Pine and California streets. ☎ **800-241-3333** *or 415-296-7465. Fax: 415-291-0288.* www.ritzcarlton.com. *Parking: $50. Rack rates: Well, if you have to ask . . . $495–$8,000. Special occasion packages available. AE, DC, DISC, MC, V.*

St. Regis Hotel
$$$$ SoMa

With the recent entry of the 40-story, purpose-built St. Regis Hotel onto the five-star scene, you can rest assured that pampering has reached, well, new heights. A distinctive addition to the skyline, the hotel itself (floors 22–40 are residences) is awash in understated, unquestionable great taste and comfort, from the handsome lobby bar to the lose-yourself-in-luxe bedrooms with deep soaking tubs, huge plasma screen TVs, and digitized remote control so one needn't rustle the high-thread-count sheets to close the window coverings or signal the butler. The fitness center and spa are the best in town. I also like the fact that each floor holds just 18 rooms. Views begin from the eighth floor. The hotel's fine-dining room, **Ame** (see Chapter 10), is now a destination in itself. All in all, the St. Regis is swell.

See map p. 98. 125 Third St., between Market and Mission streets. ☎ **415-284-4000**. *Fax: 415-284-4100.* www.starwoodhotels.com/stregis. *Parking: $45. Rack rates: $407–$749 double. AE, CB, DC, DISC, MC, V.*

San Remo Hotel
$ North Beach/Fisherman's Wharf

Staying in this 1906 building is something like bunking at a pal's home because you're going to have to share the bathrooms. Rooms are small but adorable (they look like something your grandmother may have done up), and all the hotel guests are relaxed and friendly, thrilled to have found such a bargain close to the bay. The penthouse, with a private bath, is prized for its views. However, ambience from the low-income housing project on the next block may not be the sort you crave. Laundry facilities are available, and the Fior d'Italia (the country's oldest Italian restaurant) has moved in downstairs. The rooms have no air-conditioning, televisions, or phones.

See map p. 84. 2237 Mason St., near Chestnut Street, 2 blocks from the Cannery. ☎ **800-352-7366** *or 415-776-8688. Fax: 415-776-2811.* www.sanremohotel.com. *Parking: $15 at a garage 2 blocks north. Rack rates: $55–$85. AE, DC, MC, V.*

The Serrano Hotel
$$–$$$ Union Square

A stellar example of what a boutique hotel should be, the Serrano is beautiful, relaxed, friendly, and well appointed. It's a terrific hotel for tourists as well as business travelers, who don't mind sacrificing square footage when they're receiving great value for money. The small rooms are full of color and amenities, and double-paned windows effectively work to reduce street noise. Guest rooms on upper floors even have city views. The Spanish Revival lobby is a gem — seating groups are arranged under the handsome beamed ceiling, and it's a convivial place in the early evening when complimentary wine is served and a tarot-card reader drops by to entertain. The only drawback, and it's minor, is the proximity to Ellis Street, which can seem dicey at times. In fact, it's just a 3-block walk to Union Square and 2 blocks to the Powell Street cable-car turnaround, so don't let this deter you. **Ponzu,** the hotel's restaurant, is excellent and a popular pre-theater spot.

See map p. 98. 405 Taylor St., at O'Farrell Street. ☎ **866-289-6561** *or 415-885-2500. Fax: 415-474-4879.* www.serranohotel.com. *Parking: $39. Rates: $159–$299. Check the Web site for packages. AE, DC, DISC, MC, V.*

Tuscan Inn
$$–$$$ North Beach/Fisherman's Wharf

The pet-friendly Best Western Tuscan is a welcome change compared to the rest of the chain hotels on Fisherman's Wharf. Personality doesn't abound, but the just-remodeled rooms are fairly large by local standards, and kids like the location. The concierge is enthusiastic and friendly, and all the amenities you expect are available with the added plus of an early-evening wine reception where you can meet your neighbors. In warm weather, enjoy dining al fresco at the hotel restaurant. The new Argonaut, the Tuscan's only rival on the wharf in this comfort zone, outdoes this property in style, but I'll bet the rates here will be better.

See map p. 84. 425 North Point, between Mason and Taylor streets. ☎ **800-648-4626** *or 415-561-1100. Fax: 415-561-1199.* www.tuscaninn.com. *Parking: $35. Rack rates: $159–$239. Ask about AAA, corporate, and senior discounts. AE, CB, DC, DISC, MC, V.*

Union Street Inn
$$–$$$ The Marina/Cow Hollow

This B&B has six richly appointed rooms and a choice location on a prime shopping street. If you want a bit less urban color, this is a fantastic retreat. The charming managers serve as concierge and cook a full breakfast as part of the package. Guest rooms are large, but beware of the steep stairs to the front door, which make this an impractical choice for anyone who has difficulty walking.

See map p. 84. 2229 Union St., between Fillmore and Steiner streets. ☎ **415-346-0424.** *Fax: 415-922-8046.* www.unionstreetinn.com. *Parking: $15 at a lot 1½ blocks away. Rack rates: $179–$289. AE, DISC, MC, V.*

Washington Square Inn
$$–$$$ North Beach/Fisherman's Wharf

The European atmosphere in North Beach makes this little hotel a wonderful choice, and if you plan to walk the neighborhoods, you won't find a better location. The rooms in the lower price bracket are small, but amenities such as fresh flowers, continental breakfast, afternoon tea, and evening wine and hors d'oeuvres in the antiques-filled lobby make them a terrific deal. Recent upgrades include flat screen televisions and free Wi-Fi. The staff will help you with your bags, but otherwise, the front-desk service is so-so. The hotel is non-smoking and there is a two-night minimum on weekends.

See map p. 84. 1660 Stockton St., at Filbert Street, across from Washington Square Park. ☎ **800-388-0220** *or 415-981-4220. Fax: 415-397-7242.* www.wsisf.com. *Parking: $25. Rack rates: $149–$289. AE, DC, DISC, JCB, MC, V.*

Westin St. Francis
$$–$$$$ Union Square

It's all about location. A prime corner across from Union Square and a glittering, bustling lobby are what give the historic St. Francis its air of excitement and glamour. But underneath all this is a really big, impersonal hotel — albeit one with 24-hour room service, concierges, shops, dining opportunities, and Westin's branded "Heavenly" beds. In any case, stick to the original (main) building. Its moderate-sized standard doubles are furnished with gorgeous reproductions and romantic antique chandeliers, although bathrooms are on the small side. Ask for a view or a corner room to get some natural light, and avoid rooms by the ever-busy elevators. Deluxe and Grandview rooms are the best in the house, while the standard queens are just large enough for a single traveler. My suggestion is to stay at the Orchard Hotel instead and drop by the St. Francis to ride in the glass elevator and have a look around. The good news is the hotel was sold in 2006 and a renovation is rumored.

See map p. 98. 335 Powell St., across from Union Square. ☎ **800-937-8461** *or 415-397-7000. Fax: 415-774-0124.* www.westin.com. *Parking: $40 with a $9 surcharge for oversized vehicles. Rack rates: $129–$569. AE, DC, DISC, JCB, MC, V.*

White Swan Inn
$$$ Union Square

The 26 guest rooms in this English-style B&B are designed to be lingered in. You'll want to take advantage of the four-poster beds and fireplaces in the spacious rooms. A continental breakfast buffet is included in the rates, as is afternoon tea and evening wine and hors d'oeuvres served downstairs in the parlor. You'll think you're visiting a well-to-do British aunt. Back rooms are sunnier; the queen rooms have showers only. Just as in the White Swan's neighboring inn, Petite Auberge, advance reservations are imperative here and smoking is not allowed.

See map p. 98. 845 Bush St., between Mason and Taylor streets. ☎ **800-999-9570** *or 415-775-1755. Fax: 415-775-5717.* www.jvdhospitality.com. *Parking: $32. Rack rates: $139–$249. AE, DC, MC, V.*

W San Francisco
$$$–$$$$ SoMa

Ultramodern and light on the froufrou, W precisely aims its glossy high style and service at hip business travelers. Of course, they generally head for the airport on Fridays, leaving the vaguely masculine, moderate-sized rooms available to the rest of us. Marvel at the handsome chrome-and-frosted-glass bathroom, the deluxe amenities, the CD player, and the dataports. A lap pool, fitness room, restaurant, cafe, bar, room service, and well-trained staff add heft to an already solid package. If you can snag a corner room, do — there's more space.

See map p. 98. 181 Third St., at Howard Street. ☎ *877-946-8357 or 415-777-5300. Fax: 415-817-7860.* www.whotels.com. *Parking: $45. Rack rates: $529–$589. AE, DC, DISC, JCB, MC, V. Dogs welcome.*

Runner-Up Hotels

Having trouble finding a bed? If the hotels listed earlier in this chapter are filled up, try booking in one of the following accommodations. They may have saved you some room.

The Argent Hotel

$$$–$$$$ SoMa   This is a sizable, run-of-the-mill convention hotel with larger-than-average rooms and many extras — irons, hair dryers, quality bath products, and so on. What earns it a place in this chapter, besides its stellar location near Yerba Buena Gardens and the Museum of Modern Art, are the nearly floor-to-ceiling windows providing great views from rooms and suites above the 14th floor. A restaurant, fitness center, sauna, and pretty garden also help elevate The Argent beyond the ordinary, but look for a deal on Priceline. *See map p. 98. 50 Third St., near Market Street.* ☎ *877-222-6699 or 415-974-6400. Fax: 415-543-8268.* www.argenthotel.com. *Parking: $38. Rack rates: $265–$449. Check Web site for deals. AE, DC, DISC, JCB, MC, V.*

The Cartwright Hotel

$–$$$ Union Square   Standard guest rooms in this low-key hotel are on the small side (reserve a deluxe king if you're claustrophobic), but the two-bedroom suites will suit a family. All the guest rooms have been recently redone. Along with high-end in-room amenities, free Wi-Fi, and an afternoon wine reception, the hotel provides a substantial continental breakfast. European in feel, the Cartwright is well located for Union Square and Chinatown, well managed, and you'll find friendly, helpful staff. *See map p. 98. 524 Sutter St., near Powell Street.* ☎ *800-919-9779 or 415-421-2865. Fax: 415-398-6345.* www.cartwrighthotel.com. *Parking: $30. Rack rates: $109–$189 double. AE, DC, DISC, MC, V.*

Galleria Park Hotel

$$$ Union Square   This is a terrific, small hotel in a clever location close to Chinatown, the Financial District, and Union Square. Unlike most downtown properties, this one has on-site parking that is handy for travelers who need quick access to their automobiles. The hotel's experienced concierge is a gold mine of information and assistance. There's a workout room on-site and a rooftop jogging track/garden. As this book went to press, a complete room renovation was planned for late 2006. *See map p. 98. 191 Sutter St., at Kearny Street.* ☎ *800-792-9639 or 415-781-3060. Fax: 415-433-4409.* www.galleriapark.com. *Parking: $33. Rack rates: $119–$209. AE, CB, DC, DISC, MC, V.*

Kensington Park Hotel

$–$$ Union Square   This 88-room property is beginning to look a little frayed, although the larger-than-average rooms are slowly being renovated. The bathrooms are already among the handsomest in the area. The 11th floor is now an executive floor (ask for a Royal Court room) with upgraded linens, robes, and continental breakfast. Workout facilities are available, and the staff is delightful. The hotel has no air-conditioning. *See map p. 98. 450 Post St., between Mason and Powell streets.* ☎ *800-553-1900 or 415-788-6400. Fax: 415-399-9484.* www.kensingtonparkhotel.com. *Parking: $35. Rack rates: $149–$200. AE, CB, DC, DISC, JCB, MC, V.*

King George Hotel

$–$$ Union Square   Check the Web site for deals that could be as low as $99 including parking. The guest rooms are miniscule, as are the baths, but the entire hotel was remodeled in 2002 and they did a good job. The bar is exceedingly low-key and pleasant — a proper English tea is served on weekends that is popular enough to require reservations. The hotel is in the process of updating its rooms. *See map p. 98. 334 Mason St., at Geary Street.* ☎ *415-781-5050. Fax: 415-391-6976.* www.kinggeorge.com. *Self-parking: $28. Rack rates: $159–$189. AE, CB, DC, DISC, JCB, MC, V.*

The Warwick Regis Hotel

$$–$$$$ Union Square   This is the closest you can get to a French chateau downtown. If circa–Louis XVI armoires, brocade fabrics, crown-canopied beds, and marble-tiled bathrooms get your heart racing, you're going to adore this hotel. Twice-daily housekeeping, fresh flowers, great amenities, a restaurant/bar, and 24-hour room service are wrapped up in an intimate atmosphere. *See map p. 98. 490 Geary St., at Taylor Street.* ☎ *800-827-3447 or 415-928-7900. Fax: 415-441-8788.* www.warwickhotels.com. *Parking: $30. Rack rates: $119–$3,299. AE, DC, DISC, JCB, MC, V.*

Index of Accommodations by Neighborhood

SoMa

The Argent Hotel ($$$–$$$$)
Hotel Milano ($–$$$)
Hotel Palomar ($$$$)
St. Regis Hotel ($$$$)
W San Francisco ($$$–$$$$)

Union Square

Andrews Hotel ($–$$)
Campton Place ($$$$)
The Cartwright Hotel ($–$$$)
Chancellor Hotel ($$)
Clift ($$$$)
Commodore Hotel ($–$$)
Galleria Park Hotel ($$$)
Golden Gate Hotel ($)

Handlery Union Square Hotel ($$$)
Hotel Adagio ($$)
Hotel Bijou ($–$$)
Hotel Monaco ($$$)
Hotel Rex ($$–$$$)
Hotel Triton ($$$)
Inn at Union Square ($$–$$$)
Kensington Park Hotel ($–$$)
King George Hotel ($–$$)
The Maxwell ($–$$$)
Monticello Inn ($$)
The Orchard Hotel ($$$)
Petite Auberge ($$–$$$)
The Serrano Hotel ($$–$$$)
The Warwick Regis Hotel ($$–$$$$)
Westin St. Francis ($$–$$$$)
White Swan Inn ($$$)

Index of Accommodations by Price

$

Andrews Hotel (Union Square)
Cartwright Hotel (Union Square)
Castle Inn (Russian Hill)
Commodore Hotel (Union Square)
Cow Hollow Motor Inn & Suites
(The Marina/Cow Hollow)
Golden Gate Hotel (Union Square)
Hayes Valley Inn (Civic Center/
Hayes Valley)
Hotel Bijou (Union Square)
Hotel Milano (SoMa)
Kensington Park Hotel (Union Square)
King George Hotel (Union Square)
The Marina Courtyard Motel
(The Marina/Cow Hollow)
The Marina Courtyard Motel
(The Marina/Cow Hollow)
The Maxwell (Union Square)
San Remo Hotel (North
Beach/Fisherman's Wharf)

$$

Andrews Hotel (Union Square)
The Cartwright Hotel (Union Square)
Castle Inn (Russian Hill)
Chancellor Hotel (Union Square)

Commodore Hotel (Union Square)
Cow Hollow Motor Inn & Suites
(The Marina/Cow Hollow)
Hotel Adagio (Union Square)
Hotel Bijou (Union Square)
Hotel Bohème (North
Beach/Fisherman's Wharf)
Hotel Del Sol (The Marina/
Cow Hollow)
Hotel Milano (SoMa)
Hotel Rex (Union Square)
Inn at Union Square (Union Square)
King George Hotel (Union Square)
The Marina Courtyard Motel
(The Marina/Cow Hollow)
The Maxwell (Union Square)
Monticello Inn (Union Square)
Petite Auberge (Union Square)
The Serrano Hotel (Union Square)
Tuscan Inn (North Beach/
Fisherman's Wharf)
Union Street Inn (The Marina/
Cow Hollow)
The Warwick Regis Hotel
(Union Square)
Washington Square Inn (North
Beach/Fisherman's Wharf)
Westin St. Francis (Union Square)

$$$

The Argent Hotel (SoMa)
Argonaut Hotel (Fisherman's Wharf)
Cartwright Hotel (Union Square)
Cow Hollow Motor Inn & Suites
(The Marina/Cow Hollow)
Embarcadero Hyatt Regency
(The Embarcadero)
Galleria Park Hotel (Union Square)
Handlery Union Square Hotel
(Union Square)
Harbor Court Hotel
(The Embarcadero)
Hotel Bohème (North
Beach/Fisherman's Wharf)
Hotel Griffon (The Embarcadero)
Hotel Milano (SoMa)
Hotel Monaco (Union Square)
Hotel Palomar (SoMa)
Hotel Rex (Union Square)
Hotel Triton (Union Square)
Hotel Vitale (The Embarcadero)
Inn at Union Square (Union Square)
The Maxwell (Union Square)
Nob Hill Lambourne (Nob Hill)
The Orchard Hotel (Union Square)
Petite Auberge (Union Square)
The Serrano Hotel (Union Square)
Tuscan Inn (North Beach/
Fisherman's Wharf)

Union Street Inn (The Marina/
Cow Hollow)
The Warwick Regis Hotel
(Union Square)
Washington Square Inn (North
Beach/Fisherman's Wharf)
Westin St. Francis (Union Square)
White Swan Inn (Union Square)
W San Francisco (SoMa)

$$$$

The Argent Hotel (SoMa)
Argonaut Hotel (Fisherman's Wharf)
Campton Place (Union Square)
Clift (Union Square)
Embarcadero Hyatt Regency
(The Embarcadero)
The Fairmont Hotel (Nob Hill)
Hotel Palomar (SoMa)
Hotel Vitale (The Embarcadero)
The Huntington Hotel (Nob Hill)
Nob Hill Lambourne (Nob Hill)
St. Regis Hotel (SoMa)
Ritz-Carlton (Nob Hill)
The Warwick Regis Hotel
(Union Square)
Westin St. Francis (Union Square)
W San Francisco (SoMa)

Chapter 10

Dining and Snacking in San Francisco

. . . .

In This Chapter

▶ Assessing the latest dining trends

▶ Savoring the local flavor

▶ Reserving your table

▶ Finding the best places for a leisurely meal or snack

. . . .

*W*hether you're a genuine gourmet or a fledgling foodie, San Francisco has more culinary options than you can shake a nice bunch of organic basil leaves at. But no matter where you rank yourself on the scale of serious eating, there's no excuse to waste a meal in this city. Fast-food counters, chain restaurants, marketing enterprises masquerading as dining establishments — you'll find them here, but do yourself a favor and pass 'em by. Instead, take advantage of the fresh, local ingredients and skilled chefs that keep San Francisco in the culinary spotlight, and I guarantee you'll dine to your heart's content.

Getting the Dish on the Local Scene

Restaurants debut in this town with great hoopla, but what's hot today may be out of business by the time you turn this page. At the moment, the newest trend is sharing. I don't mean spilling your life story — I mean sharing plates of food with your tablemates. Although this isn't news in your average Chinese restaurant, it is in other eateries, so if you sup at Rose Pistola or Lulu, for example, be advised that those hefty portions really are meant for the entire table. On the other end of the spectrum, small plates, an offshoot of the Spanish penchant for tapas, are all the rage, and they, too, are meant to be shared. This can get nasty if three plump scallops arrive and you're part of a party of four, so try to dine with at least one vegetarian or be prepared to cover the tabletop with a lot of little dishes.

Finding the trendiest tables

San Francisco has no lack of sizzling white-tablecloth restaurants. Getting last-minute reservations at **Jardinière** (☎ 415-861-5555), or at two of the city's newer sophisticated purveyors of fine dining, **Ame** (☎ 415-284-4040) and **Quince** (☎ 415-775-8500; see listings later in this chapter), is tough. Call ahead — way, way ahead — if you have your heart set on supping at any of these bastions of chic. Wrangling a table at the always-sublime **Dining Room at the Ritz-Carlton** (☎ 415-773-6168) is equally challenging with Ron Siegel (the kitchen god who bested Japanese television phenom "Iron Chef") at the helm. And despite the increase to 200 seats with the move to the Ferry Building, it's a three-week wait for dinner at **Slanted Door** (☎ 415-861-8032; see listing later in this chapter). You might try for lunch instead. For anyone traveling up to Yountville in order to eat at **The French Laundry** (☎ 707-944-2380), one of the most coveted reservations in the country, bookings are accepted two months to the day in advance. OpenTable.com (see "Making reservations," later in this chapter) has exactly two tables available online with a separate page devoted to the reasons why you're going to get frustrated getting your hands on one. Determined eaters who can't wait to spend $210 on a prix fixe (okay, it's an amazing experience) should mark their calendars and exercise their dialing fingers, while giving OpenTable.com a try as well.

Cooking up San Francisco cuisine

When it comes to cuisine, international influences are the inspiration for most Bay City menus. This is not odd considering the ethnic makeup of the city's population, but it may throw you for a loop when your menu runs the gamut from East to West with a little Southern comfort thrown in for good measure. Those restaurants serving tapas are the most keen to take advantage of various culinary styles, and it's a clever way for a young chef to show his or her stuff. These small plates are also a pleasing way to order a meal. You don't have to choose between dishes that sound equally appealing, because the prices are low enough, and the portions modest enough, to sample them all.

California cuisine, of course, will always have a presence here, although it's being usurped by Modern American or New American cuisine. California cuisine features fresh, seasonal ingredients prepared in simple and light ways. New American cuisine, on the other hand, also uses seasonal ingredients, but the preparations are influenced by whatever foreign cuisines interest the chef. Although the subtleties may be lost on you if you don't deconstruct your meals, I mention this because many new restaurants describe their cooking in these terms.

Another welcome dining trend has to do with accommodating those who are organizationally challenged. Many excellent restaurants in town, including **Boulevard** and **Gary Danko** (see listings later in this chapter), accommodate walk-ins with counter seats or service in their bar areas. This is your best chance to eat at these top spots if you don't have reservations.

San Francisco Dining

A-16 **2**
Absinthe **44**
Ame **27**
B-44 **26**
Bistro Aix **3**
Bodega Bistro **32**
Boulevard **21**
Butterfly **9**
Café du Nord **41**
Café Kati **47**
Canteen **29**
Chow **39**
Citizen Cake **45**
Cortez **30**
East Coast West
  Delicatessen **7**
Enrico's Sidwalk
  Café **16**
Gary Danko **8**
Gold Mountain **15**
Grand Café **31**
Green's **4**
Hawthorne Lane **36**
Hayes Street Grille **43**
Home **5, 40**
Isa **3**

Jardinière **46**
Kay Cheung **17**
Kokkari Estiatorio **18**
Le Charm **33**
Le Colonial **28**
Lichee Garden **14**
L'Osteria del Forno **13**
Lulu **34**
Mamacita **1**
Merenda **5**
Moose's **11**
Ozumo **22**
Pazzia **37**
Quince **48**
R&G Lounge **25**
Rose Pistola **12**
Slanted Door **19**
Superclub **35**
Tablespoon **6**
Tadich Grill **24**
Teatro Zin Zanni **10**
Town Hall **23**
Tres Agaves **38**
Yank Sing **20**
Zuni Café **42**

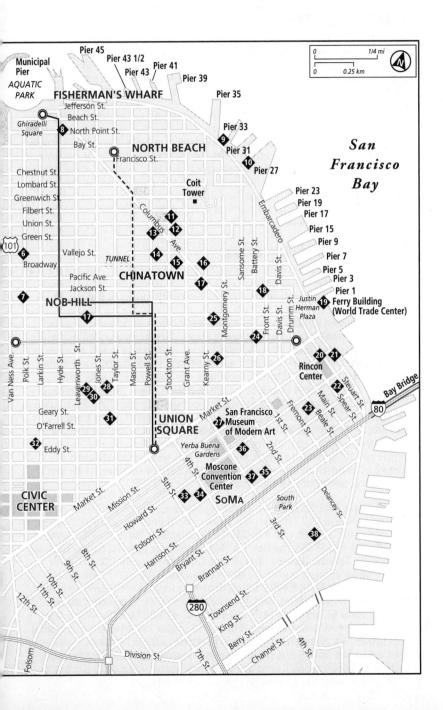

Making reservations

If you really want to experience some of the high-profile restaurants while you're in town, make sure you book a table before you get here. It's not that the hostess takes pleasure in turning you away on a Friday night at 8 p.m. — but did you notice all the other people drinking in the bar who also thought they could amble in and get a table?

 Besides picking up the phone, you can contact a vast number of restaurants through the **OpenTable** Web site (www.opentable.com). I've used this free Internet site many times, always with excellent results. You may also put your hotel concierge to work by requesting that he assist you with dinner reservations. If you're really desperate, you can show a little chutzpah like my old friend Josephine, who has been known to march up to the host, look him in the eye, and announce she has reservations, even when that's not entirely accurate. The caveat here is to make sure your dining partners don't buckle under pressure.

Exploring the dining zones

Cafes and restaurants often congregate on certain blocks, making it easy to stroll down the street until an enticing odor or empty table calls out to you. One of my absolute favorite dining destinations is **Belden Place** in the Financial District, a 1-block alley closed to traffic off Bush and Pine streets between Kearny and Montgomery. Weekdays, in good weather, the outdoor tables are coveted lunch spots. Two standouts on multicultural Belden are **Plouf** (☎ 415-986-6491), a delightful French restaurant specializing in fish and shellfish, and **B-44** (☎ 415-986-6287; see listing later in this chapter), a Spanish charmer specializing in paella and Catalan dishes. **North Beach** is awash in Italian cafes, Italian restaurants of all persuasions, and some inexpensive little eateries. The family-style **La Felce,** 1570 Stockton St., at Union (☎ 415-392-8321); and **Capps Corner,** 1600 Powell, at Green (☎ 415-989-2589), are among the last of the breed, where complete meals are no understatement. You order a bottle of Chianti and watch as your table fills with antipasti, then a tureen of minestrone, followed by huge platters of spaghetti, chicken cacciatore, and spumoni for dessert.

The **Mission District** gourmet ghetto continues to explode, especially around Valencia and 16th streets, where you'll find the popular creperie **Ti Couz,** 3108 16th St. (☎ 415-252-7373), and **Bar Tartine,** 561 Valencia St. (☎ 415-487-1600), the new Cal/Med brasserie opened by the brilliant team from **Tartine Bakery** at 18th and Guerrero streets (☎ 415-487-2600). Mexican-food lovers should try **Pancho Villa,** 3071 16th St. at Valencia (☎ 415-864-8840), which draws a crowd with its inexpensive and fresh burritos, tacos, and specialty platters, or **Taqueria Cancun,** 2288 Mission St. between 18th and 19th (☎ 415-252-9560), which stays open until 2 a.m. on weekends. The mood in this neighborhood is casual and urban; it's populated by students, artists, a large Hispanic community, and a fair number of street people. Parking requires patience and luck, but there's a BART stop at 16th and Mission — a rather dicey station, so you may want to take a cab on the way home.

Dining near North Beach and Chinatown

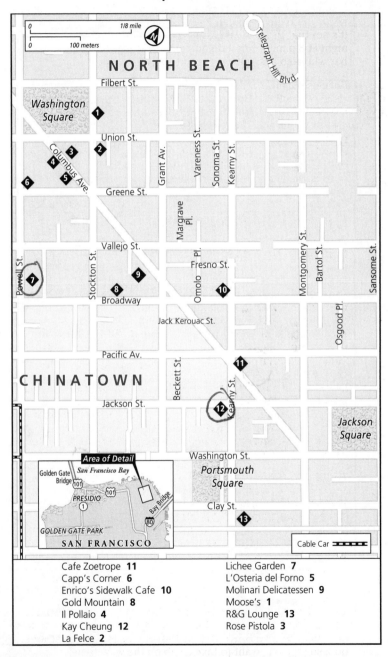

Cafe Zoetrope **11**
Capp's Corner **6**
Enrico's Sidewalk Cafe **10**
Gold Mountain **8**
Il Pollaio **4**
Kay Cheung **12**
La Felce **2**

Lichee Garden **7**
L'Osteria del Forno **5**
Molinari Delicatessen **9**
Moose's **1**
R&G Lounge **13**
Rose Pistola **3**

Dining near Union Square, SoMa, and Nob Hill

Ame **21**
B-44 **12**
Café de la Presse **18**
Café Mason **11**
Canteen **3**
Citizen Cupcake **12**

Cortez **6**
Dottie's True Blue Café **8**
Grand Café **10**
Harry Denton's Starlight Room **5**
Hawthorne Lane **23**
Kokkari Estiatorio **13**

CABLE CAR LINES

California Line ——————
Powell-Mason Line – – – – – – – – ·
Powell-Hyde Line ——————
Cable Car Turnaround ◎

CHINATOWN

Grant Ave.
Columbus Ave.
Kearny St.
Montgomery St.
Sansome St.
Battery St.
Front St.
Davis St.
Drumm St.

Pine St.
Chinatown Gateway
Claude Ln.
Bush St.
Sutter St.
Campton Pl.
Post St.
Maiden La.
Geary St.

SOUTH OF MARKET (SOMA)

Market St.
Third St.
New Montgomery St.
2nd St.
Mission St.
Fremont St.
Beale St.
1st St.
Howard St.
Folsom St.

Le Colonial **4**
Mixt Greens **17**
Palio Paninoteca **14**
Pazzia **22**
Sears Fine Food **7**
Shalimar **8**

Specialty's Café & Bakery **19**
Tadich Grill **15**
Top of the Mark **1**
Town Hall **20**
Uncle Vito's Pizzadeli **2**

You can take the N-Judah streetcar to Irving Street and Ninth Avenue near Golden Gate Park to find another great couple of blocks of moderately priced and high-quality restaurants. **Chow,** 215 Church St. (☎ 415-552-2469; see listing later in this chapter), has a location here, and you can't go wrong at **P.J.'s Oyster Bed,** 737 Irving St. at Ninth (☎ 415-566-7775). Some good Japanese and Thai restaurants are also nearby, including **Ebisu,** 1283 9th Ave. (☎ 415-566-1770).

Discovering off-the-beaten-track restaurants

Restaurants are mining new territory as well, as evidenced by the dozens of places opening in neighborhoods most visitors would have shunned once upon a time. The blocks around **Dolores, Valencia,** and **Guerrero streets** in the **Mission District** from 16th to 23rd streets are just one example. Storefronts and former corner markets have become the domain of chefs hoping to create the next big thing food-wise. **Delfina,** 3621 18th St. at Guerrero (☎ 415-552-4055; see listing later in this chapter), is one of the area's pioneers, but if you can't wrangle a table there, line up at **Dosa,** 995 Valencia St. near 21st Street (☎ 415-642-3672), for South Indian cuisine, **Limon,** 524 Valencia St. near 16th (☎ 415-252-0918), a Peruvian restaurant so good it had to move to larger digs in 2004, or **The Last Supper Club,** 1199 Valencia St. at 23rd Street (☎ 415-695-1199), an Italian joint designed to make you nostalgic for your Sicilian grandmother, whether you had one or not.

A section of **Potrero Hill** is also drawing lots of interest from professional eaters and cooks. Mosey around 18th Street between Missouri and Connecticut streets where the savvy folks behind Plouf have opened a trio of little places that keep the neighbors fat and happy. **Chez Maman,** 1453 18th St. (☎ 415-824-7166), is open daily for crepes, while **Chez Papa,** 1401 18th St. (☎ 415-255-0387), serves rustic French food that's delicious and amazingly inexpensive. Their Moroccan/Spanish entry, **Baraka,** 288 Connecticut St. (☎ 415-255-0387), offers around 25 small plates in a romantic, candlelit room. You'll need to take a cab or drive to Potrero Hill.

Sampling San Francisco's ethnic eats

Certain neighborhoods in San Francisco are hubs for particular regional cuisines, as is the case in other big cities. You can find several ethnic enclaves, with **Chinatown** the most obvious example. Head to **North Beach,** thick with trattorie and bakeries, for authentic Italian. Not to be outdone, the **Mission District** serves up terrific, inexpensive *taquerias,* and you can see Central American cafes alongside new gourmet restaurants. The tasty, authentic fare is worth the trip.

Over in the **Richmond District** (see Chapter 8), you'll notice a clutch of Russian bakeries, delicatessens, and restaurants, most notably **Katia's, A Russian Tea Room,** 600 Fifth Ave., at Balboa Street (☎ 415-668-9292), open Wednesday through Friday for lunch and Wednesday through Sunday for dinner. You can also find many more Asian and

The Mission District

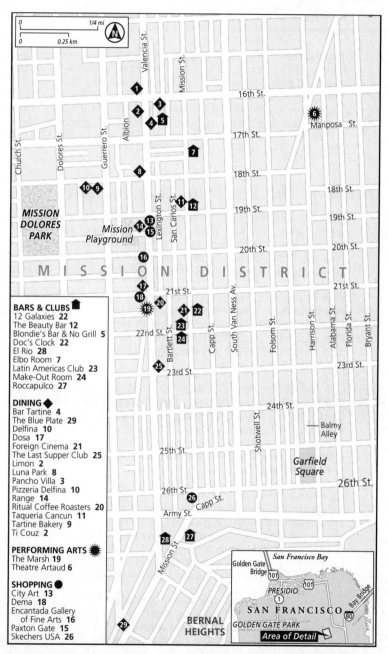

BARS & CLUBS 🏴
12 Galaxies **22**
The Beauty Bar **12**
Blondie's Bar & No Grill **5**
Doc's Clock **22**
El Rio **28**
Elbo Room **7**
Latin Americas Club **23**
Make-Out Room **24**
Roccapulco **27**

DINING ◆
Bar Tartine **4**
The Blue Plate **29**
Delfina **10**
Dosa **17**
Foreign Cinema **21**
The Last Supper Club **25**
Limon **2**
Luna Park **8**
Pancho Villa **3**
Pizzeria Delfina **10**
Range **14**
Ritual Coffee Roasters **20**
Taqueria Cancun **11**
Tartine Bakery **9**
Ti Couz **2**

PERFORMING ARTS ☀
The Marsh **19**
Theatre Artaud **6**

SHOPPING ●
City Art **13**
Dema **18**
Encantada Gallery
  of Fine Arts **16**
Paxton Gate **15**
Skechers USA **26**

Chinese eateries in the Richmond District. Another local Asian favorite is the **Mayflower,** 6255 Geary Blvd., near 27th Avenue (☎ **415-387-8338**), open daily for excellent dim sum, lunch, and dinner. Call for evening reservations.

Japantown is bargain-town when it comes to dining. Inside the **Japan Center** on Post Street (at Webster Street) are a number of noodle houses and sushi bars with more across the way. **Mifune,** 1737 Post St., Suite 375 (☎ **415-922-0337**), upstairs in the Japan Center, is a perennial favorite for big bowls of udon noodles in broth with slices of beef or chicken and vegetables. It's open until 9:30 p.m. Sunday to Thursday, and 10 p.m. Friday to Saturday. **Isuzu,** 1581 Webster St. (☎ **415-922-2290**), is a great spot for sushi or tempura.

Trimming the Fat from Your Budget

Do not head to the nearest fast-food counter, even if your travel budget doesn't allow for a $100 dinner for two every night. You can limit the stress on your credit card, and save your waistline, if you share an appetizer and dessert, or order beer instead of wine, or better yet, bring a favorite bottle of *vino* (you'll have to pay a corkage charge) or skip the alcohol entirely. (The markup on wine is usually outrageous!) If you've read all about a certain restaurant you're dying to try that's way too expensive, have lunch there instead of dinner, if it's open; you'll get the same quality of food, but for less money. Or you can eat brunch or have an inexpensive picnic lunch and contribute your savings toward a really nice dinner. See the following paragraph for places to get a quick but delicious meal or snack.

The best choice for inexpensive, flavorful dishes is to try out one of the city's many ethnic restaurants. Taxi to the **Tenderloin** for Vietnamese and Indian/Pakistani; the **Mission District** for cheap Mexican, Salvadoran, and Cambodian food; to Geary and Clement streets in the **Richmond District** for Vietnamese, Chinese, and Thai; and to **Japantown** for tempura and noodles. Your wallet will thank you and your taste buds will still be satisfied.

So, what are you in the mood for? Chinese? California-Mediterranean? Catalan tapas? *Pho?* There's no reason to go hungry seeking the right restaurant. Due to space considerations, the recommendations in this chapter only scratch the surface of my favorite places. What you have here is a representative cross-section of the best the city has to offer, in a variety of price ranges and neighborhoods. And unless the kitchen is having an off night, there's not a lemon in the bunch.

Restaurants that I've designated with the Kid Friendly icon have items on the menu that most kids like, and they'll treat your children with respect. If things like crayons at the tables and booster seats are important to your little ones, call the restaurants directly for more information.

Experiencing dinner as theater

Foreign Cinema in the Mission District (☎ 415-648-7600; see listing later in this chapter) screens films on a wall in their patio, which is handy if you don't have much to say to your date. But for live entertainment to accompany your meal, stay tuned.

San Francisco has always had its fair share of fair maidens, many of whom shave twice daily, and there is no better or safer place to gawk at "gender illusionists" than at **AsiaSF**, 201 Ninth St., at Howard (☎ 415-255-2742), a SoMa nightclub/restaurant. The "waitresses" do double duty, taking your order for small plates of fusion dishes (such as duck quesadillas) and then lip-synching to your favorite tunes while strutting down the vinyl bar. You'd think that the gimmick would bury the food, but in fact, the place manages to do a fine job in every area. There's even a disco in the basement, so you can shake your thang afterward, should you be so inclined.

Down at **Pier 29** on the Embarcadero, look for a stylized 1926 *Spiegelent* (a circular, tented pavilion), the home of **Teatro ZinZanni** (☎ 415-438-2668; www.teatrozinzanni.org). Tickets are $110 to $135, and shows are Wednesday through Sunday. This is an immensely hilarious dinner show with a twist: The audience is part of the proceedings. Don't worry — you won't be asked to get up and recite. Along with an acceptable, if not stellar, five-course meal (it reminds me of hotel wedding suppers), diners are regaled by a talented group of performers, who combine cabaret, opera, acrobatics, comedy, and improv in most unusual ways. The cast changes periodically, and strangely enough, Joan Baez has appeared in the show off and on, so it's worth investigating who's in the lineup when you come to town. This isn't a cheap date, but it's something to consider if you're celebrating or looking for an evening out of the ordinary.

And for something completely different, slip into **supperclub**, 657 Harrison St. between 2nd and 3rd streets (☎ 415-348-0900; www.supperclub.com), an offshoot of the Amsterdam original. Be prepared to spend your entire evening here, lounging barefoot against the pillows that surround your bed/seating area, drinking, eating, watching, listening, participating, and giving yourself over to whatever the experience offers as every night it changes somewhat. Expect performance art, wandering masseuses, costumes, drag queens, DJs, and who knows what else. A set five-course meal of varying consistency is served for $60 on Sunday, Tuesday, Wednesday, and Thursday, and for $70 on Friday and Saturday. Secure reservations at least one month in advance.

The dollar signs attached to the restaurant recommendations in this chapter give you an idea of how much you'll have to shell out for dinner for one person, including appetizer, main course, dessert, one drink, tax, and tip.

If a place is marked with $, a meal there will run $25 or less. At $$ places, expect to spend between $26 and $50. Restaurants with $$$ will cost from $51 to $80. Feel like going for broke? You'll sup like royalty and then fork over lots more than $80 at places with $$$$. To locate a restaurant based on its cost, location, or cuisine, see the indexes at the end of this chapter.

Dining and dancing

The **Top of the Mark** in the Mark Hopkins InterContinental Hotel, 1 Nob Hill, at Mason and California streets (☎ 415-616-6916), has it all — views, music, dancing, and a convivial crowd of suits. The hotel serves a $59 prix-fixe dinner on Friday and Saturday nights; with 7:30 p.m. reservations (the band starts at 9 p.m.), a night on the town is a done deal. **Harry Denton's Starlight Room,** in the Sir Francis Drake Hotel on Union Square, 450 Powell St. (☎ 415-395-8595), attracts tons of hotel guests and locals who appreciate the Starlight Orchestra, the drop-dead views, and the adult prom-night atmosphere. It's a glorious room for drinking expensive glasses of whatever, dancing, and having a little bite. Reservations on the weekend are advised. A more youthful and hip group congregates at **Cafe du Nord,** housed below the Swedish American Hall, 2170 Market St., at Sanchez (☎ 415-861-5016; www.cafedunord.com). The basement-level club serves dinner (sandwiches, salad, chicken, and steak), but the draw is the live music. Check the Web site to see which shows are "all ages" (usually offered upstairs), if you have teens along for the ride. Cafe du Nord is open seven days a week, good to know on a Monday when you want something fun to do and there doesn't seem to be anywhere to go at night.

San Francisco's Best Restaurants

Absinthe
$$$ Civic Center/Hayes Valley   FRENCH/BRASSERIE

I recommend this warm-hearted restaurant for a cozy dinner with your beloved (or even just a really good friend) — the restaurant is close enough to Union Square that if you don't find quite what you want near your hotel, it's just a short cab ride away. You can't miss with a selection from the oyster bar or a crisp Caesar salad to start. Depending on the day, the chef may be cooking like a French *grandmère,* with coq au vin or a confit of duck, house-made sausage, and pork cassoulet ready to satisfy your hunger pangs. A hot spot for preconcert dining, you may want to book a table after the curtain, in order to savor the romantic room and seasonal menu. Weekend brunch is busy, too, but you can walk in for lunch if you're shopping in the neighborhood.

See map p. 120. 398 Hayes St., at Gough Street. ☎ 415-551-1590. www.absinthe. com. Reservations recommended, especially on weekends. Muni to Van Ness Ave. and walk north 2 blocks to Hayes Street. Turn left. Main courses: $20–$27. AE, DC, MC, V. Open: Tues–Fri 11:30 a.m. to midnight, Sat 11 a.m. to midnight, Sun 11 a.m.– 10 p.m.

Ame
$$$$ SoMa   NEW AMERICAN

Husband and wife Hiro Sone and Lissa Doumani, of the brilliant Terra in St. Helena, were enlisted to create this new restaurant at the stunning St.

Where to eat when you don't have reservations

Not every restaurant accepts reservations, and among those that do, some keep tables for walk-ins. Others accommodate free spirits at a bar or in the bar. If it's getting late and you forgot or didn't get around to deciding where to eat, try any of the following:

Restaurants that don't take reservations: Chow, Park Chow, L'Osteria del Forno, Pizzeria Delfina

Restaurants that serve in the bar or at a counter: Absinthe, A-16, Bistro Aix, Boulevard, Chez Papa, Foreign Cinema, Gary Danko, Grand Café, Hawthorne Lane, Hayes Street Grill, Home, Jardinère, Kokkari, Ozumo, Rose Pistola, Slanted Door, Tablespoon, Tadich Grill, Town Hall

---

Regis Hotel. The pairing is another perfect match. There's no need now to speed to the Napa Valley for Sone's signature sake-marinated, broiled black cod and shrimp dumplings in shiso broth — a true blessing considering the price of gasoline. Start with the delicious burrata cheese bruschetta and spring vegetable "bagna cauda," if only to admire the beauty of the composition — that is, if the sashimi bar doesn't waylay you first. The quietly luxe room feels deceptively casual; the service meets the high standards of the globally inspired menu.

See maps p.120 and p.124. 689 Mission St. at Third Street in the St. Regis Hotel. ☎ *415-284-4040.* www.amerestaurant.com. *Reservations recommended. Muni to the Montgomery Street Station or the 15-Third, 30-Stockton, or 45-Union/Stockton bus. Main courses: $22–$36. AE, DC, DISC, MC, V. Open: Daily 11:30 a.m.–2 p.m. and 6–10 p.m.*

A-16
$$ **The Marina/Cow Hollow** **SOUTHERN ITALIAN**

A-16 refers to the highway through the Campanga region of Italy (Naples being the major city), and the menu at this stylishly spare restaurant not only reflects the cuisine of southern Italy but also uses ingredients from the area. Favorite dishes include *burrata*, a delicious mozzarella with a soft center; various house-cured *salumi;* and among a handful of excellent main courses, halibut trimmed with Meyer lemons and almonds. You'll also find a choice lineup of authentic Neapolitan pizzas and pasta dishes. I love the varied seating options here — an outdoor patio, butcher-paper-covered tables, banquettes, and stools at the bar where you can watch the chefs in action.

See map p. 120. 2355 Chestnut St., between Scott Street and Divisidero. ☎ *415-771-2216.* www.a16sf.com. *Reservations accepted. 22-Fillmore, 28–19th Avenue, 30-Stockton, or 43-Masonic bus. Main courses: $10–$23. AE, MC, V. Open: Wed–Fri 11:30 a.m.–2:30 p.m., Sun–Thurs 5–10 p.m., Fri–Sat until 11 p.m.*

B-44
$$ Financial District SPANISH

You won't find such authentic, homey Spanish food of this ilk outside of Barcelona — the cod cheeks are a treat, a variety of paellas are suffused with treasures, and you can make a happy meal of tapas, starting with my favorite, *morcilla*, sausage and white beans. There's not a lace fan or flamenco guitarist to be found within a mile of this modern spot, so don't come expecting a Spanish-themed evening. But if you want to feel like you're eating something out of the ordinary, you'll be well rewarded.

See maps p. 120 and p. 124. 44 Belden Place, off Bush Street. ☎ *415-986-6287.* www.b44sf.com. *Reservations recommended. Walk on Stockton Street north from Union Square to Bush Street and turn east for 2 blocks. Main courses: $15–$21. AE, MC, V. Open: Mon–Fri 11:30 a.m.–10:30 p.m., Sat 5–10:30 p.m., Sun 4–9 p.m.*

Bistro Aix
$–$$ The Marina/Cow Hollow FRENCH/BISTRO

This casual French-style bistro caters to lucky neighborhood residents who don't have to look for parking. Dining alfresco is a delight any season in the heated, covered patio out back — it's the perfect setting to enjoy a bottle of wine and plates of crispy-skinned chicken, fresh pasta, grilled sirloin, and perfectly dressed salads. The $19 prix-fixe menu, served from 6 to 8 p.m. Sunday through Thursday, would be a bargain even if the food were half as good.

See map p. 120. 3340 Steiner St., between Chestnut and Lombard streets. ☎ *415-202-0100.* www.bistroaix.com. *Reservations recommended. 22-Fillmore, 28-19th Avenue, 30-Stockton, or 43-Masonic bus. Main courses: $11–$19; prix-fixe menu $19. AE, DC, MC, V. Open: Mon–Thurs 6–10 p.m., Fri–Sat 6–11 p.m., Sun 5:30–9:30 p.m.*

The Blue Plate
$$ The Mission District CALIFORNIA

Eat here and then go home and regale your less-adventurous friends about the fabulous little restaurant you discovered in an out-of-the-way neighborhood in San Francisco. Worth the ride from wherever you are, Blue Plate exemplifies the best of intimate, staff-driven local places with fresh, usually organic ingredients and a quirkiness in design that even dour people can appreciate. My friend Vicki, who is a regular, always orders the Sonoma duck confit (or tries to — the menu changes daily), but plenty of other diners can't pass on the smoked bacon and cornmeal fried oysters over greens to start, or the meatloaf with mashed potatoes. Vicki's boys (husband included) consistently order a few sides of macaroni covered in Spanish goat's cheese, whether they need it or not. Sit in the back room by the patio, or on the patio itself, weather permitting.

See map p. 127. 3218 Mission St., north of 29th Street by the Bank of America parking lot. ☎ *415-282-6777.* www.blueplatesf.com. *Reservations recommended. J-Church Muni to 30th and Dolores, turn left on Mission Street; or take a cab. Main courses: $14–$28. AE, DISC, MC, V. Open: Mon–Thurs 6–10 p.m., Fri–Sat 6–10:30 p.m.*

Boulevard
$$$$ The Embarcadero AMERICAN

Housed in an elegant turn-of-the-century building with views of the Bay Bridge (from tables in the very back only), this popular favorite of both visitors and locals serves excellent, generous plates of seasonal comfort food, such as tender lamb chops and lamb *osso buco* accompanied by local asparagus in season. Start with the pan-seared foie gras while you can — before the food police run it off the menu. Noisy but comfortable, the place caters to an upscale, older crowd. Counter and bar seating is available for those without reservations, but call three or four weeks in advance for a prime-time table.

See map p. 120. 1 Mission St., at Steuart Street. ☎ **415-543-6084.** www.boulevard restaurant.com. *Reservations advised three weeks in advance. Take any Muni streetcar to the Embarcadero Station and walk 1 block east to Mission Street. Main courses: $29–$40. AE, CB, DC, MC, V. Open: Mon–Fri 11:30 a.m.–2 p.m., Thurs–Sat 5:30–10:30 p.m., Sun–Wed 5:30–10 p.m.*

Butterfly
$$$ The Embarcadero PAN-ASIAN

This is a beautiful restaurant on the water, a comfortable place to take in the bay, with drinks and maybe some oysters before the sun sets. Butterfly started in the Mission (where the original is now a bar/lounge), and its roaring success led the chef-owner, Robert Lam, to salvage this room with a view when the last owners couldn't weather the economic downturn. Lam's use of local ingredients in recipes that pick and choose from various Asian cuisines makes for unusual eating. If you're in the mood to try something different, order his crispy, fried whole fish with kimchi, black bean sauce, and Chinese sausage. You won't know what to admire more — the shimmering water or your dinner plate.

See map p. 120. Pier 33 on the Embarcadero at Bay Street. ☎ **415-864-8999.** www. butterflysf.com. *Reservations recommended. F-Market streetcar. Main courses: $16–$38. AE, MC, V. Open: Mon–Fri 11:30 a.m.–3 p.m., Sun–Wed 5–10 p.m., Thurs–Sat 5–11 p.m., happy hour Mon–Fri 3–5 p.m., brunch Sat–Sun 11 a.m.–3 p.m.*

Cafe Kati
$$$ Japantown CALIFORNIA

As in all the best spots, the menu here changes depending on what's available locally, but it always reflects the unique influence of Chef Kirk Webber, who likes to include a little something Eastern and a little something Western. Thus, you may find seafood steamed in red Thai curry and a marinated skirt steak with onion rings sharing the table and giving patrons great pleasure. Wine lovers should investigate BYOB Tuesdays, when Webber serves a $30 prix fixe with no corkage charge.

See map p. 120. 1963 Sutter St., between Fillmore and Webster streets. ☎ **415-775-7313.** www.cafekati.com. *Reservations advised two weeks in advance. 3-Jackson, 4-Sutter, 22-Fillmore, or 38-Geary bus. Main courses: $20–$28. AE, DISC, MC, V. Open: Daily 5:30–10 p.m., Sun brunch 11 a.m.–2 p.m.*

Canteen

$$ Union Square   CALIFORNIA

Miniscule Canteen is the domain of the much-admired chef Dennis Leary, whose bona fides include four years at Rubicon prior to opening this 20-seat upscale diner. The fact that you'll need a reservation even to eat at the counter (there are but four tiny booths), should clue you in that this is an unusual venture. Leary does the shopping as well as all the cooking, and his menu changes to reflect what appeals on a weekly basis. If you're staying around Union Square, breakfast here is stellar, especially the smoked salmon omelet or stuffed pancake. Work the phones to land a dinner seat or come for lunch and see what all the fuss is about.

See maps p. 120 and p. 124. 817 Sutter St., next to the Commodore Hotel. ☎ *415-928-8870.* www.canteensf.com. *Reservations accepted (and needed) for dinner only. Main courses: $20–$25. AE, DC, MC, V. Open: Mon–Fri 7–11 a.m., Wed–Fri 11:30 a.m.–2 p.m. and 6–10 p.m., weekend brunch 8 a.m.–2 p.m.*

Chow

$ The Castro   AMERICAN

If there weren't so many people eagerly waiting for a table at this noisy, casual, and friendly joint, it might qualify as a quick-bite place. But after you score a table, it's more fun to sit a while and savor the straightforward pasta dishes, brick-oven-roasted chicken, thin-crusted pizzas, and yummy desserts (love that ginger cake). A great price performer, too. Their second location, Park Chow, 1240 Ninth Ave., near Golden Gate Park, is just as terrific and just as busy.

See map p. 120. 215 Church St., at Market Street. ☎ *415-552-2469. Reservations not accepted. J-Church or F-Market streetcar to Church Street. Main courses: $7.75–$15. MC, V. Open: Sun–Thurs 11 a.m.–11 p.m., Fri–Sat 11 a.m. to midnight.*

Cortez

$$$ Union Square   MEDITERRANEAN

Hotel restaurants aren't the formal, grown-up, boring affairs they once were, and at least around Union Square, they're lately *the* places to be. Among them is this destination for couture tapas in the Hotel Adagio. The buzz is palpable from the bar and the Mondrian-meets-Miro dining room. The surprise (if you're mistrusting of glitz) is that the small plates — such as prawns a la plancha or a salad of frisee, roasted beets, and Point Reyes blue cheese — are beautifully presented and totally delicious.

See maps p. 120 and p. 124. 550 Geary St., in the Hotel Adagio. ☎ *415-292-6360.* www.cortezrestaurant.com. *Reservations advised. Main courses: $6–$17. AE, MC, V. Open: Daily 5:30–10:30 p.m.*

Delfina
$$ Mission District TUSCAN ITALIAN

This wonderfully friendly and now-renowned restaurant defines what's incredible about the city's neighborhood eats. Dishes such as the Niman Ranch flatiron steak, a pristine salmon with warm lentil salad, or bitter greens combined simply with walnuts and pancetta are full of flavor and feature the freshest ingredients, a smattering of herbs, and thoughtful preparation. For more casual eating, the Stoll's recently opened **Pizzeria Delfina** (☎ **415-437-6800**) is next door. Open from 11 a.m. Tuesday through Sunday (dinner only on Mon), it's the happening place for Neopolitan-style pizza and yummy antipasti. Look for the line on the sidewalk — no reservations are taken here.

See map p. 127. 3621 18th St., between Dolores and Guerrero streets. ☎ *415-552-4055.* www.delfinasf.com. *Reservations advised three weeks in advance. J-Church Muni line to 18th Street and then walk east 2 blocks. Main courses: $11–$24. MC, V. Open: Sun–Thurs 5:30–10 p.m., Fri–Sat 5:30–11 p.m.*

Enrico's Sidewalk Cafe
$$ North Beach CALIFORNIA/ITALIAN

Dining on a patio with a view of the bawdy section of Broadway would liven up any evening, but at this cosmopolitan bar/restaurant you also get live jazz and a menu of solid seasonal fish and meat dishes. You can easily make a meal of small plates from Enrico's long list of appetizers, and there's pizza for low-maintenance eaters. Casual and fun.

See maps p. 120 and p. 123. 504 Broadway, at Kearny Street. ☎ *415-982-6223.* www.enricossidewalkcafe.com. *Reservations recommended. Powell-Mason cable-car line or 30-Stockton bus. Main courses: $16–$35. AE, MC, V. Open: Sun–Thurs 11:30 a.m.–11 p.m., Fri–Sat 11:30 a.m. to midnight.*

Foreign Cinema
$$$ Mission District NEW AMERICAN/FRENCH

Mission District regulars nearly lost their *empanadas* when the shiny, chic Foreign Cinema opened in 1999. The expansive dining room — plus outdoor patio where foreign films are screened on a concrete wall — would throw anyone at first, but some oysters from the raw bar followed by an elegant plate of endive and smoked trout helped lower resistance to the inevitable changes in the neighborhood. Eight years later, the restaurant continues to be a must-stop for hip gourmands.

See map p. 127. 2534 Mission St., between 21st and 22nd streets. ☎ *415-648-7600.* www.foreigncinema.com. *Reservations highly recommended. BART to 24th Street. Main courses: $16–$30. AE, DISC, MC, V. Open: Mon–Thurs 6–10 p.m. (until 11 p.m. Fri–Sat), weekend brunch 11 a.m.–3 p.m.*

Gary Danko
$$$$ **Russian Hill** **NEW AMERICAN/FRENCH**

The ovens were barely lit at this fine-dining center before the food and wine cognoscenti were all over Danko's like a hollandaise, proclaiming it among the best restaurants not only in town but in the country. They were right. Choose your own three-course (or more if you like) meal from the menu — perhaps a composed lobster salad followed by day boat scallops and ending with a mango Napoleon or selections from the cheese cart — then let the kitchen make magic. If you don't mind eating at the bar, you can actually walk in without reservations.

See map p. 120. 800 Northpoint, at Hyde Street. ☎ *415-749-2060.* www.garydanko. com. *Reservations advised four weeks in advance. Powell-Hyde cable-car line. Prix-fixe menu from $61–$89. DC, DISC, MC, V. Open: Nightly 5:30–10 p.m.*

Grand Cafe
$$–$$$ **Union Square** **CALIFORNIA/FRENCH**

Living up to its name in every aspect, this vast, high-ceilinged, muraled bistro is abuzz with activity and energy. People gravitate to the Petit Cafe pre- and post-theater for brick-oven pizzas, sandwiches, and desserts, and to the dining room for a rib-eye steak or a lovely, fragrant bouillabaisse.

See maps p. 120 and p. 124. 501 Geary St., at Taylor Street. ☎ *415-292-0101. Reservations accepted. Muni Metro to Powell Street, walk 2 blocks to Geary and 2 blocks south to Taylor. Main courses: $14–$25; Petit Cafe $7–$12. AE, DC, DISC, MC, V. Open: Mon–Fri 7–10:30 a.m., Sat 8 a.m.–2:30 p.m., Sun 9 a.m.–2:30 p.m., Mon–Fri 11:30 a.m.–2:30 p.m., Sun–Thurs 5:30–10 p.m., Fri–Sat 5:30–11 p.m.; Petit Cafe open daily 11:30 a.m.–11 p.m., until midnight Fri and Sat.*

Green's
$$–$$$ **The Marina/Cow Hollow** **VEGETARIAN**

If you haven't eaten in a gourmet vegetarian restaurant, or if your vegetarian dining has been limited to alfalfa sprouts and tofu, you're in for a marvelous culinary experience. The Saturday-evening four-course prix-fixe menu is a deal, especially when you factor in the gorgeous views that come with the meal. This attractive, bright room is a brilliant destination for lunch if you're exploring the Marina.

See map p. 120. Fort Mason, Building A, off Marina Boulevard at Buchanan Street. ☎ *415-771-6222.* http://greensrestaurant.com. *Reservations highly recommended at least two weeks in advance. Take the 30-Stockton bus to Laguna and transfer to the 28–19th Avenue into Fort Mason. Main courses: $16–$23; prix-fixe menu (Sat only) $48. AE, DISC, MC, V. Open: Sun 10 a.m.–2 p.m., Tues–Sat noon– 2:30 p.m., Mon–Sat 5:30–9 p.m., Sun 10:30 a.m.–2 p.m.*

Hawthorne Lane
$$$$ SoMa CALIFORNIA/ASIAN

This classy but relaxed, art-filled restaurant in a 1-block alley near the Museum of Modern Art always delivers the goods. The Cal-Asian menu is beautifully executed (if you're lucky, the Chinese-style roasted duck with steamed green-onion buns will be on the menu); the chef, Bridget Batson, is garnering terrific reviews; and the service is impeccable, a boast not many other restaurants can make. With a nod to the small plates trend, you can now order appetizer-sized portions of some main dishes. The bar attracts a grown-up crowd, so if you're early for your reservation, take advantage and have a drink. (You may even see a local celeb like Boz Scaggs.) And dress up a little — it's a nice place.

See maps p. 120 and p.124. 22 Hawthorne Lane, off Howard Street between Second and Third streets. ☎ **415-777-9779.** www.hawthornelane.com. *Reservations recommended two weeks in advance. Any Muni streetcar to Montgomery Street Station; 30-Stockton or 45-Union/Stockton bus. Main courses: $14–$36. AE, DISC, MC, V. Open: Mon–Fri 11:30 a.m.–1:30 p.m.; Sun–Thurs 5:30–9 p.m., Fri–Sat 5:30–10 p.m.*

Hayes Street Grill
$$ Civic Center/Hayes Valley SEAFOOD

This 30-year veteran of the food biz remains one of the premier fish restaurants in the city. Whatever's been caught that morning will be prepared simply, carefully, and with integrity. The nonfish selections are equally delicious, and walk-ins can eat at the bar. The restaurant quiets down considerably around 8 p.m. when the opera/symphony/ballet-goers dash off to the show.

See map p. 120. 320 Hayes St., between Gough and Franklin streets. ☎ **415-863-5545.** www.hayesstreetgrill.com. *Reservations recommended. Take any Muni Metro to the Civic Center Station and walk north on Gough. Main courses: $18–$24; $25 prix fixe after 7:30 p.m. AE, DISC, MC, V. Open: Mon–Fri 11:30 a.m.–2 p.m., Mon–Thurs 5–9:30 p.m., Fri–Sat 5:30–10:30 p.m., Sun 5–8:30 p.m.*

Home
$–$$ Castro AMERICAN

When Union Square hotel restaurants start giving your wallet an inferiority complex, catch the F-Market streetcar to the corner of Market and Church streets and you'll be at Home. Start in the patio for a cocktail, and then head to the slightly moody dining room for better-than-home cooking such as baked ziti or pot roast that'll make you cry or at least ask for the recipe. Saturday and Sunday brunch features a do-it-yourself Bloody Mary bar, and the daily early-bird special is a 3-course prix fixe for $11! A second Home, good as the first, can be found in Cow Hollow at 2032 Union St., between Webster and Buchanan (☎ **415-931-5006**).

See map p. 120. 2100 Market St. at Church Street. ☎ **415-503-0333.** *J-Church or F-Market streetcar. Main courses: $10–$17. AE, DISC, MC, V. Open: Sun–Thurs 5–10 p.m., Fri–Sat until 11 p.m., Sat and Sun brunch 10 a.m.–2 p.m.*

Isa
$$ The Marina/Cow Hollow   FRENCH

I had a running argument with my cousin Irene over who made the wisest picks at this stellar chef-owned-and-operated find. My crab salad was full of freshly cracked crabmeat, but Irene's baked goat's cheese, surrounded by pesto and perfectly ripe tomato, elicited a bit of a fork fight. We reached an impasse between the grilled flatiron steak and the potato-wrapped sea bass, but we agreed that based on price, atmosphere, service, and taste, this was among the best meals we've shared in San Francisco. Luke Sung, the genius behind the stove, has been recognized as a Rising Star Chef of the Year by the James Beard Foundation two years in a row, and I can't argue with that.

See map p. 120. 3324 Steiner St. at Chestnut Street. ☎ *415-567-9588. 30-Stockton bus. Main courses: $12–$18. MC, V. Open: Mon–Thurs 5:30–10 p.m., Fri–Sat until 10:30 p.m.*

Jardinière
$$$$ Civic Center   CALIFORNIA/FRENCH

This is where the upscale crowd sups before the opera, ballet, or symphony. Expect sophisticated surroundings, a lively bar, and highly touted, high-priced food. The risotto is heaven sent. A jazz combo plays upstairs Sunday through Tuesday.

See map p. 120. 300 Grove St., at Franklin Street. ☎ *415-861-5555.* www. jardiniere.com. *Reservations required. Muni Metro to Civic Center; walk 4 blocks north on Franklin. Main courses: $24–$41. AE, DC, MC, V. Open: Sun–Wed 5–10:30 p.m., Thurs–Sat 5–11:30 p.m.*

Kay Cheung
$ Chinatown   CHINESE

For a fresh and interesting selection of dim sum or live seafood, this small, pleasant room can't be beat for quality or price. Most of the tables seat eight, so you'll probably end up sitting with Chinatown regulars — a terrific opportunity to chat up folks who really know their dumplings.

See maps p. 120 and p. 123. 615 Jackson St., at Kearny Street. ☎ *415-989-6838. Reservations accepted. 15-Third bus. AE, MC, V. Main courses: $6–$11. Open: Daily 9 a.m.–2:30 p.m., 5:30–10 p.m.*

Kokkari Estiatorio
$$$ Financial District   GREEK

Your average Mediterranean shipping tycoon would feel perfectly comfortable underneath the beamed ceilings of this richly appointed taverna. The California-meets-Greek menu does feature some familiar dishes, such as moussaka, but takes them to Mount Olympus–style heights. Order the Yiaourti Graniti (yogurt sorbet with tangerine ice) for dessert even if you're full.

See maps p. 120 and p. 124. 200 Jackson St., at Front Street. ☎ *415-981-0983.* www.kokkari.com. *Reservations required. 2, 3, or 4 bus; transfer to 42-Downtown loop; exit at Sansome and Jackson streets and walk 2 blocks west to Front. Main courses: $16–$34. AE, DISC, MC, V. Open: Mon–Fri 11:30 a.m.–2:30 p.m., Mon 5:30 p.m.–10 p.m., Fri –Sat 5:30–11 p.m.*

Le Charm
$$ SoMa   FRENCH BISTRO

Bargain-hunter alert! The Parisian-inspired three-course prix-fixe dinner for $28 is the real deal at this popular little sponge-painted bistro. Diners choose from a menu that may include a roasted quail served on salad greens, gnocchi with wild mushrooms, and, in season, a dessert soup of fresh apricots and cherries. Le Charm is also a winner for lunch, especially if the weather is decent and you can get a table outside in the garden.

See map p. 120. 315 Fifth St., between Folsom and Howard streets (near Yerba Buena Center). ☎ *415-546-6128.* http://lecharm.com. *Reservations accepted. Powell Street Muni; 27-Bryant or 30-Stockton bus. Main courses: $18–$25. AE, MC, V. Open: Mon 11:30 a.m.–2 p.m., Tues–Fri 11:30–2 p.m., 6–9:30 p.m., Sat 5:30–10 p.m., Sun 5–8:30 p.m.*

Le Colonial
$$$ Union Square   FRENCH-VIETNAMESE

Walking into this tall, whitewashed building sitting off by itself in an alley downtown, you immediately feel transported to another era. The pressed-tin ceiling, the fans, the potted palms, the rattan furniture — it could all easily feel contrived, but it doesn't. The look, the service, and the haute Vietnamese cuisine — starring a beautiful piece of sea bass steamed in a banana leaf — are all well executed. The enticing upstairs lounge is a great place to begin or end the evening. Share the tasting platter of Vietnamese specialties, add one of their exotic cocktails, and there's an evening I could get behind. Many inexpensive Vietnamese diners are nearby in the Tenderloin, but one eats here not just for the food but for the ambience.

See maps p. 120 and p. 124. 20 Cosmo Place, off Taylor Street between Sutter and Post streets. ☎ *415-931-3600.* www.lecolonialsf.com. *Reservations advised. From Union Square, walk 2 blocks southwest on Post then north on Taylor. Cosmo Place is just off Taylor Street. Main courses: $20–$35. AE, DISC, MC, V. Open: Sun–Thurs 5:30–10 p.m., Fri–Sat 5:30–11 p.m.*

Lichee Garden
$ Chinatown   CHINESE

This is a particularly reliable family-style Cantonese restaurant, popular with the locals, with a huge menu filled with familiar dishes (like Egg Foo Young), lots of seafood, and every Chinese dish you remember from child-hood (unless you were raised in China). They also serve a good dim sum lunch. Prices are inexpensive (Peking duck being the biggest extrava-gance), service is fine, and the room is bright and lively.

See maps p. 120 and p. 123. 1416 Powell St., near Broadway. ☎ *415-397-2290. Reservations accepted. Powell-Mason cable car. Main courses: $6.50–$25. MC, V. Open: Daily 7 a.m.–9:15 p.m.*

L'Osteria del Forno
$ North Beach   ITALIAN

A tiny storefront with an equally tiny kitchen, L'Osteria manages to dish up fine thin-crusted pizzas, pasta dishes that change daily, and a tender roast pork loin cooked in milk. It's equally satisfying to make a meal of antipasti. This is one North Beach restaurant that feels and tastes authentic.

See maps p. 120 and p. 123. 519 Columbus Ave., between Green and Union streets. ☎ *415-982-1124. No reservations accepted. Powell-Mason cable-car line; 30-Stockton bus. Main courses: $10–$15. No credit cards. Open: Sun–Mon and Wed–Thurs 11:30 a.m.–10 p.m., Fri–Sat 11:30 a.m.–11 p.m.*

Lulu
$$ SoMa   MEDITERRANEAN

With the buoyant feel of a lively Provençal bistro, the mouthwatering scent of the oak-fired rotisserie, and a lengthy menu of appealing dishes, Lulu seduces on many levels. If you're anywhere near Yerba Buena Center, don't think twice about having lunch or dinner at this local institution. Most dishes are meant to be shared, such as the daily rotisserie specials, the wonderful rosemary-scented chicken, and an antipasti plate of your own design. Dinnertime can be pretty noisy, but you'll be surrounded by a buzz of happiness from the throng at the bar, emanating throughout the cavernous room.

See map p. 120. 816 Folsom St., at 4th Street. ☎ *415-495-5775.* www.restaurant lulu.com. *Reservations advised. 45-Union/Stockton or 30-Stockton bus. Main courses: $16–$30. AE, DC, DISC, MC, V. Open: Daily 11:30 a.m.–3 p.m., Mon–Thurs 5:30 p.m.–10 p.m., Fri–Sat 5–11 p.m., Sun 5–10 p.m.*

Luna Park
$$ Mission District   NEW AMERICAN

The funky abstract art, rustic red walls, and gold velvet drapes announce that décor is in the eye of the decorator, but it's all part of the fun. The exceedingly well-priced menu attracts people from all parts of the city, making weekend nights especially loud, but that does make it comfortable for families with kids. Start with the tuna "poke" appetizer or one of the five beautiful green salads and then consider the lamb shank, beef brisket stew, or oven-roasted sea bass. Attention campers: Make-your-own s'mores light up the dessert list!

See map p. 127. 694 Valencia St., at 18th Street. ☎ *415-553-8584.* www.luna parksf.com. *Reservations advised for dinner. BART to 16th Street and walk west to Valencia and south 2 blocks. Main courses: $13–$26. MC, V. Open: Mon–Fri 11:30–2:30 p.m., Sat–Sun 11:30 p.m.–3 p.m., Mon–Thurs 5:30–10:30 p.m., Fri–Sat 5:30–11:30 p.m., Sun 5:30–10 p.m.*

Mamacita
$$ The Marina/Cow Hollow MEXICAN

It was a mournful day when Café Marimba suddenly closed and left the Marina bereft of a decent tortilla. Fortunately, Mamacita has come to everyone's rescue, not only occupying the very same building, but serving south-of-the-border treats that surpass expectation. Don't miss the carnitos tacos, an irresistible heap of slow-cooked pork, roasted hominy, avocado, and cream, so delectable-looking that it's a toss-up whether to admire them or finish 'em off in a bite or two. Larger plates, such as seared Ahi, are equally good, but you'll run the risk of not having room for dessert — and who wants to miss out on cinnamon churros? This place gets crowded and noisy as the evening wears on; arrive early if you don't have reservations.

See map p. 120. 2317 Chestnut St., between Scott and Divisadero streets. ☎ *415-346-8494.* www.mamacitasf.com. *Reservations advised. 30-Stockton bus. Main courses: $10–$21. AE, MC, V. Open: Daily 5:30–10:30 p.m. Bar open until midnight.*

Moose's
$$$ North Beach CALIFORNIA/MEDITERRANEAN

Popular with politicos, socialites, and local luminaries, the great thing about Moose's, besides the food, is that even the little people have a great time eating here. Although a splendidly prepared appetizer of steak tartare followed by the venison will definitely leave a little draft whistling through your wallet, the smooth, professional staff and bright décor guarantee a memorable, very San Francisco meal. Look for the daily changing Chef's Menu, three courses for $32 before 7:30 p.m. Afterwards, hang out at the bar listening to the evening's jazz pianist.

See maps p. 120 and p. 123. 1652 Stockton St., across from Washington Square. ☎ *415-989-7800.* www.mooses.com. *Reservations recommended. Powell-Mason cable-car line; 30-Stockton bus. Main courses: $11–$39. AE, DISC, JCB, MC, V. Open: Thurs–Sat 11:30 a.m.–2:30 p.m., Sun 10 a.m.–2:30 p.m., Mon–Thurs 5:30–10:30 p.m., Fri–Sat 5:30–11:30 p.m., Sun 5–10:30 p.m.*

Ozumo
$$$ The Embarcadero SUSHI/JAPANESE

High-quality sushi is available in a number of local restaurants, but the very contemporary Ozumo also offers a beautiful selection of Japanese dishes, featuring grilled meats and vegetables. Reserve a table in the back for views, and if you're coming for sushi, let the chef guide you. The sake tasting menu is an eye-opener and highly recommended.

See map p. 120. 161 Steuart St., near Mission Street. ☎ *415-882-1333.* www.ozumo.com. *Reservations recommended. Any Muni streetcar to Embarcadero Station. Main courses: $13–$38. AE, DISC, MC, V. Open: Mon–Fri 11:30 a.m.–2 p.m., Sun–Wed 5:30–10 p.m., Thurs–Sat 5:30–10:30 p.m., Kanpai 4–7 p.m.*

Pazzia
$ SoMa NORTHERN ITALIAN

Have an authentic Northern Italian moment at this colorful, tiny place, a quick walk from Yerba Buena Center and the Museum of Modern Art. The tempting pizza, delicious pasta dishes, and heartier entrees provide something to please everyone. The staff is pleasant to kids and grown-ups alike; if you're in the area, there's no better pick for the price.

See maps p. 120 and p. 124. 337 Third St. ☎ **415-512-1693.** www.pazzia.city search.com. *Reservations advised. Muni to Montgomery Street station; 15-Third, 30-Stockton, or 45-Union/Stockton bus. Main courses: $7–$16. AE, DISC, MC, V. Open: Mon–Fri 11:30 a.m.–2:30 p.m., Mon–Thurs 6–10 p.m., Fri–Sat 6–10:30 p.m.*

Quince
$$$ Pacific Heights MODERN ITALIAN

Not long after opening at the end of 2003, Quince became, and remains, one of the more sought-after reservations in town. Chef/owner Michael Tusk, an alumnus of Chez Panisse and Oliveto, and his wife Lindsey, have created a refined retreat where every dish feels nurtured. The menu changes daily, but if a crudo appears under the first-course selections, don't be shy, even if you think you don't like raw fish. The house-made pasta in any form will be equally inspired. Unlike so many new restaurants in town that equate noise with buzz, Quince offers a grown-up dining experience in calm surroundings.

See map p. 120. 1701 Octavia St. at Bush. ☎ **415-775-8500.** *Reservations necessary. Take a cab. Valet parking available. Main courses: $15–$30. AE, MC, V. Open: Mon–Thurs 5:30–10 p.m., Fri–Sat 5–10 p.m.*

R&G Lounge
$ Chinatown CHINESE

Downstairs, you get excellent Hong Kong Chinese dishes in a setting that reminds me of an airport lounge, with lackluster service. The small dining room upstairs is more attractive, so talk your way to a table up there. In either case, you'll have a chance to order live spot shrimp from the downstairs tank and fresh, crisp vegetables such as Chinese broccoli and *yin choy* (a leafy green vegetable with a red root, often boiled and then braised with garlic).

See maps p. 120 and p. 123. 631 Kearny St., between Sacramento and Clay streets. ☎ *415-982-7877. Reservations accepted. 15-Third bus. Main courses: $7.25–$9.50. AE, MC, V. Open: Daily 11 a.m.–9:30 p.m.*

Range
$$ Mission District CALIFORNIA

Range is a prime example of the modern San Francisco neighborhood restaurant. Opened by a kitchen-savvy husband and wife team (Cameron and Phil West), their small, seasonal menu features flavor over flash, backed by charming service. The coffee-rubbed pork shoulder is a favorite, while Range's delicate take on meat and potatoes — pan-roasted, thinly sliced bavette steak (cut from the short loin) with narrow fingerlings — satisfies on a more primal level. Two simple yet warm dining rooms, fronted by an attractive bar, allow for conversation, a nice touch given how often restaurants seem designed to make that impossible.

See map p. 127. 842 Valencia St., between 19th and 20th streets. ☎ *415-282-8283.* www.rangesf.com. *Reservations recommended. 14 bus or taxi as parking is difficult. Main courses: $17–$20. MC, V. Open: Sun–Thurs 5:30–10 p.m., Fri–Sat 5:30–11 p.m.*

Rose Pistola
$$$ North Beach   ITALIAN

Walk by the sidewalk tables covered in gaily printed cloths, and you'll feel the pull of this solidly established restaurant. From the couples praying for a few bar stools to free up, to the parties sipping wine in the more private and quieter dining areas in the back, the scene is intense, but the sophisticated Mediterranean food often deserves the hype it gets. A former waiter suggests that you go for lunch or dinner during the week; on weekends, the kitchen is so crazed that your order may not get all the attention it deserves.

See maps p. 120 and p. 123. 532 Columbus Ave., between Union and Green streets. ☎ *415-399-0499.* www.rosepistolasf.com. *Reservations recommended two weeks in advance. Powell-Mason cable-car line; 30-Stockton bus. Main courses: $14–$33. AE, DISC, MC, V. Open: Daily 11:30 a.m.–4 p.m., Sun–Thurs 5:30 p.m.–11 p.m., Fri–Sat 5:30 p.m.–midnight.*

Slanted Door
$$ The Embarcadero   VIETNAMESE

After colonizing the Mission District and then moving temporarily to a space on Brannan Street while the original building was to be remodeled, the city's premier Vietnamese eatery landed in the city's premier location — the glorious Ferry Building. Savvy travelers and locals didn't let the room remain empty for even a moment, and they pour in for the buttery steamed sea bass, caramelized chicken, and plates of "shaking" beef. Even if dinner reservations seem impossible to come by, call at 5:30 p.m. the evening you want to dine and see whether there is a cancellation. You may get lucky. You even need a reservation for lunch, especially since chef Charles Phan was named Best Chef in California by the James Beard Foundation in 2004.

See map p. 120. 1 Ferry Building, Embarcadero and Market. ☎ *415-861-8032.* http://slanteddoor.com. *Reservations a must. BART or Muni to the Embarcadero Station. Main courses: $16–$30. AE, MC, V. Open: Daily 11:30 a.m.–2:30 p.m., Sun–Thurs 5:30–10 p.m., Fri–Sat 5:30–10:30 p.m.*

Tablespoon
$$ Russian Hill AMERICAN

This urbane, Manhattan-like dining room only seats 45 (plus 12 at the bar), and in such close confines you'll have a chance to examine what the guy next to you is eating. Chances are it'll be delectable as the chef/co-owner, Robert Riescher, left the renowned Erna's Elderberry House for an opportunity to operate on his own. The menu changes daily, but with luck he'll be plating a topless ravioli dish with tender shreds of braised lamb shank and mustard greens in a pool of onion broth. It is awesome and the focus of one of my few regrets in life, because I wasn't the one who ordered it. Service is also professional and smart.

See map p. 120. 2209 Polk St., at Vallejo Street. ☎ *415-268-0140. Reservations recommended. Powell-Hyde cable car to Vallejo, walk 2 blocks to Polk. Main courses: $18–$21. AE, MC, V. Open: Mon–Sat 6 p.m.–midnight, Sun 5 –10 p.m.*

Tadich Grill
$$ Financial District SEAFOOD

If you're making the rounds of old San Francisco, lunch here or at Sam's Grill, 374 Bush St. (☎ 415-421-0594), is mandatory. This turn-of-the-last-century watering hole, with waiters to match, features a daily printed menu advertising dishes so old-fashioned (had Lobster Newburg lately?) that they're probably the next big thing (like Liberals or bright colors). Order defensively: Stick with whatever fresh fish is available and the delicious creamed spinach.

See maps p. 120 and p. 124. 240 California St., between Front and Battery streets. ☎ *415-391-1849. Reservations not accepted. Take any Muni streetcar to the Embarcadero Station. Main courses: $12–$18. MC, V. Open: Mon–Fri 11 a.m.– 9:30 p.m., Sat 11:30 a.m.–9:30 p.m.*

Town Hall
$$$ SoMa NEW AMERICAN

The latest destination spot to wow the city that knows how to eat (I saw Robin Williams there), Town Hall oozes confidence like Tom Cruise at the end of a rope. Heavy-hitters from the local cuisine scene, most prominently the Rosenthal brothers of Postrio fame, automatically raised the restaurant's profile, and their cooking will keep it in the big leagues. If you like New Orleans–style dishes — multiflavored, multitextured, ample portions — you'll love their cornmeal-fried oysters with baby spinach, covered in a jazzy bacon dressing, and the scallops with andouille sausage jambalaya. There's nothing shy about this food, and you don't have to share unless you really want to.

See maps p. 120 and p. 124. 342 Howard St., at Beale Street. ☎ *415-908-3900.* www. townhallsf.com. *Reservations advised. 1-Calif., 12-Folsom, or 14-Mission bus. Main courses: $19–$26. AE, MC, V. Open: Mon–Fri 11:30 a.m.–2:30 p.m., Sun–Thurs 5:30 –10 p.m, Fri–Sat 5:30–11 p.m.*

Dim sum 101

I wasn't sure what to expect the first time I tried dim sum, way back when. I'll admit — and only because you were kind enough to buy this book — that I was a little hesitant. The idea of eating these Chinese dumplings, filled with ingredients I couldn't identify at first, was a bit scary. But I'm delighted to report that I quickly overcame my initial wariness and now adore dim sum. If you haven't tried it, I urge you to do so.

In many Chinese restaurants, dim sum is served from late morning until around 2 p.m., but not later. In fact, if you arrive past 1 p.m., you run the risk of the kitchen losing interest in providing much of anything to eat. It's best to arrive around 11 a.m. Dim sum generally enters on carts wheeled about the room by waitresses. (Otherwise, you order from a menu.) Ask for a table near the kitchen in order to get first crack at whatever's on its way around the room. The ladies with their carts will stop by your table and show you what they have. If it looks appealing to you, nod or say, "Yes"; if not, just say, "No, thanks." It's okay to order slowly — finishing one plate, sipping tea, and then ordering something else. By the way, if you run out of tea, open the teapot lid.

Here's a rundown of dim sum that first-timers will definitely enjoy:

- **Har gau:** Shrimp dumplings encased in a translucent wrapper and steamed

- **Sui mai:** Rectangles of pork and shrimp in a sheer noodle wrapper

- **Gau choi gau:** Chives, alone or with shrimp or scallop

- **Jun jui kau:** Rice pearl balls with seasoned ground pork and rice

- **Law mai gai:** Sticky rice with bits of meat and mushrooms wrapped in a lotus leaf

- **Char siu bau:** Steamed pork buns — bits of barbecued meat in a doughy roll

- **Guk char siu ban:** Baked pork buns — bits of barbecued meat in a glazed roll

- **Chun guen:** Spring rolls — smaller, less-crowded version of egg roll

- **Gau ji:** Potstickers — a thick, crescent-shaped dough filled with ground pork

Where to go

Yank Sing, on the Embarcadero at Rincon Center, 101 Spear St. (☎ **415-957-9300;** www.yanksing.com), or 49 Stevenson St., near First Street (☎ **415-541-4949;** lunch only), is considered by those in the know to be one of the premier dim sum houses in town. It's also the most expensive in town, although you get a lot in terms of quality and surroundings.

In Chinatown, **Gold Mountain,** 644 Broadway, near Stockton Street (☎ **415-296-7733**), is typical of the cavernous dim sum parlors that serve hundreds of families on the weekends.

Lichee Garden (see review earlier in this chapter) is another very good spot for dim sum in the sometimes-confusing array of Chinatown choices. It's the favorite of one of San Francisco's most prominent chefs, as well as plenty of Chinatown workers on their morning break.

Tres Agaves
$$ SoMa   MEXICAN

Margaritas reach new heights of succulence in this brick, extremely loud new hot spot near the ballpark. You'll need to toss back a few to find the noise level amusing, but for those of us who crave something more fulfilling than a burrito, sacrifices must be made. Main plates here will feed two, especially when starting the evening with some addictive pork riblets or the masa cakes stuffed with onion and mushrooms (can't drink on an empty tummy, now, can we?). The carnitas (slow-roasted pork) plate is delicious and it's hard to stop filling the small, homemade tortillas with the slightly spicy meat and accompaniments that include two kinds of beans, a crunchy jicama and cabbage salad, and various salsas.

See map p. 120. 130 Townsend St., near 2nd Street. ☎ 415-227-0500. www.tres agaves.com. *Reservations recommended. Main courses: $12–$22. AE, MC, V. Open: Mon–Fri 11:30 a.m. to 3 p.m., Sat and Sun brunch 10:30 a.m.–3 p.m., Sun–Wed 4 – 10 p.m., Thurs–Sat until 11 p.m. Late-night menu until 1 a.m. weeknights and 2 a.m. weekends.*

Zuni Cafe
$$ Civic Center/Hayes Valley   CALIFORNIA

There's always a palpable buzz from the smartly dressed crowd hanging about Zuni's copper bar drinking vodka, snarfing oysters, and waiting for their table to empty. Everything from the centrally located brick oven is terrific, but Zuni's signature roast chicken with bread salad for two is downright divine. Don't opt for an outside table; the view on this section of Market Street isn't all that pleasant.

See map p. 120. 1658 Market St., between Franklin and Gough streets. ☎ 415-552-2522. Reservations recommended. Muni Metro F-Market to Van Ness, walk 2 blocks southwest. Main courses: $13–$29. AE, MC, V. Open: Tues–Sat 11:30 a.m.–6 p.m., Sun 3–5 p.m., Tues–Sat 6 p.m.–midnight, Sun 11 a.m.–3 p.m., 5–11 p.m.

Dining and Snacking on the Go

With the exception of Fisherman's Wharf, where people attempt to walk while balancing bread bowls filled with questionable clam chowder, street food is practically nonexistent in San Francisco. (Although, in a very weak moment, and for research purposes only, I once bought a hot dog from a cart on PIER 39.) But that doesn't mean you should head to the closest fast-food chain for a meal on the go. Instead, head to one of the many sandwich counters, Asian bakeries, Italian delis, coffeehouses, or pastry shops that provide a grand variety of delicious foodstuffs quickly and for reasonable to downright cheap prices.

Whether you're feeling a bit peckish or positively peaked, you'll find something tempting to tide yourself over until the next big meal.

Have food, will travel

Just 2 long blocks west of the Ferry Building on the Embarcadero, next to Pier 5, is a bench-lined, refurbished wooden wharf with fine views that practically begs for an impromptu picnic lunch. Plenty of other spots around the city exist in which to unpack a brown bag, too.

You can generously fill your lunch pail at **Molinari Delicatessen,** a second-generation, family-run Italian delicatessen with a fantastic assortment of cheeses, inexpensive Italian wines, and friendly people who make excellent sandwiches to go. It's located at 373 Columbus Ave. in North Beach (☎ **415-421-2337;** www.molinarideli.com) and is open Monday through Friday 8 a.m. to 6 p.m. and Saturday 7:30 a.m. to 5:30 p.m.

Also in North Beach, on the corner of Columbus and Kearny, is a Parisian-inspired, Italian cafe owned by the director Francis Ford Coppola. Surprisingly, **Café Zoetrope** (☎ **415-291-1700;** www.cafe zoetrope.com) — part wine bar, part kitchen store — serves the most delicious muffuletta (comprised of olive salad, mortadella, and provolone) outside of New Orleans, a sandwich that once made my husband so ecstatic he squirreled away half to eat the following day. The cafe is open from 11 a.m. until 10 p.m. weekdays (closed Mon) and opens at noon on the weekends, staying open until 10 p.m. Saturday and 9 p.m. Sunday.

In the Financial District at **Palio Paninoteca,** 505 Montgomery St., near California Street (☎ **415-362-6900;** www.palipaninoteca.com), $7 gets you a panino large enough for two. Fillings range from grilled vegetables or meats to smoked prosciutto with Gorgonzola, mascarpone, and arugula. It's closed weekends. Weekdays, it's open from 6:30 a.m. to 4 p.m. Prefer a salad? **Mixt Greens,** 120 Sansome St., at Bush (☎ **415-433-6498**), provides a lovely range of made-to-order, truly gourmet salads that you can eat on premises or take away.

Closer to Union Square, with another two locations in the Financial District, is **Specialty's Café & Bakery,** 1 Post St., at Market (☎ **415-896-2253** or 877-502-2837; www.specialtys.com). This spot is popular for a vast array of fresh sandwiches served on made-from-scratch breads. It's closed on weekends. Weekdays, it's open from 6 a.m. to 7 p.m.

The Ferry wonderful Building

If you only had a few hours to spend in San Francisco, I'd send you to the splendidly remodeled Ferry Building on the Embarcadero at the foot of Market Street. A landmark completed in 1898, the building gradually fell into disuse after the Bay Bridge opened in 1936, allowing commuters from the East Bay to drive, rather than ferry, into the city. The revitalization of the Embarcadero seems complete now that the clock tower shines beaconlike in the evening, and the Ferry Building marketplace is a hub once more, drawing in people from around the Bay Area. Open every day (a few shops are closed on Sun), the light-filled space has been populated with the best local purveyors of food and food-related items. For purposes of grabbing a quick bite, food to go, a picnic, or a complete meal, you can find something satisfying just by making a tour of the open-front shops. Some highlights: **The Hog Island Oyster Company** oyster bar, with gorgeous bay views from the counter; **Mastrelli's Delicatessen,** the sister store to Molinari's in North Beach, where you can order freshly made sandwiches to go; and **Golden Gate Meat Company,** a small counter that sells organic meats but also has lunch specials — my pastrami sandwich emitted such a delicious odor and looked so luscious, I actually had people stopping me to ask where I'd bought it. You'll also find a Japanese deli, a French rotisserie, chocolate, gelato, cookbooks, and gifts.

Down on the farm — farmers' market, that is

Saturday and Tuesday mornings bring the **Ferry Plaza Farmers' Market** in front of and behind the Ferry Building (open from 8 a.m.–1:30 p.m.). A jumble of basket- and canvas-sack-wielding couples pick over the heirloom tomatoes and grab the last of the wild strawberries while juggling coffee and a cellphone. The simple beauty of the organic vegetables and flowers makes a walk around the market an enormous pleasure, despite the crowds. The **Hayes Street Grill** and **Rose Pistola** restaurants cook gourmet breakfasts from their outdoor booths on Saturdays, and other vendors sell items such as bottles of olive oil, jars of local honey, and exotic orchid plants. This is also a great place to gather picnic food — fresh bread, artisan cheeses, and fruit — for later in the day. The F-Market streetcar almost drops you at the door.

Snacking at the wharf

Let's be frank. **PIER 39/Fisherman's Wharf** is the most touristy part of town. The restaurants that crowd Jefferson Street exist for the people who are here today and gone tomorrow. I've learned to accept this, if not to embrace it, and I'm not going to sneer at anybody who spends part of a day here on the way to Alcatraz or just to see what all the fuss is about.

But let's say that this person is hungry. Let's say that this person has heard about all the crab vendors and the sourdough bread, and thinks to himself, "That sounds like lunch to me." This is what I'd suggest: Buy a bottle of beer, buy a little round of sourdough bread, and ask one of the guys at a crab stand (try **Fisherman's Grotto No. 9**) to cook, clean, and crack a live crab for you. Then take these goodies and lots of napkins through the doors marked "Passageway to the Boats," walk down this relatively quiet area, sit on the dock, and have a good time. *Remember:* The local Dungeness crab season is from November through May. In the summer, the crabs are flown in from Alaska or parts east.

Most recently, **Boudin Bakery** (the sourdough bread people) built a nifty new demonstration bakery/cafe/museum on Fisherman's Wharf (160 Jefferson St. at Taylor Street; ☎ 415-928-1849). You can watch bread being prepared from a glass-walled catwalk suspended above the action, take a tour, sample the wares, and tuck into your soup at indoor and outdoor tables. Boudin created San Francisco's distinctive sourdough loaves in 1849, and for an icon, they taste pretty darn good.

Unless you purchase a freshly cracked crab, rest assured that the $5.25 crab cocktail you ordered is made of canned crab — or even imitation crab.

Flour power

You can have a swell time hunting and gathering among the bakeries in North Beach. For starters, drop by **Liguria Bakery,** on the corner of Stockton and Filbert streets (☎ 415-421-3786), for a sheet of plain focaccia, or maybe one topped with green onions or tomato. They're all delicious and wrapped for portability. Liguria is open every day by 8 a.m. and closes when the last piece of focaccia is sold, usually by 2 p.m. I also love **Victoria Pastry Co.,** 1362 Stockton St., at Vallejo (☎ 415-781-2015), which sells a large selection of Italian sweets (the chewy almond cookies are good enough to give as a gift) and slices of its justly popular cakes.

Citizen Cake, 399 Grove St., in Hayes Valley (☎ 415-861-2228), creates the kind of homemade cookies, cakes, and desserts that ignites a love/hate relationship between your taste buds and your hips. The spacious cafe also serves lunch and dinner Tuesday through Friday (8 a.m. – 10 p.m.) and brunch and dinner on the weekends (Sat 10 a.m.–10 p.m.; Sun 10 a.m.–5 p.m.) It's located near the stylish Hayes Street shopping blocks, which makes eating and spending so efficient. Now inhabiting the back of the top floor of the Virgin Megastore, 2 Stockton St. at Market Street (☎ 415-399-1565), is **Citizen Cupcake.** Here you can gaze at the street scene below over coffee and mini scones, a beer and a sandwich, or even a sake and a salad. Teens would especially enjoy a pit stop here.

A small chain of **Boulangerie Bay Bread** bakery/cafes has popped up in the Haight-Ashbury, Cow Hollow, Fillmore, and Russian Hill neighborhoods, with my favorite being **Boulange de Polk,** 2310 Polk St., at Green Street (☎ 415-345-1107). Along with lovely French pastries (the *cannelés de Bordeaux* are swoon-worthy), you can order savory tarts, sandwiches, and salads to take away or eat at one of the coveted outdoor tables.

Chinese bakeries

Chinese bakeries, which sell savory as well as sweet items, abound in **Chinatown,** in the **Sunset District** on Irving Street, and in the **Richmond District** on Clement Street. For snacking on the premises or on the go, delicious baked or steamed pork buns (baked buns are golden brown, and steamed buns are white) are ideal and a big hit with kids. If you want something on the sweet side, custard tarts and sesame-seed-covered balls of rice surrounding a bit of sweet bean paste are standard issue. Look also for *bo lo bow,* slightly puffy and sweet bread with a crust that resembles the outside of a pineapple, or *chung yow bow,* green-onion bread. You may have to point to whatever looks appetizing because the folks behind the counter don't necessarily speak English.

Coffee and tea, if you please

Places to sit and sip are as prevalent as pigeons in this caffeine-crazed piece of paradise. Coffeehouses — and I'm not even including the mega-chains — nestle in every neighborhood, seemingly on every block. I don't think drinking coffee as a lifestyle was invented in North Beach, but based on sheer numbers, it could have been. Regulars, of course, have their favorite blends and favorite tables, but no one will argue against hanging out at **Mario's Bohemian Cigar Store** on the corner of Columbus and Union Street (☎ 415-362-0536). Along with excellent coffee (Graffeo), you can graze on a mouth-watering chicken parmigiana on focaccia. **Caffé Trieste,** on Vallejo and Grant streets (☎ 415-982-2605; www.caffetriseste.com), is a mob scene on Saturday afternoons, when the owners and friends take a turn at the microphone to sing. Coffee is served daily with or without opera.

Although that Seattle-based coffee Goliath continues to snap up real estate in a quest to make everyone drink frappaccinos, we have our own local chain to kick around. Actually, **Peet's Coffee and Tea** is worshipped by caffeine aficionados, and if you love really strong coffee, it's worth dropping by one of their many stores. The one closest to Union Square is in the Financial District at 22 Battery St., at Bush (☎ 415-981-4550; www.peets.com). You can also try the shop on Chestnut Street between Steiner and Pierce streets in the Marina (☎ 415-931-8302) or the newest one in the Ferry Building (☎ 415-593-3831). They're all open daily. In Hayes Valley, the community coffee klatch takes place in front of a custom furniture workshop at 30 Linden St., an alley off Gough Street. Look for the seemingly makeshift bar, indicating the **Blue Bottle Coffee Co.** You can eavesdrop or make new friends while waiting in line for a good strong cuppa.

Self-described coffee snobs have little choice but to drop by **Ritual Coffee Roasters,** 1026 Valencia St. in the Mission (☎ 415-641-1024). The beans come from Portland Oregon's Stumptown Coffee and in all honesty, they make the best cappuccino I have had in town (thanks, Bev). The roomy storefront has a glass case filled with treats, free wireless, and it's open until 11 p.m. Monday through Saturday and until 9 p.m. Sunday.

The peaceful **Imperial Tea Court,** 1411 Powell St., near Broadway (☎ 415-788-6080), is a must-stop in which to rest your feet and take stock of your life — or maybe just the last half hour — over a pot of exotic leaves and blossoms that would make Celestial Seasonings blush. This is the place to sample the highest-quality teas as they were meant to be brewed — and the staff will be happy to show you how it's done. Open Wednesday through Monday 11 a.m. to 6:30 p.m.

Breakfast of champions

Touring is hard work; you need a good breakfast. Around Union Square you can find lots of restaurants serving in the morning, including **The Grand Café** (☎ 415-292-0101) on Geary and **Sears Fine Food** (☎ 415-986-1160) on Powell, both across from Union Square, and open daily; and my favorite, **Dottie's True Blue Café,** 522 Jones St., between Geary Boulevard and O'Farrell Street (☎ 415-885-2767). Open Wednesday through Monday only, Dottie's is a tiny diner that offers daily specials as well as the basics — eggs, pancakes, sausage — all prepared with great flair. The baked goods are so delicious you may want to purchase some to go. Expect to wait in line on the weekends. When the lines at Dottie's and Sears appear too daunting, just walk over to **Café Mason,** 320 Mason St. between Geary and O'Farrell (☎ 415-544-0320), for all kinds of fruit-enhanced pancakes, eggs any way, or maybe yogurt and fresh fruit. For Union Square, the prices are reasonable and the food's fine. Across from the Chinatown gate is **Café de la Presse,** 352 Grant Ave. (☎ 415-398-2680), very European in feel, with excellent lattes, croissants, newspapers, and lots of windows. Lines here move faster than you might think.

Bechelli's, in the Marina/Cow Hollow neighborhood at 2346 Chestnut St., between Divisadero and Scott streets (☎ 415-346-1801), serves a substantial breakfast until 3 p.m. during the week, and until 4 p.m. Saturday and Sunday. To my mind, the booths, scruffy leatherette chairs, and beat-up, horseshoe-shaped wooden counter add to the charm of this neighborhood institution, but more importantly, the breakfast menu is nearly as huge as the portions. Buttermilk pancakes, French toast, homemade corned beef hash, and lots of omelets potentially will hold you for a good part of the day. Kids often enjoy bellying up to the counter, and the place has a very relaxed, family-friendly atmosphere. No reservations; credit cards are accepted.

Around the Embarcadero on Battery Street, **Il Fornaio** (☎ 415-986-0100; www.ilfornaio.com) offers an array of baked goods that are sold from a takeaway counter just inside. On the weekends, the restaurant opens at 9 a.m. for brunch.

If you don't mind traveling to Golden Gate Park to hunt down an early-morning meal, take the N-Judah streetcar to Ninth Avenue, walk toward the park, and at the corner of Lincoln and Ninth avenues you'll find **The Canvas Café/Gallery** (☎ 415-504-0060), open daily. As the name implies, inside are paintings by local artists plus simple food for breakfast (oatmeal, bagels, frittatas); sandwiches, salads, pizza, and Mediterranean *mezza* (appetizer) or fondue platters to share for lunch; and afternoon pick-me-ups including wine and beer. It's exactly where you want to stop before or after a day in the park.

Finally, if you have a soft spot for diners — and I mean the real thing, not *Happy Days* replicas — make your way to the end of Geary Boulevard (the name changes to Point Lobos Avenue) where it meets the Great Highway. The little joint overlooking the old Sutro Baths is **Louis,** 902

Point Lobos Ave. (☎ 415-387-6330), which opened in 1937 and has an endless view of the Pacific Ocean. Louis serves breakfast and lunch daily from 6:30 a.m., nothing to write home about, but there's something comfortable and familiar about the décor (linoleum, worn booths) and a big plate of eggs over easy, country ham, and hash browns. This is a fine place to eat before hiking along the Coastal Trail, golfing at Lincoln Park, or heading to Golden Gate Park. Cash and traveler's checks only.

Pizza and other cheap eats

Although I'm known to criticize fast food, I consider pizza an exception. Good pizza can make a perfectly satisfying, easygoing, low-rent meal. And although San Francisco doesn't have the reputation of either New York or Chicago in the pizza department, you won't have any difficulty finding a ready slice in any neighborhood.

Uncle Vito's Pizzadelli, on the corner of Bush and Powell streets (☎ 415-391-5008), serves credible pie with a big selection of toppings, good salads, and enough pasta dishes to carbo-load for the next day's adventures. Uncle Vito's is inexpensive and convenient to Nob Hill and Union Square, so you'll see lots of foreign tourists here, attempting to put together just the right combination of pizza and beer. When shopping on Fillmore Street, stop by **Dino's Pizzeria** (☎ 415-922-4700) to check up on sports scores and dig into one of Dino's thick-crusted, cheesy creations. It's on the corner of Fillmore and California, where you'll often find Dino at the door eyeing passersby and chatting up the regulars.

If too much exposure to coddled food makes you long for a touch of grease, you can find a couple places to deal with your craving for hamburgers, fries, and a shake. **Mo's Grill,** which makes many kinds of burgers, is South of Market at Folsom and Fourth streets, on the southwest side of Yerba Buena Gardens (☎ 415-957-3779). You can also find a branch in North Beach on Grant Street, between Vallejo and Green (☎ 415-788-3779). Because I have a soft spot for '50s-patterned Formica and bright colors, my favorite place to chew the fat is **Burger Joint** in the Mission on 807 Valencia St. (☎ 415-824-3494). And, despite my protestations against fast food, **Taylor's Refreshers** at the Ferry Building makes a great burger and a greater milkshake. Anyway, they aren't *that* fast.

North Beach also shelters at least two eateries specializing in roasted chicken, the oldest being **Il Pollaio,** 555 Columbus Ave., between Union and Green streets (☎ 415-362-7727). A very casual place to sit down for savory chicken and other meats and salads, this is where you go when the kids start rolling their eyes if you mention dim sum or sea bass. It's also a good choice when you're tired of spending too much money on dinner.

Adventure eaters in the mood for Indian food will barely feel a strain on the pocketbook at **Shalimar,** 532 Jones St., between Geary and O'Farrell (☎ **415-928-0333**), another Formica-tabled hole-in-the-wall in the Tenderloin/Union Square area. Order at the counter, sit at your table, watch for your food to come up, and then enjoy delicious curries, savory nan bread, and tandoori. It's open daily for lunch and dinner; cash only. Another highly recommended restaurant in the Tenderloin, and attractive enough for a date, is the **Bodega Bistro,** 607 Larkin St. at Eddy (☎ **415-921-1218**). The *pho ga,* Vietnamese chicken noodle soup, is simply wonderful, due in part to brilliant chicken stock. Another can't miss is the papaya salad, but in fact, the dishes here are some of the best in the category. If you are uncomfortable in the neighborhood, come for lunch. Cash only.

The real dill

Oh, happy day. A genuine delicatessen, with bagels imported directly from New York, exists right here in San Francisco. You don't know how we suffered until **Miller's East Coast West Delicatessen** started with the chicken soup and the matzo balls, not to mention the pastrami, the pickled herring, and the brisket (every bit as good as mine, if not better). Located at 1725 Polk St. (☎ **415-563-3542**) and open daily, this is also a fine place to get sandwiches to take with you for the trip home — I wouldn't want you to go hungry.

Index of Establishments by Neighborhood

The Castro
Chow (American, $)
Home (American, $–$$)

Chinatown
Gold Mountain (Chinese, $)
Kay Cheung (Chinese, $)
Lichee Garden (Chinese, $)
R&G Lounge (Chinese, $)

Civic Center/Hayes Valley
Absinthe (French, $$$)
Hayes Street Grill (Seafood, $$)
Jardinière (California/French, $$$$)
Zuni Cafe (California, $$)

The Embarcadero
Boulevard (American, $$$$)
Butterfly (Pan-Asian, $$$)

Taylor's Refreshers (Burgers, $)
Hog Island Oyster Company (Seafood, $)
Il Fornaio (California/Italian, $–$$)
Ozumo (Japanese/Sushi, $$$)
Slanted Door (Vietnamese, $$
Yank Sing (Dim Sum, $$)

Financial District
B-44 (Spanish, $$)
Kokkari Estiatorio (Greek, $$$)
Plouf (French, $$)
Tadich Grill (Seafood, $$)

Japantown
Cafe Kati (California, $$$)
Isuzu (Japanese, $)
Mifune (Japanese, $)

The Marina/Cow Hollow

A-16 (Italian, $$)
Bechelli's (Breakfast, $)
Bistro Aix (French, $–$$)
Green's (Vegetarian, $$–$$$)
Isa (French, $$)
Mamacita (Mexican, $$)

The Mission District

Bar Tartine (California/
Mediterranean, $$)
Blue Plate (California, $$)
Burger Joint (Burgers, $)
Delfina (Tuscan Italian, $$)
Dosa (Indian, $)
Foreign Cinema (New American/
French, $$$)
The Last Supper Club (Italian, $)
Limon (Peruvian, $)
Luna Park (New American, $$)
Pancho Villa (Mexican, $)
Pizzeria Delfina (Pizza, $)
Range (California, $$)
Taqueria Cancun (Mexican, $)
Ti Couz (Crepes, $)

Nob Hill

Uncle Vito's Pizzadelli (Pizza, $)

North Beach

Café Zoetrope (Italian, $)
Capp's Corner (Italian, $$)
Enrico's Sidewalk Cafe
(California/Italian, $$)
Il Pollaio (Chicken, $)
La Felce (Italian, $$)
L'Osteria del Forno (Rustic Italian, $)
Moose's (California/
Mediterranean, $$$)
Rose Pistola (Italian, $$$)

Pacific Heights

Dino's Pizzeria (Pizza, $)
Quince (Modern Italian, $$$)

Potrero Hill

Baraka (Moroccan, $$)
Chez Maman (Crepes, $)
Chez Papa (French, $$)

Richmond/Sunset Districts

Canvas Café Gallery
(Mediterranean, $)
Ebisu (Japanese, $$)
Katia, A Russian Tearoom (Russian, $)
Louis (Breakfast/Burgers, $)
Mayflower (Chinese, $$)
PJ's Oyster Bed (Seafood, $$)

Russian Hill

East Coast West Delicatessen
(Jewish, $)
Gary Danko (New American/
French, $$$$)
Tablespoon (American, $$)

South of Market (SoMa)

Ame (New American, $$$$)
Asia SF (California/Asian, $$)
Hawthorne Lane (California/
Asian, $$$$)
Le Charm (French, $$)
Lulu (Mediterranean, $$)
Mo's Grill (Burgers, $)
Pazzia (Northern Italian, $)
supperclub (New American, $$$$)
Town Hall (New American, $$$)
Tres Agaves (Mexican, $$)

The Tenderloin

Bodega Bistro (French Vietnamese, $)
Shalimar (Indian, $)

Union Square

Café de la Presse (French, $)
Café Mason (Breakfast, $)
Canteen (California, $–$$)
Cortez (Mediterranean, $$$)
Dottie's True Blue Café (Breakfast, $)
Grand Cafe (California, $$–$$$)
Le Colonial (French-Vietnamese, $$$)
Sear's Fine Food (Breakfast, $)

Index of Establishments by Cuisine

American
Boulevard (The Embarcadero, $$$$)
Chow (The Castro, $)
Home (The Castro, $–$$)
Tablespoon (Russian Hill, $$)

Asian/Latin
Asia de Cuba (Union Square, $$$$)

Breakfast
Bechelli's (The Marina/Cow Hollow, $)
Café Mason (Union Square, $)
Dottie's True Blue Café
(Union Square, $)
Louis (Richmond/Sunset, $)
Sear's Fine Food (Union Square, $)

Burgers
Burger Joint (Mission District, $)
Louis (Richmond/Sunset, $)
Mo's Grill (SoMa, $)
Taylor's Refreshers (Embarcadero, $)

California
The Blue Plate (Mission District, $$)
Cafe Kati (Japantown, $$$)
Canteen (Union Square, $$)
Grand Cafe (Union Square, $$–$$$)
Range (Mission District, $$)
Zuni Cafe (Civic Center/
Hayes Valley, $$)

California/Asian
AsiaSF (SoMa, $$)
Hawthorne Lane (SoMa, $$$$)

California/French
Grand Café (Union Square, $$–$$$)
Jardinière (Civic Center/
Hayes Valley, $$$$)

California/Italian
Enrico's Sidewalk Cafe
(North Beach, $$)
Il Fornaio (Embarcadero, $–$$)

California/Mediterranean
Bar Tartine (Mission District, $$)
Moose's (North Beach, $$$)

Chicken
Il Pollaio (North Beach, $)

Chinese
Gold Mountain (Chinatown, $)
Kay Cheung (Chinatown, $)
Lichee Garden (Chinatown, $)
Mayflower (Richmond/Sunset, $$)
R&G Lounge (Chinatown, $)

Crepes
Chez Maman (Potrero Hill, $)
Ti Couz (Mission District, $)

Dim Sum
Yank Sing (Embarcadero, $$)

French
Absinthe (Civic Center/
Hayes Valley, $$$)
Bistro Aix (The Marina/
Cow Hollow, $–$$)
Café de la Presse (Union Square, $)
Chez Papa (Potrero Hill, $$)
Foreign Cinema (Mission District, $$$)
Gary Danko (Russian Hill, $$$$)
Isa (The Marina/Cow Hollow, $$)
Le Charm (SoMa, $$)
Plouf (Financial District, $$)

French-Vietnamese
Bodega Bistro (Tenderloin, $)
Le Colonial (Union Square, $$$)

Greek

Kokkari Estiatorio (Financial District, $$$)

Indian

Dosa (Mission District, $)
Shalimar (Union Square, $)

Italian

A-16 (The Marina/Cow Hollow, $$)
Café Zoetrope (North Beach, $)
Capp's Corner (North Beach, $$)
Delfina (Mission District, $$)
La Felce (North Beach, $$)
The Last Supper Club (Mission District, $)
L'Osteria del Forno (North Beach, $)
Pazzia (SoMa, $)
Qunice (Pacific Heights, $$$)
Rose Pistola (North Beach, $$$)

Japanese

Ebisu (Richmond/Sunset, $$)
Isuzu (Japantown, $)
Mifune (Japantown, $)
Ozumo (Embarcadero, $$$)

Jewish

East Coast West Delicatessen (Russian Hill, $)

Mediterranean

Canvas Café Gallery (Richmond/Sunset, $)
Cortez (Union Square, $$$)
Lulu (SoMa, $$)

Mexican

Mamacita (The Marina/Cow Hollow, $$)
Pancho Villa (Mission District, $)
Taqueria Cancun (Mission District, $)
Tres Agaves (SoMa, $$)

Moroccan

Baraka (Potrero Hill, $$)

New American

Ame (SoMa, $$$$)
Foreign Cinema (Mission District, $$$)
Gary Danko (Russian Hill, $$$$)
Luna Park (Mission District, $$)
supperclub (SoMa, $$$$)
Town Hall (SoMa, $$$)

Pan Asian

Butterfly (Embarcadero, $$$)

Peruvian

Limon (Mission District, $)

Pizza

Dino's Pizzeria (Pacific Heights, $)
Uncle Vito's Pizzadelli (Nob Hill, $)
Pizzeria Delfina (Mission District, $)

Russian

Katia, A Russian Tearoom (Richmond/Sunset, $)

Seafood

Hayes Street Grill (Civic Center/Hayes Valley, $$)
Hog Island Oyster Company (Embarcadero, $)
PJ's Oyster Bed (Richmond/Sunset, $$)
Tadich Grill (Financial District, $$)

Spanish

B-44 (Financial District, $$)

Sushi

Ozumo (Embarcadero, $$$)

Vegetarian

Green's (The Marina/Cow Hollow, $$–$$$)

Vietnamese

Slanted Door (Embarcadero, $$)

Index of Establishments by Price

$

Bechelli's (Breakfast, The Marina/
Cow Hollow)

Bistro Aix (French, The Marina/
Cow Hollow)

Bodega Bistro (French-Vietnamese,
Tenderloin)

Burger Joint (Burgers,
Mission District)

Café de la Presse (French,
Union Square)

Café Mason (Breakfast, Union Square)

Café Zoetrope (Italian, North Beach)

Canvas Café Gallery (Mediterranean,
Richmond/Sunset)

Chez Maman (Crepes, Potrero Hill)

Chow (American, The Castro)

Dino's Pizzeria (Pizza, Pacific Heights)

Dosa (Indian, Mission District)

Dottie's True Blue Café (Breakfast,
Union Square)

East Coast West Delicatessen
(Jewish, Russian Hill)

Gold Mountain (Chinese, Chinatown)

Hog Island Oyster Company
(Seafood, Embarcadero)

Home (American, Castro)

Il Fornaio (California/Italian,
Embarcadero)

Il Pollaio (Chicken, North Beach)

Isuzu (Japanese, Japantown)

Katia, A Russian Tearoom
(Russian, Richmond/Sunset)

Kay Cheung (Chinese, Chinatown)

The Last Supper Club (Italian,
Mission District)

Lichee Garden (Chinese, Chinatown)

Limon (Peruvian, Mission District)

L'Osteria del Forno (Rustic Italian,
North Beach)

Louis (Breakfast/Burgers,
Richmond/Sunset)

Mason (American, Union Square)

Mifune (Japanese, Japantown)

Mo's Grill (Burgers, SoMa)

Pancho Villa (Mexican,
Mission District)

Pazzia (Northern Italian, SoMa)

Pizzeria Delfina (Pizza,
Mission District)

R&G Lounge (Chinese, Chinatown)

Sear's Fine Food (Breakfast,
Union Square)

Shalimar (Indian, Union Square)

Taqueria Cancun (Mexican,
Mission District)

Taylor's Refreshers (Burgers,
Embarcadero)

Ti Couz (Crepes, Mission District)

Uncle Vito's Pizzadelli (Pizza,
Nob Hill)

$$

AsiaSF (California/Asian, SoMa)

A-16 (Southern Italian, The
Marina/Cow Hollow)Baraka
(Moroccan, Potrero Hill)

Bar Tartine (California/Mediterranean,
Mission District)

B-44 (Spanish, Financial District)

Bistro Aix (French, The Marina/
Cow Hollow)

Blue Plate (California, Mission
District)

Canteen (California, Union Square)

Capp's Corner (Italian, North Beach)

Chez Papa (French, Potrero Hill)

Delfina (Tuscan Italian,
Mission District)

Ebisu (Japanese, Richmond/Sunset)

Enrico's Sidewalk Cafe
(California/Italian, North Beach)

Grand Cafe (California, Union Square)

Green's (Vegetarian, The Marina/
Cow Hollow)

Hayes Street Grill (Seafood,
Civic Center/Hayes Valley)

Home (American, Castro)

Il Fornaio (California/Italian,
Embarcadero)

Isa (French, The Marina/Cow Hollow)
La Felce (Italian, North Beach)
Le Charm (French, SoMa)
Lulu (Mediterranean, SoMa)
Luna Park (New American,
Mission District)
Mamacita (Mexican, The Marina/
Cow Hollow)
Mayflower (Chinese,
Richmond/Sunset)
PJ's Oyster Bed (Seafood,
Richmond/Sunset)
Plouf (French, Financial District)
Range (California, Mission District)
Slanted Door (Vietnamese,
Embarcadero)
Tablespoon (American, Russian Hill)
Tadich Grill (Seafood, Financial
District)
Tres Agaves (Mexican, SoMa)
Yank Sing (Dim Sum, Embarcadero)
Zuni Cafe (California, Civic Center/
Hayes Valley)

$$$

Absinthe (French, Civic Center/Hayes
Valley)
Butterfly (Pan Asian, Embarcadero)
Cafe Kati (California, Japantown)
Cortez (Mediterranean, Union Square)

Foreign Cinema (New American/
French, Mission District)
Grand Café (California/French,
Union Square)
Green's (Vegetarian, The Marina/
Cow Hollow)
Kokkari Estiatorio (Greek,
Financial District)
Le Colonial (French-Vietnamese,
Union Square)
Moose's (California/Mediterranean,
North Beach)
Ozumo (Japanese/Sushi,
Embarcadero)
Quince (Modern Italian,
Pacific Heights)
Rose Pistola (Italian, North Beach)
Town Hall (New American, SoMa)

$$$$

Ame (New American, SoMa)
Boulevard (American,
The Embarcadero)
Gary Danko (New American/
French, Russian Hill)
Hawthorne Lane (California/
Asian, SoMa)
Jardinière (California/French,
Civic Center/Hayes Valley)
supperclub (New American, SoMa)

Part IV
Exploring San Francisco

The 5th Wave   By Rich Tennant

In this part . . .

Now you get to the main course. This part tells you about the landmarks and neighborhoods that define San Francisco to the world. And you know what? Most of them are worthy of their star billing.

How do you take in everything? That depends on how much time you have. If you have only a day or two, a guided tour may be the best way of at least seeing, if not savoring, the sites. Or you can pick and choose from a list of a few places to see, spend some quality time at each of those sites, and plan on coming back to the city another time to catch the rest. If you have three or more days to wander, take a look at my suggested itineraries for an idea of how to absorb as much of the city as possible.

Don't forget the shopping opportunities while the pleasure of browsing in one-of-a-kind stores is still possible. An entire shopping chapter awaits, and it's filled with suggestions of where to find interesting clothes, gifts, and foods that you won't find in your local mall. Leave room in your suitcase — it'll be heavier on the trip home.

You'd think it would be enough for me to help you plan your trip to San Francisco, a marvel among big cities, but no . . . I toss in a few extra treats for your dining and sightseeing pleasure. Chief among them are trips to the gorgeous Napa and Sonoma valleys, where the sights and scents of grapes and olives act like a restorative. Closer still is Berkeley, a microcosm of Northern California life that revolves around the university and a vibrant dining scene. Finally, nature boys and girls will have a veritable field day hiking or relaxing on the coast in verdant Point Reyes and Inverness.

Chapter 11

Discovering San Francisco's Best Attractions

. . . .

In This Chapter

▶ Finding the most popular attractions in San Francisco

▶ Breaking in to Alcatraz

▶ Riding the cable cars

▶ Crossing the Golden Gate Bridge

▶ Indulging history, architecture, sports, and nature lovers

▶ Taking a guided tour by land or sea

. . . .

Something is bringing you to San Francisco. Perhaps you've been overcome by recollections of old Rice-A-Roni commercials ("the San Francisco treat [ding ding!]") that became synonymous with cable cars. Or maybe visions of the Golden Gate Bridge spanning the icy waters of the bay are pulling you to the left coast. Are the views from your window a bit too flat? Is the thrill-seeker in you ready for the action our hills provide to drivers and passengers alike? Did you manage to schedule a week off from work, and coming to San Francisco just seemed like a good idea? Whatever your reasons for choosing this city, I don't think you'll be bored, and I know you won't be disappointed.

You may be curious to understand firsthand why this city is different from any other urban center in the United States and why its residents are so passionate about where they live. After a few days making your way around, you may glean some of the reasons, the most apparent of which is the sheer beauty of the setting. There's more of course. You never know what you'll see when you look carefully. Take those cable cars, for example: Sure, they're a fun ride, but as you climb aboard, observe the gripman (or gripwoman — there's one) and the other passengers, and note how the neighborhoods change as you head from Union Square through North Beach or past Nob Hill. Even watching the passersby on the pavement is an experience. I'll always remember how

Saving on entrance fees

Your timing has to be right, but if you're in the neighborhood take advantage of free museum days. Entry to the **California Academy of Sciences** and the **Exploratorium** is free on the first Wednesday of every month; the **Asian Art Museum**, the **Museum of Modern Art (MoMA)**, and the **Legion of Honor** are gratis on the first Tuesday of every month. Every Thursday after 5 p.m., admission is reduced at the Asian and at MoMA, and they stay open until 9 p.m.

heads turned (and kept turning) to follow a gorgeous girl in her black leather pants as she sashayed up Mason Street. It was certainly the first time I've ever been on a cable car that intentionally moved backward!

The following list gives you a quick reference of the features that make San Francisco, well, San Francisco.

San Francisco's Top Attractions

Alcatraz Island
Fisherman's Wharf

Hollywood movies, including *Birdman of Alcatraz, Escape from Alcatraz,* and *The Rock,* have recast what is essentially an early-20th-century ruin in San Francisco Bay into a hugely popular tourist site. Even if you're familiar with this former military fort and federal prison only from vague references to its famous prisoners — Al Capone, "Machine Gun" Kelly, Robert (the Birdman) Stroud — you'll find the self-guided tour of the cell house strangely moving. I credit this to the excellent audio guide that includes remembrances narrated by former guards and prisoners, and to the low-key manner in which Alcatraz is presented. No attempt is made to glamorize the inmates or to condemn the system. This was a cold, isolated, maximum-security prison housing the most hardened criminals of the day, which coincidentally offered them glimpses of an enticing city, perhaps invoking longing and regret. Imagining what life here was like isn't all that difficult, but at the moment you begin to feel inklings of pity for the incarcerated, a vividly told story of an attempted prison escape reminds the listener that these inmates were, for the most part, remorseless. Before or after the cellblock tour, you're invited to view an orientation video and, during fall and winter, you can tour the island itself on a walking path that begins near the ferryboat landing. (The trail is closed from mid-Feb through early Sept during bird-nesting season.) Rangers are around for questions, and they often give talks on the history of the prison and famous escapes. Bring a jacket as well as comfortable shoes for the steep walk to the cell house. A tram is available once an hour to take wheelchair users or anyone unable to make the walk up to the prison. The Alcatraz experience takes about two and a half hours, including the ferry ride.

To get the full effect of what being an inmate may have been like, try the **Alcatraz After Hours tour.** The prison becomes especially sinister when the sun goes down, so use discretion before deciding to bring kids along. The tour is offered Thursday through Sunday only; the ferry departs at 6:15 p.m. and 7 p.m. (4:20 p.m. during the winter).

During the summer, you must reserve tickets far in advance for the ferry ride to the island, and tickets purchased are valid only on the date and time indicated on the ticket. Order tickets over the Web site, or call ☎ 415-981-ROCK to purchase tickets over the phone.

See maps p. 164 and p. 171. Pier 33, at Fisherman's Wharf for location of ferry departures. ☎ 415-981-ROCK. www.alcatrazcruises.com *or* www.nps.gov/alcatraz.com. *Open: Winter daily 9:30 a.m.–2:15 p.m.; summer daily 9:30 a.m.–4:15 p.m. Ferries run approximately every half hour; arrive at least 20 minutes before sailing time. F-Market streetcar, Powell-Mason cable car (the line ends a few blocks away), or 30-Stockton bus. Admission (includes ferry and audio tour): $19 adults, $17 seniors 62 and older, $11 children 5–11. Night tour fares are $26 adults, $23 seniors and kids 12–17, $14 children 5–11.*

Asian Art Museum
Civic Center

The new Asian Art Museum holds one of the largest collections of Asian art in the Western world, covering 6,000 years and encompassing the cultures of Japan, China, Korea, and Southeast Asia. Formerly housed in Golden Gate Park, the Asian gathered public and private funds to renovate the interior of the old Beaux Arts Main Library and create 37,500 square feet of exhibition space (and if that doesn't invigorate Civic Center, I'm not sure what will). Although the collection remains more than enough reason to visit, the renovation has also attracted plenty of attention. It is designed by Gae Aulenti, the Milanese architect who renovated the former d'Orsay train station in Paris into the popular Musée d'Orsay. The Asian is compact, and it won't take you more than a few hours to see all the galleries. **Cafe Asia** on the first floor is open from 10 a.m. for drinks and Asian-influenced dishes served cafeteria style.

Getting around and in with Citypass

Citypass (www.citypass.net) is a booklet of discounted tickets to six major attractions, including the **Museum of Modern Art, Palace of the Legion of Honor** and **de Young museums, Aquarium of the Bay, Exploratorium,** the **California Academy of Sciences** or **Asian Art Museum,** and a Blue & Gold Bay Cruise, and includes a seven-day Muni Passport, making it quite a bargain for those who are ambitious enough to use all the coupons. It's $49 for adults, $39 for kids, and you can purchase it online or at the participating attractions.

San Francisco's Top Sights

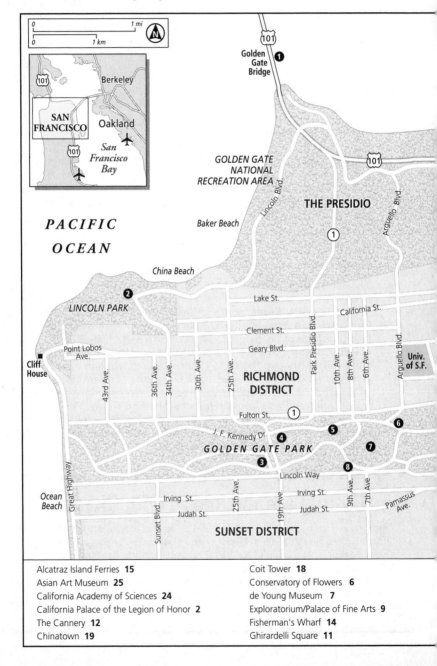

Alcatraz Island Ferries **15**
Asian Art Museum **25**
California Academy of Sciences **24**
California Palace of the Legion of Honor **2**
The Cannery **12**
Chinatown **19**

Coit Tower **18**
Conservatory of Flowers **6**
de Young Museum **7**
Exploratorium/Palace of Fine Arts **9**
Fisherman's Wharf **14**
Ghirardelli Square **11**

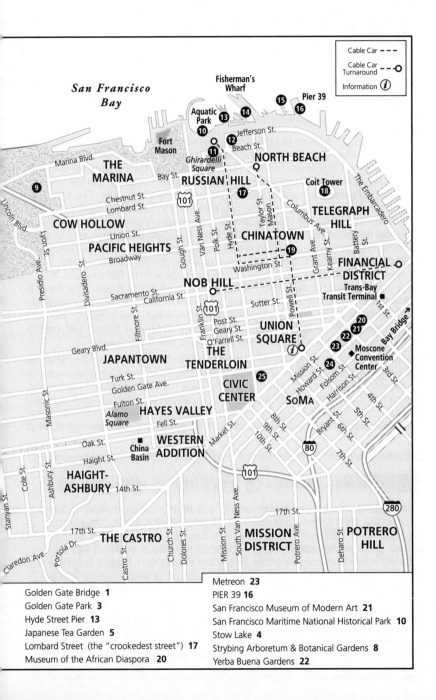

San Francisco Bay

Cable Car ---
Cable Car Turnaround ---O
Information (*i*)

Fisherman's Wharf

Pier 39

15 **16**

Aquatic Park **13** **14**

10

Fort Mason

12 Jefferson St.

11 Beach St.

Ghirardelli Square

NORTH BEACH

Marina Blvd.

THE MARINA

Bay St.

RUSSIAN HILL

Coit Tower **18**

9

Chestnut St.
Lombard St.

(101)

17

Taylor St.
Mason

Columbus Ave.

TELEGRAPH HILL

COW HOLLOW

Union St.

Van Ness Ave.

Polk St.

Hyde St.

CHINATOWN

Grant Ave.

Kearny St.

Battery St.

Lincoln Blvd.

Lyon St.

PACIFIC HEIGHTS

Broadway

Gough St.

19

Washington St.

FINANCIAL DISTRICT O

Presidio Ave.

Divisadero St.

NOB HILL

Sacramento St.
California St.

Fillmore St.

Franklin St.

(101)

Sutter St.

Powell St.

Trans-Bay Transit Terminal ■

The Embarcadero

Bay Bridge

20

Geary Blvd.

Post St.
Geary St.
O'Farrell St.

UNION SQUARE

(*i*)

21

22

23

1st St.

JAPANTOWN

Masonic St.

Turk St.
Golden Gate Ave.

THE TENDERLOIN

25

Mission St.

Howard St.

Folsom St.

24

Moscone Convention Center

2nd St.

3rd St.

Fulton St.

Alamo Square

CIVIC CENTER

SoMa

Harrison St.

4th St.

Oak St.

HAYES VALLEY

Fell St.

China Basin ■

WESTERN ADDITION

Market St.

8th St.
9th St.
10th St.

Bryant St.

5th St.

6th St.

7th St.

Haight St.

HAIGHT-ASHBURY

14th St.

(80)

Cole St.

Ashbury St.

Stanyan St.

(101)

17th St.

(280)

Claredon Ave.

Portola Dr.

17th St.

THE CASTRO

Church St.

Dolores St.

Castro St.

South Van Ness Ave.

Mission St.

MISSION DISTRICT

Potrero Ave.

Deharo St.

POTRERO HILL

See map p. 164. 200 Larkin, at Fulton Street. ☎ **415-581-3500.** www.asianart.org.
Muni or BART to Civic Center station. Public parking lot across the street. Open:
Tues–Sun 10 a.m.–5 p.m., Thurs until 9 p.m. Admission: $10 adults, $7 seniors 65 and
over, $6 students and kids 12–17, free for kids under 12. $5 every Thurs after 5 p.m.
and free first Tues of the month.

Cable Cars
Union Square/Financial District

San Francisco's most notable icon is probably the cable car. These cher-
ished wooden cars creak and squeal up and around hills while passengers
lean out into the wind, running the risk of getting their heads removed by
passing buses. San Francisco's three existing lines comprise the world's only
surviving system of cable cars, and they are a delight to ride. The sheer joy
of whizzing down a hill with the bay glistening in the foreground will linger
in your memory. But these legendary icons aren't just fun, they're also a
useful means of transportation. The **Powell-Mason line** wends its way from
the corner of Powell and Market streets through North Beach and ends near
Fisherman's Wharf. If you only have time to ride the cars once, this is the
one I'd recommend. It will take you most of the way to Fisherman's Wharf,
or, if you prefer, you can hop off when you get to North Beach. The **Powell-
Hyde line,** which starts at the same intersection, ends up near the **Maritime
Museum** and **Ghirardelli Square.** The somewhat less thrilling, but less
crowded **California line** begins at the foot of Market Street and travels
straight up California Street over **Nob Hill** to Van Ness Avenue.

I thought I had a foolproof method of avoiding the crowds at the cable-car
turnarounds (which is literally where the cars are turned around at
the end of the line) by waiting 2 blocks from the Powell Street turnaround,
but after forcing my visiting brother to watch as one car after another
passed us by ("And you do this professionally?" he said), my only other
suggestion is to get up early to ride. (It turns out we were waiting at what

Maximum prison to maximum attraction

Alcatraz Island was first discovered in 1775. Due to its strategic location in San
Francisco Bay, the U.S. Army took notice and began building a military fortress atop
"The Rock." From 1850 to 1933, it served as a military post and army prison, housing
Civil War, Spanish-American War, and, finally, civilian prisoners. In 1934, it was converted into a maximum-security prison. The prison was home to famous gangsters
such as Al Capone; Robert Stroud, the so-called Birdman of Alcatraz (because he was
an expert on ornithological diseases — he never kept birds on Alcatraz); and
"Machine Gun" Kelly. Twenty-nine prisoners tried to escape from Alcatraz — two
made it ashore, only to be captured almost immediately, and five presumably drowned,
although their bodies were never recovered. All 29 attempts are said to have failed. The
prison closed in 1963, due to deterioration of the buildings and prohibitive maintenance
costs. Alcatraz became part of the Golden Gate National Recreation Area in 1972.

The steel wheels tour

The famous cable cars you see going up and down the hills of downtown San Francisco were invented in 1869 by Andrew Hallidie. Hallidie saw the need for a new mode of transportation when he witnessed a horse-drawn streetcar slide backward down one of the many steep slopes that make up San Francisco's unique topography. Here's how the cable-car system works: A steel cable is housed just under the street in a rail, kind of like an inside-out train rail (it's the cable that makes that clickity-clacking sound). Powered by electricity, this cable constantly runs through the rail. Each cable car has a lever that, when pulled back, closes a pincerlike "grip" on the cable. The person who pulls the lever is called a *gripper* — some would call this person a driver, but he doesn't drive, he "grips" the cable. The cable car is then attached to the cable that runs through the rail under the pavement, and the car begins to move at a constant 9 mph — the speed at which the cable is set to travel.

the hotel doormen refer to as "Fantasy Island.") You can also try walking a few more blocks to the next stop. (Stops are indicated by brown signs with a white cable car on them.) Although at first it will appear that there's no room among the zillions of passengers already on the car, by magic a foothold may open up. Otherwise, go get in line with a coffee. Cars run from 6:30 a.m. to 12:30 a.m. The fare is $5 per person one-way, payable on board; Muni Passports are accepted. For more information, call Muni at ☎ 415-673-6864 or log on to www.sfmuni.com. See Chapter 8 for more details, including a route map on p. 80.

Chinatown

Crowded with pedestrians and crammed with exotic-looking shops and vegetable markets whose wares spill onto the sidewalks, Chinatown is a genuinely fascinating destination. Take your time as you walk through this enclave, housing the largest Chinese population outside of Asia — it's easy to miss something. The **Dragon Gate arch** at Grant Avenue and Bush Street (just a few blocks north of Union Square) marks the entry to Chinatown. To get a more authentic experience, avoid the visiting hordes and explore the side streets and alleys off Grant Avenue. If you stay for lunch or dinner, your adventure will take about a half-day. Walking from Union Square is the more sensible way to get here, but you can also reach Chinatown by taking the 30-Stockton bus — quite an experience during rush hour; parking is nearly impossible, but if you want to try it, your best bet is on Kearny Street at Portsmouth Square. (See Chapter 10 for dining suggestions and Chapter 12 for where to shop.) While you're in Chinatown, don't miss the following highlights.

The Chinese Historical Society of America is a good place to begin your Chinatown tour. A museum and research center, the Historical Society documents the fascinating story of the Chinese in California through photographs, art, and changing exhibits. Its bookstore stocks fiction and nonfiction titles on Chinese themes.

Chinatown

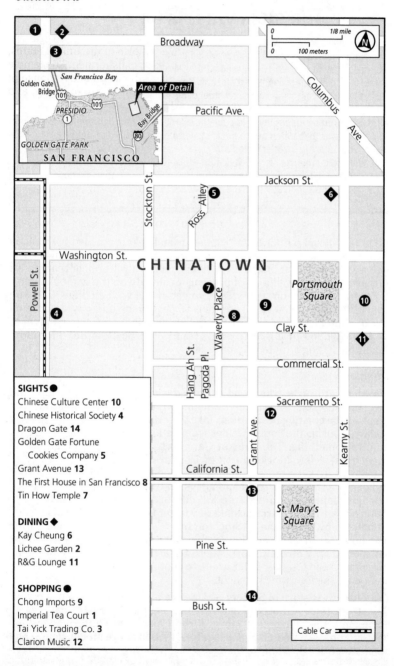

SIGHTS ●
Chinese Culture Center **10**
Chinese Historical Society **4**
Dragon Gate **14**
Golden Gate Fortune
   Cookies Company **5**
Grant Avenue **13**
The First House in San Francisco **8**
Tin How Temple **7**

DINING ◆
Kay Cheung **6**
Lichee Garden **2**
R&G Lounge **11**

SHOPPING ●
Chong Imports **9**
Imperial Tea Court **1**
Tai Yick Trading Co. **3**
Clarion Music **12**

See map p. 168. 965 Clay St. ☎ **415-391-1188.** www.chsa.org. *Admission: $3 adults, $2 seniors, $1 children 6–12; free first Thurs of the month. Open: Tues–Fri noon– 5 p.m., Sat–Sun noon to 4 p.m.*

Tin How Temple, one of the oldest Chinese temples in the United States, is dedicated to the Goddess of Heaven, protector of fishermen. The temple is open to the public, but please keep in mind this is an active house of worship. Be prepared to climb a narrow staircase to the top floor, and make an offering or buy some incense on your way out.

See map p. 168. 125 Waverly Place, off Clay Street between Stockton and Grant streets. No phone. Admission: Free. Open: 9 a.m.–4 p.m. daily.

Golden Gate Fortune Cookies Company is a working factory where you can buy bags of fresh, inexpensive almond and fortune cookies. You may find the cramped quarters somewhat claustrophobic, but watching rounds of dough transmogrify into cookies is fun.

See map p. 168. 956 Ross Alley, between Jackson and Washington streets near Grant Avenue. No phone. Admission: Free. Open: Daily 10 a.m.–7 p.m.

Portsmouth Square, a park above the Portsmouth Square parking garage on Kearny Street between Washington and Clay streets, marks the spot where San Francisco was originally settled and is the site of the first California public school, which opened in 1848. A compact but complete playground attracts all the neighborhood preschoolers and, in the morning, elderly Chinese people practice their tai chi exercises. The landscape includes comfortable benches, attractive lampposts, and young trees. The distinctly San Francisco view includes the **Transamerica Pyramid** looming above the skyline. The garage below is a good place to know about if you're driving. Interestingly, the garage's fourth floor is most likely to have empty spaces, because in Cantonese, the word for *four* sounds like the word for *death.* Superstitious Chinese won't park there.

The pedestrian bridge over Kearny Street leads directly into the third floor of the Chinatown Hilton, where you'll find the **Chinese Culture Center.** A gift shop leads to the gallery, where changing exhibits may feature photographs from pre-earthquake Chinatown, Chinese brush painting, or embroidered antique clothing and household items. The Center also offers two-hour docent-led heritage walks for groups of 4 or more by reservation; $17 adults and $8 kids under 12.

See map p. 168. 750 Kearny St. ☎ **415-986-1822.** www.c-c-c.org. *Admission: Free. Open: Tues–Sun 10 a.m.–4 p.m.*

Coit Tower
Telegraph Hill (near North Beach)

Erected in 1933 with funds bequeathed to the city by Lillie Hitchcock Coit, this 210-foot concrete landmark is visible from much of the city. But everyone needs to take a closer look to see the beauty of the tower. The décor inside features walls with dramatic murals inspired by and commissioned during the Great Depression. Take an elevator to the top for panoramic views of the city and the bay. This diversion will probably take about 30 minutes from start to finish.

See map p. 164. Atop Telegraph Hill. ☎ *415-362-0808. Take the 39-Coit bus, or walk from Lombard Street where it meets Telegraph Hill Boulevard (2 blocks east of Stockton Street). Parking: The drive up and the parking lot are always a mass of cars. Admission to top of tower: $4.50 adults, $2.50 seniors, $1.50 kids 6–12. Open: Daily 10 a.m.–5 p.m.*

Exploratorium/Palace of Fine Arts
Marina District

Scientific American magazine rates the Exploratorium as "the best science museum in the world," and it's certainly an intriguing space that appeals to all ages. The hands-on exhibits explore topics such as technology, human perception, and natural phenomena. Well-written text accompanies the exhibits to enhance the learning experience. Don't worry about feeling like a science dunce if you're visiting with children; a well-informed volunteer is ready to field any questions you can't answer. Expect to spend two hours minimum exploring the museum, especially if you're traveling with kids. Allow more time, and make advance reservations, if you want to experience the popular Tactile Dome, a pitch-black geodesic dome that you have to feel your way through. A walk around the grounds of the **Palace of Fine Arts,** which now houses the Exploratorium but was originally built for the 1915 Panama-Pacific International Exposition, is a great way to unwind after exploring the museum. Better yet, if the weather's balmy, bring a picnic and stay a while.

See map p. 164. 3601 Lyon St., at Marina Boulevard. ☎ *415-561-0360.* www. exploratorium.edu. *30-Stockton bus to Marina stop. Parking: Free and easy. Admission: $13 adults; $10 students, youth 13–17, and seniors; $8 kids 4–12; free kids 3 and under; free for all first Wed of the month; tactile dome: $16 (includes general admission) all ages. Open: Summer (Memorial Day to Labor Day) daily 10 a.m.–6 p.m., Wed until 9 p.m.; winter Tues–Sun 10 a.m.–5 p.m.*

Fisherman's Wharf

Don't be confused when you arrive at Fisherman's Wharf and see lots of people wandering around, none of whom appear to fish for a living. This was once a working set of piers, but today it's a seemingly endless outdoor shopping mall masquerading as a bona fide destination. Some people enjoy examining the refrigerator magnets and cable-car bookends stocked in one olde shoppe after another; others, dazed in the presence of so much kitsch, plan their escape. Still, because most folks stop by the wharf for one reason or another, here's a rundown of what's there.

No matter the weather, tourists crowd **PIER 39,** a multilevel, Disneyesque shopper's dream (or nightmare). Arcades, lined with deafening video games, anchor the pier on each end. You can also find T-shirt and sweatshirt shops and plenty of fried food. Join the mob if you want to see the views of Alcatraz visible from the end of the pier or watch the huge sea

Fisherman's Wharf and Vicinity

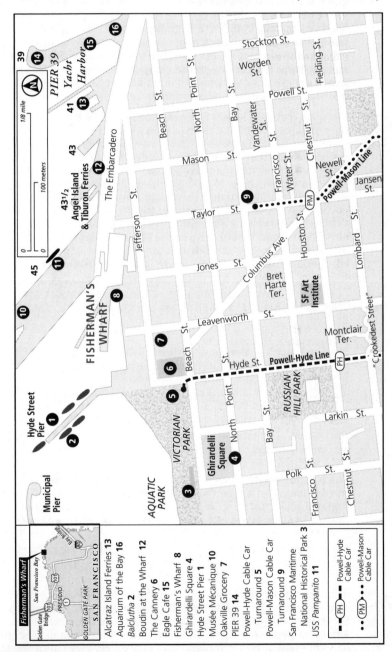

Fisherman's Wharf

GOLDEN GATE PARK
PRESIDIO
SAN FRANCISCO
Golden Gate Bridge
San Francisco Bay
Bay Bridge

Alcatraz Island Ferries **13**
Aquarium of the Bay **16**
Balclutha **2**
Boudin at the Wharf **12**
The Cannery **6**
Eagle Cafe **15**
Fisherman's Wharf **8**
Ghirardelli Square **4**
Hyde Street Pier **1**
Musée Mécanique **10**
Oakville Grocery **7**
PIER 39 **14**
Powell-Hyde Cable Car
  Turnaround **5**
Powell-Mason Cable Car
  Turnaround **9**
San Francisco Maritime
  National Historical Park **3**
USS *Pampanito* **11**

PH ▬ ▬ ▬ Powell-Hyde
         Cable Car
PM ••••••• Powell-Mason
         Cable Car

Municipal Pier
AQUATIC PARK
VICTORIAN PARK
Hyde Street Pier
Ghirardelli Square
FISHERMAN'S WHARF
Powell-Hyde Line
Powell-Mason Line
RUSSIAN HILL PARK
SF Art Institute
"Crookedest Street"
The Embarcadero
PIER 39
Yacht Harbor
Angel Island & Tiburon Ferries

Stockton St.
Worden St.
Powell St.
Beach St.
North Point St.
Bay St.
Vandewater St.
Chestnut St.
Fielding St.
Mason St.
Francisco St.
Water St.
Newell St.
Jansen St.
Taylor St.
Houston St.
Lombard St.
Jones St.
Columbus Ave.
Bret Harte Ter.
Jefferson St.
Leavenworth St.
Montclair Ter.
Hyde St.
Beach St.
North Point St.
Larkin St.
Bay St.
Ghirardelli Square
Polk St.
Francisco St.
Chestnut St.

N

1/8 mile
100 meters

39
41
43
43½
45

lions that loaf around on the west side of the pier (follow the barking). Catch the ferry to Alcatraz or for bay cruises as well. If you're hungry, stop by the only authentic place to eat, the **Eagle Cafe** (☎ **415-433-3689**), open daily from 7:30 a.m. to 9 p.m. on the second floor. This inexpensive breakfast and lunch joint opened in 1920. If you're arriving by car, park on adjacent streets or on the wharf between Taylor and Jones streets. *Note:* The parking garage charges $5.50 per hour! Do your best to avoid these price gougers and don't bring a car here. Besides, taking the F-Market down the Embarcadero is much more fun (see Chapter 8).

The giant fish bowl known as the **Aquarium of the Bay** is dedicated to the creatures that inhabit the San Francisco Bay ecosystem (so don't go looking for tropical species). After a brief introduction to the underwater world, facilitated by the Aquarium's loquacious band of naturalists, visitors descend to a moving walkway that slowly leads through two clear tunnels surrounded by 700,000 gallons of filtered bay water. Many thousands of fish swim by (some seemingly chasing their lunch), and if you've ever wanted to be practically face to face with a *Prionace glauca,* this is your big chance. The last exhibit contains touch pools, always a hit with children. Should a trip to the Monterey Bay Aquarium be in your future, you can easily skip this smaller cousin, but for something with an educational component on the wharf, this is a refreshing stop.

See map p. 171. PIER 39 Fisherman's Wharf. ☎ *800-SEA-DIVE.* www.aquarium ofthebay.com. *Admission: $14 adults, $7 seniors and kids 3–11, $34 for a family ticket. Open: Mon–Fri 10 a.m.–6 p.m., Sat–Sun 10 a.m.–7 p.m.; summer daily 9 a.m.–8 p.m.*

The **San Francisco Maritime National Historical Park** is a small two-story museum overlooking the bay and Alcatraz. It takes only 15 minutes or so to examine the model schooners, figureheads, and photographs illustrating the city's maritime heritage, although children may lose interest after the first five minutes. Still, it's sweet and admission is free. The museum will be closed for remodeling, however, until mid-2008

See map p. 171. Bathhouse Building at the foot of Polk Street. ☎ *415-561-7100.* www.nps.gov/safr.

The **National Park Service** has also opened a new **visitor center** inside the Argonaut Hotel (see Chapter 9), which partners with the Maritime National Historical Park. Along with exhibits and an educational center, the ranger-staffed desk can answer questions about special events on the Hyde Street Pier.

See map p. 84. Hyde and Jefferson streets. ☎ *415-447-5000.* www.nps.gov/ safr/local. *Admission: Free. Open: Daily 9:30 a.m.–5:30 p.m.*

If you have small children along (or anyone interested in history), you won't want to miss touring the **USS *Pampanito.*** This submarine saw active duty during World War II and helped save 73 British and Australian prisoners of war. The family pass (for two adults and up to four children) also gets you into the **Hyde Street Pier** (see following).

See map p. 171. Pier 45. ☎ *415-561-6662. Admission: Submarine with 20-minute audio tour $9 adults, $5 seniors and students, $3 children 6–12, free for kids under 6; family pass $20. Open: Winter daily 9 a.m.–6 p.m., summer until 8 p.m.*

At the **Hyde Street Pier,** 2 blocks east of the Maritime Museum, you can roam around on a number of historic, refurbished ships. Of particular note is the 112-year-old *Balclutha,* a square-rigger with an interesting past. During the year, activities that take place on the *Balclutha* include concerts, sea chantey singalongs, and children's events. Call for a schedule. Touring the vessels takes at least an hour or so.

See map p. 171. ☎ *415-556-6435. Admission: $5 adults, free for kids 17 and under. Pier open: Daily 9:30 a.m.–5:30 p.m.*

Ghirardelli Square, which is the site of the original Ghirardelli chocolate factory, across the street from the Maritime Park, offers one of the more pleasant shopping-mall experiences in the area. Granted landmark status in 1982, the series of brick buildings is home to a roster of special events, including an annual chocolate-tasting benefit in September. Street performers entertain regularly in the West Plaza. Open daily 10 a.m. to 6 p.m. in winter, to 9 p.m. in summer.

See maps p. 164 and p. 171. Bordered by Polk and Hyde streets to the east and west, Beach and Bay streets to the north and south. ☎ *415-775-5500.* www.ghirardelli sq.com. *Admission: Free. Open: Sun–Thurs 10 a.m.–6 p.m., and Fri–Sat until 9 p.m.*

Go 1 block east of Ghirardelli Square and you find what was once the largest peach-canning facility on earth. Today, **The Cannery at Del Monte Square** features shops, jugglers, musicians, and food, including a small farmers' market Friday and Saturday mornings from 8 a.m. until noon. Visitors especially enjoy **Lark in the Morning** (☎ 415-922-HARP), a music haven with an array of early music and modern instruments. Gift shoppers of a practical bent and people with newly formed blisters will also love **Sock Heaven** (☎ 415-563-7327), which, as the name implies, sells foot coverings, in both silly and conventional patterns. If the kids get wiggly (or if the weather is ugly and you need something to keep them occupied), head to the **Basic Brown Bear Factory** (☎ 866-5BB-BEAR), which is located on the first floor of the South Building. Customers stuff and help sew teddy bears to take home, and you can take a tour of the factory, which recently relocated from its longtime Potrero Hill lair. **The Oakville Grocery** (☎ 415-614-1600), a favorite stop for folks heading up Hwy 29 in the Napa Valley, is a welcome new addition on the corner of Leavenworth and Jefferson. A counter overlooks the sidewalk and it's a good place for people-watching while snacking on pizza, one of the pretty salads, a made-to-order sandwich, or irresistible sweet from the pastry case. In the back there's a wine bar if you aren't in a hurry.

See map p. 171. At the foot of Polk Street, on the western edge of the Embarcadero. ☎ *415-556-3002. Take the Powell-Hyde cable-car line to the last stop; the F-Market streetcar; or the 19-Polk, 30-Stockton, 42-Downtown Loop, or 47–Van Ness bus. Parking: Pricey lots and garages; street parking is difficult. Admission: Free. Open: Daily 10 a.m.–5 p.m.*

Golden Gate Bridge

This quintessential San Francisco landmark spans 1⁷⁄₁₀ miles and soars hundreds of feet above the water. Bundle up against the windy conditions, and then set out from the **Roundhouse** on the San Francisco side of the bridge lot (see "Especially for hikers," later in this chapter, for information on walking to the bridge). It can get pretty noisy, but the views can't be beat. Remember that the only way to return from the other side is on foot, so know your limits before crossing the whole bridge and finding out you're too tired to make it back. Afterward, take some time to climb below the bridge to see the 5-acre garden there. The 28–19th Avenue or the 29-Sunset bus deposits you across from the viewing area, right by a parking lot. If you're driving, take 19th Avenue or Lombard Street and pay attention to the sign that indicates when to exit for the parking lot. Otherwise, enjoy your drive across the bridge: There's a $5 toll upon your return to the city.

See map p. 164. Highway 101 North. www.goldengatebridge.org. *Admission: Free for pedestrians; $5 toll per car. Open to pedestrians: Daily 5 a.m.–3:30 p.m.*

Golden Gate Park

Once nothing but a sand-covered tract, today's glorious Golden Gate Park features 1,017 acres of greenery and cultural attractions. San Franciscans can be spotted doing just about everything here, from playing soccer to sailing model yachts to throwing family reunions. On Sundays, when John F. Kennedy Drive is closed to street traffic, bicyclists ride with impunity, and in-line skaters converge for dance parties. From April through the middle of October, also on Sundays, the **Golden Gate Park Band** plays in April through October, Sundays from 1 to 3 p.m. in the **Spreckles Temple of Music,** between the new **de Young Museum** and the **California Academy of Sciences** construction site. (If they aren't there, the musicians may have decamped to the lawn in the Strybing Arboretum.) A massive **Children's Playground** and a beautifully restored carousel sit just past the grand park entrance on Stanyan Street (off Waller Street). This remodeled entrance, for some reason, reduced the rather large number of street people who used to hang out there (the Haight seems to attract youthful transients and burnouts) but didn't completely eliminate the panhandling. In any event, don't let that keep you away. Another entrance at Ninth Avenue on Lincoln Way brings you to the **Strybing Arboretum** and the **Japanese Tea Garden.**

Joggers and parents pushing baby strollers make regular use of the path around man-made **Stow Lake.** It's the perfect place to take advantage of a sunny day by renting a paddleboat and having a picnic. The **boathouse** (☎ 415-752-0347) also rents bikes and in-line skates by the hour, half-day, and full-day. If you aren't driving, it's a bit of a walk to the boathouse, which is west of the Japanese Tea Garden on Martin Luther King Drive. It's open daily from 9 a.m. to 4 p.m.

See map p. 175. www.parks.sfgov.org. *The N-Judah Muni Metro streetcar drops you off on Ninth Avenue and Judah Street; from there it is a 3-block walk to the park. Numerous bus lines drive close to or into the park, including the 44-O'Shaughnessy, which you can catch on Ninth Avenue, the 21-Hayes, the*

Golden Gate Park

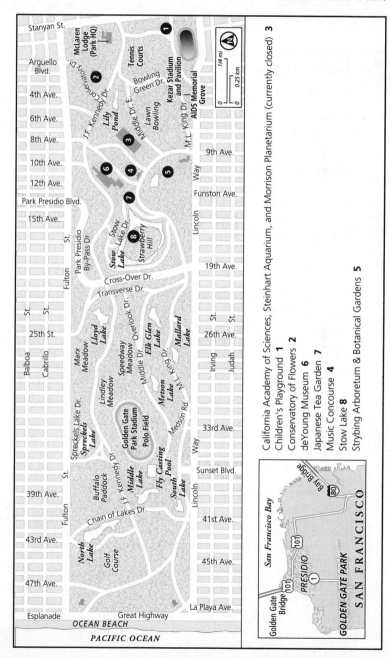

71-Haight-Noriega, and the 5-Fulton. You can also transfer to the 44-O'Shaughnessy from the 38-Geary bus on Sixth Avenue. Open daily. Contact individual attractions for hours and admission prices.

California Academy of Sciences
Golden Gate Park

The Academy features an aquarium and traveling exhibits on everything from dinosaurs to spiders, which complement the informative permanent natural history exhibits. However, it's closed for renovation until 2008. See the "Especially for kids" section, later in this chapter, for information on the Academy's temporary digs downtown.

The Conservatory of Flowers
Golden Gate Park

A fixture in guidebooks and tourist brochures, and nearly as recognizable as the Golden Gate Bridge, the postcard-perfect Victorian Conservatory of Flowers closed in 1995 after sustaining massive damage during a storm. Prefabricated in Ireland in 1875 and erected in the park around 1878, the cost to repair the glass and wood greenhouse topped $25 million, all of which was privately donated. Construction was finished in 2003, and the Conservatory is back to its exquisite self, with lines of delighted visitors snaking past the entrance. Rare orchids, ferns, tropical plants, and a 100-year-old philodendron rescued from the wreckage are on exhibit.

See map p. 175. Conservatory: Just off John F. Kennedy Drive, near the Stanyan Street entrance. ☎ **415-666-7001.** www.conservatoryofflowers.org. *Admission: $5 adults, $3 seniors and youth 12–17, $1.50 kids 5–11, free for children under 5. Free first Tues of the month. Open: Tues–Sun 9 a.m.–4:30 p.m.*

The de Young Museum
Golden Gate Park

San Francisco Chronicle publisher, M. H. de Young founded the city's first fine arts museum in 1895. Its eclectic permanent collection today includes American paintings as well as sculpture, textiles, African and Oceanic objects, furniture, and contemporary crafts housed in a sprawling, copper-clad three-story complex that opened in October 2005. If you want to make some sense of the collection, consider taking one of the free docent tours offered daily at 10 a.m., 11 a.m., 1 p.m., and 2 p.m. A highlight of the building is the 144-foot tower offering unobstructed views (if the sky is clear) of the neighborhoods beyond the park. Access to the tower is free, even if you don't intend on touring the museum. The museum's cafe is the only sit-down restaurant in the park. Not inexpensive, the menu (salads, sandwiches, a few mains such as steamed halibut) features local producers and seasonal produce.

See map p. 175. 50 Hagiwara Tea Garden Dr., off John F. Kennedy Drive. ☎ **415-863-3330.** www.deyoungmuseum.org. *Admission: $10 adults, $7 seniors, $6 students and kids 13–17, free for children under 13. $2 discount with Muni transfer or fast pass. Open: Tues–Sun 9:30a.m.–5 p.m., until 8:45 p.m. Fri.*

The Strybing Arboretum and Botanical Gardens
Golden Gate Park

This splendid oasis houses over 6,000 species of well-tended plants, flowering trees, and theme gardens. It is exceptionally lovely in late winter when the rhododendrons blossom and wild iris poke up in corners, and there is no more peaceful a place when it's rainy and gray outside. You can catch a free docent tour offered daily at 1:30 p.m.; I recommend it for those, like myself, who are arboreally and botanically challenged when trying to identify any but the most basic of flowers and trees. Plan to spend at least half an hour here just wandering around.

See map p. 175. Ninth Avenue at Lincoln Way, left of the tour bus parking lot by the Music Concourse. ☎ *415-661-1316, ext. 314, for docent tour information.* www.sf botanicalgarden.org. *Admission: Free. Open: Mon–Fri 8 a.m.–4:30 p.m., Sat–Sun 10 a.m.–5 p.m.*

Japanese Tea Garden
Golden Gate Park

Enjoying this tranquil spot, with colorful pagodas, koi ponds, bridges, and a giant bronze Buddha, you feel like you've been transported for a moment to the Orient. Young children find this part of the park particularly memorable — they can climb over a steeply arched wooden bridge here, just as I did when I was much younger and lots more limber than I am today. The Tea Garden's beauty is slightly marred by its gift shop, full of miniature license plates and other junk. Bus tours overrun this major destination during the day, so try to get here before 10 a.m. or after 4 p.m. during the summer to avoid the onslaught. You can partake of Japanese tea and snacks in the teahouse for $2.95 per person. I think the garden is worth the small admission fee, but you won't be missing anything if you pass on the tea and crackers.

See map p. 175. The garden entrance is to the left of the de Young Museum. ☎ *415-752-4227. Admission: $3.50 adults, $1.25 seniors and children 6–12. Open: Daily 8:30 a.m.–6 p.m.*

Lombard Street
Russian Hill (near North Beach)

Lombard Street, or to be exact, the part of Lombard with the moniker "crookedest street in the world," begins at Hyde Street below Russian Hill. This whimsical, flower-lined block attracts thousands of visitors each year. If you intend to drive this red-brick street (it's one-way, downhill, so take the curves slowly), go early in the morning before everyone else revs up their rentals. If you stop to take a picture from your car, you'll be holding up traffic and everyone will hate you. Better yet, walk down the stairs to admire the flowers, the houses with their long-suffering tenants, and the stellar view.

See map p. 164. Between Hyde and Leavenworth streets. Take the Powell-Hyde cable-car line.

Museum of the African Diaspora
SoMa

If you walk down 3rd Street toward Yerba Buena Center, you can't fail to notice the multi-story photo mosaic marking one of latest additions to the South of Market culture klatch. MoAD packs quite a bit into its relatively small exhibition space, and while it won't take more than an hour to tour, you'll find much to think about. Photographs, video, and some very cool interactive displays and technological touches focus upon the themes of origins, movement, adaptation, and transformation in relation to Africa, and thus, in relation to our own selves and communities. Take the kids.

See map p. 164. 685 Mission St. at 3rd Street. ☎ *415-358-7200.* www.moadsf.org. *Take any Muni streetcar to the Montgomery Street Station or the 15-Third, 30-Stockton, or 45-Union/Stockton bus. Admission: $8 adults, $5 seniors and students. Open Wed–Mon 10 a.m.–6 p.m., until 9 p.m. Thurs.*

San Francisco Museum of Modern Art
SoMa

The handsome Museum of Modern Art (MoMA) houses an impressive collection of 20th-century paintings, sculptures, and photographs. The beautiful interior exudes a warmth that makes viewing the exhibits even more enjoyable. Among the Diebenkorns and Rauschenbergs, you may be surprised to see Jeff Koons's gold-and-white sculpture of Michael Jackson and his chimp pal, Bubbles (an acquisition I think better suited to a Las Vegas hotel lobby, but obviously the curators know something I don't). The exhibits, the excellent museum cafe, and the artfully stocked museum store keep you there for a good half-day.

See map p. 164. 151 Third St., 2 blocks south of Market near Howard Street. ☎ *415-357-4000.* www.sfmoma.org. *Take any Muni streetcar to the Montgomery Street Station or the 15-Third, 30-Stockton, or 45-Union/Stockton bus. Admission: $13 adults, $8 seniors, and $7 students with ID; half-price Thurs 6–9 p.m.; free for kids under 12; free to all first Tues of the month. Open: Thurs 11 a.m.– 8:45 p.m., Fri–Tues, 11 a.m.–5:45 p.m.; closed Wed and major holidays; open at 10 a.m. during the summer.*

Yerba Buena Gardens and Center for the Arts
SoMa

This 22-acre complex is a microdestination in a setting that once attracted nothing but parking lots and derelicts. It includes a collection of galleries showing a rotating exhibition of contemporary visual and performance art by local artists, lovely gardens, a stage for dance troupes including ODC/ San Francisco and Smuin Ballets/SF, and a film/video theater. Interactive amusements include an ice-skating rink, a bowling alley, a children's garden and carousel, and an arts/technology studio for older kids. An unrelated entertainment behemoth in a separate building across the street — **the Metreon** — houses restaurants, retail shops, an IMAX theater, games, and multiplex movie screens. If you take in all that Yerba Buena Center has

Yerba Buena Gardens

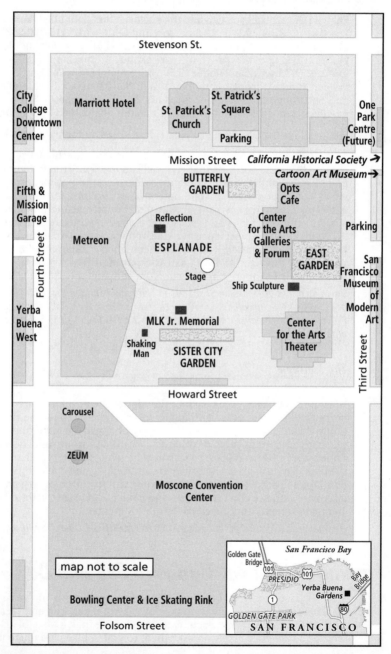

to offer, you can easily spend the entire day in this area. Parking is expensive; use public transportation if possible.

East of the carousel you can find the enclosed, but light-filled, **Yerba Buena Ice-Skating Rink** and the 12-lane **Bowling Center** (☎ 415-820-3532; www. skatebowl.com). Public skating session times vary, so you should phone before trekking over with your figure skates. Admission is adults $7, seniors and children 12 and under $5.50. Skate rental is $3. The Bowling Center is open Sunday through Thursday 10 a.m. to 10 p.m., until midnight Friday and Saturday. Admission for adults is $3.50 per game or $20 per hour; evenings and weekend afternoons it's $6 per game or $30 per hour.

Wednesdays from 7:15 to 9:15 p.m. is free skate-rental night for 18-plus.

Zeum (☎ 415-820-3320; www.zeum.org) is a wonderful art/technology center with hands-on labs that give visitors the opportunity to create animated video shorts with clay figures; learn about graphics, sound, and video production in the second-floor studio; and interact with the gallery exhibits. The center is rare in that it's the only attraction specifically designed for older kids and teens that delivers some intellectual stimulation and doesn't rely on video games. Even your standard-issue bored adolescent would find it difficult not to succumb to a Zeum offering. It's open Wednesday through Sunday 11 a.m. to 5 p.m. and Tuesdays in the summer. Admission is $8 for adults, $7 for seniors and students, $6 for kids 5 to 18.

See map p. 179. 701 Mission St., between Third and Fourth streets. ☎ *415-749-2228 or 415-978-ARTS (box office).* www.yerbabuenaarts.org. *Take a streetcar to the Powell or Montgomery Street station, or take the 14-Mission or 15-Third bus, among others.*

The Metreon
SoMa

Noisy and lit like a Vegas casino, the Metreon was once touted by Sony corporation as the next big thing in entertainment. For some reason, no doubt related to the profit motive, Sony changed its mind and sold the place to shopping mall developers Westfield Group and Forest City Enterprises early in 2006. While it's unclear what exactly will change inside the four stories of glass and brushed metal, eating and spending will surely continue to be the big themes here along with the interactive game arena, a favorite with the city's teenagers and young adults. On the third floor are 15 movie screens and the city's first IMAX theater.

See map p. 164. Mission at Fourth Street. ☎ *800-METREON. Open: Daily 10 a.m.–10 p.m.*

Finding More Cool Things to See and Do

Just because you've visited the top sights doesn't mean you've seen it all. This section offers ideas on how to entertain children and teens, how to get a taste of San Francisco history and more than a taste of art, where to take your hiking shoes, where to grab a bike, and much more.

Especially for kids

San Francisco has enough family activities to exhaust even the most energetic clan. Along with those I list in this section, consider an afternoon at the ballpark (see "Especially for sports fans," later in this chapter), which has an exciting play area just for kids that's open whether or not the Giants are in town. The easy walk to Fort Point (see "Especially for hikers," later in this chapter) appeals to kids as well, because it takes in the Golden Gate Bridge and there's a cool Civil War–era fort to explore.

The best Web site for finding out what's available for children is **GoCityKids** (www.gocitykids.com). The calendar of events is kept up to date and really mines what's going on in and around the city.

The **San Francisco Zoo,** Sloat Boulevard and 45th Avenue (☎ **415-753-7080;** www.sfzoo.org), has been renovating like mad, ridding itself of old-fashioned cages and exhibits, and embracing animal conservation. You'll find a new African Savanna exhibit and Lemur Forest, an innovative, noteworthy primate center, an historic merry-go-round, an expanded children's petting zoo, and — this is the clincher — a sizable children's playground near the Sloat Boulevard entrance. Stroll the more than 65 acres to see the animals, and then park your tired body on a bench within yelling distance and let the under-10 members of the family climb to their heart's content. Take note of the Carousel hot dog parlor across Sloat Boulevard, marked by a fiberglass, chef-hatted dachshund. Formerly one of many Doggie Diners in town, this puppy was the center of heated controversy between those who wanted to grant it landmark status and those who wanted it moved so the site could be turned into a parking lot. Judging from its shiny cherry paint job, the doggy won. Zoo admission is $11 for adults, $8 for seniors and kids 12 to 15, $5 for kids 3 to 11, free for babes 2 and under, and free the first Wednesday of each month. The zoo is open daily from 10 a.m. to 5 p.m. To get there, take the L-Taraval Muni streetcar.

Another kid-pleaser, the **Musée Mécanique,** Pier 45 at the end of Taylor Street (☎ **415-346-2000;** www.museemecanique.org), contains a fantastic collection of lovingly restored and maintained mechanical marvels that were the forerunners of pinball machines. Among the treasures, you can try your hand at World Series Baseball, have your fortune told, and giggle wildly with Laughing Sal, all for a quarter a pop. The museum is housed close to PIER 39, having moved from smaller, more charming quarters near the Cliff House. Admission is free, but bring along a roll of quarters. The museum is open Monday through Friday from 10 a.m. to 7 p.m., Saturday and Sunday from 10 a.m. to 8 p.m. To get there, take the F-Market streetcar or the Powell-Mason cable car.

China Beach has picnic facilities and awe-inspiring views of the Golden Gate Bridge. It's also one of the few safe swimming beaches in town, but the water is chilly, so designing sand castles and picnicking are better activities. The 29-Sunset bus stops at 25th Avenue and El Camino del Mar. From there, walk about 6 blocks north to the beach.

The Zoo and Lake Merced Area

San Francisco has no shortage of parks and playgrounds in nearly every neighborhood, but they do range in quality. In the Nob Hill/Russian Hill area, **Lafayette Park** is appealing for its small but nicely equipped and fenced-in playground, walking paths, and views. It's on Clay Street between Washington, Laguna, Gough, and Sacramento streets. Take the 1-California or 12-Folsom-Pacific buses to get there. You have to make a little effort to reach **Mountain Lake Park,** which is close to the Richmond District side of the Presidio on Lake Street (between 8th and 12th avenues), but this is one of the best parks in town for the entire family. The playground is two-tiered; the street-level half is for the under-6 set, while the bottom half is fun even for young-at-heart teens. Hiking trails and a small beach make this spot even more attractive. To get there, take Muni bus 1AX, 1BX, or 28–19th Avenue.

Young Performers Theatre (YPT) at Fort Mason presents children's plays most weekend afternoons, starring members of the YPT acting classes. The performances are most suitable for kids 10 and under. You can find a schedule of events on the Web (www.ypt.org). Tickets are $6 for kids and $9 for adults. Make reservations in advance by phoning YPT at ☎ **415-346-5550** or e-mail them at reservations@2ypt.com. The theater is located in Room 300, Building C, at Fort Mason. To get there, take the 22-Fillmore, 30-Stockton, or 42-Downtown bus.

The temporary quarters for the **California Academy of Sciences,** 875 Howard St., between Fourth and Fifth streets (☎ **415-321-8000;** www. calacademy.org), are better than not having a substitute site for this beloved organization, but they are pretty cramped. Nevertheless, young kids should still enjoy an outing to this urban science center. There's still an aquarium for the penguins, fish, and frogs, Sssssnake Alley for the boas and other slithery creatures, a two-story coral reef tank, a special Nature Nest play area for preschoolers, and 500 square feet of exhibit space for a variety of ants. A gift shop and a cafe are on the premises so you can spend a good long morning here. If you only have time on this trip to visit either the Exploratorium or the Academy of Sciences, until the new building debuts sometime in 2008, I'd head for the Exploratorium. Admission is $7 for adults; $4.50 for seniors, students, and kids 12 to 17; $2 for kids 4 to 11, and free for kids 3 and under. The first Wednesday of the month is free for all. Open daily from 10 a.m. to 5 p.m. To get there, from the Powell Street Muni station walk northeast on Market to Fourth Street, turn right, and walk 2 blocks to Howard Street.

Especially for teens

The South of Market neighborhood works well as a teenage playground encompassing Yerba Buena Gardens, the Metreon, and the many places to shop. From here, it's a quick walk to Market Street, where you can catch the N-Judah Muni streetcar to the Haight-Ashbury. After your kids have seen Haight Street, they've seen it all.

The **Cartoon Art Museum,** 655 Mission St., between Second and Third streets (☎ **415-227-8666;** www.cartoonart.org), takes the funny papers seriously. Exhibits in the museum's five galleries, a half-block from Yerba Buena Gardens, trace the history of cartoon art from political jabs to underground comics. Temporary shows highlight individual artists such as Edward Gorey, and forms such as television cartoon animation. The museum shop has a sophisticated selection of books for enthusiasts. Admission is $6 for adults, $4 for seniors and students, and $2 for children 6 to 12. The first Tuesday of the month is "pay what you wish day." The museum is open Tuesday through Sunday from 11 a.m. to 5 p.m. To get there, take any streetcar to the Montgomery Street station and walk 1 block east to Mission Street.

San Francisco Centre, on the corner of Market and Fifth streets, is a nine-story mall containing many familiar names beloved by teenaged girls, including a huge **Nordstrom** department store. At the end of 2006, it will be neighboring a 357,740-square-foot Bloomingdale's (and that's a lot of hangers), anchor tenant at the humungous new mall consuming the spot where the Emporium once ruled downtown. Your young shopper may be just as happy exploring the stores around Union Square (see

Chapter 12), and at least there you'll get a little fresh air on your way in and out of the revolving doors.

Teenagers adore the **Metreon** because the technology stores contain all the latest widgets, some of which they can audition. When they tire of gawking at stuff, the video games in the Airtight Garage can occupy as many minutes as you'll allow or that they can pay for. And when you've had enough, you can coax them away from the flashing screens with promises of food at one of the many cafes.

Zeum was designed for 8- to 18-year-olds and is staffed by savvy teens. Even recalcitrant 15-year-olds can find something engaging to do here, whether or not they admit it.

I saved the best for last. Take your teen to Haight Street for some shopping (and shock) therapy. The N-Judah streetcar deposits you a few blocks south of Haight, and it beats parking. One of the best music stores in town, **Amoeba Records,** is here, and both the used and new clothing stores — in particular stop by Villains, 1672 Haight St. (☎ **415-626-5939**) — stock the coolest stuff around. I don't mean to make too much of the street scene, but youthful runaways and poseurs do congregate in this neighborhood and it can feel equally attractive, poignant, and scary to adolescents. At the very least, you'll have something interesting to talk about on the ride back to your hotel.

Especially for history buffs

In this case, you'll have to settle for fairly recent history, given that not a whole lot was happening around here until the Gold Rush. The next major event was the 1906 earthquake.

One of the historic sites related to the earthquake that you can visit is at the corner of Market and Kearny streets: **Lotta's Fountain** (given to the city in 1875 by popular entertainer Lotta Crabtree). This gold-painted landmark served as a community bulletin board where people left notes for missing family and friends after the disaster.

To find out about San Francisco's rise during the quest for gold, take the free Gold Rush City walking tour offered by City Guides on Sundays at 2 p.m. and Wednesdays at noon. Meet by the flower stand at Clay and Montgomery streets. The walk encompasses **Jackson Square** (Jackson and Montgomery streets), a National Historic Register Landmark admired for its many restored Gold Rush–era brick warehouses. Call ☎ **415-557-4266** for details.

The Cable Car Museum explains everything you'd want to know about our 130-year-old road warriors, through photographs, models, actual cable cars, and a close-up look at the mechanisms that make them click. The museum is inside the cable-car barn, 1201 Mason St., at Washington (☎ **415-474-1887;** www.cablecarmuseum.com). Admission is free, and the museum is open daily, April through September 10 a.m. to 6 p.m. and

October through March until 5 p.m. To get there, take the Powell-Mason or Powell-Hyde cable-car lines.

Mission Dolores, 16th and Dolores streets (☎ **415-621-8203**), is a fine example of Mission architecture and the oldest building in the city. This is the sixth of the 21 missions founded under the auspices of Franciscan Missionary Junipero Serra and built by Native Americans. Services were first held on the site a few days before the Declaration of Independence was signed. A $1 self-guided audio tour takes 40 minutes. Admission is free, but donations are gratefully accepted; the mission is open daily from 9 a.m. until noon, and from 1 to 4 p.m. To get there, take the J-Church streetcar, which stops 1 block east.

The **Wells Fargo History Museum** is located at 420 Montgomery St., at California Street (☎ **415-396-2619;** www.wellsfargohistory.com/museums). Wells Fargo opened one of its first offices on this site in 1852, ready to handle business generated by the Gold Rush. Among the displays are mining equipment, an antique stagecoach, and gold nuggets. Be sure to try out the telegraph machine on the first floor, especially if you have kids in tow. The museum is open weekdays from 9 a.m. to 5 p.m., and admission is free.

Especially for art lovers

The **Legion of Honor,** Lincoln Park between Clement Street and 34th Avenue in the outer Richmond District (☎ **415-750-3600;** www.thinker.org), exhibits an impressive collection of paintings, drawings, decorative arts, and one of the world's finest collections of Rodin sculptures, including an original cast of *The Thinker.* The grounds around the Palace are a draw as well. Admission is $10 for adults, $7 for seniors over 65, $6 for children 13 to 17, and free for children under 13, and free on the first Tuesday of the month. The museum is open Tuesday through Sunday from 9:30 a.m. to 5 p.m. To get there, take the 38-Geary bus to 33rd Avenue, and then transfer to the 18–46th Avenue bus for a ride to the museum entrance.

Union Square from Grant Avenue to Mason Street and Geary to Post Street is home to a number of fine-arts dealers. Of note are the **Catharine Clark Gallery** (☎ **415-399-1439**) and **Toomey Tourell** (☎ **415-989-6444**), both located in the canvas-rich building at 49 Geary St., at Grant Street, as well as the **John Berggruen Gallery** at 228 Grant St., between Sutter and Post (☎ **415-781-4629**). The galleries are closed on Mondays.

First Thursdays is a somewhat new program sponsored by the San Francisco Art Dealers Association to get people inside member galleries. They open on the first Thursday of the month around Union Square, serving wine and maybe a little cheese from 5:30 to 7:30 p.m. For a list of participating galleries, call ☎ **415-921-1600**.

Combine a walk along the Marina with a tour of the galleries housed at **Fort Mason Center** (☎ 415-441-3400; www.fortmason.org). They include the **Museo ItaloAmericano** and **SFMoMA's Artists Gallery,** which displays original art for sale and for rent. The galleries are fairly small but often have quirky exhibits. Wandering around Fort Mason is a good way to round out your excursion. A small admission fee is charged by the **Museo ItaloAmericano,** but the Artists Gallery is free. Open Tuesday through Saturday from 11:30 a.m. to 5:30 p.m. To get there, take the 30-Stockton, 47–Van Ness, or 28–19th Avenue bus, which run nearby.

Especially for architecture lovers

When you visit the **Alamo Square Historic District,** you may feel a touch of déjà vu. That's because this is where the famous picture of the Victorian row houses was photographed. The "painted ladies," which front the San Francisco skyline, are still sought by photographers, probably on a daily basis. You'll find this historic block between Steiner, Scott, Hayes, and Grove streets, west of the Civic Center. The 21-Hayes bus takes you right there from Market and Hayes streets.

The **Haas-Lilienthal House** (☎ 415-441-3000), an 1886 Queen Anne Victorian, is open to the public for one-hour tours on Wednesdays and some Saturdays from noon to 3 p.m. and Sundays from 11 a.m. to 4 p.m. Located at 2007 Franklin, at Jackson Street, this is the only local example of a home from this period that's open to the public. To get there by bus, take the 12-Folsom, the 27-Bryant, the 42–Downtown Loop, the 47–Van Ness, the 49–Van Ness/Mission, or the 83-Pacific. Admission is $8 for adults and $5 for seniors 65 and older and for children under 12.

You may also want to check out the **New Main Library,** 100 Larkin St. (☎ 415-557-4400), between Grove and Fulton streets. Natural light streams in from a five-story atrium skylight and windows that encircle the stacks. If you have kids along, browse the children's section. The library even has — gasp! — a gift shop. Take any Muni streetcar to the Civic Center station and walk a block west on Grove Street.

While you're in the Civic Center neighborhood, drop by the refurbished **City Hall** on Van Ness Avenue, between McAllister and Grove streets. The building debuted in 1915, but it's never looked better. Not only did the structure get a seismic retrofitting (de rigueur in this earthquake-prone town) and a good cleaning, but the dome and ornamental balcony railings were regilded, creating an impressive landmark and adding golden highlights to the view. The rotunda is breathtakingly beautiful and worth going through the metal detectors to view.

For more architectural wonders, check out the walking tours later in this chapter.

Especially for bicyclists

If your reflexes are good and you have a reliable helmet, try touring San Francisco from the seat of a two-wheeler. You can rent bikes and helmets from quite a few locations around town.

For a ride in beautiful Golden Gate Park, stop by one of the nearby bike stores such as **Avenue Cyclery,** 756 Stanyan St. (☎ 415-387-3155) or from inside the park at **Wheel Fun** at Stow Lake (☎ 415-668-6699). The **Bike Hut** at South Beach, on the Embarcadero at Pier 40 (☎ 415-543-4335), is the place to find high-quality bikes to pedal along the waterfront. It's open everyday from 10 a.m. to 6 p.m. Rentals are a mighty reasonable $5 per hour or $20 per day. And if you're considering a bike trip across the Golden Gate Bridge, the nice guys at **Blazing Saddles** (☎ 415-202-8888) at either the North Beach location (1095 Columbus Ave.) or the Fisherman's Wharf location (Pier 41) will provide you with all the information and encouragement you need to tackle this route. The equipment for kids and adults is shiny and well maintained. Rental prices are $7 per hour or $28 per day and include helmets, locks, front packs, rear racks, maps, and advice. Three-hour guided bike tours are also available at $55 for adults and $40 for kids up to 12 years old. This includes the ferry ticket to return to the city.

Pedaling across the Golden Gate Bridge into Sausalito, where you can have something to eat, do a little sightseeing in this arty, touristy town, and then return by ferry, can be good fun and in truth, you don't really need a chaperone. The **Blue & Gold Fleet** (☎ 415-705-5555; www.blue andgoldfleet.com) and **Golden Gate Ferry** (☎ 415-923-2000) depart the Sausalito ferry dock at least half a dozen times a day. Call for a schedule. One-way Blue & Gold Fleet fares are $8.50 for adults and $4.50 for children 5 to 11; one-way Golden Gate Ferry fares are $6.45 for adults, $3.20 for children 3 to 12 (kids ride free on weekends), and $3.20 for seniors. The 9-mile ride to Sausalito can be challenging, partly due to the windy conditions and partly due to the other bicyclists you're competing with for space.

For more information on biking in the area, contact the San Francisco Bicycle Coalition (☎ 415-431-BIKE), or browse their Web site at www.sfbike.org.

Especially for hikers

A surprisingly good amount of hiking opportunities can be found within the city, in the Presidio, along the bay, through Golden Gate Park, and along the Pacific Coast. Committed hikers should head to the Marin Headlands for the best trails and views. Muni runs a bus (76–Marin Headlands) from downtown to the Headlands parking lot on Sundays and holidays. Check www.sfmuni.com for a schedule and route information.

Golden Gate National Recreation Area

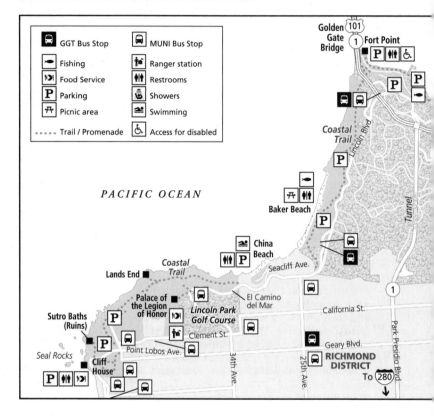

Angel Island, a federal and state wildlife refuge that is the largest of San Francisco Bay's three islets, is 8 miles from San Francisco and is accessible only by ferry (a 20-minute journey) or private boat. Plan to spend the entire day on the island if you decide to go during the week — the ferry departs San Francisco sometime after 10 a.m., and the only return trip departs sometime after 3 p.m. (The schedule changes seasonally.) On the weekends, you have the choice of four return trips. You can bring a picnic or get something at the small store and cafe that operate near the dock. Check out the beautiful 12 miles of hiking trails, climb up Mt. Livermore for yet another spectacular view of the Golden Gate Bridge, or take the one-hour tram tour past the historic sites, including the former immigration station. Mountain-bike rentals are also available on Angel Island, but only during the spring and summer months. Call **Blue & Gold Ferry** (☎ **415-705-8200**) for a current ferry schedule. Round-trip fares are $15 for adults and $8.50 for children 6 to 12. For recorded information about the island, call ☎ **415-435-1915.** Ferries leave from Pier 41 in Fisherman's Wharf.

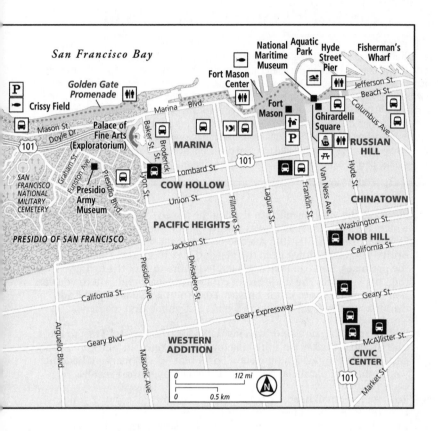

Crissy Field (☎ **415-561-7690** general information or 415-561-7752 for weekend workshops and classes; www.crissyfield.org), the Bay Area's newest national park, is comprised of 100 acres between the bay and the Presidio. The park features a tidal marsh, sheltered picnic area, bike path, walking trail, cafe, bookstore, and education center. It's a beautiful spot; an easy, flat walk; and wheelchair accessible. Begin with a visit at the Crissy Field Center and ask for an activity book for a self-guided walk or join one of the interpretive hikes offered most weekends. Stop at the Warming Hut at the western end of the park by the fishing pier for a snack and some inspired gift shopping. Foodies will be suitably impressed to discover that the cafe menu was developed with input from Alice Waters, of Chez Panisse fame. The 28–19th Avenue, 29-Sunset, and 43-Masonic buses stop nearby.

Fort Point (☎ **415-556-1693**), which dates from 1857, lies under the Golden Gate Bridge at the tip of the peninsula. Along with Civil War–era cannons, you can see surfers who appear to be risking their lives much more than the soldiers once stationed here did. From the Hyde Street

A short history of Angel Island

Originally a Miwok Indian hunting and fishing ground, Spanish, British, and Mexican ships harbored at various times at Angel Island beginning in 1775. Before the Civil War, the U.S. government turned the island into a military base, remnants of which are still visible. Between 1910 and 1940, Angel Island was used as a detention center mainly for Asian immigrants, which earned it the nickname "Ellis Island of the West." The immigration station at China Cove is open for tours and provides a poignant glimpse into an era when anti-Asian and anti-immigration policies placed hundreds of Chinese into forced detention for weeks, months, and sometimes years. Poems carved into the walls of the barracks by lonely and isolated detainees were rediscovered in 1970 and inspired the ongoing preservation effort by the California legislature.

Pier, take the easy 3½-mile stroll along the paved Golden Gate Promenade, which hugs the coast as it passes through the Marina Green and Crissy Fields. Or take the 28–19th Avenue or 29-Sunset bus to the Golden Gate Bridge and climb down from the viewing area to a short trail leading to the premises. You can take a self-guided audio tour of the fort if you like, then backtrack to the Hyde Street cable-car turnaround, where you can hop on a cable car to Union Square. Fort Point is usually open Friday through Sunday from 10 a.m. to 5 p.m., but phone first to check.

 If you're a hiking novice or walking with kids, the **Coastal Trail** to the Cliff House probably isn't the hike for you. It's rigorous and can be dangerous. The trailhead, a bit east of Fort Point, is well marked. Heading south, the trail parallels the Pacific Ocean through the Presidio.

 You can see small beaches below the trail on this hike, but if you're tempted to feel sand beneath your toes, follow the marked paths to get there. Don't climb over any rocky cliffs; the land here isn't stable enough to guarantee your safe return.

When you reach Baker Beach, about 1½ miles from Fort Point, be prepared for the nude sun worshippers, if there is any sun. As you continue on the trail, you'll pass the Lobos Creek Water Treatment Plant. From there it's a short way to El Camino Del Mar, a street leading through Sea Cliff, a fancy residential neighborhood. At the end of El Camino Del Mar, you'll pick up the trail near the Lincoln Golf Course. If you continue along this trail, with the land and the views rewarding your every step, eventually you'll arrive at the Cliff House, which has been serving refreshments to visitors since 1863. It's undergone a pretty dramatic renovation and now has one casual and one fancier restaurant plus a bar, all with the views that keep tourists as well as locals enthralled. Prices are high so keep walking down the Great Highway until you reach the **Beach Chalet** restaurant and brewery (☎ **415-386-8439**). After lunch you can return toward the Cliff House and catch the 38-Geary bus at La Playa and Balboa Street, or continue to Judah Street and take an N-Judah streetcar downtown.

Named in honor of Sierra Club founder and conservationist John Muir, 553-acre **Muir Woods** is what's left locally of the redwood forests that once dominated the coast of Northern California. Although not as sizable as Redwood National Forest further north, these old-growth redwoods are beautiful, and a range of trails suits hikers of all levels. From the Golden Gate Bridge, take the Stinson Beach/Highway 1 exit west and follow the signs. Parking is limited, so set out early in the day on weekends or go during the week. Muir Woods Park is open from 8 a.m. until sunset. For additional information call ☎ **415-388-2595.**

Especially for sports fans

The San Francisco Giants Major League Baseball team opened the fabulous, 40,000-seat **AT&T (formerly Pac Bell, formerly SBC) Park** stadium on the bay in April 2000. The ballpark is sweet — sightlines are clear, you don't freeze to death like you did at Candlestick, the food is pretty good, and home runs splash into the bay. Season-ticket holders have bought up all the best seats, but buying bleacher tickets to any but the most sought-after games (Giants versus Dodgers contests, for example) shouldn't be impossible, because they're sold only on game days. To purchase regular tickets or tickets from season-ticket holders unable to make it to a particular game, log on to the Web site (www.sfgiants.com) before you arrive, or call ☎ **877-473-4849** to charge tickets by phone. Transportation to the ballpark is simple — take Muni to the Embarcadero Station and transfer to the King Street extension. In or out of season, the stadium is open for 75-minute tours everyday but game days at 10:30 a.m. and 12:30 p.m. Admission is $10 adults, $8 seniors, and $6 kids 12 and under.

The San Francisco 49ers play at **3Com Park.** Home games have been sold out for years, but if you want to try your luck, the ticket office number is ☎ **415-656-4900.** Scalpers sell tickets outside the park, but these are often counterfeit. The best method of transport to the park is by Muni bus. The 9X–San Bruno Express bus leaves from Sutter Street near Union Square; the 28X–19th Avenue bus runs along 19th Avenue; and the 47X–Van Ness cruises Van Ness Avenue.

You can also head across the bay to watch Oakland's professional teams play. For information on schedules and availability, and to order tickets, visit the sites listed in the "Checking out sports on the Web" sidebar.

 Getting seats to home games isn't impossible, but you have to use some creativity. A terrific source for last-minute concert and sports tickets (as well as lots of other things) is the Web site www.craigslist.org. Craig Newmark, an actual person who lives in San Francisco, created this Web

---

Checking out sports on the Web

In addition to the following specific sites, where (in most cases) you can purchase tickets online, swing by the Bay Area's general sports site at www.bayinsider. com.

✔ **Golden State Warriors:** www.nba.com/warriors

✔ **Oakland A's:** www.oaklandas.com

✔ **Oakland Raiders:** www.raiders.com

✔ **San Francisco 49ers:** www.sf49ers.com

✔ **San Francisco Giants:** www.sfgiants.com

---

site in 1995, and it quickly became a community asset. Craigslist is now nationwide, and it's free to use.

Golfers have a great selection of public courses on which to play, including gorgeous (and inexpensive) **Lincoln Park** (☎ 415-221-9911), the newly redesigned **Harding Park** (☎ 415-664-4690; www.harding-park. com), and the **Presidio Golf Course** (☎ 415-561-4661; www.presidio golf.com). The links in the Presidio only opened to the public in 1995, although the 18-hole, par-72 course was originally built in 1895. Both Harding Park and the Presidio have restaurants and pro shops, and there's a putting green at the Presidio.

Seeking Some Spiritual Pursuits

San Franciscans aren't merely a hedonistic group of left-wing free-thinkers, despite what you may have heard. As a matter of fact, most pray on a daily basis. Sometimes they pray for a parking space, but mostly they thank God that they live in San Francisco.

Arrive a good half-hour early to claim a seat at the 9 a.m. Sunday services (an hour early for the 11 a.m. services) at **Glide Memorial United Methodist Church,** 330 Ellis St. (☎ 415-674-6000). The Reverend Cecil Williams, a genuinely great man, lets the multiethnic gospel choir do most of the sermonizing, and they're wildly effective. A cross-section of friendly San Franciscans packs the pews, clapping, singing, and celebrating. It's church, it's theater, and it's amazing.

Grace Cathedral, the magnificent Episcopal Church at the top of Nob Hill, 1100 California St., between Taylor and Jones streets (☎ 415-749-6300), has an outdoor stone terrazzo labyrinth that may promote a meditative moment. It's open to visitors daily, anytime. You can rent a labyrinth audio tour, complete with walking music provided by the Grace Choir, at the gift shop.

Old First Presbyterian Church, 1751 Sacramento St., at Van Ness Avenue (☎ **415-474-1608**), sponsors a concert series leaning heavily toward the classical that's low cost and high quality. You can call for a list of upcoming events or check the Internet (www.oldfirstconcerts. org). Getting from downtown to the church is a snap on the California Street cable-car line.

Completed in 1970, **St. Mary's Cathedral,** 1111 Gough St., between Ellis and Geary (☎ **415-567-2020**), is worth a look for its modern architecture and soaring interior space. Inside, be sure to lift your eyes toward heaven to admire the cross-shaped skylight.

Going for Garden and Park Respites

San Franciscans cherish the city's open spaces. If you know where to look, you'll find little parks and secret gardens in some unlikely places. At the end of Market Street in the Embarcadero, two simple gardens grace the seventh floor of One Market Plaza. Elevators to the gardens are situated in the Spear and Steuart Street lobbies. Upon exiting, walk toward the bay; you'll find two patios surrounded by well-tended expanses of lawn and flowers overlooking a classic bay view.

At **Rincon Center** (corner of Mission and Steuart streets) you'll find a courtyard garden with benches sitting among a generous array of orna-mental hedges, azaleas, and seasonal plantings. You can get a snack inside and enjoy it in the garden. A few blocks away, at 100 First St., you'll find the award-winning second-floor garden in the Delta Tower, which is a lush respite from the madness of the Transbay Terminal and Mission Street. The black granite and green glass fountain sculpture pro-vide a soothing counterpoint to the street traffic. **Yerba Buena Gardens** features willow trees, a sweep of bright-green lawn, and a variety of blos-soms. Behind the garden's 22-foot waterfall is a memorial to Martin Luther King, Jr., featuring a series of glass panels etched with quotations from Dr. King's speeches and writings.

Levi's Plaza, between the Embarcadero and Sansome Street, consists of the company's multiple buildings and two plazas separated by Battery Street. The centerpiece of the hard plaza is a fountain you can walk through on paving stones — a big favorite with kids. The soft plaza across the street is really a park with fir trees and grass. The company displays letters and products in a visitor center at 1155 Battery St., open weekdays from 9 a.m. to 6 p.m. and Saturdays from 10 a.m. to 5 p.m.

Cross the plaza to Sansome Street and look for the bottom of the Filbert Steps, a steep staircase that rises to Montgomery and Filbert streets. Around the midpoint of the stairway you'll find a sight so profoundly San Francisco that you'll immediately understand what all the fuss is about. This is the **Grace Marchand Garden;** its roses and ferns add a wild elegance to the hillside. The residents don't like the tourists who clog the steps, especially on weekends, but that's the price they have to pay for living next to a minor landmark. In any case, this is a garden to admire from outside the wooden fence only.

Seeing San Francisco by Guided Tour

I used to feel self-conscious about taking a guided tour in a new city. Many travelers, myself included, shy away from the idea of being herded on and off large buses like curious sheep. But I've finally embraced my inner tourist and learned to appreciate organized outings. Actually, guided tours are a sensible way to get your bearings in an unfamiliar place. You may not have much time to explore on your own and just want to catch the major sights in one day. Or perhaps you have difficulty getting around, or you don't want to drive. Maybe you need an overview to find out what interests you in San Francisco, or you're traveling alone and want some company.

Fortunately, you can find almost as many varieties of guided tours as there are varieties of people in San Francisco. Not all of them have you peering out a dirty bus window at some landmark while straining to hear the muffled voice of your guide over the microphone, or worse, an out-of-date tape. In San Francisco, guided tours happen on foot and ferry boats as well as on buses and even zebra-striped Land Rovers. And they cover special interests, as well as the major sights. If you think a tour listed in this chapter is for you, call the companies or individual guides for their brochures, or ask your hotel to send you information. Most tours require advance reservations.

 Hotels generally have preferred companies that they recommend for bus tours. The hotel often gets a small kickback for every reservation, so it may not have your best interests in mind. If you favor one tour company over another, book it yourself or request that company specifically when you speak to the concierge. Don't leave the decision up to the hotel.

The bus stops here: Touring on wheels

If you want to be sure you at least catch a glimpse of San Francisco's major attractions, orientation tours may be just the ticket. Some tour operators spiff up the menu with motorized cable cars or double-decker buses, whereas other companies use lower-profile minibuses that appeal to visitors who don't want to stand out in a crowd.

Union Square), catch the L-Taraval or N-Judah streetcar, each of which travels through some well-kept residential neighborhoods. Get off at Sunset Boulevard in the outer Sunset District. On Sunset Boulevard, at Taraval Street or Judah Street, depending on which streetcar you rode, pick up a 29-Sunset bus going to the Presidio (*not* to California and 25th Avenue, which doesn't enter the former military base). The spectacular views on this part of the ride include the Pacific Ocean and the Golden Gate Bridge. In fact, the bus stops by a viewing area where you can get off the bus and walk across the bridge and back if that's on your to-do list. The ride also includes a look at a pet cemetery inside the Presidio.

The 29-Sunset terminates at Letterman Hospital in the Presidio, but you can then catch the 43-Masonic bus from the same bus shelter, which takes you down Lombard Street and over to Chestnut Street in the Marina district. From there, the 30-Stockton meanders along Chestnut over to Van Ness Avenue, and then travels down Van Ness to North Point Street, close to Aquatic Park and Ghirardelli Square. The route then goes through North Beach and Chinatown, then back to Union Square. Alternatively, you can walk to PIER 39 and catch the F-Market streetcar for a ride down the Embarcadero and up Market Street. Allow three hours without breaks.

Two if by sea: Touring by boat

Boat cruises provide a view of the city from an unusual vantage point and are the only way to experience the bay in all its glory. You have quite a few options for riding the waves of the bay, one of which is the commuter ferries. Ferries pick up passengers from Fisherman's Wharf (Pier 41) and the Ferry Building.

The Blue & Gold Fleet (☎ 415-705-5555; www.blueandgoldfleet.com) operates ferries to and from Marin County. This is also the only company that will take you to Alcatraz Island. Blue & Gold's one-hour bay cruise ($20 for adults, $16 for seniors and kids 12–18, $12 for kids 5–11) sails under the Golden Gate Bridge; past Sausalito, Angel Island, and Alcatraz; and then back to Fisherman's Wharf. This tour will be a satisfying, if brief, encounter with the bay. Check the Web site for discounts on tickets.

You want something a little more exciting than a ferry? Try sailing on *The Ruby* (☎ 415-861-2165; www.rubysailing.com). This 60-foot steel sloop, which holds about 30 passengers, skims the white caps in the bay daily with a lunch cruise from 12:30 to 3 p.m. and an early-evening sail with hors d'oeuvres from 6 to 8:30 p.m. The cost is $35 per person (including food); beer and wine are available at an additional cost. Kids under 10 are $20. Reservations are necessary. The Ruby is docked by The Ramp at the foot of Mariposa Street at Third Street. The 22-Fillmore or 15-Kearny bus drops you off a block away.

Hornblower Dining Yachts (☎ 888-467-6256; www.hornblower.com) let you sup as you sail, offering dinner and weekend brunch cruises around the bay. Cruises last from one and a half hours for brunch to three hours for the nightly dinner/dance. The food is hotel-like, but this is a festive way to dine — surrounded by superb views. Dinner rates per person are $84 Sunday and Tuesday through Thursday, $99 Friday, $103 Saturday. Saturday- and Sunday-brunch cruises cost $59. Kids are half-price. Reservations are required.

The bright yellow amphibious vehicles you may see bouncing around bayside neighborhoods belong to **Bay Quackers San Francisco Duck Tours** (☎ 415-431-3825; www.bayquackers.com). Their 80-minute tours leave every two hours beginning at 9 a.m. from the Anchorage Mall at Fisherman's Wharf and end up in the bay motoring around McCovey Cove. If you time it right, you could enjoy an unusual view of a Giants' baseball game. It's most definitely an entertaining ride and the water portion lasts just long enough to see the views but not get bored. Tickets are $35 adults, $32 seniors/students, $25 kids under 13. $100 buys a family ticket for two adults and two children.

Taking a walk on the wild side: Walking tours

Friends of the Library sponsor **City Guides walking tours** (☎ 415-557-4266; www.sfcityguides.org). You may choose from 26 different tours, all for free! All you have to do is pick the tour that interests you and show up at the proper corner on time. You can get an insider's view of Chinatown, admire San Francisco's collection of beautifully restored Victorian homes on the Landmark Victorians of Alamo Square tour, or explore the haunts of the original 49ers on the Gold Rush City walk. Tours run about two hours on average. Highly recommended!

The Victorian Home Walk (☎ 415-252-9485; www.victorianwalk.com) combines a trolley-car excursion with a walking tour through a number of celebrated neighborhoods. During the two-and-a-half-hour tour, you see an array of houses in areas where tour vans are prohibited from entering. The guide promises the walk isn't strenuous. The cost is $20. Tours leave daily at 11 a.m. from the lobby of the Westin St. Francis, 335 Powell St., between Geary and Post streets in the Union Square neighborhood.

San Francisco Architectural Heritage conducts a Pacific Heights walk (☎ 415-441-3000 for reservations) on Sundays at 12:30 p.m. beginning at the Haas-Lilienthal house. The two-hour tour through this swanky neighborhood costs just $8 for adults and $5 for seniors and children under 12.

HobNob Tours (☎ 866-851-1123; www.hobnobtours.com) gives you the lowdown on Nob Hill while pointing out the highlights of one of the city's more significant 'hoods. Sure, the gossip and scandal provided is on the historic side, but it's still fascinating. The two-hour tours leave from the Fairmont Hotel lobby weekdays at 10 a.m. and 1:30 p.m. for $30 per person.

Eating your way through San Francisco

Shirley Fong-Torres, a local writer and personality, has been operating Chinatown food tours for 20 years. The three-and-a-half-hour walk manages to demystify the exotic rather irreverently. It includes running commentary about the history of this fascinating neighborhood and stops at an artist's studio, a one-room temple, a market, an herbal shop, and a tea company, where you're treated to a tasting. Shirley's company, **Wok Wiz Chinatown Walking Tours & Cooking Center,** 654 Commercial St., between Kearny and Montgomery streets (☎ **415-981-8989;** www. wokwiz.com), schedules the tours daily at 10 a.m. They cost $40 for adults and $35 for kids under 11 (dim sum lunch included).

The popular North Beach neighborhood reaches new heights of giddiness on Saturdays when food writer GraceAnn Walden (www.graceann walden.net) leads **Mangia! North Beach,** a four-and-a-half-hour, $80 walking, eating, shopping, and history tour. GraceAnn and her followers traipse in and out of a deli, a chocolate shop, a bakery, bookshop, pottery store, and two churches, before ending with a multi-course family-style lunch at one of her favorite restaurants. Lots of samples, lots of tidbits about the Italians, and lots of fun. Call ☎ **415-925-9013** to make reservations. If you're interested in Latin culture, inquire about GraceAnn's **Latino Mission Tour and Mural Walk** ($85), which includes lunch at a Nuevo Latino restaurant.

Seeking out special-interest tours

Learn all there is to know about gay and lesbian history from the Gold Rush to the present day while **Cruisin' the Castro** (☎ **415-255-1821;** www.cruisinthecastro.com). Tours meet at the rainbow flag on the corner of Market and Castro streets, Tuesdays through Saturdays at 10 a.m. Reservations are necessary. The cost, which includes lunch, is $45 adults and $35 kids 3 to 12.

The **Precita Eyes Mural Arts Center,** 2981 24th St., near Harrison Street (☎ **415-285-2287;** www.precitaeyes.org), a not-for-profit arts center, features more than 75 murals on the Mission District walking tours that it sponsors (including the very colorful Balmy Alley). The 6-block walk departs Saturdays and Sundays at 1:30 p.m. from the center itself. The cost is $12 for adults, $5 for seniors, and $2 for children under 12. A slightly different walk leaves from **Café Venice,** 3325 24th St., near the 24th Street BART station, on Saturdays at 11 a.m.

Someday, no one's gonna care where Janis Joplin or members of The Grateful Dead crashed back in the day, but while you still have your memories (or memory, as the case may be) check it out on the **Haight-Ashbury Flower Power Walking Tour** (☎ 415-863-1621). The two-hour walk — a combination of hippy lore and Victorian appreciation — is offered at 9:30 a.m. on Tuesdays and Saturdays for a mere $15 per walker. If you have your own group of at least four, you can inquire about alternate days and times.

An easy way to explore the redwood groves of Muir Woods (see "Especially for hikers," earlier in this chapter) is with Sierra Club guide Tom Martell, of **Tom's Scenic Trailwalking** (☎ 415-381-5106). He'll pick you up (and drop you off) at your hotel, provide a picnic lunch, and drive up to six adventurers to the lovely redwoods just beyond the Golden Gate Bridge for a 2- to 4-mile hike. Cost for the three-and-a-half-hour walk with lunch is $50.

Chapter 12

Shopping the Local Stores

. . . .

In This Chapter

▶ Locating San Francisco's big-name shops and specialty boutiques
▶ Discovering the main shopping neighborhoods
▶ Hunting down bargains

. . . .

*A*lthough most people think of Union Square as the hub of San Francisco shopping — and for good reasons — the downtown area has plenty of competition. Nearly every San Francisco neighborhood boasts a thriving "Main Street" of locally owned boutiques, cafes, and bookstores. You can find retailers with unique arts and crafts, clothing stores that eschew chain-mentality fashion, even housewares havens that reflect the style of the local clientele. Shopping in San Francisco is never mundane. Depending on where you head, you can try on a different attitude as easily as a different outfit.

Surveying the Scene

If you know where to look, you can do some very interesting shopping around here. Oh, plenty of people complain about the city being Starbucked and Gapped to death, but they aren't looking beyond the obvious retail centers. Not all the entrepreneurs in San Francisco are franchisees or part of some conglomerate — some are actually opening boutiques with a personal stamp. In particular, check out Valencia Street for postmodern streetwear and décor; Hayes Street for shoes, clothing, and mod furnishings; Sacramento Street for contemporary clothing, antiques, and kids' clothes and furnishings; upper Grant Street for local designers; upper Polk Street for home furnishing and decoration design trends; and Haight Street for vintage, mod, and skateboarding gear.

You'll find that stores are generally open Monday through Saturday from 10 a.m. to 6 p.m. and on Sunday from noon to 5 p.m., even on many holidays. Shops around Fisherman's Wharf tend to stay open later, as do most department stores.

Sales tax in San Francisco is 8.5 percent, and the salesperson will add it at the register for all goods. You don't have to pay the sales tax if the store ships something out of state for you, but shipping can cost as much as or more than the tax, unless you're purchasing a very expensive item.

San Francisco Shopping

Anne Fontaine **28**
Apple Store **34**
Belden Place **24**
Bell'occhio **12**
Biordi Art Imports **16**
Bloomingdale's
  Westfield San
  Francisco Centre **36**
Books, Inc. **1**
Britex Fabrics **30**
Burton's Pharmacy **2**
Carol Doda's
  Champagne &
  Lace **5**
Chong Imports **22**
City Lights
  Bookstore **17**
Clarion Music Center **23**
The Collector's Cave **4**
Dandelion **38**
DSW Shoe
  Warehouse **32**
Elaine Magnin **41**
Enchanted House **15**
Flight 001 **11**
Forrest Jones **42**
Gaia Tree **11**
Gallery of Jewels **3**
Golden Gate Fortune
  Cookie Co. **21**

Goodbyes **41**
Gump's **29**
Imperial Tea Court **18**
Isda & Co. Outlet **39**
Jeremy's **39**
Kiehl's **8**
Knitz & Leather **15**
La Place du Soleil **20**
La Tulipe Noir **19**
Laku **13**
MAC **10**
Macy's **31**
Mrs. Dewson's Hats **9**
Mudpie **6**
Neiman Marcus **33**
Nest **7**
Old Vogue **15**
Ooma **15**
Original Levi's Store **26**
Paolo Iantorno **11**
Pollanco **11**
Rolo Garage **37**
Saks Fifth Avenue **25**
San Francisco Centre **35**
Tai Yick Trading
  Company **18**
Wilkes Bashford **27**
XOX Truffles **14**

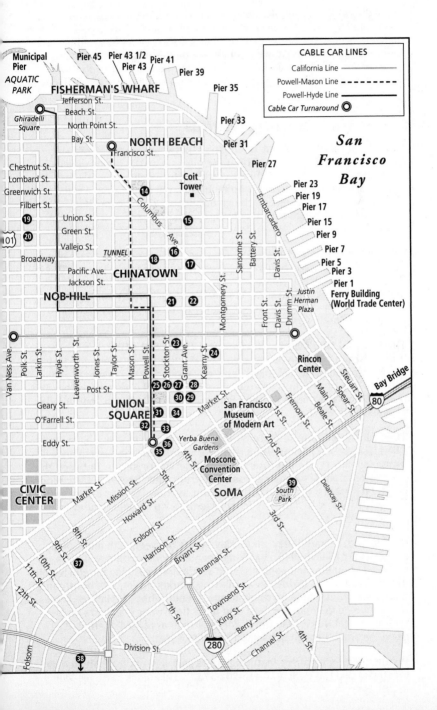

CABLE CAR LINES

California Line ————
Powell-Mason Line – – – –
Powell-Hyde Line ————
Cable Car Turnaround ◉

Municipal Pier
AQUATIC PARK
Pier 45   Pier 43 1/2   Pier 41
Pier 43   Pier 39
FISHERMAN'S WHARF
Pier 35
Jefferson St.
Beach St.
Ghiradelli Square
North Point St.
Pier 33
Bay St.
NORTH BEACH   Pier 31
Francisco St.
Pier 27
Chestnut St.
Lombard St.
Greenwich St.
Coit Tower
Pier 23
Pier 19
Pier 17
Filbert St.
19
Union St.   14
Green St.   15
20   Vallejo St.
TUNNEL   18   16
Broadway   17
Pacific Ave.
Jackson St.   CHINATOWN
NOB-HILL
21   22
23
24
Rincon Center
UNION SQUARE
25 26 27 28
30 29
31   34
32   33
35   36
Yerba Buena Gardens
San Francisco Museum of Modern Art
Moscone Convention Center
SoMa
CIVIC CENTER
South Park   39
37
38

San Francisco Bay

Pier 15
Pier 9
Pier 7
Pier 5
Pier 3
Pier 1
Ferry Building (World Trade Center)
Justin Herman Plaza
Bay Bridge
Embarcadero

The worldwide chain-store invasion has not, unfortunately, passed San Francisco by. In fact, we accept the blame for the Gap frenzy — the headquarters is near the Embarcadero — and if you see a Pottery Barn or a Gymboree in your midst, well, those companies originated in the Bay Area, as well. But you can find plenty of unique emporiums that will bring some excitement to the chase. Here's a short list of great places.

Checking Out the Big Names

Gump's, in Union Square at 135 Post St., between Kearny Street and Grant Avenue (☎ 415-982-1616; www.gumps.com), is famous for its Asian antiques, silver, and china, as well as for longevity — it's been in business since 1861. Anyone who receives a gift from Gump's will shower impressed thanks on the giver because of the name itself. It's open Monday through Saturday from 10 a.m. to 6 p.m. and Sunday, noon to 5 p.m.

Looking for the perfect place for one-stop shopping? Then head over to **Macy's West** on Union Square, at Stockton and O'Farrell streets (☎ 415-954-6271). At 700,000 square feet, this eight-story, glass-fronted fashion behemoth is bigger than some towns. It's open Monday and Wednesday 10 a.m. to 8 p.m., Tuesday and Thursday through Saturday 10 a.m. to 9 p.m., and Sunday from 11 a.m. to 7 p.m.

The Original Levi's Store, 300 Post St. (☎ 415-501-0100), is a showcase for more than 501s — you'll see some wild designs stitched onto jackets and jeans. One corner of this three-story monument to denim is dedicated to alterations, in case your shrink-to-fits still need a tuck here and there. It's open Monday through Saturday 10 a.m. to 8 p.m., and Sunday 11 a.m. to 7 p.m.

The brandacious **Apple Store** on the corner of Stockton and Ellis streets (☎ 415-392-0202) schedules a roster of workshops for current and future Mac users and has Internet access on the premises. Between this place, the Virgin Megastore across the street, and Niketown a few blocks north on Post Street, you could lose your average teen for a few hours. It's open Monday to Saturday from 10 a.m. to 9 p.m., and Sunday from 11 a.m. to 6 p.m.

Bell'occhio, 8 Brady Alley, off Market Street between 12th and Gough streets (☎ 415-864-4048), has long been a favorite with decorators, wedding planners, and sophisticated shoppers searching for elusive bits of European flavor. Hidden in an alley off Market Street, this bewitching little shop stocks cunning decorations, French ribbons, Mariage Frères tea, imported face powder, and odd finds the owner discovers on her travels. To get there, take the F-Market streetcar to Civic Center. It's open Tuesday through Saturday 11 a.m. to 5 p.m.

Polanco, a bright gallery featuring crafts and artwork from Mexico, is located at 393 Hayes St. (☎ 415-252-5753). This block in Hayes Valley also has a few terrific clothing and home-décor shops, so if you're in the neighborhood, it's worth a side trip. The gallery is open Monday through Saturday 11:30 a.m. to 6:30 p.m., and Sunday 1 to 6 p.m.

Dandelion, 55 Potrero Ave., at Alameda (☎ **415-436-9500**), isn't a store you'll find by accident. You have to have heard about this place from a devoted customer, with its out-of-the-way location close to the Design Center south of Market Street. The owners seem to be magnets for beautiful objects. Their prices are very fair, their taste impeccable. The 9–San Bruno bus from Market and Ninth streets can take you right here. It's open Monday through Saturday 10 a.m. to 6 p.m. Famed *San Francisco Chronicle* journalist Herb Caen's favorite clothing store, **Wilkes Bashford,** 375 Sutter St., between Stockton Street and Grant Avenue, near Union Square (☎ **415-986-4380**), was often mentioned in his columns. And San Francisco's natty former mayor, Willie Brown, purchases his Brioni suits here. The store sells sophisticated clothing for women as well. It's open Monday through Saturday 10 a.m. to 6 p.m., and Thursday to 8 p.m.

For CDs, vinyl (remember that?), and an in-depth selection of previously owned music, the cognoscenti shop at **Amoeba Records,** 1855 Haight St. (☎ **415-831-1200**), in the musically famous neighborhood of the same name. Open Monday through Saturday from 10 a.m. to 10 p.m., and Sunday from 11 a.m. to 9 p.m.

When those cognoscenti stroll down Haight Street, they often wear really cool clothes from **Rolo,** a locally grown retailer with six stores around town. The flagship store, which carries streetwear for both men and women, is south of Market at 1235 Howard St. (☎ **415-431-4545**). It's open Monday through Saturday from 11 a.m. to 8 p.m., and Sunday 11 a.m. to 7 p.m.

Market Street continues its upward trajectory (at least from 5th Street toward the Bay) with the opening of the humungous **Bloomingdale's,** centerpiece of the new Westfield San Francisco Centre next to the older one (where Nordstrom is located) on 5th and Market streets. Along with all the usual suspects one expects to find in an upscale mall, this one also has a day spa on the 5th floor, a gourmet grocer in the basement, movie theaters, and dining establishments with good pedigrees including **Out the Door,** a take-away from the Slanted Door family.

Going to Market

Farmers' market aficionados will find Saturdays at the **Ferry Building** at the foot of Market Street more than satisfying. The majority of producers bring organically grown foodstuffs, and you'll discover unusual varieties of fruits and vegetables including heirloom tomatoes in season. The perfume of the salt air, ripe fruit, and a whiff of lavender wafting past your nostrils are deeply pleasurable; combined with the bay views, a busker

playing standards on his saxophone, and a plethora of tastes, the scene
is magical. Inside the building, permanent shops, most of which are open
seven days a week, stock everything you'd need for a feast plus all kinds
of tempting items including books, chocolates, olive oil, kitchen necessities, wine, and imported packaged foods. If you find yourself hungry, this
is where the **Slanted Door** has moved (see Chapter 10) or you can sit
down at the **MarketBar** on the east end, visit **Taylor's Refreshers** for fast
food I heartily approve of, or attempt to get a counter seat at the **Hog
Island Oyster Bar.**

Discovering the Best Shopping Neighborhoods

Looking for that perfect little doodad for Aunt Hermione back home? Or
do you just like to browse and see what catches your fancy? Following is
a rundown of the city's best shopping areas, with a few highlights in
each. Happy hunting!

Union Square

You're never far from a department store in this neighborhood. From
one spot in the middle of Union Square, you can see **Neiman Marcus**
(☎ 415-362-3900) on Stockton and Geary streets (open: Mon, Thurs,
and Fri 10 a.m.–8 p.m.; Tues and Wed 10 a.m.–6 p.m.; Sat 10 a.m.–7 p.m.;
Sun noon–6 p.m.) and **Saks Fifth Avenue** (☎ 415-986-4300) on the
corner of Powell and Post streets (open: Mon–Sat 10 a.m.–7 p.m.
[Thurs open until 8 p.m.]; Sun 11 a.m.–6 p.m.). Then there's **Levi's**
(see "Checking Out the Big Names") on Post and Stockton, and **Macy's**
(see "Checking Out the Big Names") everywhere else. Ah . . . shopping!

A half-block north of Neiman's on Stockton Street is Maiden Lane, which
is lined with designer shops. There's also a back entrance to **Britex
Fabrics** (☎ 415-392-2910), probably the most well-stocked notions and
fabric store in the country (open: Mon–Sat 9:30 a.m.–6 p.m.; Sun noon–
5 p.m.). The front door is at 146 Geary St.

Parallel to Stockton eastward is Grant Street. One of the newest stores
here is also one of my favorites in the world, **Anne Fontaine,** 118 Grant
St. (☎ 415-677-0911). If you appreciate gorgeously made and tailored
white blouses (plus a few other nonwhite must-haves), you'll be one
wide-eyed consumer. Walk another block east and 2 blocks north and
watch for tiny **Belden Place** between Bush and Pine streets (see Chapter
10). A covey of delicious little restaurants lines the alley, and any one of
them makes a satisfying place to stop for a meal. At lunchtime on fair
days, Belden, which is closed to auto traffic, is filled with cafe tables,
giving the street a partylike atmosphere (open: Mon–Sat 10 a.m.–6 p.m.;
Sun noon–5 p.m.).

Be careful of the multitude of shady salespeople who operate questionable electronics/camera, luggage, and gift shops on certain blocks of
Mason and Market streets around Union Square. (You'll probably know

them when you see them: Most offer too-good-to-be-true deals, and some have someone standing outside the store scoping out potential customers.) Out-of-town customers have been known to discover inflated charges on their credit cards after shopping at these places, so buyer beware.

Chinatown

Chinatown is known for its amusing trinkets and inexpensive clothing. But most of the souvenirs sold in the shops that line Grant Avenue are not the must-haves you come to San Francisco seeking. If you venture off Grant Avenue, however, shop to your heart's content in Chinese herbal shops with strange remedies and unique jewelry stores full of jade of varying quality. The merchants in the less touristy stores don't always speak English, and they may seem less than friendly, but don't let that stop you from looking around.

 The "going-out-of-business" signs you see taped to the windows of several Chinatown stores are nearly as old as the grandmothers walking about with babies tied to their backs. These stores have been running their farewell sales for years. Don't expect any bargains.

If you can't tear yourself away from Grant Avenue, the best place to find inexpensive (or expensive) gifts and housewares is **Chong Imports,** 838 Grant Ave., in the Empress of China building between Clay and Washington streets (☎ **415-982-1432**). This basement-level treasure house stocks a little of everything. It's open daily from 10 a.m. to 9 p.m.

At the **Clarion Music Center,** 816 Sacramento St., near Grant Avenue (☎ **415-391-1317;** www.clarionmusic.com), check out the amazing instruments, including traditional Chinese instruments like moon-shaped guitars, plus Chinese lion dance masks. It's open Monday through Friday from 11 a.m. to 6 p.m., and Saturday from 9 a.m. to 5 p.m. Call for a Friday night world concert series schedule.

Tai Yick Trading Company, 1400 Powell St., at Broadway (☎ **415-986-0961**), sells teapots, dishes, lamps, porcelain and pottery vases, and statues at reasonable prices. The owners are helpful and friendly, and native San Franciscans swear that this is the best store of its kind in town. It's open daily from 9:30 a.m. to 6:30 p.m.

The Imperial Tea Court, 1411 Powell St., near Broadway (☎ **415-788-6080**), noted as a tranquil place to rejuvenate yourself, sells everything you need to brew a proper cup of Chinese tea. It's open Wednesday through Monday from 11 a.m. to 6 p.m.

Legend has it that fortune cookies were invented at the Japanese Tea Garden in Golden Gate Park. If you want to watch these cookies being made, head to the **Golden Gate Fortune Cookie Company** in Chinatown (see Chapter 11). They make wonderful gifts to take back home. The factory is at 956 Ross Alley, between Jackson and Washington streets near Grant Avenue. It's open daily from 10 a.m. to 7 p.m.

Haight Street

The scruffiness of this area used to bother me when I lived nearby in the early '80s, but I've changed and so has the neighborhood. Clothing is the big draw for shoppers, whether vintage or cutting edge, and you'll locate apparel and shoes for all ages and stages. In particular, look for **Behind the Post Office,** 1510 Haight St. (☎ 415-861-2507), for accessories from local designers; **Kids Only,** 1608 Haight St. (☎ 415-552-5445), for your flower child; **Ambiance,** 1458 Haight St. (☎ 415-552-5095), for pretty dresses, stylish shoes, and somewhat retro handbags; and **Villains Vault,** 1653 and 1672 Haight St. (☎ 415-864-7727 or 415-626-5939), for streetwear and shoes. Most stores on Haight Street are open from 10 a.m. to 7 p.m. daily.

North Beach

North Beach is more than just a food-and-drink mecca — you can find all sorts of curiosities and clothing off Columbus Street. The section of Grant Avenue (completely different from the street of the same name in Chinatown) from Union to Greenwich streets has a more Continental accent, with stylish boutiques for clothes and accessories. Among the finds — and there are many — head to **Knitz & Leather,** 1429 Grant Ave. (☎ 415-391-3480), for handmade sweaters and leather jackets (open: Mon–Tues 11 a.m.–6 p.m., Wed–Sat 11 a.m.–5 p.m. and Sun noon–5 p.m.). **Old Vogue,** 1412 Grant St. (☎ 415-392-1522), is a better organized and higher-quality vintage shop than most of those on Haight Street, while **Ooma,** 1422 Grant St. (☎ 415-627-6963), displays the goods of local designers. Members of your party not interested in clothes may find the oriental antiques at the **Enchanted House** more to their liking. It's at 1411 Grant Ave. (☎ 415-981-5870).

You don't need to comb Italy for ceramics when you can shop at **Biordi Art Imports,** 412 Columbus Ave., at Vallejo Street (☎ 415-392-8096). You'll find the most beautiful hand-painted Majolica dishes and serving pieces nearly too pretty to actually use. It's open Monday through Saturday from 9:30 a.m. to 6 p.m.

City Lights Bookstore, 261 Columbus Ave. (☎ 415-362-8193; www.city lights.com), is famous for its Beat Generation roots, but it's also a book fiend's paradise. The first all-paperback bookstore in San Francisco, this city institution dates to 1953, when it was opened by Beat poet Lawrence Ferlinghetti. At the time, most people thought hardcover books were superior to paperbacks in terms of both the quality of the content as well as the quality of the paper. Ferlinghetti challenged this attitude and made great literature available to everyone by stocking his bookstore with less-costly paperback editions. The San Francisco Board of Supervisors recently designated the store a cultural and architectural landmark, assuring a long and happy life for the building. Ferlinghetti's brainchild is also on its way to becoming a national historic site. It's open daily from 10 a.m. to midnight.

Admirers of chocolate can wedge themselves into **XOX Truffles,** 754 Columbus Ave. (☎ **415-421-4814**), a tiny store devoted to nickel-sized truffles in a huge assortment of flavors. These bites of bliss are all hand-made under the direction of a handsome French chef, who removed himself from the rigors of the restaurant world to bring pleasure to us chocoholics. Open Monday through Saturday from 9 a.m. to 6 p.m.

Union and Chestnut streets

According to a survey, one out of four visitors to San Francisco plans on visiting Union Street between Fillmore Street and Van Ness Avenue in the Marina district. Folks who love wandering in and out of specialty shops will think they've hit pay dirt. Muni buses 22-Fillmore, 41-Union, 42–Downtown Loop, and 45-Union/Stockton all run on Union Street.

Carol Doda, who shaped a career out of her chest long before implants were considered accessories, runs a lingerie shop, **Carol Doda's Champagne and Lace,** at 1850 Union St. (☎ **415-776-6900**). She carries bras in regular and hard-to-find sizes, plus lots of other fun things. It's open daily from 12:30 a.m. to 6:30 p.m., Sunday until 5 p.m.

Cover yourself with beautiful adornments crafted by local artists at **Gallery of Jewels,** 2101 Union St. (☎ **415-929-0259**), open Monday through Friday 10:30 a.m. to 6:30 p.m. and Sunday 11 a.m. to 6 p.m. You'll find unique pieces of jewelry as well as purses and hats on occasion.

Because man apparently does not live by cashmere alone, you may be interested in perusing **The Collectors Cave** at 2072 Union St. (☎ **415-929-0231**), which displays all kinds of new and old comic books, action figures, and sports cards for serious and not-so-serious collectors. It's open Tuesday through Sunday from 10 a.m. to 6 p.m.

Mudpie, 1694 Union St. (☎ **415-771-9262**), sells expensive children's clothes and gifts. Sticker shock is slightly alleviated in the downstairs saleroom, where everything is half-price. It's open Monday through Saturday 1 a.m. to 5 p.m.

Another highly attractive, healthy shopping area is **Chestnut Street** in Cow Hollow, patronized by highly attractive and healthy locals with plenty of discretionary cash. Neither Chestnut nor Union Street, a few blocks south, has been able to fight off the invasion by some of the more ambitious chain stores, but local neighborhood and merchant groups are vigilant enough to keep them at a minimum. Muni bus 30-Stockton or 43-Masonic will get you to Chestnut Street.

Among the Banana Republic, Pottery Barn, and Williams-Sonoma stores lining the area is an anomaly, **Burton's Pharmacy,** 2016 Chestnut St. (☎ **415-567-1166**), one of the few remaining independent drugstores left. It's open weekdays from 9 a.m. to 6:30 p.m., Saturday 9:30 a.m. to 6 p.m.

On the other end of Chestnut is another independent, **Books, Inc.,** 2251 Chestnut St. (☎ 415-931-3633), which has a broad inventory of reading material for the entire family. It's open Sunday through Thursday 9 a.m. to 10 p.m., and Friday and Saturday 9 a.m. to 11 p.m.

Pacific Heights

The tony neighborhood of Pacific Heights offers shoppers Fillmore Street, which is chock-full of clothing boutiques and other cool places to shop. Between Jackson and Sutter streets, you won't be able to put your credit card away.

Kiehl's manufactures high-end, high-quality cosmetics and hair products for men and women. Their shop at 2360 Fillmore St. (☎ 415-359-9260) is one of only two freestanding retail outlets in the country. It's open Monday through Saturday 10 a.m. to 7 p.m., Sunday 11 a.m. to 6 p.m.

Nest, 2300 Fillmore St., at Clay Street (☎ 415-292-6199), is yet another home store, but one that carries many old French decorative items, including quilts and linens. It's open Monday through Saturday 10:30 a.m. to 6:30 p.m., Sunday 11 a.m. to 6 p.m.

You don't see many hat shops left in the world, so a visit to **Mrs. Dewson's Hats,** 2050 Fillmore St. (☎ 415-346-1600), is a must if your chapeau is a little tattered. This place is home to the "Willie Brim," a fedora named after Mayor Willie Brown. It's open Tuesday through Saturday from 11 a.m. to 6 p.m., and Sunday noon to 4 p.m.

Polk Street

The stretch of road from Filbert to Broadway on the Russian Hill end of Polk Street has blossomed into a hot spot for dining and shopping. Along with a second location for **Nest** (see the preceding section), two little shops for the home, **La Place du Soleil,** at 2356 Polk St. (☎ 415-771-4252; open: Tues–Sat 11 a.m.–6 p.m., Sun noon–5 p.m.), and **La Tulipe Noire,** at 2418 Polk St. (☎ 415-922-2000; open: Tues–Sun 11 a.m.–7 p.m.), will seemingly transport you to a street in the fourth arrondissement of Paris.

Sacramento Street

Some exclusive antiques shops and also some of the best secondhand stores in town can be found in the section of Sacramento Street between Spruce and Divisadero streets in Presidio Heights. The 1-California bus takes you within 1 block of Sacramento Street.

Before housewares were considered a lifestyle choice, **Forrest Jones,** 3274 Sacramento St. (☎ 415-567-2483), was stocking an array of kitchen tools, linens, lovely porcelain lamp bases and vases, cookbooks, glassware, and other necessities. The variety of goods crowded about makes the store very appealing. It's open Monday through Saturday 10 a.m. to 6 p.m., Sunday 11 a.m. to 5 p.m.

Elaine Magnin's needlepoint shop, 3310 Sacramento St. (☎ 415-931-3063), is the place to go if you wield a mighty needle and are seeking some new patterns. It's open Monday through Saturday 10 a.m. to 5 p.m.

If you want to see what the swells have cleaned out of their closets (the locals are going to hate me for this), head to **GoodByes**, 3464 Sacramento St., between Walnut and Laurel streets (☎ 415-346-6388). This is the place for gently worn men's and women's clothing. It's open Monday through Saturday from 10 a.m. to 6 p.m., Thursday until 8 p.m., and Sunday from 11 a.m. to 5 p.m. A second store for women only is across the street (☎ 415-674-0151).

Hayes Street

Naming the hippest shopping street in the city would be difficult, but if forced, I'd have to say Hayes Street. Start at Grove and Gough, where you'll find the expanded **MAC** (Modern Appealing Clothing) store at 387 Grove St. (☎ 415-863-3011; open: Mon–Sat 11 a.m.–7 p.m., Sun noon–6 p.m.). From there, head 1 block south to Hayes Street and start walking toward the Pacific. You'll find a wealth of stuff here for all facets of your life unless you live like a Spartan or a monk, in which case you may want to stop at the **Gaia Tree**, 575 Hayes St. (☎ 415-255-4848; open: Mon–Tues 10 a.m.–7:30 p.m., Wed–Sat 10 a.m.–8 p.m., Sun noon–6 p.m.), for a yoga mat or maybe a facial or a massage. See, there's just no escaping commerce. To see all the things you needed to buy before you got on the plane, stop in **Flight 001**, 525 Hayes St. (☎ 415-487-1001), where they sell those little spray bottles of Evian so you won't dry up on the flight home. If your feet hurt, stop in one of the many shoe stores here, including **Paolo Iantorno**, 524 Hayes St. (☎ 415-552-4580), which sells beautiful Italian-made creations for men and women to decorate whatever's below your ankles. The shop also stocks gorgeous handbags. Besides regular weekday hours, many of the stores on these blocks are open Sunday afternoons.

Valencia Street

In the last ten years, Valencia Street in the Mission District has been developing into the shopping district for those who eschew the mainstream. The blocks from 19th to 23rd streets still hold plenty of storefront churches and used-appliance dens, but the cafes and restaurants that ventured here in the first wave of gentrification have been joined by sellers of youthful fashions, local art, and goods for the home. Of note is **Paxton Gate**, 824 Valencia St. (☎ 415-824-1872; open: Mon–Fri noon–7 p.m., Sat–Sun 11 a.m.–7 p.m.), part entomological display, part garden store, but neither description does this place justice. Almost next door is **City Art** (☎ 415-970-9900; open: Wed–Sun noon–9 p.m.), a co-op gallery featuring San Francisco artists and photographers. And don't pass by **Encantada Gallery of Fine Arts**, 904 Valencia St. (☎ 415-642-3939; open: Tues–Sun noon–6 p.m., until 8 p.m. Fri–Sat), which has a wonderful collection of Mexican art and pottery, as well as a changing exhibit of paintings and mixed media. One of my favorite local designers for women's clothing, Dema, has a store and workshop at 1038 Valencia St. (☎ 415-206-0500). Dema's patterns and colors are spirit raisers. My favorite hat was fashioned at **Laku,** a teensy store at 1069 Valencia St. (☎ 415-695-1462; open: Tues–Sat 11:30 a.m.–6:30 p.m., Sun noon–5 p.m.), which also sells handmade, fanciful slippers for babies and big people. From downtown, use BART, exit at the 24th Street Station, and walk 1 block west. Most of the Valencia Street shops are closed on Mondays.

Hunting for bargains in SoMa and beyond

The discount manufacturers based South of Market (SoMa) have made bargain shopping in San Francisco a popular pursuit. Although outlets can be found around SoMa and beyond, the area between Townsend and Bryant streets and Second and Fourth streets is great for bargains.

The hip retailer Rolo has an outlet for sale merchandise called **Rolo Garage,** 1301 Howard St., at Ninth Street (☎ 415-861-1999). It's open Monday through Saturday from 11 a.m. to 7 p.m and Sundays noon to 6 p.m.

Two worthwhile stores are off Second Street between Bryant and Brannan streets in South Park, a little sub-neighborhood south of Market, once infamous for ties to the dot-com industry. **Isda & Co. Outlet,** 28 South Park (☎ 415-512-1610; open: Mon–Sat 10 a.m.–6 p.m.), carries its fashionable women's wear suitable for the office and after-hours at great prices, while **Jeremy's,** 2 South Park (☎ 415-882-4929; open: Mon–Sat 11 a.m.–6 p.m., Sun until 5 p.m.), is filled with last season's markdowns, returns, and display items from department stores and some famous names.

Did your son outgrow his sneakers yesterday? Did you? You're gonna go wild in the **Skechers USA** outlet in the Mission at 2600 Mission St. (☎ 415-401-6211). It's open Monday through Saturday 10 a.m. to 8 p.m., Sunday 10 a.m. to 7 p.m. If you or someone in your party needs something dressier, dance over to the **DSW Shoe Warehouse** near Union Square, 111 Powell St. (☎ 415-445-9511). It's open Monday to Saturday 9:30 a.m. to 9 p.m., Sunday until 8 p.m.

Index of Stores by Merchandise

Antiques
The Enchanted House (North Beach)
Gump's (Union Square)
La Tulipe Noire (Polk Street)

Arts and Crafts
City Art (Valencia Street)

Encantada Gallery of Fine Arts (Valencia Street)
Polanco (Hayes Valley)

Beauty Products
Gaia Tree (Hayes Street)
Kiehl's (Pacific Heights)

Books
Books, Inc. (Union/Chestnut streets)
City Lights (North Beach)

Clothing, Children's
Kids Only (Haight-Ashbury)
Macy's West (Union Square)
Mudpie (Union/Chestnut streets)
Neiman Marcus (Union Square)

Clothing, Menswear
Bloomingdale's (SoMa)
Goodbyes (Sacramento Street)
MAC (Hayes Street)
Macy's West (Union Square)
Neiman Marcus (Union Square)
Jeremy's (SoMa)
Old Vogue (North Beach)
Original Levi's Store (Union Square)
Rolo (SoMa)
Rolo Garage (SoMa)
Saks Fifth Avenue (Union Square)
Villains Vault (Haight-Ashbury)
Wilkes Bashford (Union Square)

Clothing, Womenswear
Anne Fontaine (Union Square)
Behind the Post Office (Haight-Ashbury)
Bloomingdale's (SoMa)
Dema (Valencia Street)
Goodbyes (Sacramento Street)
Isda & Co. Outlet (SoMa)
Jeremy's (SoMa)
Knitz & Leather (North Beach)
MAC (Hayes Street)
Macy's (Union Square)
Neiman Marcus (Union Square)
Old Vogue (North Beach)
Ooma (North Beach)
Original Levi's Store (Union Square)
Rolo (SoMa)
Rolo Garage (SoMa)
Saks Fifth Avenue (Union Square)
Villains Vault (Haight-Ashbury)
Wilkes Bashford (Union Square)

Computers
Apple Store (Union Square)

Edibles
Ferry Plaza Marketplace (Embarcadero)
Golden Gate Fortune Cookie Company (Chinatown)
Imperial Tea Court (Chinatown)
XOX Truffles (North Beach)

Fabric/Yarn
Britex (Union Square)
Elaine Magnin Needlepoint (Sacramento Street)

Gifts
Biordi Art Imports (North Beach)
Burton's Pharmacy (Union/Chestnut streets)
Chong Imports (Chinatown)
The Collectors Cave (Union/Chestnut streets)
Dandelion (SoMa)
Ferry Plaza Marketplace (Embarcadero)
Flight 001 (Hayes Street)
Gump's (Union Square)
Show Biz (North Beach)

Hats
Laku (Valencia Street)
Mrs. Dewson's Hats (Pacific Heights)

Home Decor and Housewares
Bell'occhio (Civic Center)
Forrest Jones (Sacramento Street)
La Place du Soleil (Polk Street)
Nest (Pacific Heights)
Paxton Gate (Valencia Street)
Tai Yick Trading Company (Chinatown)

Jewelry
Gallery of Jewels (Union/Chestnut streets)

Lingerie

Bloomingdale's (SoMa)
Carol Doda's Champagne and Lace
(Union/Chestnut streets)

Luggage

Flight 001 (Hayes Street)
Macy's (Union Square)

Music

Amoeba Records (Haight-Ashbury)
Clarion Music Center (Chinatown)

Shoes

Ambience (Haight-Ashbury)
Bloomingdale's (SoMa)
DSW Shoe Warehouse (Union Square)
Macy's (Union Square)
Neiman Marcus (Union Square)
Paolo Iantorno (Hayes Street)
Saks Fifth Avenue (Union Square)
Skechers USA (SoMa)
Villains Vault (Haight-Ashbury)

Chapter 13

Following an Itinerary: Four Great Options to Make Your Day

In This Chapter

▶ Making the most out of three to five days
▶ Showing the kids a good time
▶ Taking a food-lover's holiday

*V*isitors naturally want to pack as much as possible into a sightseeing trip, in case they don't have a chance to return. Having been in that position myself, I've come to the conclusion that travel isn't pleasurable if all you do is run around checking off sights as if you're grocery shopping. My idea of a good time is visiting one or two important sights in a day (or sometimes just walking past the front portal and waving) and then finding somewhere to sit and watch the world pass by. (I must admit that I felt foolish for missing the Eiffel Tower on my first visit to Paris — and I was in the neighborhood.) You may prefer a compromise between these approaches, in which case I suggest you decide in advance what you *must* see, and then fit in whatever else you can based on how much time and energy you have.

On that note, the following suggested itineraries are intended for first-time visitors who want to catch as much as possible without completely exhausting themselves or their companions. I've packed in a lot, but you can pick and choose (or completely ignore) parts of each.

San Francisco in Three Days

Three days is barely enough to "get" San Francisco, so I'm going to keep you within the city limits for the entire time. The following list takes you step by step through the city:

✔ **Day 1:** Find Market Street and catch one of the historic F-Market streetcars (see Chapter 8) heading toward PIER 39 and Fisherman's Wharf. If you haven't eaten breakfast, the **Eagle Café** on the second floor of the pier serves a big, delicious one with views. If it happens to be a Saturday, exit at the **Ferry Plaza Farmers' Market.** A few of the local restaurants — Hayes Street Grill, Rose Pistola — have booths where you can buy something savory to eat for your morning meal, or you can make yourself quite happy with coffee and fresh pastries from **Frog Hollow Farms** inside the building. When you reach **PIER 39,** greet the sea lions (follow the barking) and continue to the end of the pier for a dead-on view of Alcatraz Island. Walk to **Aquatic Park** to complete a tour of **Fisherman's Wharf** (see Chapter 11). You'll pass the **Hyde Street Pier** and the **Maritime National Museum** — pop in if you like ships — as well as **Ghirardelli Square.** On Bay Street, catch a 30-Stockton bus to Chestnut Street. If it's not too soon to shop or eat, **Mamacita** (see Chapter 10) is a great choice for Mexican food. The bus ends up at Beach Street, and your task is to walk from the **Palace of Fine Arts** through Crissy Field and the Presidio to the **Golden Gate Bridge.** Follow the joggers along the bay; there's a path. The 29-Sunset bus will also take you there and back. End the afternoon around **Union Square,** window shopping along Stockton and Sutter. Change your clothes, then go to the **Top of the Mark** (see Chapter 10) for an aperitif and a grand view. For dinner, see what's cooking on **Belden Place** (see Chapter 10), and if you still have a bit of steam left, drop by **Biscuits and Blues** (see Chapter 16) for a musical nightcap.

✔ **Day 2:** This day starts with another transportation highlight. Fling yourself on a Powell-Hyde cable car (see Chapter 8) for the brief ride to Lombard Street. Walk down via the staircases on either side and, heading north, find the **San Francisco Art Institute** at 800 Chestnut St. Inside the campus, follow the signs to the cafe for breakfast or a snack. This is a funky place with unobstructed views of the bay and a menu of sandwiches, bagels, and vegetarian entrees priced for starving artists. Follow Filbert Street to **Washington Square Park** in North Beach, a modest pocket of green with plentiful benches on the perimeter and the twin spires of Saints Peter and Paul's Church solidly cutting into the sky to the north. Park yourself on a bench, maybe with a latte in hand from **Mario's Bohemian Cigar** on the corner. Then stroll around North Beach if you like, or walk up Grant Avenue past Union Street and follow the signs to **Coit Tower** (see Chapter 11). From there, return to North Beach for a leisurely lunch at **Moose's** (see Chapter 10), which is on the east side of the park, or pick up a sandwich at one of the delis and have a picnic of sorts in Portsmouth Square (above the parking garage on Kearny Street between Washington and Clay; see Chapter 11), a short walk away. Spend the afternoon exploring **Chinatown** (see Chapter 11). If you're in the mood for Chinese cuisine for dinner, see Chapter 10 for suggestions. Then head back to North Beach for a performance of *Beach Blanket Babylon* (see Chapter 15).

✔ **Day 3:** Enjoy a walk in the park — **Golden Gate Park** (see Chapter 11) — where you can row a boat on Stow Lake, hunt for Bison, and smell the flowers in the **Strybing Arboretum.** Find lunch over on Ninth Avenue and then stroll down Irving Street, a typical neighborhood shopping block. Alternatively, exit the park on Stanyon Street and take in the Haight-Ashbury, also a typical neighborhood — for San Francisco. In the afternoon, a trip to the **Museum of Modern Art** (see Chapter 11) finishes the artistic portion of your vacation. Take a rest stop in **Yerba Buena Gardens** (see Chapter 11) across the street. Then dine around **Union Square** if you're ambitious enough to see an 8 p.m. show at ACT or another theater. Otherwise, hail a cab and head to a Mission District restaurant such as **Delfina** or **Foreign Cinema** (see Chapter 10), and pretend you're a local. Night owls can finish the evening at a salsa dance club such as **El Rio,** or hang out with the hipsters at the **Make-Out Room** (see Chapter 16).

San Francisco in Five Days

For a four- or five-day trip, you can add the following days to the itinerary in the preceding section:

✔ **Day 4:** By now, you've already covered a fair portion of the city; it's probably time to hug a tree (you *are* in Northern California, after all). Rent a car or take a guided tour (see Chapter 11) and cross the Golden Gate Bridge into **Marin.** Hike **Muir Woods** in the morning (take the Stinson Beach exit) and have lunch by Muir Beach at the English Tudor–style **Pelican Inn,** located at the end of Muir Wood Road at Highway 1 (☎ **415-383-6000;** www.pelicaninn.com). The inn is a short walk from the beach, which lies below a hikable hill. Stop in **Sausalito** on your way back to the city for an ice cream or just a walk along the bayfront — the San Francisco skyline is quite the sight, but Sausalito itself, though postcard pretty, is quite touristy. This evening, eat dinner in Japantown at either **Mifune** in the Japan Center for noodles or **Isuzu** for sushi or tempura (see Chapter 10), and maybe see what's playing at the cineplex around the corner.

✔ **Day 5:** This may be the morning to get in your trip to **Alcatraz Island** (see Chapter 11) or to trek to the **Palace of the Legion of Honor** (see Chapter 11) for another dose of culture. For lunch try the **Tadich Grill** (see Chapter 10), the oldest restaurant in California (although it's been in its current location only since 1967). The menu of favorites, such as lobster thermidor, is accompanied with a side of local history and an active bar. Then spend the afternoon catching up on shopping, or stroll down to Pier 5 near the Ferry Building (to the east of Broadway), where you can hang out on benches and watch skateboarders or just admire the view. In the evening, splurge with a fancy dinner — **Ame** or **Quince** are two good choices (see Chapter 10) — followed by the late show at Jazz at Pearl's (see Chapter 16).

San Francisco for Families with Kids

How to keep the kids engaged and happy (for example, not asking what time it is, what they're doing tomorrow, and when they're eating) depends on their ages and interests. Here's a list to meet any need:

✔ **For families with little kids:** A day around **Golden Gate Park** is ideal. The **Japanese Tea Garden** is memorable, you can't miss with either a bike ride or the paddle boats around Stow Lake, and youngsters with energy to spare will gravitate toward the big, imaginatively designed playground. When lunch beckons, you can feed the family reasonably at **Park Chow** on Ninth Avenue, just a block from the park entrance. The **zoo** (see Chapter 11) is a logical alternative for a morning's activity as well; it's easy to reach on a streetcar and, on your return downtown, you may head to **Yerba Buena Gardens** for lunch and then to the **California Academy of Sciences** at their South of Market building (see Chapter 11). If a quieter afternoon seems like a better idea, consider a **ferryboat ride** to Sausalito and back.

✔ **For families with slightly older progeny:** Spend a delightful day taking the cable car to **Fisherman's Wharf** (see Chapter 8), where PIER 39 holds sway, with its many shops and video games. You can avoid the scene, if you prefer, with strategically timed tickets to **Alcatraz** (see Chapter 11); think about bringing along sandwiches or snacks because most of the food around the pier is overpriced and underwhelming. If you can stave off starvation until your return from solitary confinement, hustle everyone over to **North Beach** on the Mason-Powell cable car and eat at **Il Pollaio** (see Chapter 10). **Chinatown** is convenient to North Beach and kids love browsing in the shops. For dinner, **Lichee Gardens** (see Chapter 10) is a good family-style Chinese restaurant, or you can eat at one of the North Beach eateries such as **La Felce,** 1570 Stockton St., at Union (☎ 415-392-8321), where antipasti, pasta, and roast meats satisfy diverse tastes.

✔ **For families with kids of varied ages:** Yerba Buena Gardens (see Chapter 11) is a godsend. Teens are usually more than happy to hang out in **Metreon's Airtight Garage** and at **Zeum,** while younger siblings can ride the merry-go-round and then run around the gardens. Skating or bowling works for everyone, and there is plenty of food to be had within walking distance. For a step above the center's offerings, **Pazzia** (see Chapter 10) is an excellent choice for dinner.

San Francisco for Foodies

You could come here and spend a week honing your talents in the kitchen at **Tante Marie's Cooking School** (☎ 415-788-6699; www.tante marie.com) and that would certainly qualify you as a foodie. Or you could imitate my friend Bev, who flies up from Los Angeles on a regular basis to raid **North Beach** for supplies and then orders huge meals at the restaurant of the moment. Because the cooking classes run from 10 a.m. to 4 p.m. and 6 to 10 p.m., let's make like Bev for a day instead.

Wake up and smell the cappuccino and a raisin roll at a local favorite, **Caffe Greco,** 423 Columbus Ave., in North Beach (☎ 415-397-6261). While you sip, make a mental note of how much room you have in your suitcase for imported Italian delicacies, then walk a block to **Molinari's** delicatessen on the corner of Columbus and Vallejo Street (☎ 415-421-2337). If you have some way of refrigerating fresh sausages and cheese, you can take better advantage of the selection here — otherwise, consider ordering a sandwich to go for later. Drop by **Liguria** (see Chapter 10) for a sheet of pizza focaccia, which will make you the envy of your fellow airplane passengers on the ride home. If you need a new pizza stone, go to **A. Cavalli & Co.,** 1441 Stockton St., which also sells Italian cards and maps, as well as cooking utensils.

Don't miss immersing yourself in San Francisco's cultural diversity by eating as much dim sum as possible and stocking up on the wealth of ingredients available in its ethnic enclaves. Bev's favorite, **Mayflower** in the Richmond District, 6255 Geary Blvd. (☎ 415-387-8338), makes fine dumplings and won't be mobbed like the dim sum places in Chinatown (few tourists venture this far out on Geary Boulevard). After lunch, walk or take a bus north down Clement Street, 1 block west of Geary, and stop by **Green Apple Books,** 506 Clement St., to peruse a sizable selection of used cookbooks. You can find many produce, fish, and meat markets along Clement, as well as housewares stores; **May Wah,** 547 Clement St., is worth a look, as is **Kamei,** 606 Clement St. If you're serious about eating, you'll probably be ready for a snack or at least coffee by this time. Bev fights for parking on Valencia Street in order to down an espresso at **Ritual Coffee** while musing over taquerias. Fortunately, **Pancho Villa** (see Chapter 10) tosses together a steak and prawn quesadilla that is unparalleled for quality and price. Because you'll find it in the Mission District, you'll also want to visit **La Palma,** 2884 24th St., at Florida (☎ 415-647-1500), for fresh tortillas, dried chiles, and other essentials for cooking Mexican food. Make your way to Civic Center on the F-Market and stop at **Yum,** 1750 Market St. (☎ 415-626-9866), for more additions to your pantry. You'll find a glorious selection of spices, and Blanxart chocolate from Catalonia (the best). Finally, head south of Market to the **Wine House** at 535 Bryant St., between Third and Fourth streets, where the staff is very knowledgeable. For dinner, consider a new leading destination such as **Range** (see Chapter 10) or a high-end experience such as **Gary Danko** (see Chapter 10). If you have another day, or you're ready for more, see Chapter 14 for additional dining destinations.

Chapter 14

Going Above and Beyond San Francisco: Three Day Trips

. . . .

In This Chapter

▶ Crossing the bridge to Berkeley

▶ Shining a light at Point Reyes

▶ Drinking in the Wine Country

. . . .

*I*f you have the time to spare, or want to break up your trip with a glimpse of the rest of Northern California, here are three fabulous day trips that will show you some of the region around San Francisco.

Day Trip #1: Berkeley

As you approach Berkeley, a mere 20 minutes over the Bay Bridge, you'll know you aren't in San Francisco anymore. The weather is an immediate giveaway — although the temperature isn't dramatically different, San Francisco's ever-present summer fog disappears. Berkeley is also smaller, and much of its cultural life revolves around the University of California at Berkeley (UCB) campus. One thing both cities have in common is a devotion to fine dining. In fact, one excellent reason to visit Berkeley is to eat a great meal.

Getting there

You can use BART to reach Berkeley, but taking a car is better. Most people drive over the Bay Bridge and follow the signs to Highway 80. The exits include Ashby Avenue, University, and Gilman. If you intend to begin your day on Fourth Street (see "Shopping delights" later in this chapter), take the University Avenue exit. If the University is your first stop, an alternate route is Highway 24, exiting on scenic Claremont Avenue. Claremont intersects College Avenue, which leads directly to the campus while avoiding the less handsome flatlands of Berkeley.

Berkeley

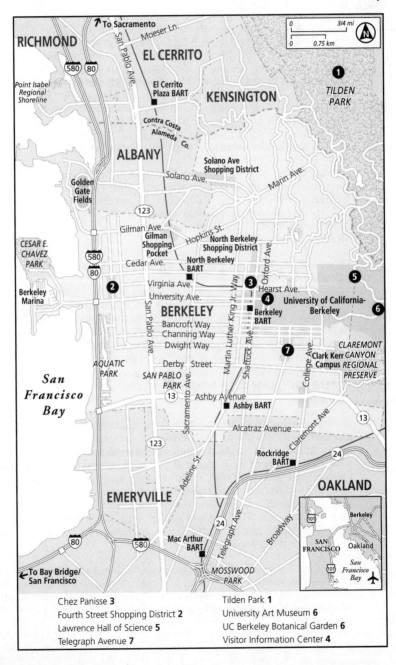

RICHMOND

To Sacramento

Moeser Ln.

EL CERRITO

580 80

San Pablo Ave.

Point Isabel
Regional
Shoreline

El Cerrito
Plaza BART

KENSINGTON

TILDEN
PARK

①

Contra Costa
Alameda Co.

ALBANY

Solano Ave
Shopping District

Solano Ave.

Marin Ave.

Golden
Gate
Fields

123

Gilman Ave.

Gilman
Shopping
Pocket

Hopkins St.

North Berkeley
Shopping District

CESAR E.
CHAVEZ
PARK

580

80

Cedar Ave.

North Berkeley
BART

Oxford Ave.

⑤

Berkeley
Marina

②

Virginia Ave.

University Ave.

③

Hearst Ave.

④

University of California-
Berkeley

⑥

BERKELEY

Bancroft Way
Channing Way
Dwight Way

Martin Luther King Jr. Way

Berkeley
BART

Shattuck Ave.

CLAREMONT
CANYON
REGIONAL
PRESERVE

Clark Kerr
Campus

⑦

College Ave.

San
Francisco
Bay

AQUATIC
PARK

San Pablo Ave.

Derby Street

SAN PABLO
PARK

13

Ashby Avenue

Ashby BART

Sacramento Ave.

Alcatraz Avenue

13

123

Adeline St.

Rockridge
BART

Claremont Ave.

24

EMERYVILLE

OAKLAND

24

Mac Arthur
BART

Telegraph Ave.

Broadway

101

Berkeley

SAN
FRANCISCO

Oakland

80

580

MOSSWOOD
PARK

San
Francisco
Bay

101

To Bay Bridge/
San Francisco

0   3/4 mi
0   0.75 km

Chez Panisse **3**
Fourth Street Shopping District **2**
Lawrence Hall of Science **5**
Telegraph Avenue **7**

Tilden Park **1**
University Art Museum **6**
UC Berkeley Botanical Garden **6**
Visitor Information Center **4**

If you visit on a Thursday, you get free admission to UCB museums and the botanical garden.

Seeing the sights

To my mind, an ideal day in Berkeley revolves around lunch or dinner at **Chez Panisse** (see "Dining locally" later in this chapter). The food is as close to perfect as food gets. If your reservation is for dinner, you can easily spend your time shopping on **Fourth Street** (see "Shopping delights" later in this chapter), walking around **Tilden Park,** and seeing what's up at the UCB campus. If you've made lunch reservations, tour UCB in the morning and hike in Tilden Park or check out the merchandise on **Telegraph Avenue** or Fourth Street in the afternoon.

The attractive, active campus of **University of California at Berkeley** is the biggest sight in Berkeley, so to speak. The **Visitor Information Center** is at 101 University Hall, 2200 University Ave., at Oxford Street (☎ **510-642-5215**). You can join a free 10 a.m. campus tour there Monday through Friday. Weekend tours leave from the Campanile at 10 a.m. Saturdays and 1 p.m. Sundays.

Other notable UCB stops include the **Hearst Museum of Anthropology** (☎ **510-642-6271;** www.hearstmuseum.berkeley.edu; open: Wed–Sat 10 a.m.–4:30 p.m., Sun noon–4 p.m.; admission: $4 adults, $3 seniors, $1 students with student ID, free Thurs), the **Berkeley Art Museum** at 2621 Durant Ave. and 2626 Bancroft Way (☎ **510-642-0808;** www.bampfa.berkeley.edu; open: Wed–Sun 11 a.m.–5 p.m.; admission: $8 adults, $5 seniors, students and children, free Thurs), and the 307-foot-tall **Sather Tower** (also known as the Campanile) in the center of campus, where you can take an elevator to the top for excellent views of Berkeley and the bay (open: daily; admission: $2 adults, $1 seniors, free for kids under 18).

Above the campus in the lush hills is the **UC Berkeley Botanical Garden,** 200 Centennial Dr. (☎ **510-643-2755;** www.botanicalgarden.berkeley.edu; admission: $3 adults, $3 seniors 65 and older, $1 kids 3–18, free Thurs). It features 13,000 plants, including cactus and rose gardens. It's a good place for an easy hike. Open daily 9 a.m.– 5 p.m. Farther up the road, the kid-friendly **Lawrence Hall of Science** (☎ **510-642-5132;** www.lawrencehallofscience.org; open: daily 10 a.m.– 5 p.m.; admission: $9.50 adults, $7.50 seniors and students, $5.50 kids ages 3–4) brings science up close and personal. This is an excellent hands-on museum that has activities for kids from 3 to 12.

The campus is bounded by shops, cafes, and well-stocked bookstores. To get a sense of Berkeley street life, walk along **Telegraph Avenue** from Bancroft to Ashby, and get your fill of cappuccino, street vendors, psychic readers, and the occasional weirdo.

Shopping delights

Close to the University exit off I-80 is **Fourth Street,** a mecca for shoppers from all over the Bay Area. It started out small, with a few outlet stores and a popular diner, but over the years it developed into a full-fledged destination for fashion, food, and home décor. Begin by oohing over the gorgeous accessories for home and garden at **The Gardener,** 1836 Fourth St. (☎ 510-548-4545; www.thegardener.com; open: Mon–Sat 10 a.m.–6 p.m., Sun 11 a.m.–6 p.m.), and keep heading on down the block.

Dining locally

Each of these restaurants is a great place to dine while you're in Berkeley, and Chez Panisse is definitely a "destination" eatery.

Bette's Oceanview Diner
$ AMERICAN

You can sit down here for a homey breakfast or lunch featuring tender baked goods, tasty salads, and Bette's famous pancakes. Expect crowds and a long wait on the weekends. Next door, Bette's sells takeout sandwiches, salads, and desserts, to take care of impatient hungry people.

1807 Fourth St., Berkeley. ☎ *510-644-3230. No reservations. Main courses: $6.50–$11. MC, V. Open: Mon–Fri 6:30 a.m.–2:30 p.m., Sat–Sun 6:30 a.m.–4 p.m.*

Cafe Rouge
$–$$ MEDITERRANEAN

Those living in the Fourth Street neighborhood don't have many reasons to stray. Everything you need is nearby, including a lovely meal in this French-style bistro opened by a kitchen alumnus of Chez Panisse. Meat eaters will be charmed by the menu (go admire the butcher counter in the back), while mollusk fans can turn to the oysters. Desserts shine as well.

1782 Fourth St., Berkeley. ☎ *510-525-1440.* www.caferouge.net. *Reservations advised. Main courses: $15–$32. MC, V. Open: Monday is lunch only. Tues–Sun 11:30 a.m.–9:30 p.m., Fri–Sat 11:30 a.m.–10:30 p.m.*

Chez Panisse and Chez Panisse Café
$$$–$$$$ CALIFORNIA/FRENCH

Alice Waters, the owner of Chez Panisse, is an icon in the food world, respected for adhering to her vision of food as a gift we give daily to our loved ones (including you) and for serving beautifully constructed dishes. Eating here in the cafe or restaurant is one of the nicer things you'll do for yourself. Dinner downstairs is $45 to $75 prix fixe, depending on the night. The cafe is moderately priced, comparatively speaking, but expect to spend a lot more than you think prudent for lunch. It's worth it.

1517 Shattuck Ave., Berkeley. ☎ *510-548-5525.* www.chezpanisse.com. *Advance reservations a must for dinner in the restaurant; recommended for dinner in the cafe. Main courses: $50–$85 prix fixe downstairs; $17–$25 in the cafe. AMEX, DISC, MC, V. Open: Restaurant Mon–Sat first seating begins 6–6:30 p.m. and second seating 8:30–9:30p.m.; cafe Mon–Thurs 11:30 a.m.–3 p.m. and 5–10:30 p.m., Fri–Sat 11:30 a.m.–3:30 p.m. and 5–11:30 p.m.*

Day Trip #2: Point Reyes and Inverness

A scenic one-hour drive through the small towns of Marin County and Samuel P. Taylor State Park leads you to **Point Reyes National Seashore,** a mix of wild coastline and forest of unequivocal appeal to hikers, nature lovers, and wildlife-watchers. The rocky shore along this part of the coast is a direct result of earthquake activity — you can even get a close-up look at the San Andreas Fault. **Point Reyes Station,** the minuscule town nearby, is a bit of a tourist magnet on the weekends, so you can find a selection of excellent restaurants and interesting shops within its 4-block radius. **Inverness,** a tiny community on Tomales Bay, a few miles farther north, has a handful of picturesque inns and B&Bs. For more information, log onto www.pointreyes.net, which has links to other Web sites of interest.

Deciding when to visit

When planning your trip, remember the **Point Reyes Lighthouse** is closed Tuesdays and Wednesdays. If you can come later in the week (avoiding the crowded weekends), you'll be treated to relatively empty roads, even during the summer. The best times to view seasonal flora and fauna in the **Point Reyes National Seashore** area are as follows:

- ✔ **Wildflowers:** February through July

- ✔ **Elephant seals:** November through March

- ✔ **Harbor seals:** Mid-March through mid-June

- ✔ **Gray whales:** January through March

And another word of advice: Bring warm clothes. The weather in Point Reyes is often cold and sometimes foggy in the summer.

Getting to the Point

To reach Point Reyes, cross the Golden Gate Bridge and exit on San Anselmo/Sir Francis Drake Boulevard. Then turn left, heading west on Sir Francis Drake, and stay on this road as it passes through the high-priced burgs of San Anselmo, Ross, Woodacre, and Lagunitas. It takes about an hour (with light traffic) to reach seashore headquarters.

Point Reyes National Seashore

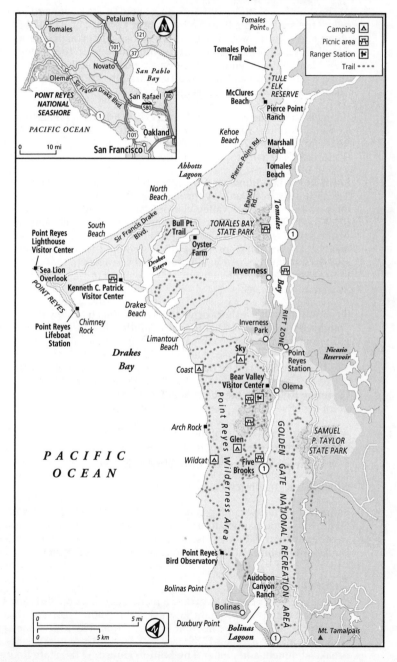

Seeing the sights

At the junction of Highway 1 and Sir Francis Drake Boulevard in Olema, follow the signs to the **Bear Valley Visitor Center** (☎ 415-464-5100), about one minute away. The Center has maps, informative park rangers, a book/gift section, and some interesting exhibits on the ecology of the area. Many trails begin here, including an under-1-mile earthquake trail along the San Andreas Fault. Another park attraction is **Kule Loklo,** a Coast Miwok Native Indian village replica.

Hiking is the prime activity in the park, but a drive to **Limantour Beach** is another option. You get to the beach by turning left on Bear Valley Road and left again on Limantour Road. Swimming is not recommended (besides, it's usually too cold), but you can bird-watch and picnic here.

Point Reyes Lighthouse is a big attraction in these parts all year long but especially from January through March when migrating gray whales pass by. From the Bear Valley Visitor Center, the lighthouse is a 21-mile drive along Sir Francis Drake Boulevard past dairy farms and pastures. At the end of the road is a parking lot. The lighthouse is a half-mile walk away and down 300 steps. The cliffs all around this area are not stable enough to climb on, and you'll see lots of warnings to that effect. **Sea Lion Overlook** near the lighthouse is the place to watch those creatures as well as harbor seals.

From this stop, it's a short drive to **Drake's Beach** (follow the signs as you drive to or from the lighthouse). Another fine visitor center with park rangers is on the beach parking lot, next to a cafe specializing in fried foods. As is the case at all the area beaches, no lifeguard is on duty and the undertow can be dangerous, so swimming is not encouraged. At the end of Drake's Beach, past the Point Reyes Lifeboat Station, is **Chimney Rock.** The **Elephant Seal Overlook** nearby is a good vantage point for observing elephant seals in the winter months.

At the northernmost tip of the seashore at **Tomales Point** is the **Tule Elk Reserve,** where over 500 of these once-nearly-extinct creatures live on 2,600 protected acres. The reserve is a 30-minute drive from Inverness. Stay on Sir Francis Drake Boulevard until you reach Pierce Point Road, which takes you directly into the reserve.

Some wonderful swimming beaches are located along Tomales Bay in Inverness. If you happen to be making this trip in August in warmer weather, with or without kids, look for signs along Sir Francis Drake Boulevard leading to **Chicken Ranch Beach** or **Shell Beach.**

Dining locally

If you're hungry or want to gather a picnic, continue on Sir Francis Drake Boulevard until it meets Point Reyes–Petaluma Road. Drive across the little bridge and you'll be in Point Reyes Station. The **Pine Cone Diner,** 60 Fourth St. (☎ 415-663-1536; www.pineconediner.com), is open for breakfast, lunch, and dinner. **The Station House,** 11180 State Route 1

(☎ **415-663-1515;** www.stationhousecafe.com), is also popular and moderately priced (and there's live music on Fri and Sat nights). The kitchen uses lots of locally produced foods. For takeout, **Tomales Bay Foods,** 80 Fourth St. (☎ **415-663-9335**), has a small but fantastic menu of salads and sandwiches to go. It shares a building with Cow Girl creamery and a shop with lovely hand-woven clothing.

Spending the night

If you want to turn your day trip into an overnight, here's a good choice for accommodation. For more inn or B&B choices, contact **Point Reyes Lodging** (☎ **800-539-1872;** www.ptreyes.com).

Manka's Inverness Lodge
$$$–$$$$ **Inverness**

Inverness consists of a few stores and restaurants, private homes, and some inns. At the high end is Manka's, a handsomely rustic, romantic 80-year-old former hunting and fishing lodge that looks as if Ralph Lauren would feel at home there. Rooms contain fireplaces, comfy beds, privacy, and that woodsy feeling Red Riding Hood's grandmother must have known and loved. Manka's is also renowned for its $58 to $88 gourmet prix-fixe dinners served Thursday through Monday — it's by far the best place in town to eat.

Argyle Road, Inverness. ☎ **415-669-1034.** www.mankas.com. *Look for the sign pointing to Argyle Road, off Sir Francis Drake Boulevard. Rack rates: $215–$615 double; two-night minimum on weekends. Call months ahead for reservations. MC, V.*

Day Trip #3: The Wine Country

About an hour's drive north of San Francisco is the gorgeous Napa Valley, America's most celebrated wine-producing region. Less than 30 miles from end to end, this fertile area brims with world-class wine-tasting rooms, excellent restaurants, and marvelous resorts and inns.

Just to the west of Napa Valley along Highway 12 is the peaceful Sonoma Valley. Sonoma Valley is quieter and somewhat less tourist-oriented — but equal to its neighbor as a grape-lover's paradise. Although both valleys are vacation destinations, many visitors arrive for a day of wine tasting and then turn around and head back to San Francisco. That's not the ideal way to get the most out of this bucolic piece of earth. If at all possible, stay a few days to relax and renew before heading back to tackle the big city.

Planning a visit to the Wine Country

Earlier in this book, I warn you against renting a car during your stay in San Francisco. In this section, I recant — for your Wine Country trip,

The Wine Country

anyway — because the best way to tour Napa Valley or Sonoma Valley is by car. If you don't want to drive, you can join an organized tour. But if you want to spend a night or two in Sonoma or in one of the towns near Napa, or if you want to visit smaller, less commercial wineries than those the tour companies choose, you'll need to drive yourself.

Getting to the Wine Country

You can take one of two roads to get there. The faster, less scenic route is across the San Francisco–Oakland Bay Bridge (I-80). The more scenic path crosses the Golden Gate Bridge and meanders up through Marin County on U.S. 101. For the return trip, from Napa, I highly recommend taking I-80 rather than U.S. 101 over the Golden Gate Bridge, especially if you're traveling on a weekend. But to get back from Sonoma, use the Golden Gate Bridge.

If you decide to go the Bay Bridge route to Napa, drive east over the bridge (I-80) and then north to the Napa/Highway 29 exit near Vallejo.

Highway 29 is the main road through the Napa Valley. The trip takes approximately 70 minutes.

If you decide to go over the Golden Gate Bridge, continue on U.S. 101 north to Novato, where you need to pick up Highway 37 east. Then, if you're interested in a pleasant drive and aren't in a big hurry, take Highway 121 (the Sonoma Highway) north toward Sonoma and then east to Napa, if that's your destination, where you'll end up on Highway 29. If Sonoma is your destination, take Highway 12. Make sure to have a map handy. This drive takes about 90 minutes.

Contact the **Napa Valley Conference & Visitors Bureau,** 1310 Napa Town Center, Napa, CA 94559 (☎ **707-226-7459;** www.napavalley.com), for maps to help get you on your way.

Picking the best time to visit

The most popular seasons for touring Napa and Sonoma valleys are summer and fall. The summers are hot in Wine Country, which is one reason why it's a favorite with fog-bound San Franciscans. September and October are extremely busy due to the *crush,* or grape harvest, when the sweet aroma of *must* (crushed grapes) fills the air.

Wine Country is delightful any time of year. In the winter, restaurants aren't jammed and traffic is light. Spring is beautiful and still relatively uncrowded. However, if the forecast calls for rain, I recommend you save this trip for another time. If you do plan to visit Wine Country during summer or autumn, make lodging reservations early.

You'll meet with a lot more traffic and tourists on the weekends than on the weekdays. Also, Golden Gate Bridge traffic heading north on Friday afternoons and south on Sunday afternoons is amazing, and I don't mean that in a positive way. Let the guys with their weekend plans sit and stew on 101. Go while everyone else is at work.

Looking out for your safety

Although you may taste wines all along the 35-mile route through Napa and on the scenic roads through Sonoma, the rules of drinking and driving (and common sense) still apply. All those sips add up more quickly than you think. Every tasting room has containers for spitting out the wine so you can taste without actually letting it go to your head.

 Highway 29 is dangerous, even if you're not drinking. This two-lane thoroughfare through Napa Valley has been the scene of many accidents, especially at night.

Taking an escorted Wine Country tour

A good option if you don't feel comfortable driving, or if you're on a tight schedule, is a one-day Wine Country tour to the Napa and Sonoma valleys offered by San Francisco companies. On these six- to nine-hour tours, you can usually visit two to three wineries and have lunch in one of the picturesque villages along the way. The downside of a tour like this is that you won't see some of the great wineries that aren't part of the tour itinerary, you won't have time to relax in places that catch your eye, and you may not be able to choose where you want to eat.

But if you're interested in the escorted tours, you have two main options: a tour that starts in San Francisco or a tour that starts in the Wine Country. Here are a few good tours that leave from San Francisco:

- ✔ **Great Pacific Tour Company** (☎ 415-626-4499; www.greatpacific tour.com) picks you up at your San Francisco hotel and delivers you back after tastings at two Sonoma wineries, a picnic lunch, and a tour of Domaine Chandon, a sparkling wine producer in Napa. The cost, including lunch, is $83 for adults, $81 for seniors, and $71 for children 5 to 11.

- ✔ **California Wine Tours** (☎ 800-294-6386; www.californiawine tours.com) offers several Wine Country outings from Napa and Sonoma, and one originating in San Francisco. Customers take the 8:55 a.m. ferry to Vallejo where they are met by limo for a six-hour excursion that includes five very diverse wineries, including V. Sattuoi where you can picnic. The price is $72 per person, which includes round-trip tickets on the ferry.

- ✔ **Tower Tours** (☎ 866-345-8687; www.towertours.net) takes you to Napa and Sonoma valleys for the day, with stops at three wineries and lunch in Yountville or the town of Sonoma with a little time to shop. The charge is $59 for adults and $39 for children. Save $5 by booking online.

And here are some of the best tours originating in the Wine Country:

- ✔ **Wine Country Jeep Tours** (☎ 800-539-5337; www.jeeptours.com) will plan a custom three- to four-hour winery tour that can include some off-road trailblazing and a picnic lunch. The cost is $75 per person and another $25 each for each additional hour.

- ✔ **Napa Winery Shuttle** (☎ 707-257-1950; www.wineshuttle.com), a small family-run enterprise, gets my vote for value and flexibility. You and your shuttle driver plan the itinerary, although the company does have some favorite wineries it likes to show off. The price is $52 per person for the day — approximately 10 a.m. to 4 or 5 p.m.

- ✔ The **Napa Valley Wine Train** (☎ 800-427-4124 or 707-253-2111; www.winetrain.com), like a gourmet restaurant on wheels, choo-choos 36 miles through the valley, from the town of Napa to the village of St. Helena and back. You can get a lunch, Sunday brunch, or dinner tour starting in price from $89. These tours primarily involve dining and admiring the gorgeous scenery. Two trips that include stops at a winery are the Grgich Hills Private Winery Tour and Tasting, a luncheon ride that costs $110 per person, and the

Domaine Chandon Winery excursion at $115 per person. Onboard the train is a wine-tasting car with an attractive bar and knowledgeable host. The three-hour tours depart from the train station in downtown Napa, at 1275 McKinstry St. You must make reservations for the train. If you don't want to drive to Napa, for $145, **Grayline** (☎ **888-428-6937** or 415-558-9400; www.graylinesanfrancisco. com) will bus you to and from your hotel to the wine train station in Napa for the excursion.

Mapping out your winery journey

A single day in Wine Country can't do the area justice and will leave you wanting more. But if that's all the time you have, plan to visit no more than three to four wineries, one before lunch and two or three after, followed by a late-afternoon snack or an early dinner.

If you spend two days and a night, you'll have the chance to do some other enjoyable activities such as checking out **Copia** (see "Napa excursions" later in this chapter), biking down a sleepy road, or taking a spa treatment. You could also cut down on your winery visits the first day and take advantage of whatever your inn has to offer, such as a swimming pool, a garden walk, or just some peace and quiet. On your second day, have a substantial breakfast and consider one of the 11 a.m. reservation-only winery tours, such as the one offered by **Benziger.** To occupy any extra time you may have left in your schedule, there's always **outlet shopping** in Napa and along Highway 29 past St. Helena.

Creating a wine-tasting itinerary isn't easy, because there are so many vineyards to choose from. The wineries suggested in this chapter are great for first-time tasters, because they make a special effort to accommodate visitors. These vineyards offer tours, exhibits, and/or an extra-friendly staff. But there are plenty more vineyards to choose from, so get a map of the area and, time permitting, explore those back roads.

Touring the wineries on your own

For wine-tasting newbies, the first winery you visit should be one that offers an in-depth tour, so you can familiarize yourself with the winemaking process. If you're traveling from north to south, **Sterling Vineyards** in Calistoga is a good bet, as is **Robert Mondavi** in Oakville. In Sonoma, the tram operators at **Benziger** are both knowledgeable and accessible.

If you're already somewhat of a connoisseur, ask your local wine merchant for suggestions on smaller wineries that you may enjoy.

The Napa Valley is home to more than 380 wineries (Sonoma has around 250), some owned by corporations and others by individuals so seduced by the grape that they abandoned successful careers to devote themselves to *viticulture* (the cultivation of grapes). Although there's no correlation between the size of a winery and the quality of the product — which has more to do with the talents of the *vintners* (winemakers) and

Becoming a wine connoisseur: The basics

Cabernet sauvignon, pinot noir, and zinfandel grapes (grown for red wines), and chardonnay and sauvignon or fumé blanc grapes (grown for white wines), are the most prominent grape varieties produced in the area. Telling the difference between them takes a great deal of knowledge. Each one of these varieties contains identifiable flavors and aromas you can only begin to recognize through careful sipping.

Reading the label on the bottle is the best way to tell the difference between cabernet and pinot. The label identifies the type of grape used if the wine contains at least 75 percent of that variety, among other bits of information. The appellation of origin indicates where the grapes were grown. The label may state that the grapes were grown in either a viticulture area, such as the Carneros region of the Napa Valley, in a certain county, or just in the state itself. Check the vintage date as well, which explains when at least 95 percent of the grapes were crushed. Also make a note of the vintage date, because many wines taste better aged, and some years produce better grapes than others.

variables such as weather and soil conditions — the bigger wineries offer more to visitors in terms of education and entertainment.

You can greatly enhance your knowledge of wine by tasting correctly — and what better classroom than a French-style chateau smack in the middle of a vineyard? Remember that wine appreciation begins by analyzing color, followed by aroma, then taste. You do this with your eyes first, then your nose, then your mouth. Don't be shy about asking questions of the person pouring — he'll cheerfully explain all, because the more you discover about the product, the more likely you are to become a steady customer. And that makes everybody happy!

You won't be able to get a deal on wine that you purchase directly from the wineries. They sell their wines at the full retail price so as not to undercut their primary market, the wine merchants. If you can't get a particular vintage at home, most wineries may be able to mail-order it for you (depending on the laws in your home state).

Wineries in Napa Valley

Wineries in Napa (less so in Sonoma) are developing new ways to market wine tasting as an educational/culinary event — and an expensive one at that. In what I think is an effort to eradicate the notion that this is a great way to cage free alcohol, most wineries charge at least a nominal tasting fee and many are promoting sit-down food and wine pairings for real money. Rubicon Estate (formerly Niebaum-Coppola) is a case in point; you can't even drive onto the property without paying $25 at the gate per adult, just so they know you *really, really* want to be there (the fee covers a tour and five tastes). Wine tasting has become very serious business in these parts.

Napa Valley

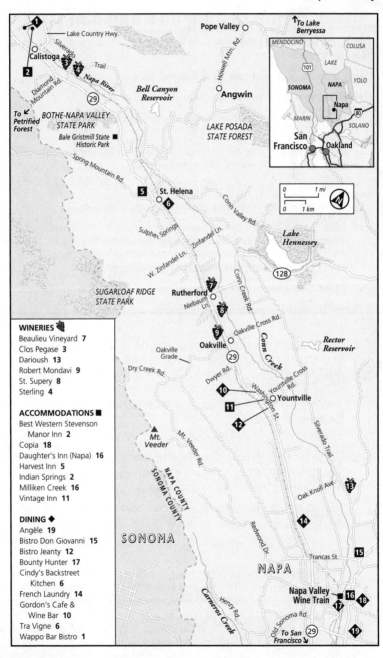

WINERIES
Beaulieu Vineyard **7**
Clos Pegase **3**
Darioush **13**
Robert Mondavi **9**
St. Supery **8**
Sterling **4**

ACCOMMODATIONS
Best Western Stevenson
  Manor Inn **2**
Copia **18**
Daughter's Inn (Napa) **16**
Harvest Inn **5**
Indian Springs **2**
Milliken Creek **16**
Vintage Inn **11**

DINING ◆
Angèle **19**
Bistro Don Giovanni **15**
Bistro Jeanty **12**
Bounty Hunter **17**
Cindy's Backstreet
  Kitchen **6**
French Laundry **14**
Gordon's Cafe &
  Wine Bar **10**
Tra Vigne **6**
Wappo Bar Bistro **1**

Wine tasting do's and don'ts

When you taste wines, keep in mind the following suggestions and you'll fit right in — even if it's your first time:

✓ **Before the pour, sniff your glass.** It should have a clean aroma.

✓ **Do not pour the wine yourself.** Winery staff will pour it for you.

✓ **Taste wines in the appropriate order.** Whites first, reds second, and dessert wines last.

✓ **Swirl the wine to coat the inside of the glass.** Swirling introduces more oxygen and helps open up the wine flavors and aromas.

✓ **Smell the wine.** Notice the different aromas — spice, fruit, flowers.

✓ **Take a sip and cover the back of your tongue with the wine.**

✓ **Taste, then spit.** Wine tasting is one of the few sports where spitting is not only allowed, it's encouraged. (Just make sure you hit your target, a bucket, or some other container available for this purpose.) Tasting, then spitting, is also a nifty way to sample many wines without becoming cloudy-headed.

✓ **Do not bring a bottle of wine from one winery into another.**

Start in Calistoga and work your way down the valley along Highway 29 to make your return to San Francisco a bit shorter. But don't take this drive on a summer weekend. The bumper-to-bumper traffic on Highway 29 will ruin your day.

Beaulieu Vineyard

At this well-regarded, hospitable establishment, the vintners pass out glasses of sauvignon blanc as you walk in, to get you in the right mood. After you've enjoyed a glass, you can take a free half-hour tour of the production facility, open daily from 11 a.m. to 4 p.m. Each tasting thereafter is $5, or $25 for five delicious reserve vintages.

1960 St. Helena Hwy. (Highway 29), Rutherford, CA 94573. ☎ *800-264-6918 or 707-967-5230.* www.bvwines.com. *Open: Daily 10 a.m.–5 p.m.*

Clos Pegase

The official tour takes only about 30 minutes and is offered at 11 a.m. and 2 p.m. You can spend the rest of your time at this winery joyfully studying the art collection, walking around the sculpture garden, or picnicking on the vast lawn. You need to reserve a picnic table, but reservations aren't required for the complimentary tour. Wine tasting is $2.50 for current releases and $2 each for reserve wines.

1060 Dunaweal Lane (between Highway 29 and the Silverado Trail), Calistoga, CA 94515. ☎ **800-726-6136** or 707-942-4981. www.clospegase.com. Open: Daily 10:30 a.m.–5 p.m.

Darioush

A Persian palace (think Persepolis) in Napa? No, you haven't had one too many, you've found Darioush. This eye-catching — to say the least — building, clad in travertine stone mined in Iran, opened in 2004; the winery itself has been producing since 1997. Tastings are offered of course ($15 for a flight of four wines), but tours must be arranged in advance and I'd make the call if only to drool over Darioush Khaledi's private wine cellar. If it's available, try the 2004 signature Chardonnay, which has an amazing pearish, creamy consistency from start to finish. Saturdays through Thursday a wine and cheese tasting is offered ($35) and every Friday is a cheese intensive featuring Cowgirl Creamery's best ($65). A tip from one of the staff is to try and avoid visiting on a Saturday in the summer. The valley is lots calmer during the week.

4240 Silverado Trail, Napa, CA 94558. ☎ **707-257-2345.** www.darioush.com. Open: Daily 10:30 a.m.–5 p.m.

Robert Mondavi

Mondavi was the first winery to conduct public tastings, and it continues to take pride in educating people about wine. A menu of tours is offered, from the daily 75-minute To Kalon tour at $25 a pop (☎ **888-RMONDAVI,** ext. 82001, for same-day reservations) to a $100 Harvest of Joy tour that includes a three-course lunch. For fees ranging from $50 to $110, you can benefit from seminars on grape growing, essence tasting, and wine and food pairing. Reservations are required for tours and seminars. During July and August, you can catch a Saturday evening concert. The shows sell out quickly, so call ☎ **888-769-5299** or visit Mondavi's Web site for a schedule and tickets.

7801 St. Helena Hwy. (Highway 29), P.O. Box 106, Oakville, CA 94562. ☎ **800-RMONDAVI** or 707-226-1395. www.robertmondavi.com. Open: Daily 10 a.m.–5 p.m.

St. Supery

Find out about aromas common to certain varietals with the self-guided interactive tour featuring "SmellaVision." You'll also hear about growing techniques at the winery's demonstration vineyard. Have $10 on hand for the tasting fee. On the weekends, you can get a half glass of the really good stuff in the Divine Wine room (the reserve tasting room) for $15. A Winemaker's tour and tasting is now offered for $45 per person at 1 p.m. Monday through Thursday. Tickets can be purchased online.

8440 St. Helena Hwy. (Highway 29), Rutherford, CA 94573. ☎ **800-942-0809.** www.stsupery.com. Open: Daily 10 a.m.–5 p.m.

Sterling

Arrive at this hilltop winery by aerial tram and swoon over the spectacular vista. Wine tasting is included in the ticket price of $15 ($20 weekends and holidays; $10 for under 21s). After you reach the winery, take the self-guided tour that leads you through the entire operation and into the tasting room, where the friendly staff serves you wine at tables rather than at a bar. For grander palates, a $45 reserve tasting and guided tour is offered at 11 a.m. daily. Plan on spending at least one hour here.

1111 Dunaweal Lane (½ mile east of Highway 29), P.O. Box 365, Calistoga, CA 94515. ☎ *800-726-6136 or 707-942-3349.* www.sterlingvineyards.com. *Open: Daily 10:30 a.m.–4:30 p.m.*

Wineries in Sonoma Valley

The Sonoma Valley includes the towns of Sonoma, Glen Ellen, and Kenwood and is frequented a bit less than the Napa Valley because of its smaller size. Day-trippers may enjoy the relaxed, more intimate atmosphere of Sonoma Valley. You can drive here in just over an hour, tour a few wineries, shop, have a great meal, and be back in the city — traffic willing — in time for dinner. You may choose to spend the night, in which case you can find many B&Bs and hotels, plus a few resorts sprinkled around the country roads.

Enter the Sonoma Valley by Highway 121; then turn north on Highway 12. This path takes you directly into the charming town of Sonoma. (If you want to go directly to Glen Ellen, take Highway 116 instead.)

This tour includes stops at some smaller wineries that are too delicious to miss; all provide a little wine education and tastings. You'll see country roads bedecked by acres of grapes, old oaks, and flowers. And although the destinations are noteworthy, the drive alone is splendid.

Arrowood

Arrowood is an intimate, high-end, and somewhat exclusive winery with a small production but national distribution. You need to make an appointment for daily tours of 40 to 90 minutes in duration at fees from $20 to $30. Call a day or two in advance. If you don't care for a tour, you can still sit on the verandah overlooking grapevines and mountains and try some great wines. There is a $3 tasting fee.

14347 Sonoma Hwy., Glen Ellen, CA 95442. ☎ *800-938-5170 or 707-938-5170.* www.arrowoodvineyards.com. *Open: Daily 10 a.m.–4:30 p.m.*

Benziger

Tractor-pulled trams take visitors up the flower-lined path of this 85-acre ranch for a 45-minute tram tour ($10; reservations required). The winery, owned by the Benziger family since 1981, is situated near Jack London State Park. The tram operators explain how vines work, how insects are controlled, and how the sun and soil together affect the

Sonoma Valley

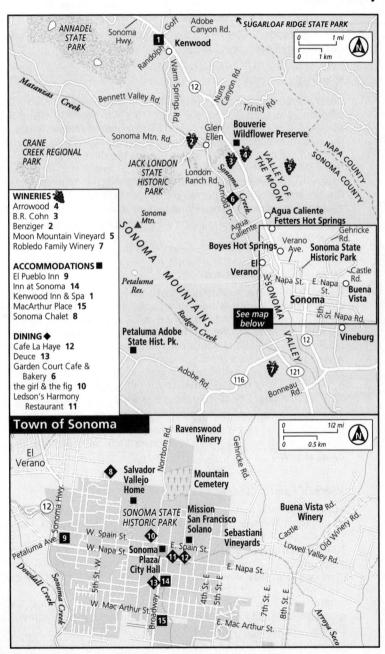

WINERIES
Arrowood **4**
B.R. Cohn **3**
Benziger **2**
Moon Mountain Vineyard **5**
Robledo Family Winery **7**

ACCOMMODATIONS ■
El Pueblo Inn **9**
Inn at Sonoma **14**
Kenwood Inn & Spa **1**
MacArthur Place **15**
Sonoma Chalet **8**

DINING ◆
Cafe La Haye **12**
Deuce **13**
Garden Court Cafe & Bakery **6**
the girl & the fig **10**
Ledson's Harmony Restaurant **11**

Town of Sonoma

taste of the wine. You can choose from two tasting opportunities, one of which is complimentary; the other which costs $10 for the reserve wines.

1883 London Ranch Rd., Glen Ellen, CA 95442. ☎ **888-490-2739.** www.benziger. com. *Take Highway 12 to Arnold Drive and turn left on London Ranch Road. Open: Daily 10 a.m.–5 p.m.*

B.R. Cohn

Cohn's remodeled tasting room, gift shop, and new picnic area flanked by olive trees are just down the road from Arrowood. Tasting fees are a modest $5 for current releases and $10 for limited release wines, including the signature 2002 Olive Hill Estate Cabernet. Along with the wines, some of which are only available at the winery, the olive oil produced here is of the highest quality and makes a great gift. Friendly staff members who are happy to talk wine and olives preside over the relaxed tasting room. Doobie Brothers music plays on the speakers and is available in the gift shop because owner Bruce Cohn is their manager.

15000 Sonoma Hwy., Glen Ellen, CA 95442. ☎ **800-330-4064.** www.brcohn.com. *Open: Daily 10 a.m.–5 p.m.*

Moon Mountain Vineyard

A long drive up the mountain rewards with stunning views and some delicious organic estate wines only available on-site. You must make an appointment to visit, but the phone call is well worth the effort. The tasting room is inside a turret, too intimate to accommodate the busloads that reach more accessible wineries. You'll have a chance to ask questions while touring the tank room and caves or tasting the Bordeaux-style offerings. Fellow tasters are likely to be serious wine students who have sought out what is one of the less ostentatious yet sophisticated wineries in either Napa or Sonoma. The tasting fee is just $10.

1700 Moon Mountain Rd., Sonoma, CA 95476. ☎ **707-996-5870.** www.moon mountainvineyard.com. *Take Highway 12 toward Glen Ellen. Moon Mountain Road is between Agua Caliente and Madrone roads. Open: Mon–Sat 10 a.m.–4 p.m. by appointment.*

Robledo Family Winery

The modest little tasting room here, comfortably furnished with handsome pieces from Michoacan, Mexico, epitomizes old-fashioned American success stories. Reynaldo Robledo, Senior, who arrived in the valley as a 16-year-old migrant worker, combined hard work and a gift for nurturing grape vines into ownership of three vineyards, a vineyard management company, and this winery. His children are actively involved in the business, and you'll meet at least one behind the bar, pouring tastes of their estate Sauvignon Blanc, Pinot Grigio, Pinot Noir, and Merlot. A small producer, the majority of the bottles are sold directly to consumers through their wine club or at the winery.

21901 Bonness Rd., Sonoma, CA 95479. ☎ ***707-939-6903.*** www.robledofamily winery.com. *Take Arnold Drive and turn on Hwy 116 toward Petaluma. Open: Mon–Sat 10 a.m.–5 p.m., Sun 11 a.m.–4 p.m.*

Taking advantage of other fun stuff in the valleys

Wine Country offers many other activities besides wine tasting. If you're staying overnight, be sure to check out the following sites, sports, and downright sumptuous pleasures in Napa and Sonoma.

Napa excursions

Copia: The American Center for Wine, Food, and the Arts, 500 First St., Napa (☎ **707-259-1600;** www.copia.org), opened in the fall of 2001 and has quickly become one of the must-see attractions in the valley. Copia celebrates the finer things in life in a modern museum-like setting, but it's neither solemn nor overly reverential. One permanent exhibit, an interactive presentation on the role of food and wine in American society, is accessible and amusing. In addition, there's a state-of-the-art theater for concerts, lectures, and films; a full roster of wine and food courses are offered year-round; and a 500-seat concert terrace overlooking the Napa River, surrounded by Copia's orchard and organic gardens, provides warm-weather amusement. A fine restaurant, Julia's Kitchen (open for lunch Wed–Mon and dinner Thurs–Sun), wine bar, and, of course, a gift shop round out the experience. Check the Web site for programming during your trip, and try to take in an exhibit, a class, a concert, or a meal — all four if time allows. Admission is $5 adults, $4 seniors and students, free for children 12 and under. It's open daily 10 a.m. to 5 p.m. except Tuesdays.

Art turns up in the most unexpected places, but none more so than the **di Rosa Preserve** (☎ **707-226-5991,** ext. 25; www.dirosapreserve.org). This is a 217-acre indoor/outdoor gallery located 6½ miles west of Napa on Highway 121, displaying over 2,000 works amid meadows, hanging from trees, and throughout the former winery. Rene di Rosa, a former journalist and viticulturist, owns the property. Guides conduct one-hour introductory and two-and-a-half-hour tours Tuesday through Saturday (reservations required); admission is $10 and $15.

Ride horseback through the countryside with the help of the **Sonoma Cattle Company and Napa Valley Trail Rides** (☎ **707-255-2900;** www. napasonomatrailrides.com). The one-person stable with just four, well-nurtured horses, offers two-hour rides on Thursdays and Sundays at 10 a.m. through Skyline Wilderness State Park, 2201 Imola Ave. off Highway 29. Rides, which include 30 minutes of instruction, are $90 and available for adults and kids 8 years old and up. Soaring over the vineyards under a colorful balloon, with just a few other souls sharing your basket, is a breathtaking experience. **Bonaventura Balloon Company** (☎ **800-FLY-NAPA** or 707-944-2822; www.bonaventuraballoons.com) is one of Napa's most trusted operators, with a range of packages from

$198 per person. Or call **Napa Valley Aloft/Adventures Aloft** (☎ 800-944-4408 or 707-944-4408; www.nvaloft.com), whose early-morning lift-off includes a preflight snack and a postflight brunch with bubbly. However, at $195 to $250 per person (depending on the number of persons and the extras you choose), you may decide to keep those feet on the ground.

If you want to join the many bicyclists you see pedaling Napa's scenic roads, **St. Helena Cyclery,** 1156 Main St., St. Helena (☎ 707-963-7736; www.sthelenacyclery.com), will set you on the Silverado Trail for $10 per hour or $30 per day. **Getaway Adventures BHK** (Biking, Hiking, and Kayaking), 1117 Lincoln Ave., Calistoga (☎ 800-499-BIKE or 707-942-0332), runs day trips with lunch and winery tours.

Wind down after a busy day with a mud bath. People have been immersing themselves in Calistoga mud for more than 150 years, but if you're prone to claustrophobia, get a massage only. You can reserve a tub and a follow-up massage at **Dr. Wilkinson's Hot Springs,** 1507 Lincoln Ave. (☎ 707-942-4102; www.drwilkinson.com); **Indian Springs Resort and Spa,** 1712 Lincoln Ave. (☎ 707-942-4913; www.indiansprings calistoga.com); or **Calistoga Spa Hot Springs,** 1006 Washington St. (☎ 707-942-6269). A mud bath and 50-minute massage is $175 at Indian Springs, and you get use of the pool.

Hop on the city of Napa's free downtown trolley for a 40-minute tour or a ride to Copia, the local outlet mall, or other stops. Trolley routes and times vary by day. Monday through Wednesday trolleys run every 45 minutes from 11 a.m. to 7:53 p.m. On Thursday through Saturday, two trolley loops operate every 30 minutes: the Red Loop runs from 11 a.m. to 7:57 p.m., and the Green Loop runs from 11:15 a.m. to 8:12 p.m. On Sundays the trolley runs every 45 minutes from 11 a.m. to 7:53 p.m. Find a trolley stop at 1st and Main streets. Call ☎ 707-255-7631 for more info.

Sonoma activities

Massage therapists abound in the valley, many of whom were well trained at the **California Institute of Massage and Spa Services,** 772 W. Napa St. (☎ 707-939-9431), located near the Sonoma Plaza. This is not a fancy facility, but the treatment rooms are comfortable, clean, and quiet. A 60-minute therapeutic massage is currently $75.

Olives are also an important crop in Wine Country, and olive oil tastings have become a popular activity. You can debate the merits of various extra-virgin olive oils in Glen Ellen at **The Olive Press,** 14301 Arnold Dr. (☎ 888-965-4839 or 707-939-8900; www.theolivepress.com). The press runs 24 hours between October and March. Watch the process from the tasting room while sampling award-winning olive oil and browsing olive-themed merchandise.

Jack London State Historic Park, 2400 London Ranch Rd. (☎ 707-938-5216; www.jacklondonpark.com), is where the prolific author of *The*

Call of the Wild lived before his death in 1916 at age 40. You can walk on trails to the ruins of Wolf House, London Lake, and Bath House, and visit the museum/library, which displays first editions of London's works and some of his personal memorabilia. Open daily from 9:30 a.m. to dusk. The park charges a $6-per-vehicle entrance fee.

The Goodtime Touring Co. (☎ **888-525-0453** or 707-938-0453; www. goodtimetouring.com) meets customers off the Sonoma Plaza to embark on guided four-and-a-half-hour picnic/winery rides for $99, which includes lunch and tasting fees. Bike rentals alone are also available for $25 per day.

If you have an intense interest in food, sign up for a three- to four-hour class at **Ramekins,** 450 W. Spain St., Sonoma (☎ **707-933-0450**), a small B&B and culinary school next to the General's Daughter restaurant. During the day, take in the demonstration classes; then in the evening, glean culinary tips from some major Bay Area chefs. Students have lots of opportunities to sample the goods with a few glasses of wine. Call for a catalog. You can register over the phone, in person, or on the Web at www.ramekins.com.

Spending the night

Although country inns and bed-and-breakfasts interspersed with spas and motels are sprinkled throughout both valleys, supply and demand keep the room rates and the occupancy on the high side. Even if you plan to look for a hotel in San Francisco at the last minute, you need to make reservations in the Wine Country as far in advance as possible, especially for stays between May and October. Most lodgings have a two-night minimum on the weekends during the high season. The good news: Parking is free at all the accommodations I list in this section.

Here is a breakdown of what the dollar signs represent in the following hotel listings (*Note:* This is a slightly different scale from San Francisco proper.):

- ✔ $: Under $150
- ✔ $$: $151 to $225
- ✔ $$$: $226 to $300
- ✔ $$$$: Over $300

Finding a substantial and well-prepared meal won't be as hard as finding a room, although you still need to make reservations. Some great chefs have settled their lives and businesses around the valleys, perhaps realizing that well-to-do tourists and urbanites with second homes love to eat out. Eating out is also one of the few evening activities in Wine Country — there's not much else to do after 10 p.m.

Contact **The Napa Valley Conference & Visitors Bureau,** 1310 Napa Town Center, Napa, CA 94559 (☎ **707-226-7459;** www.napavalley.com), for information on accommodations.

The **Sonoma Valley Visitors Bureau** is located on the Sonoma Plaza at 453 First St. E. (☎ **707-996-1090;** www.sonomavalley.com). They keep an availability sheet of hotel/B&B/motel rooms in case you didn't make reservations.

In the Napa Valley

Best Western Stevenson Manor Inn
$–$$$ Calistoga

Situated just east of town, this pleasant motel offers great value in an expensive neighborhood. The motel-basic rooms are boosted up a notch by fireplaces or whirlpool tubs, cable TV, fridges, coffeemakers, and hair dryers, as well as on-property extras including a pool, hot tub, sauna, and steam rooms. Guest rooms with two queen-size beds won't crowd the family, and kids under 12 stay free.

1830 Lincoln Ave. (west of Silverado Trail), Calistoga. ☎ *707-942-1112. Fax: 707-942-0381.* www.callodging.com. *Rack rates: $99–$229 double. Rates include continental breakfast. AE, CB, DC, DISC, MC, V. Check the Web site for Internet-only discounts. Guests get 10 percent off services at a nearby spa.*

Daughter's Inn
$$$–$$$$ Napa

Downtown Napa has a good selection of B&Bs in converted Victorians, with this family-run inn among the best. It's a smart choice for couples seeking a little romance, but who also want a location that's close to restaurants and whatever nightlife is available in the revitalized town of Napa. Daughter's Inn has a total of ten individually designed TV-free rooms, five in the mansion and five in a slightly more private new building in the garden. The focal points in all are the cushy beds and in-room Jacuzzis (heart-shaped in the Poppy suite), just so you understand in what direction you're headed. In the heat of the summer, a more resortlike hotel with a pool would probably be preferable, but in snuggling weather, Daughter's Inn provides nearly everything you need.

1938 First St., Napa. ☎ *866-253-1331.* www.daughtersinn.com. *Rack rates: $225–$329 double. Rates include a full breakfast. MC, V.*

Harvest Inn
$$$–$$$$ St. Helena

This Tudor-inspired complex was renovated in 1999, making all the rooms light, attractive, comfortable, and roomy enough for a family. Very recently 20 new rooms have been added. Two pools and two Jacuzzis are set in lovely gardens against a dramatic backdrop of mountains and vineyards.

Lots of little luxuries help justify the price, including feather beds, fireplaces, CD players, and VCRs. The midvalley location is central to everything.

1 Main St., St. Helena. ☎ *800-950-8466 or 707-963-9463. Fax: 707-963-4402.* www.harvestinn.com. *Rack rates: $259–$599 double; $399–$675 suite. Rates include continental breakfast. AE, DC, DISC, MC, V.*

Indian Springs
$$$–$$$$ Calistoga

Each of these comfortable, old-fashioned bungalows has a kitchen with a refrigerator and microwave, and picnic tables and barbecue grills are nearby. The resortlike atmosphere is perfected with *surreys* (bikes with bench seats and awnings) and Ping-Pong tables for guests to use. Lounge chairs surround a warm, Olympic-size mineral pool. The spa, which is located in a bathhouse from 1913, offers a full range of services with experienced practitioners. Booking a bungalow in the summer isn't easy, but try edging out the families who come here year after year by calling 48 hours ahead to find out whether you can get in on a cancellation.

1712 Lincoln Ave., Calistoga. ☎ *707-942-4913. Fax 707-942-4919.* www.indianspringscalistoga.com. *Rack rates: $185–$325 double studio or 1-bedroom; $265–$375 2-bedroom; $450–$600 3-bedroom. MC, V.*

Milliken Creek
$$$$ Napa

Cushy, chic, and romantic, the airy, large rooms in this intimate new inn resemble photos out of *Metropolitan Home.* No luxury has been overlooked, from Frette bed linens and L'Occitane bath products to candlelight turndown service. The 3-acre creekside gardens are equally stunning and private; you'll find it difficult to tear yourself away, although many excellent small wineries await along the Silverado Trail.

1815 Silverado Trail, Napa. ☎ *888-622-5775 or 707-255-1197. Fax: 707-942-2653.* www.millikencreekinn.com. *Rack rates: $325–$675 double. Rates include breakfast and afternoon wine and cheese. DC, MC, V.*

Vintage Inn
$$$–$$$$ Yountville

This big, attractive French-country inn is conveniently situated near some of the finest restaurants in the valley. Recently refurbished in a French Renaissance décor, rooms are clustered throughout the lovely flowering grounds and are equipped with fireplaces, fridges, Jacuzzi tubs, and coffeemakers. Tennis courts and a heated pool make this a comfortable mini-resort, good for couples exploring the area. Spa services are available next door at the Villagio, the sister inn. Check for specials and packages, which can make this a relative bargain.

6541 Washington St., Yountville. ☎ *800-351-1133 or 707-944-1112. Fax: 707-944-1617.* www.vintageinn.com. *Rack rates: $230–$630 double. Rates include continental champagne breakfast and afternoon tea. AE, CB, DC, DISC, MC, V.*

In Sonoma

El Pueblo Inn
$–$$$ Sonoma

Here's a lovable, way-better-than-average motel almost within walking distance of the Sonoma Plaza, and very well located for touring. Family-owned and -run, it has a really nice vibe, supported by very comfortable, spacious rooms in the buildings closest to reception. (The corner units there have fireplaces.) Guest rooms in the original two-story building in the back are less expensive given that the bathrooms are older and smaller. A pretty garden and pool sit next to a shaded patio and fitness room; it could get noisy in the summer as the property is right along Highway 12. If I had the kids along, I'd stay here without question. And if I was seeking affordable lodgings, ditto.

896 W. Napa St., Sonoma. ☎ *800-900-8844 or 707-996-3651.* www.elpebloinn. com. *Rack rates: $120–$235 double; Rates include a continental breakfast. MC, V.*

Inn at Sonoma
$$–$$$ Sonoma

This attractive, three-year-old Four Sisters Inn offers terrific value for money. Public and guest rooms are graciously decorated, smartly maintained, and include a generous breakfast, afternoon happy hour, and cookies. With just 19 rooms, you'll get as much attention as you require from the staff, although actually obtaining a room in summer will take advanced planning as this is a popular hotel for wedding parties. Less than 2 blocks from the Sonoma Plaza, the location makes walking to dinner a simple treat. For romantic occasions, I'd prefer a more secluded and luxurious hideaway such as the Kenwood Inn or Milliken Creek; otherwise, a room here more than satisfies.

630 Broadway, Sonoma. ☎ *888-568-9818 or 707-939-1340. Fax: 707-996-5227.* www. foursisters.com. *Rack rates: $145–$275 double; includes a full breakfast and afternoon wine. MC, V.*

Kenwood Inn and Spa
$$$$ Kenwood

If price is no object, or you want an all-out splurge, this gorgeous inn — reminiscent of villas on the Italian Riviera — is my pick over any hotel in either valley. The faux-painted buildings appear almost miragelike as you drive up the Sonoma Highway, the pale yellow stucco blending into the landscape on a sunny day. When you step inside, you'll have no desire to leave. Rooms are fitted with wood-burning fireplaces, feather beds, sensuous fabrics, and the facilities — an inviting saline pool, a separately situated Jacuzzi, a cozy bar and cafe (for guests only), and spa rooms that overlook vineyards — guarantee a feeling of sublime, luxurious seclusion.

10400 Sonoma Hwy., Kenwood. ☎ *800-353-6966 or 707-833-1293. Fax: 707-833-1247.* www.kenwoodinn.com. *Rack rates: $350–$700 double. Rates include three-course breakfast. AE, MC, V.*

MacArthur Place
$$$$ Sonoma

This divine small hotel is a renovated Victorian connected to newer buildings. The rooms are spacious and comfy, with four-poster beds that'll make you think twice about getting up. Contented guests relax at the small, well-staffed spa where the practiced hands of a masseuse work out pre-vacation tension. Manicured gardens surround a swimming pool, and a steakhouse restaurant in the 100-year-old barn supplies room service.

29 E. MacArthur St., Sonoma. ☎ *800-722-1866 or 707-938-2929. Fax: 707-933-9833.* www.macarthurplace.com. *Rack rates: $299–$399 double; $375–$499 suite. Rates include continental breakfast. AE, MC, V.*

Sonoma Chalet
$$–$$$ Sonoma

Although all you see from this Swiss-inspired farmhouse inn are mountains and the ranch next door, it's located less than a mile from the Sonoma town square. Antiques and collectibles decorate the three delightful, spacious cottages. Inside the farmhouse, the upstairs rooms have private facilities, while the two downstairs rooms share a bathroom. The simple and delicious breakfast includes fresh pastries.

18935 Fifth St. W., Sonoma. ☎ *800-938-3129 or 707-938-3129.* www.sonoma chalet.com. *Rack rates: $110–$225 double with continental breakfast. AE, MC, V.*

Dining in the valleys

Wine tasting certainly isn't the only reason to make the drive from San Francisco to Wine Country: The food here is sublime. Picking and choosing which dining rooms to include below almost hurt, but someone has to make the tough decisions. I tend to lean toward the places locals support, as tourist-oriented restaurants don't expect to see you again. (And if you're wondering why French Laundry is missing, it's because reservations are nearly impossible to get.)

In Napa

Angèle
$$–$$$ Napa   FRENCH BISTRO

Napa is experiencing a major growth spurt in hotels and especially restaurants, none with more to recommend it than this warm, casual brasserie overlooking the Napa River. Part of the historic Hatt Building development,

Angèle serves typical French fare as interpreted by a chef with access to the bounty of Northern California. My perfectly cooked *Pavé de Boeuf Haché* (yes, a hamburger) may not have been the most challenging selection, but it sure hit the spot one winter evening when a heavier meal would only have led to gout. My dining companions ate every scrap of their succulent pan-seared scallops and a tender veal stew. A high level of professionalism at every level makes this spot a standout.

540 Main St., Napa. ☎ 707-252-8115. Reservations recommended. Main courses: $19–$32. AE, MC, V. Open: Daily 11:30 a.m.–10 p.m.

Bistro Don Giovanni
$$–$$$ Napa   ITALIAN/COUNTRY FRENCH

Share a pizza, some antipasti, and a bottle of chardonnay for a delightful, light Italian meal, or go all out with the porterhouse for two. This inviting place, easily the most popular restaurant in the valley for all the right reasons, attracts a crowd that gathers at tables on the porch overlooking vineyards. It's heavenly.

4110 Howard Lane (off Highway 29), Napa. ☎ 707-224-3300. www.bistrodon giovanni.com. Reservations recommended. Main courses: $12–$28. Major credit cards accepted. Open: Sun–Thurs 11:30 a.m.–10 p.m., Fri–Sat 11:30 a.m.–11 p.m.

Bistro Jeanty
$$$ Yountville   FRENCH BISTRO

Much applauded around the Bay Area for its menu, authenticity, and vivacious dining room, this French bistro satisfies both the appetite and the spirit. Rustic dishes like lamb tongue and potato salad or rabbit and sweetbread ragout make up the seasonal menu. Both timid and adventurous eaters can find something to suit them, with typical bistro items such as steak frites and coq au vin also available.

6510 Washington St., Yountville. ☎ 707-944-0103. www.bistrojeanty. com. Reservations recommended. Main courses: $14.50–$29. MC, V. Open: Daily 11:30 a.m.–10:30 p.m.

Bounty Hunter
$$ Napa   AMERICAN

Foremost a wine shop, the wealth of bottles available to pair with the first-rate southwestern-influenced cooking pretty much obviates the need to ever drive Highway 29 again. Surrounded by the best wines available, your other difficult choice will be what to eat — the grilled whole chicken stuffed with Tecate beer? The barbecued ribs, smoky and succulent? A plate groaning with artisan cheeses and meats? This cozy former grocery in downtown Napa knows how to elevate dining into a rousing good time.

975 First St., Napa. ☎ 707-255-0622. www.bountyhunterwine.com. No reservations. Main courses: $11.50–$39. MC, V. Open: Sun–Thurs 11 a.m.–10 p.m., Fri–Sat 11 a.m.–midnight.

Cindy's Backstreet Kitchen
$$ St. Helena   CALIFORNIA

Cindy Pawlcyn (of Mustards Grill fame) opened this smaller, more low-key eatery in 2001. Given that St. Helena gets its fair share of weekend wine tasters, it's a testament to her sensibility how much this two-story house feels like a neighborhood hangout. A table in the garden is the ideal spot for a Cobb salad or curried chicken and something cold (there's a full bar as well as fresh juice drinks). In the evening, small plates, such as rabbit tostados or Piquillo peppers stuffed with cumin-scented beef seem made for a local lager. Large plates include specials from the wood-burning oven, fish of the day, and steak frites that'll have you hunkered over your dish. Use one of Cindy's root beer floats, featuring housemade vanilla ice cream, to teach kids the difference between ordinary and extraordinary.

1327 Railroad Ave. (between Hunt and Adams), St. Helena. ☎ *707-963-1200.* www. cindysbackstreetkitchen.com. *Reservations recommended. Main courses: $11–$21. AE, DC, DISC, MC, V. Open: Daily 11:30 a.m.–10 p.m., Sun–Thurs 11:30 a.m.– 9 p.m., weekends until 10 p.m. Nov–Apr.*

Gordon's Cafe and Wine Bar
$–$$ Yountville   AMERICAN

Chef-owner Sally Gordon's delicious food is served in a congenial atmosphere reminiscent of a general store. Besides comfort-food favorites at breakfast and creative sandwiches at lunch, Gordon's serves a three-course prix-fixe dinner on Friday nights, making the cafe a prime destination for food lovers. Don't be discouraged if there's a line for breakfast; just get in it.

6770 Washington St., Yountville. ☎ *707-944-8246. Reservations essential at dinner. Main courses: $3.50–$8 at breakfast and lunch; $45 prix-fixe dinner. AE, MC, V. Open: Tues–Sun 7:30 a.m.–6 p.m., Fri 7:30 a.m.–5 p.m. and 6–8:30 p.m.*

Tra Vigne
$$$ St. Helena   CLASSIC ITALIAN

This elegant (but not stuffy) restaurant is what people dream of when they dream of eating in the Italian countryside. You have two choices where to take your meal — either the more formal dining room inside or outside on the lovely courtyard patio (probably the better spot if the kids are with you). The Cantinetta delicatessen is the place to pick up wine and prepared foods to eat at the bar or to take on a picnic. Nearby at 1016 Main St. is **Tra Vigne Pizzeria,** a favorite with local families craving spaghetti and meatballs or thin-crusted pizzas in a more casual setting.

1050 Charter Oak Ave., St. Helena. ☎ *707-963-4444.* www.travignerestaurant. com. *Reservations recommended. Main courses: $16–$27. CB, JCB, DISC, MC, V. Open: Daily 11:30 a.m.–4 p.m., Sun–Thurs 4–10 p.m. Fri–Sat 4 –10:30 p.m.*

Wappo Bar Bistro
$$$ Calistoga   INTERNATIONAL

I like this pair of restaurants off the main drag for an unusual menu that spans a good part of the globe. Start an international culinary tour with spiced chickpea fritters and Vietnamese spring rolls, and then head to South America with a Brazilian seafood stew, layered with flavors, or opt for a soft landing in Italy over some tender *osso buco*. Wappo also serves on a pretty patio that lies in between its two storefronts. A glass of white wine, the Turkish *mezze* (appetizers) plate, and a table in the warmth of a Napa Valley afternoon defines one version of happiness.

1226 Washington St., Calistoga. ☎ *707-942-4712.* www.wappobar.com. *Reservations accepted. Main courses: $14–$24. AE, MC, V. Open: Wed–Mon 11:30 a.m.–2:30 p.m. and 6–9:30 p.m.*

In Sonoma

Cafe La Haye
$$ Sonoma   CALIFORNIA

This casual little cafe serves some of the best food around and, unlike many other Wine Country restaurants, it makes no attempt to pretend it's in Italy or France. Plain tables and chairs are carefully set about, as if to not disturb the art that fills the walls, making La Haye's single room resemble a gallery. The menu selection, spare but complete, features whatever's seasonal and offers organic produce. The daily risotto is fabulous, but you can't go wrong no matter what you order.

140 E. Napa St., Sonoma. ☎ *707-935-5994.* www.sterba.com/sonoma/lahaye. *Reservations advised. Main courses: $16–$29. AE, MC, V. Open: Tues–Sat 5:30–9 p.m.*

Deuce
$$ Sonoma   CALIFORNIA

With so many valley restaurants and chefs vying for attention, I think that Deuce, a popular stop for county residents, gets overlooked by travelers. Inside the yellow Craftsman-style house, which sits on the main road heading toward Sonoma Plaza, you'll be treated to especially friendly service and well-prepared food that doesn't require any translation. Lots of diners (especially those who want dessert) make do with a couple of starters, in particular the tender/crispy calamari or the irresistible lobster pot pie. For mains, the smart money is on the thick, perfectly grilled pork chop, although it's hard to pass up the cassoulet. Kids are welcome here, and the kitchen will prepare something to their liking if you ask.

691 Broadway, Sonoma. ☎ *707-933-3823.* www.dine-at-deuce.com. *Reservations advised. Main courses: $19–$25. AE, MC, V. Open: Sun–Thurs 11 a.m.–9 p.m., Fri and Sat 11 a.m.–9:30 p.m.*

Garden Court Cafe and Bakery
$ Glen Ellen   AMERICAN

Get a modest plate of bacon and eggs and lunch to go, or a tasty, filling breakfast that keeps you going most of the day. This is a completely unpretentious diner where the regulars settle back with the paper and coffee while waiting for gravy and biscuits. Atkins and South Beach dieters have lots of egg dishes to choose from — hold the housebaked breads. Well, maybe not — these are especially fine.

13647 Arnold Dr., Glen Ellen. ☎ *707-935-1565.* www.gardencourtcafe.com. *No reservations. Main courses: $4.95–$13. MC, V. Open: Wed–Mon 7:30 a.m.–2 p.m.*

the girl & the fig
$$ Sonoma   COUNTRY FRENCH

This upscale country French bistro moved to the Sonoma Hotel in 2001, adding outdoor dining to the delight of its admirers. The seasonal menu meets the needs of seafoodies, vegetarians, or carnivores with one or two dishes in each category. The grilled fig salad with arugula and local goat's cheese is a must-order when fresh figs are available.

110 W. Spain St., Sonoma. ☎ *707-938-3634.* www.thegirlandthefig.com. *Reservations advised. Main courses: $12–$25. MC, V. Open: Daily 11:30 a.m.–10 p.m.*

Ledson's Harmony Restaurant
$$$ Sonoma   CALIFORNIA/FRENCH

You can't miss this new restaurant/hotel on Sonoma's square, although the designers did such a great job blending the new building with the old architecture that it looks as though it's always been here. A hotel dining-room sensibility seems at odds with the casual Wine Country atmosphere everywhere else — when I ate here, servers were lined up by the kitchen door, and the plates of tasty food were self-conscious in their presentation. But with a pianist nightly and a vocalist weekends, Harmony has definitely enlivened the town. Six marble-bathed bedrooms above the restaurant are worthy of sensitive royalty and priced accordingly.

480 First St., Sonoma. ☎ *707-996-9779.* www.ledsonhotel.com. *Reservations advised. Main courses: $23–$30. AE, MC, V. Open: Daily 11:30 a.m.–10 p.m.*

Part V
Living It Up after Dark: San Francisco Nightlife

The 5th Wave   By Rich Tennant

"We loved Beach Blanket Babylon. It's a show featuring a bunch of people making fun of celebrities and politicians while cavorting around in big, silly hats. You know, a lot like your mother's garden club."

In this part . . .

Because San Francisco contains such a diverse populace to begin with, no single form of entertainment has come to be associated with the city in the same way that jazz is mentioned in the same breath as New Orleans or theater with New York. Instead, San Francisco offers an eclectic mix of dance, music, performance art, theater, and opera, with plenty to choose from on any given night. If you shun anything requiring a trip to a box office, you can choose from plenty of bars and clubs to keep you off the streets until the wee hours.

Even travelers with kids don't have to limit after-hours activities to dinner and a movie. A few clubs offer shows for patrons of all ages, featuring local alternative or blues bands. (Your kid will think you're very special.) A night at the theater is also a great family alternative; you can usually find something that appeals to people of all ages.

Chapter 15

Applauding the Cultural Scene

*W*hether you're up for world-class classical music or experimental theater, and pretty much everything in between, you can find it on stage in San Francisco. In this chapter, I give you the overall picture and then detail how to find out what's going on and score tickets.

Getting the Inside Scoop

Performing-arts fans can find plenty of interesting offerings in San Francisco. For drama, there's a bit of the tried and true when Broadway road companies drop into town, and our own **American Conservatory Theatre (ACT)** regularly produces works that are visually inspired and well acted. Opera is just as vibrant. Although the great Enrico Caruso never returned to San Francisco after the shock of the 1906 earthquake, plenty of other stars have aria'd their way through town, raising the local opera company to world-class heights. The **SF Symphony** is in a similar league, and while I'm bragging, I'd better mention the ballet. It, too, is as fine a company as you'll see anywhere. But don't let the big brands sway you from trying stages outside the Civic Center, including Yerba Buena Gardens, and smaller venues south of Market where experimental theater abounds.

Finding Out What's Playing and Getting Tickets

On the Web you can search sites such as **Citysearch** (www.sanfrancisco. citysearch.com) and the *San Francisco Chronicle* (www.sfgate. com/listings) for reviews and synopses; otherwise, follow your instincts (and local recommendations) when you get here. You may stumble onto something wonderful. If you're looking for something outside the mainstream (and this is a fine place to find that), a month or so before your trip sign up for the e-mail list Flavorpill SF (sf.flavorpill. net). This free weekly e-mail highlights the more-elusive cultural events gracing the town, including films, concerts, and theater.

Here are a few other Web sites to check out for what's happening now:

✔ www.sfbg.com: You can find the *Bay Guardian*'s complete entertainment listings online. Try this one first.

✔ www.sanfran.com: *San Francisco,* our very own monthly magazine, is chock-full of arts and entertainment information.

✔ www.sfweekly.com: This is the Web site for *SF Weekly,* another great lefty publication with provocative features, lots of local info, and reviews.

For tickets to any theater, dance, symphony, or concert performance, you can call the appropriate box office directly or head online and order with a credit card (charges are nonrefundable if, for some reason, you don't show up). Around Civic Center, **City Box Office,** 180 Redwood St., Suite 100 (☎ 415-392-4400; www.cityboxoffice.com), sells tickets to shows playing at the Nob Hill Masonic Center, Project Artaud Theater, Herbst Theatre, and other lesser-known stages. If you arrive in town without plans, visit **TIX Bay Area** (☎ 415-433-7827; www.theatrebay area.org/tix) for half-price tickets for same-day performances (a $1–$3 service charge is tacked on). TIX, which is also a **BASS Ticketmaster** outlet, is located on Union Square between Post and Geary streets. It's open Tuesday through Thursday from 11 a.m. to 6 p.m., Friday and Saturday until 7 p.m., and Sunday 10 a.m. to 3 p.m.

 Don't buy tickets from anyone outside TIX or a box office claiming to have discounted or scalper tickets, especially to sporting events. Folks get duped all the time, forking over real cash for counterfeit tickets. Another common scam is to sell tickets to an event that has already taken place.

The concierge at your hotel can be a source for hard-to-get tickets. The larger the hotel, the more likely it is that the concierge will be successful, but in any case, it's worth asking. If he does manage to come through, a $5 to $10 tip is appropriate, thanks.

Surfing for performing-arts information

Check out the following sites for all your performing arts needs:

- American Conservatory Theater: www.act-sfbay.org
- Best of Broadway theater info: www.bestofbroadway-sf.com
- Lamplighters light opera company: www.lamplighters.org
- San Francisco Ballet: www.sfballet.org
- San Francisco Opera: www.sfopera.org
- San Francisco Performances: www.performances.org
- San Francisco Symphony: www.sfsymphony.org

If you're flexible about your plans for the evening, go to the box office of the theater you want to attend and stand in line for last-minute cancellations by season-ticket holders or the release of tickets held for media or VIPs. With luck, you can land seats in the orchestra. Without luck, you'll have wasted an hour or so.

Don't be late to the theater, symphony, or opera. Curtains rise on time, and if you're late, you won't be seated until there's a break in the action.

 If you're attending a show at the Geary Theater, avoid the boxes on either side. They're positioned to obscure half the stage, generally the half where the action takes place.

As for what to wear, you'll see a little of everything, from tailored evening clothes to jeans. People seem to dress up a bit more Friday and Saturday nights, especially in the orchestra seats, but your Sunday best isn't necessary.

Raising the Curtain on the Performing Arts

Cable cars will get you to Union Square theaters if you're coming from North Beach; from the Marina or Union Street, take a 30-Stockton or 45-Union/Stockton bus. If you prefer to take a cab to your lodgings afterward, walk to a big hotel to catch one. You can find a number of parking garages near Union Square with fees beginning at $10 for the evening.

You can reach the **Civic Center,** where the opera, ballet, and symphony are located, by any Muni Metro streetcar or any bus along Van Ness Avenue. I wouldn't walk around this area unescorted after dark to get back to the Muni station, and taxis aren't always immediately available.

San Francisco Performing Arts

American Conservatory Theater
(Geary Theater) **11**
Beach Blanket Babylon (Club Fugazi) **2**
Curran Theater **10**
42nd St. Moon (Eureka Theatre) **3**
Golden Gate Theater **14**
Intersection for the Arts **19**
Lorraine Hansberry Theatre **6**
The Magic Theater **1**
Marines Memorial Theatre **6**
New Conservatory Theater **17**
New Langton Arts **18**
Noontime Concerts (St. Patrick's Church) **12**
Old First Presbyterian Church **4**
Orpheum **15**
The Plush Room **5**
Post Street Theater **7**
Project Artaud Theater **20**
San Francisco Ballet **16**
San Francisco Opera **16**
San Francisco Symphony **16**
Smuin Ballets/SF
(Yerba Buena Center for the Arts) **13**
Ticket Outlets:
City Box Office **8**
TIX Bay Area **9**

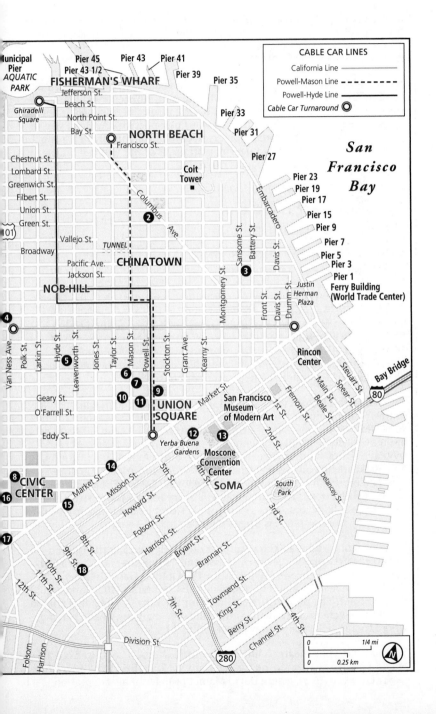

Municipal Pier
AQUATIC PARK
Ghiradelli Square

Pier 45
Pier 43 1/2
Pier 43
Pier 41
Pier 39
Pier 35

FISHERMAN'S WHARF

Jefferson St.
Beach St.
North Point St.
Bay St.

NORTH BEACH

Francisco St.

Chestnut St.
Lombard St.
Greenwich St.
Filbert St.
Union St.
Green St.

Coit Tower

Vallejo St.
TUNNEL
Broadway

Pacific Ave.
Jackson St.

CHINATOWN

NOB-HILL

Columbus Ave.

Pier 33
Pier 31
Pier 27
Pier 23
Pier 19
Pier 17
Pier 15
Pier 9
Pier 7
Pier 5
Pier 3
Pier 1
Ferry Building
(World Trade Center)

San Francisco Bay

Embarcadero

Sansome St.
Battery St.
Montgomery St.
Front St.
Davis St.
Drumm St.

Justin Herman Plaza

Van Ness Ave.
Polk St.
Larkin St.
Hyde St.
Leavenworth St.
Jones St.
Taylor St.
Mason St.
Powell St.
Stockton St.
Grant Ave.
Kearny St.

Rincon Center

Steuart St.
Spear St.

Bay Bridge

Geary St.
O'Farrell St.
Eddy St.

UNION SQUARE

Market St.

San Francisco Museum of Modern Art

Fremont St.
1st St.
Beale St.
Main St.
2nd St.

Yerba Buena Gardens

Moscone Convention Center

SOMA

South Park

Delancey St.

CIVIC CENTER

Market St.
Mission St.
5th St.
4th St.
Howard St.
Folsom St.
Harrison St.
Bryant St.
Brannan St.

3rd St.

8th St.
9th St.
10th St.
11th St.
12th St.

7th St.

Townsend St.
King St.
Berry St.
Channel St.
4th St.

Folsom
Harrison

Division St.

280

0   1/4 mi
0   0.25 km

N

CABLE CAR LINES

California Line ————
Powell-Mason Line – – – –
Powell-Hyde Line ————
Cable Car Turnaround ◎

If you feel stuck, walk to one of the many nearby restaurants and ask the host to call a taxi for you. Relax, and prepare to wait a while at the bar. If you're driving, you can park in the garage on Grove Street between Franklin and Gough streets.

South of Market and Mission neighborhood venues have troubles similar to **Civic Center.** You can usually get to the performance by public transportation, but returning late at night by bus is less interesting (or perhaps more interesting, depending on your perspective). Again, if you're attending a show in this area, don't expect to automatically hail a cab afterward. Instead, walk to a nearby restaurant or bar and call. These numbers for local cab companies can help:

- ✔ **Desoto Cab:** ☎ 415-970-1300
- ✔ **Luxor Cabs:** ☎ 415-282-4141
- ✔ **Pacific:** ☎ 415-986-7220
- ✔ **Veteran's Cab:** ☎ 415-648-1313
- ✔ **Yellow Cab:** ☎ 415-626-2345

I would never seriously compare our little theater district to the Great White Way in New York, but San Francisco has a fair number of professional stages. At least ten in varying sizes are housed around **Union Square,** and experimental theaters are scattered about the **South of Market** and **Mission** districts in converted warehouses and gallery spaces. Productions may include a musical or two, distinguished classics, and world-premiere comedies and dramas.

The **American Conservatory Theater (ACT)** is the preeminent company in town and produces a wide variety of plays during its season, which runs October to June. The acting is first-rate, and the costumes and sets are universally brilliant. The choice of material ranges from new works by playwrights such as Tom Stoppard, can't-lose American chestnuts, and Shakespeare, all the way to not-quite-ready-for-prime-time dramas that still receive a careful rendering. The lovely **Geary Theater** is home to ACT productions. You'll find it at 415 Geary St., at Mason Street (☎ 415-749-2228; www.act-sfbay.org). Ticket prices range from $35 to $80, and the box office is open every day from 10 a.m.

Broadway hits and road shows appear down the block at the **Curran Theater,** 445 Geary St., between Mason and Taylor streets (☎ 415-551-2000; www.bestofbroadway-sf.com); the **Golden Gate Theater,** 1 Golden Gate Ave., at Market Street; and the **Orpheum,** 1192 Market St., at Eighth Street. The phone number listed for the Curran Theater is shared by all three venues, and the recorded message explains what's playing, where to buy tickets, and how to get to the theaters.

You may like your theater a little more cutting-edge. If so, check out **The Magic Theatre** at Fort Mason Center, Bldg. A (☎ 415-441-8822; www.magictheatre.org), where David Mamet premiered his adaptation

Pre- and post-theater dining

You have plenty of dining choices before attending any 8 p.m. performance. After the show, however, your dining choices are somewhat more limited. On Union Square, a branch of **The Cheesecake Factory** has arrived on the eighth floor of Macy's. It's open until 11 p.m. **The Grand Cafe** (reviewed in Chapter 10) also serves until 11 p.m. from a bar menu. If you're attending an event around Civic Center and want to eat before the show, be sure to make reservations. **The Hayes Street Grill** (reviewed in Chapter 10) originally opened to accommodate the culture crowd, and this restaurant has been joined by a great many more on and around Hayes Street. Down around Yerba Buena Center, **Bacar,** 448 Brannan, between Third and Fourth streets (☎ 415-904-4100), has the most extensive wine list around and serves tempting dishes like wok-cooked Maine lobster. **XYZ** at the W Hotel, 181 Third St., at Howard (☎ 415-817-7836), has a cafe as well as a restaurant, so you can go casual or upscale, depending on how quickly you need to eat.

of *Dr. Faustus*. Tickets range from $26 to $52. Or try **Intersection for the Arts,** a 72-seat performance space in the Mission District at 446 Valencia St., between 15th and 16th streets (☎ **415-626-3311**; www.the intersection.org). You won't find anything traditional here in their exhibits, literary series, music, or interdisciplinary works of art. Ticket prices run between $9 and $15.

The Magic Theatre sets aside a limited number of tickets for "Sliding Scale" Tuesdays. Prices range from $5–$25 and reservations aren't accepted; it's first-come, first-served at the box office (open: Tues–Sat noon–5 p.m.), cash only.

The **Lorraine Hansberry Theatre,** 620 Sutter St. (☎ **415-474-8800**; www. lorrainehansberrytheatre.com), features dramas and musicals by black authors past and present such as Langston Hughes and August Wilson. Ticket prices are $25 to $32. If you are in town the month of December, don't miss the holiday gospel show, *Black Nativity*.

Another Union Square stage is tucked inside the building that houses the Kensington Park Hotel at 450 Post St. The **Post Street Theatre,** formerly Theatre on the Square, opened with the rock 'n' roll musical *Buddy: The Buddy Holly Story*. You can find out what's playing next on the Web site www.poststreettheatre.com or by contacting the box office at ☎ **415-771-6900. Marines' Memorial Theatre,** located on the second floor of the Marines' Memorial Club, 609 Sutter St. (☎ **415-771-6900**; www.marinesmemorialtheatre.com), similar in size and flavor to the Post Street Theatre, presents small off-Broadway shows and new productions, most recently the premiere of a musical based on the life of Janis Joplin.

Close to Civic Center, in an impressive former Masonic Temple built in 1911, is the **New Conservatory Theater (NCT)** complex at 25 Van Ness Ave., a half block off Market Street (☎ 415-861-8972; www.nctcsf.org). NCT, which consists of three small theaters, presents a variety of productions throughout the year. From April through August is **"Pride Season,"** during which a series of six plays with gay themes is presented. NTC also produces children's theater programming all year long.

Admirers of musical theater should keep an eye out for productions by **42nd Street Moon.** This company presents long-forgotten American musicals in concert format and gives audiences an opportunity to hear delightfully clever tunes that somehow "disappeared." Check the Web site (www.42ndstmoon.org) for shows and dates. Productions take place at the **Eureka Theatre,** 215 Jackson St., at Battery in the Financial District (☎ 415-978-2787).

Symphony and Opera

San Francisco has many venues for listening to classical music. Local papers and Web sites are your best source for event listings. You can see major groups such as the **San Francisco Symphony,** which performs in the **Louise M. Davies Symphony Hall,** 201 Van Ness Ave., at Grove Street (☎ 415-864-6000), in the Civic Center. The season runs from September through July, and tickets cost $15 to $78. Also at Civic Center is the **Herbst Theater,** 410 Van Ness Ave. (☎ 415-621-6600), home to **San Francisco Performances** (www.sfperformances.org) and other professional groups.

You can also enjoy piano and violin duos, chamber music ensembles, and singers at **Old First Presbyterian Church,** 1751 Sacramento St., at Van Ness Avenue (☎ 415-474-1608; www.oldfirstconcerts.org). These less-formal concerts are scheduled afternoons and evenings, and tickets are a mere $12 to $15. The California Street cable car takes you to within 2 blocks of the church. If you're around **Yerba Buena Gardens** at lunchtime on a Wednesday, head to **St. Patrick's Church,** 756 Mission St., which is the site for half-hour concerts produced by **Noontime Concerts** (☎ 415-777-3211; www.noontimeconverts.org). These brief shows may be solo or full orchestral performances. Admission is $5. Noontime Concerts also uses the **A.P. Giannini Auditorium** at the Bank of America headquarters, 555 California St., in the Financial District. Concerts are currently held there on the second and fourth Tuesdays of the month, but call for an updated schedule.

The San Francisco Opera opens its season with a gala in September and ends quietly in early January. Performances are produced in the **War Memorial Opera House,** 301 Van Ness Ave., at Grove Street (☎ 415-864-3330), in the Civic Center. Tickets run from $25 to $235. **Pocket Opera** (☎ 415-972-8934) delivers opera to the masses in stripped-down,

The Civic Center

English-language versions that are quite entertaining and highly professional. The season begins in February and ends in June; productions are held at different locations, including the Palace of the Legion of Honor, so you'll need to phone for a schedule or check the Web site (www.pocketopera.org).

Dance

Plenty of classical and modern dance groups raise the barre in San Francisco, the **San Francisco Ballet** being the best-known company. Their season runs from February to June, and they perform in the **War Memorial Opera House,** 301 Van Ness Ave., at Grove Street. Call ☎ **415-865-2000** for tickets. Prices run from $10 for standing room to over $100 for orchestra seats. Students, seniors (68-plus), and military personnel qualify for discounted same-day tickets, at $10 to $20. You can check for availability by phoning the box office.

You'll discover an adventurous season of modern dance, performance art, and theater at the **Project Artaud Theater,** 450 Florida St., at 17th Street (☎ 415-626-4370; www.artaud.org), in the Mission District. Ticket prices are $20 or less, depending on the day and type of show.

Some of the most interesting dance companies, including **Smuin Ballets/ SF,** appear on stage at the **Yerba Buena Center for the Arts,** 700 Howard St. (☎ 415-978-2787; www.ybca.org). It's easy to reach, and there are many fine restaurants in the neighborhood for pre- or post-theater supper.

New Langton Arts, a nonprofit, artist-run performance space in SoMa, may have an art show, a theater performance, video pieces, or all three at the same time — it's experimental and won't be mistaken for *Beach Blanket Babylon* in any case. Check it out at 1246 Folsom St., between Eighth and Ninth streets (☎ 415-626-5416; www.newlangtonarts.org). Gallery and box office hours are Wednesday through Saturday, noon to 5 p.m.

You may not want to miss ***Beach Blanket Babylon,*** by now a San Francisco ritual. The 90-minute musical revue is known for wildly imaginative hats that seem to live lives of their own. The spectacle is so popular that even after celebrating 32 years of poking fun at stars, politicians, and San Francisco itself, seats for the constantly updated shows are always sold out. Purchase tickets ($25–$80) through TIX or by mail at least three weeks in advance (especially if you want to attend a weekend performance). You must be 21 to attend evening performances; minors are only admitted for Sunday matinees, when no liquor is sold. You can enjoy this spectacle in North Beach at **Club Fugazi,** 678 Green St., between Powell Street and Columbus Avenue (☎ 415-421-4222; www.beachblanketbabylon.com). You've got to see it to believe it.

Chapter 16

Hitting the Clubs and Bars

* *

In This Chapter

▶ Checking out the hippest clubs and bars for live music
▶ Shaking your body at dance clubs
▶ Aiming for atmosphere
▶ Getting a good laugh
▶ Broadening your horizons at some unique establishments

* *

*O*ne thing I love about this city: There's no end to the good times. You can have a night at the theater, followed by a night hopping through a few bars and clubs, followed by a night listening to great jazz. There are so many places for drinking and dancing and socializing, you'll have no excuse (except maybe exhaustion) for staying in at night.

Livin' It Up with Live Music

Bars, all of which by law must remain closed from 2 to 6 a.m., are self-explanatory. Clubs are a different story altogether. South of Market, dance clubs that have different styles and names may share the same space. For example, a particular club may feature 1970s-revisited disco catering to the Velvet Elvis crowd on Friday, and then play Gothic industrial "music" for body-piercing aficionados on Monday. Take a careful look at the listings in *SF Weekly* or *Bay Guardian* to know what you're getting into. Most clubs don't get going until after 10 p.m., so plan to take cabs anywhere not within walking distance of your hotel.

Finding some cool jazz

Jazz at Pearl's, 256 Columbus Ave., at Broadway (☎ **415-291-8255;** www.jazzatpearls.com), showcases the 17-piece big band Contemporary Jazz Orchestra every Monday and local jazz musicians Tuesday through Saturday. Pearl's closed for a few months in 2003 and reopened with new owners who brought in a Spanish chef to retool the menu. The room has more of a '30s supper-club atmosphere now and a generous selection of tapas and larger plates including paellas for two. Dinner-and-show packages are $35 to $50. Show tickets are $5 to $10. The ever-cool

San Francisco Clubs and Bars

Asia SF **43**
Amber **8**
Balboa Café **1**
Bambuddha Lounge (in Phoenix Hotel) **35**
Bar of Contemporary Art **39**
The Beauty Bar **49**
Bigfoot Lodge **25**
Bimbo's 365 Club **10**
Biscuits & Blues **32**
Bix **21**
Blondie's Bar & No Grill **47**
Boom Boom Room **2**
Bubble Lounge **22**
The Café **5**
Café du Nord **6**
Club Townsend **40**
Cobb's Comedy Club **11**
DNA Lounge **46**
Edinburgh Castle **29**
Elbo Room **48**
The Empire Plush Room **28**
Endup **42**
Fillmore Auditorium **3**
Gino & Carlo's **14**
Grant & Green **15**

Great American Music Hall **34**
Hemlock Tavern **30**
The Independent **4**
Jazz at Pearl's **18**
Johnny Foley's **37**
Li-Po Cocktail Lounge **24**
Lost & Found Saloon **17**
The Marsh **50**
Martuni's **9**
Mick's Lounge **12**
The Mint Karaoke Lounge **7**
O'Reilly's **13**
Pier 23 **16**
Punchline Comedy Club **23**
The Ramp **41**
Red Room **31**
Redwood Room **33**
Rickshaw Stop **36**
The Saloon **19**
SF Weekly Warfield **38**
Slim's **45**
Spec's **19**
The Stud **44**
Tonga Room **26**
Top of the Mark **27**
Vesuvio **20**

Mission District

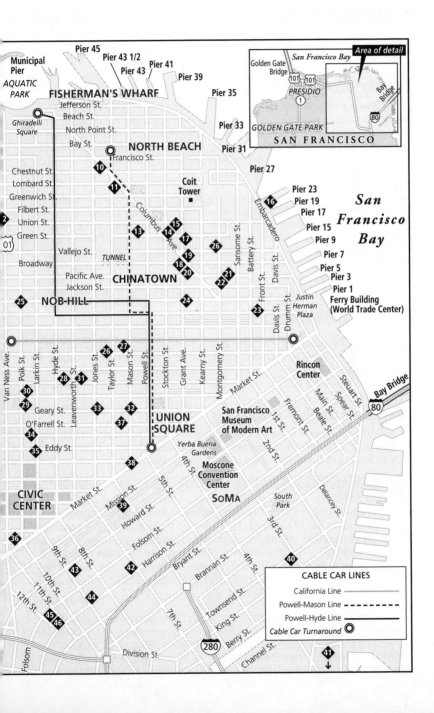

Elbo Room, 647 Valencia St., near 17th Street (☎ 415-552-7788), blasts acid jazz for a well-dressed younger crowd, or, depending on the night, you can move to Latin and funk bands. Cover starts at $5 upstairs; downstairs the bar has a fine menu of microbrews and a couple of pool tables.

Feelin' blue: Blues bars

The **Boom Boom Room,** 1601 Fillmore St., at Geary Street (☎ 415-673-8000; www.boomboomblues.com), is open every night for dancing, cocktails, and jiving. Lines often form on the weekends, so it doesn't hurt to arrive early and sip your drink slowly. The cover charge varies depending on the night and the act; it generally ranges from free to $12. Check the Web site for an events calendar.

Follow the crowds to **The Saloon,** 1232 Grant Ave., at Fresno Street near Vallejo Street (☎ 415-989-7666), as your first stop on a walking tour of North Beach blues bars. Johnny Nitro plays here Friday and Sunday nights. If you can manage to get inside, the cover is usually $4 to $5. Up the block, check out the **Lost and Found Saloon,** 1353 Grant Ave., between Vallejo and Green streets (☎ 415-981-9557). It's just as crowded weekend nights; there's no cover. **Grant & Green,** 1371 Grant Ave. (☎ 415-693-9565), is the third in the North Beach blues triumvirate. No cover here, either. If you're looking for something a little less . . . real . . . head over to Enrico's (see Chapter 10).

During the day, **Pier 23,** The Embarcadero, at Front Street (☎ 415-362-5125), serves lunch to fashionable business executives on the patio. At night, hot local blues and funk musicians, honky-tonk pianists or ska bands play for fans ages 21 to 70. There's a $5 to $10 cover on weekends.

Catching the big-name acts

You'll want to contact the box office directly or purchase tickets from **BASS** at ☎ 415-776-1999 for major musical acts. Ticket prices vary at the following clubs, depending on the performers.

The **Great American Music Hall,** 859 O'Farrell St., near Polk Street (☎ 415-885-0750; www.musichallsf.com), books everything from rhythm and blues to Cajun bands to Grammy Award–winning artists such as Bonnie Raitt. Although you'll notice the club isn't in a squeaky-clean neighborhood, safety isn't a problem because so many people are going in and out of the place. If you're driving, use the valet in front (if available) or park in the AMC 1000 garage across the street. Take a cab home after the show if you aren't driving. You can find the club schedule and order tickets on the Web site.

It won't be the Grateful Dead, but you can find out who's playing **The Fillmore,** 1805 Geary St., at Fillmore Street, by checking out its Web site (www.thefillmore.com) or by calling the box office at ☎ 415-346-6000. A pilgrimage here for die-hard rock 'n' roll fans really is meaningful. **The SF Weekly Warfield,** 982 Market St. (☎ 415-775-7722), is a huge theater that hosts big-time musicians, mostly rock 'n' roll. **Slim's,** 333 11th St., between Folsom and Harrison streets (☎ 415-255-0333; www. slims-sf.com), is a smaller, fairly comfortable club owned by singer Boz Scaggs, who plays here every now and then. A much bigger room that some grown-ups I know find extra-palatable is **Bimbo's 365 Club,** in North Beach at 1025 Columbus Ave., at Chestnut Street (☎ 415-474-0365; www.bimbos365club.com). It's a '30s-style ballroom with an ornate bar and an attendant in the ladies' restroom. Music varies from rock to alternative, and you can check the schedule at the Web site. **Bottom of the Hill,** 1233 17th St., at Texas Street (☎ 415-621-4455; www.bottomofthehill.com), is a 300- to 500-capacity venue that caters to nationally known indie rock acts with special appeal to a demographic that listens to college radio. This Potrero Hill–based club also serves bar and grill food and hosts an all-you-can-eat barbecue/music hoedown Sunday afternoons. Smokers are allowed to puff on the patio. You can get there on the 22-Fillmore or 19-Polk buses. My sources in the music biz inform me that **The Independent,** 628 Divisadero St., between Grove and Hayes streets (☎ 415-771-1421; www.theindependentsf.com), has the best sound system in the city and books the hottest indie and pop bands. Their schedule is online; the door runs from free with a two-drink minimum to $20.

Shakin' Your Groove Thang: Dance Clubs

The Ramp, 855 China Basin, off Third Street at Mariposa Street (☎ 415-621-2378; www.ramprestaurant.com), is an indoor/outdoor bar/restaurant serving salads, burgers, breakfast, and perhaps the best views over the water. Between May and October you can dance to live music on the weekends; Saturdays feature salsa bands, and Sundays bring world music (both days from 5–8 p.m.). There's no cover charge. The ultracool but friendly **Cafe du Nord and The Swedish American Hall,** 2170 Market St., at Sanchez Street (☎ 415-861-5016; www.cafedunord.com), is a basement-level club and restaurant that features indie bands or some type of live music most every evening. Cover runs from $7 to $15. Under-21 bohemians are allowed in for selected shows if accompanied by adults. **DNA Lounge,** 375 11th St., at Harrison Street (☎ 415-626-1409; www.dnalounge.com), may be blasting metal, gothic, hip-hop, synthpop . . . whatever . . . on different nights of the week. Cover is around $20 on weekends.

Swing, salsa, and ballroom dancers, and those who've never completely let go of their Ginger Rogers fantasies, will adore the **Metronome Dance Center,** 1830 17th St. (☎ 415-252-9000; www.metronomedancecenter.com). You can swoop by at 7:30 p.m. to take a class, and then stay for a dance party on Friday, Saturday, or Sunday night, or simply arrive at 9 p.m. to trip the light fantastic. This is strictly a social dancing venue; only snacks and nonalcoholic beverages are available. There's a cover charge of $7 to $16. Already have your moves down? The **Top of the**

Mark in the Mark Hopkins Hotel, 1 Nob Hill (☎ **415-616-6916;** www.top ofthemark.com), with its surround-sound view, is one of the prettiest rooms in the city. A dance floor is ringed by tables and a six-piece band plays '40s dance tunes on Friday and Saturday nights. Cover is $10 — or you can go all out and eat dinner here, too. Wednesday nights feature salsa dance lessons at 8 p.m. and live music to practice to from 9 p.m.

There's much more to local nightlife than South of Market dance halls. For a little fiesta in the Mission District, reserve a seat on **El Voladote,** the Mexican Bus (www.mexicanbus.com), as it cruises the dance clubs Friday and Saturday nights. The $38 ticket price includes cover charges at three clubs. Call ☎ **415-546-3747** for reservations two or three weeks ahead. Salsa dancing is all the rage, and the place to take a lesson or just sit back watching expert couples heat up the expansive dance floor is **Roccapulco,** 3140 Mission St. at Precita Street (☎ **415-648-6611;** www. roccapulco.com). Ten dollars gets you a one-hour lesson Wednesday, Friday, and Saturday nights at 8:30; live Latin bands play Friday and Saturday nights from 10 p.m. and Mexican specialties are available to keep your energy up. You'll want to dress the part here.

Sunday afternoons in the Mission call out for a *cerveza* on the patio at **El Rio,** 3158 Mission St. (☎ **415-282-3325**), where they pack 'em in for salsa parties ($8 admission after 3 p.m.). The rest of the week you might find DJs, a movie on the patio, a benefit for an alternative magazine, and you'll always find a mixed but congenial crowd of locals. Usually there's no cover; for special events they sometimes charge $4 or $5.

Drinking in the Atmosphere: The Best Places to Have a Drink and Mingle

San Francisco offers a special ambience. From coffee shops and dance clubs to galleries and restaurants, there's something to appeal to every persuasion. If atmosphere is what you're after, check out these favorites.

Joining the singles scene

The **Balboa Cafe,** 3199 Fillmore St., between Greenwich and Filbert (☎ **415-921-3944**), has withstood the test of time. The bar/restaurant gets lots of repeat customers — they come here after every divorce. In and around the Tenderloin, they line up to enter the **Red Room,** 827 Sutter St., between Jones and Leavenworth streets, next door to the Commodore Hotel (☎ **415-346-7666**). Look sharp. **Bambuddha Lounge,** at the Phoenix Hotel, 601 Eddy St., at Larkin Street (☎ **415-885-5088**), combines an Asian sensibility with the desire to have a really good time eating, drinking, and checking out the people around the pool. It offers innovative cocktail fare, house music nightly, and well-regarded food.

Blondie's Bar and No Grill, 540 Valencia St., between 16th and 17th streets (☎ 415-864-2419), is on the sizzling Valencia Street corridor in the Mission District. The young and the restless make good use of the free jazz jukebox. The **Make-Out Room,** also in the Mission at 3225 22nd St. (☎ 415-647-2888), attracts a very attractive young crowd and features alternative bands (cover ranges from free to about $8).

Closer to Union Square at 414 Jessie St., off 5th Street, is the brand-new **Bar of Contemporary Art** (BOCA; ☎ 415-474-7973; www.bocasf.com), a combo art gallery, drinking, dancing, and dining space with regularly changing installations. You can check out the artwork during the day and have lunch, and come back later to get sweaty with the DJs. It's open Tuesday through Saturday until the wee hours; there's a cover Friday and Saturday nights.

The Mission has its own version of the Bermuda Triangle, and, if you have the stamina to investigate, you could begin the evening at **Latin American Club,** 3286 22nd St. (☎ 415-647-2732). This bar has an unstructured feel — maybe it's the piñatas hanging from the ceiling — and you'll see lots of mid-20s to mid-30s people hanging out and drinking while they wait for things to get going at one of the nearby music clubs. Although the Make-Out Room is just across the street, walk down to Mission St. and see what's happening at **12 Galaxies,** 2565 Mission St. (☎ 415-970-9777; www.12galaxies.com), which on some nights is a little out of this world. Live music draws the local party crowd and not infrequently the club is the scene of theme bashes. The night I visited, the Devil-Ettes were out in full force, horns and all, for their five-year anniversary go-go blowout. Right next door is **Doc's Clock,** 2575 Mission St. (☎ 415-824-3627), which is the best bar in the area according to Aiden, who checks identification at the door. He also pointed out that it has the only shuffleboard in the Mission, plus charming, articulate bartenders.

Check out a four-hour, three-club tour, **Three Babes and a Bus** (www.threebabes.com), for a great time on a Saturday night. It's hassle-free — no parking to deal with and no lines. Local gals in celebratory moods usually fill the luxury tour bus, and the fun is infectious. The $35-per-person fee includes club cover charges, VIP entry, and transportation to and from Union Square. Call ☎ 800-414-0158 for reservations at least a week in advance.

Mixing with the sophisticates

A splendid Art Deco supper club, **Bix,** 56 Gold St., off Montgomery Street between Pacific and Jackson streets in the Financial District (☎ 415-433-6300; www.bixrestaurant.com), will make you want to wear a bias-cut gown (or a dinner jacket, perhaps) and appear very glamorous. The food is now better than ever, too. The **Redwood Room,** at the Clift Hotel,

495 Geary St., at Jones Street (☎ 415-929-2372), is not quite the refined place it 'twas in my mother's day, but the clientele appears as if they dropped in from a *Vanity Fair* photo shoot. The **Tonga Room** at the Fairmont Hotel, 950 Mason St., at California Street (☎ 415-772-5278), features a happy hour buffet weekdays from 5 to 7 p.m. For the price of a drink (about $7) you can enjoy hors d'oeuvres and entertainment — a tropical rainstorm hits every half hour. Okay, okay, maybe that isn't so sophisticated, but at least the hotel's posh.

The Empire Plush Room, inside the York Hotel, 940 Sutter St., between Hyde and Leavenworth streets (☎ 866-468-3399; www.yorkhotel. com/plushroom.htm), features torch and standards singers of some repute. (More than one songbird has started a career in this intimate room and ended up playing clubs in New York City.) At other times, you may find a musical revue or duo or even a comedian (Mort Sahl played here recently). Tickets, ranging from $20 to $55, can be purchased through the Web site and are $5 more expensive at the door. This is one of my favorite clubs, but then I also loved Mel Torme.

Heading to the local for a pint

Chief among our expat watering holes is **Edinburgh Castle Pub,** 950 Geary St., near Polk Street (☎ 415-885-4074), which hosts a mix of entertainment ranging from live music to readings to Quiz Night on Tuesdays. A pool table adds to its stellar reputation. There's no cover charge. Convenient to Union Square is the fine **Johnny Foley's,** 243 O'Farrell St. (☎ 415-954-0777). There's live entertainment nightly and, if you're in the mood for bangers and mash or fish and chips, this is the place to be. Missing Guinness? Head to **O'Reilly's,** 622 Green St. (☎ 415-989-6222), an Irish pub (no kidding) with the two-toned stout and weekend brunch, as well as an authentic crowd of employed locals.

Bringing the kids along

Biscuits and Blues, 401 Mason St., at Geary Street (☎ 415-292-2583), is near the theater district on Union Square in a basement room. The all-ages venue has inexpensive food ($13–$16 entrees), and the music — blues musicians of varied repute — is really good. If you dine here, you get the best seats in the house. Tickets are $5 to $15. The **Great American Music Hall,** 859 O'Farrell St., near Polk Street in the Tenderloin (☎ 415-885-0750), allows children over 6 into some shows; call for an events calendar to see who's playing an early show. Because it offers food service, **Jazz at Pearl's,** 256 Columbus Ave., at Broadway (☎ 415-291-8255), can also accommodate minors. The same is true of **Slim's** and **Bottom of the Hill.** (See "Catching the big-name acts," earlier in this chapter.)

Laughing It Up: Comedy Clubs

I probably don't have to remind you that San Francisco is where Robin Williams got his start and where Lenny Bruce once shocked the audience at The Purple Onion by using foul language. Imagine that. Although the city is no longer the hotbed of chuckles that it was in the '70s, the comedy clubs are still packin' 'em in.

Cobb's Comedy Club, 915 Columbus Ave. (☎ **415-928-4320;** www.cobbs comedy.com), features headliners Tuesday through Sunday and a three-hour marathon of comics on Wednesday nights for a mere $10. No one under 16 admitted; tickets range from $15 to $40, and there's a two-drink minimum. The **Punchline Comedy Club,** 444 Battery St., between Washington and Clay streets (☎ **415-397-7573;** www.punchlinecomedy club.com), also books local and nationally known comics nightly at 9 p.m. with a second set at 11 p.m. Friday and Saturday nights. These shows are only open to folks 18 and over; tickets range from $5 to $20, and there's a two-drink minimum. The Valencia Street corridor in the Mission District is one hot property, but before it was the place to be, it was the longtime 'hood of **The Marsh,** 1062 Valencia St. (☎ **800-838-3006** or 415-826-5750; www.themarsh.org), a complex of theaters devoted to developing work. On Saturday nights in one of these theaters (two doors down at 1074 Valencia St.), you'll find the **Mock Café,** with scheduled performers at 10 p.m. for a cover charge of $7. You won't normally find the polished acts that show up at the other clubs (although Robin Williams himself makes the occasional appearance), but you'll certainly be closer to the cutting edge of comedy. Monday nights showcase works-in-progress. Check the Web site for more events.

Defying Categorization: Unique Bars

A manicure *and* a martini can be yours at **The Beauty Bar,** 2299 Mission St., at 19th Street (☎ **415-285-0323**), where the décor is straight out of a 1959 beauty parlor. (In case you were wondering where all those enormous hair dryers with the hoods ended up, look no farther.) Wednesday through Saturday happy hour from 7 p.m. includes a manicurist making the rounds. If you spend $10 on a drink (and you will) either Friday or Saturday nights, that also buys you a mini-makeover from their friends at Urban Decay. Our local suburbanites join the fun on the weekends, and during the week around midnight, hipsters drape themselves over the chrome barstools to exude cool.

If you smoke and drink, or drink and don't mind smoke, **Amber,** 718 14th St., around Church and Sanchez streets (☎ **415-626-7827**), is the bar for you. This is a locals' hangout with high-quality booze, a comfy lounge, and excellent lighting. **Li-Po Cocktail Lounge,** 916 Grant Ave., at Washington Street (☎ 415-982-0072), is an authentic, dark, Chinatown dive, complete with dusty Asian furnishings, a huge rice-paper lantern, and a shrine to Buddha behind the bar. If you want to drink with professionals, head to North Beach and grab a bar stool at **Gino and Carlo's,** 548 Green St., between Columbus and Grant avenues (☎ 415-421-0896), which opens early so the regulars can get in a fortifying scotch before lunch. **Spec's,** 12 Saroyan Alley, off Columbus Avenue and Broadway (☎ 415-421-4112), is another North Beach institution — dark and dingy, but historic.

Literary types make a pilgrimage to **Vesuvio** in North Beach, where Jack Kerouac passed the time. It's at 255 Columbus (☎ 415-362-3370), next to Kerouac Alley, where the author used to pass out.

Fancy yourself an undiscovered singing sensation? Make your way to the back room at **Martuni's,** 4 Valencia St., at Market (☎ 415-241-0205), where customers croon and the piano player is kind.

Champagne lovers unite in the Financial District at the **Bubble Lounge,** 714 Montgomery St. (☎ 415-434-4204). The bar has over 300 sparkling wines, plush sofas, and an array of financial-center types reminiscing over their expense accounts.

If you're around Polk Street for dinner, stop in afterward at the **Bigfoot Lodge,** a retro, log-cabin-like bar with good recorded music, a cool crowd of singles, and a wooden likeness of Bigfoot, as we imagine him to be. Find all this and more at 1750 Polk St., near Washington Street (☎ 415-440-2355). Alternatively, **Hemlock Tavern,** 1131 Polk St. at Post Street (☎ 415-923-0923; www.hemlocktavern.com), brings in two indie bands most nights to play in one of the smallest enclosed spaces I've seen in public. There's another room for drinking, a pool table, and a patio for smoking. Over in Hayes Valley, you can snack on corn dogs and other foodlike products, drink, and discover what's happening in the indie music scene at **Rickshaw Stop,** 155 Fell St. at Van Ness Avenue (☎ 415-861-2011; www.rickshawstop.com). Events are scheduled Wednesday through Saturday nights and tickets are $5 to $12 at the door.

Stepping Out: The Gay and Lesbian Scene

In this section, I give you a short list of the many clubs and bars that cater to the gay and lesbian community in the city. Find specific listings in the weekly entertainment guides, *SF Weekly* and *Bay Guardian,* and look for the free *Bay Area Reporter* in bookstores, cafes, and bars around town.

The Cafe, 2367 Market St., near Castro (☎ 415-861-3846), is currently the place for both sexes to go dancing. It's also the place to stand in line on weekend nights. **The Stud,** 399 Ninth St., at Harrison Street (☎ 415-252-7883), is a long-time institution in the city. Different nights feature different music, but Tuesdays are infamous for "Trannyshack" hosted by Heklina. Cover $2 to $6 on weekends. **Endup** is another gay icon, a hang-out as well as a dance club. South of Market at 401 Sixth St. (☎ 415-646-0999), it's a San Francisco institution like the cable cars or Coit Tower. Cover is $10 to $20 these days.

To be entertained or be entertaining, try **Martuni's** piano bar (see the preceding section), which is certainly gay-friendly, but you should also make your way to **The Mint Karaoke Lounge,** 1942 Market St. in the Castro (☎ 415-626-4726). On the weekends, the hard core come in to warm up at 4 p.m., but the show goes on seven nights a week. Stop off at the ATM before you arrive, because the bar only accepts cash.

Part VI
The Part of Tens

The 5th Wave   By Rich Tennant

" Oh, look. Shake it, and it fills with tiny felons
trying to swim their way to freedom."

In this part . . .

*W*hipping up these top-ten lists was a challenge! I'm just glad I didn't have to come up with my ten favorite restaurants (too challenging) or my ten favorite parking places (the first ten available spots, wherever they are). Instead, in this part I give you my humble opinions on the greatest views, the best pastimes in foul weather, useful/playful gifts that won't damage your credit rating, and the best ways to look less like a tourist — not that I have anything against tourists, mind you.

Chapter 17

The Top Ten San Francisco Views

. . . .

In This Chapter

▶ Finding the best panoramas

▶ Golfing, dining, and drinking cocktails, with a view

▶ Checking out the view from Berkeley

. . . .

*P*eople like views. That much is clear from the wrangling that goes on to get a table with a view in restaurants, or the extra tariff imposed on a room with a view, not to mention a home with a view. San Francisco is one major view, owing to all those hills. I admit to a permanent sentimental attachment to the views of San Francisco. Following are some of my favorites.

From Twin Peaks

The mother of all views — if the weather cooperates — is from **Twin Peaks,** which sits in the center of San Francisco in a residential neighborhood at the top of Market Street. The sightline encompasses the entrance to the bay and reaches all the way 'round to Candlestick Point. If you're driving, head southwest on Market Street, which becomes Portola Drive past 17th Street. The first light past Corbett Street is a right turn only; this is Twin Peaks Boulevard, the road that takes you up the hill.

The **37-Corbett bus,** which you can catch on Market and Church streets, takes passengers near, but not all the way to, Twin Peaks. And the rest of the trip is quite a hike uphill. If you'd prefer something less strenuous and want to see one of San Francisco's beautiful "hidden" staircases, here's a tip: Exit the bus at Corbett and Clayton streets, and look for an old concrete wall on the west side of Clayton marked by a street sign that says "Pemberton." This leads to the Pemberton Stairs. You won't get to the top of Twin Peaks by climbing them, but you'll be treated to bay views in quiet, green surroundings.

From Bernal Heights Park

Look southeast from downtown and you'll spot a prominent hill with a few trees decorating the top. That's **Bernal Heights Park,** the favored dog-walking and fireworks-viewing area for the Bernal Heights neighborhood. The weather in this part of town is far superior to the weather around Twin Peaks, which can get really foggy, much to the dismay of the camera-toting folk on the tour buses. The views here are equally wonderful to my mind, partly because Bernal Hill is closer to downtown and the bay. The **67-Folsom bus** drives to the end of Folsom at Esmeralda. Exit and walk up the hill on any of a number of paths.

From Lincoln Park

Lincoln Park is one of the prettiest golf courses in creation, situated around the Palace of the Legion of Honor and above the entrance to the San Francisco Bay at Land's End. Standing in front of the museum, you can see in the distance a snippet of downtown framed within the green branches of fir trees. From here, walk west down the street. You'll be stunned by a postcard-perfect view of the Golden Gate Bridge from a unique perspective — facing north as if you're entering the bay. Take a seat on one of the benches along the street so you can survey the vista in comfort. The **18–46th Avenue bus** stops in the museum parking lot.

From the Beach Chalet Restaurant

The waves along **Ocean Beach,** at the end of Golden Gate Park on the Great Highway, are at times soothing and at times violent enough to discourage beachcombing. In either case, you'll be as comfy as a babe in his crib if you get a table upstairs in the **Beach Chalet** restaurant (☎ **415-386-8439**) overlooking the Pacific (ideally, as the sun sets). The building was designed by Willis Polk, and the first-floor visitor center is adorned by murals painted in the 1930s by the same artist who painted the frescoes at Coit Tower. The restaurant is particularly popular for its menu of house-brewed beers, and it serves throughout the day and evening starting at breakfast. If you don't want to wait for a table in the dining room (the food is so-so), you can take a seat in the bar (a much better idea) and turn toward the view, dramatic in any season. The latest addition to the building is called the Park Chalet, which looks onto, well, the park, of course. The **5-Fulton bus,** which you can pick up on Market and Powell streets, takes you to Ocean Beach, a block or so from the Beach Chalet.

Above Dolores Park

From any Muni Metro station (the Powell Street Station being the closest to Union Square) take the J-Church toward Daly City. Exit on 18th and Church streets, above Dolores Park. The city and bay views over this stretch of green on a clear day have been responsible for more than one decision to relocate to the Bay Area. After soaking in the scenery and taking a stroll through the park, walk 2 blocks north on Dolores Street until you reach **Mission Dolores** at 16th and Dolores streets, the oldest building in San Francisco.

From the Top of the Mark

If you feel like having a cocktail as you drink in a view, head to the **Top of the Mark** in the Mark Hopkins Intercontinental Hotel, 1 Nob Hill, at California and Mason streets (☎ 415-392-3434). Sometimes it's so busy you have to wait in line at the elevator, but the city views are mesmerizing when you get a table.

From the Cheesecake Factory

Union Square is a compact urban hub, immensely appealing, especially when it's crowded and bustling. Up until recently, there wasn't a handy place to be among, but not in, the madding crowd, but now **Macy's** (see Chapter 12) has alleviated that problem by installing a branch of the **Cheesecake Factory** (☎ 415-397-3333) on the eighth floor of the department store. Management shrewdly included a heated patio for diners who favor a city view in all its skyscrapered glory. The restaurant is open from 7 a.m. until 11 p.m.

From Fisherman's Wharf

If for some unfathomable reason you've skipped to this section without reading what's come before, you won't know that I, like all upstanding San Franciscans, generally avoid **Fisherman's Wharf** (see Chapter 11) like I avoid the Oakland A's. However, I recently discovered a way to escape the folks crowding the sidewalks, yet still take advantage of the views and freshly cracked crab.

The crab stands are plopped in front of their namesake restaurants along one block off Jefferson Street. Just to the left of Fisherman's Grotto #9 are glass doors marked "Passageway to the Boats," the boats being what remains of the fishing fleet. Take your cracked crab, your beer, and plenty of napkins and push through. You'll be on a pier that leads to the tiny **Fisherman's and Seaman's Memorial Chapel** on your right, with views of the bay and Telegraph Hill in front and to your left. The pier is parallel to Jefferson Street but may be gloriously close to empty even on a weekend. You can eat your crab in peace sitting on the dock of the bay, watching . . . well, you know. Close by, sea lions jump, swim, and beg in the waters below.

From Fort Point

The remains of **Fort Point,** an 1861 brick artillery fortress, occupy the land at the edge of the bay nearest the Golden Gate Bridge. I remember the first time I visited this area, because heavy fog obscured everything around me except the uppermost portion of the bridge. It was a dramatic vision. On a clear day, you'll be treated to the bridge, of course, but also to bright views of the downtown skyline and Alcatraz. The **29 bus** stops as close as the parking lot next to the bridge visitor center, a downhill walk to a particularly pretty viewpoint in the midst of eucalyptus trees. If you're up for a hike, follow the joggers past the Marina Green and through the Presidio (see Chapter 11).

From UC Berkeley Botanical Gardens

Drive to the **UC Berkeley Botanical Gardens,** high in the hills behind the campus. Find the rose garden. Beyond the plants, you can see the bay and San Francisco, small and glowing in the distance. See Chapter 14 for other ideas on what to do in Berkeley after you finish admiring the view.

Chapter 18

Ten Things to Do If It's Raining (or Just Too Foggy)

● ●

In This Chapter

▶ Making the most of a soggy day

▶ Pampering yourself at the hot springs or spa

▶ Finding entertaining indoor activities

● ●

San Francisco isn't Seattle or London by any means, but our rainy days can get in the way of enjoying the city. Actually, a foggy morning is what bothers people most — fog is always cold and damp and gray. But you don't have time to grouse about the weather. You have things to do, places to see, people to meet . . . oh, you don't like getting wet? Okay. Here are a few rainy/foggy-day options.

Taking Afternoon Tea

Afternoon tea at one of the many hotels that offers it is probably the only civilized way to keep dry. Try the cozy **King George Hotel,** 334 Mason St. (☎ 415-283-4TEA; weekends only); the **Fairmont Hotel's Laurel Court,** California and Mason streets (☎ 415-772-5260); the **Palace Hotel,** Market and New Montgomery streets (☎ 415-546-5089; Sat afternoons only); or the **Ritz-Carlton,** 600 Stockton St. (☎ 415-773-6198). **Neiman Marcus** also has a lovely, traditional tea service in the **Rotunda** restaurant, 150 Stockton St. (☎ 415-362-4777), from 2:30 to 5 p.m. daily.

Checking Out Japantown

Head to Japantown and take cover inside the **Kinokuniya Building** at 1581 Webster St., between Post Street and Geary Boulevard. Although this and the other buildings in the area isn't much to look at from the outside, inside you can get a delicious bowl of noodles at **Mifune** (see

Chapter 10), the most authentic noodle house in town, and then entertain yourself in any of a number of stores, such as **Mashiko Folkcraft** (open Wed–Mon 11 a.m.–6 p.m.) and the **Kinokuniya Bookstore** (open daily 10:30 a.m.–7 p.m.). If the sky still hasn't cleared up, take in a movie at the **Kabuki Theater** next door. This multiplex gets all the latest films. An underground parking lot is located off Webster Street. Muni buses 2-Clement, 3-Jackson, 4-Sutter, 22-Fillmore, and 38-Geary all drop you in Japantown.

Luxuriating at Kabuki Springs

Staying indoors can turn into a modest luxury at **Kabuki Springs & Spa,** 1750 Geary Blvd., at Webster Street (☎ 415-922-6000), a most respectable communal bathhouse. You can soak your feet, have a massage, and take a steam bath. Women may use the communal bath facilities on Sundays, Wednesdays, and Fridays; Tuesdays are coed; and men get the rest of the week. Shy people may not feel comfortable at first walking around the premises au naturel, but no one will bother you. Massages, facials, acupuncture, and other treatments are by appointment. To get here, take the 38-Geary bus. Open daily from 10 a.m. to 10 p.m.

Rock Climbing (Or Working Out) at the Touchstone Mission Cliffs Gym

Rather than let the kids climb the walls in your hotel room, take everyone rock climbing (indoors of course) at **Touchstone Mission Cliffs Climbing and Fitness,** located in the Mission District at 2295 Harrison St., at 19th Street (☎ 415-550-0515), and open every day. This world-class facility caters to beginners and experts of all ages and even folks who never dreamed of making like flies. *Belay* (rope handling) classes are taught regularly, so you can act as assistant to your compadres and vice versa. You don't even need any special equipment — you can rent whatever is necessary (including shoes) — and there goes your final excuse. Also on-site is a gym with locker rooms and a sauna, relief for those who prefer to keep their feet on the floor.

Watching the Weather from the Cliff House

Admire the storm from the confines of the **Cliff House,** 1090 Point Lobos Ave., on the Great Highway (☎ 415-386-3330), open every day. This newly renovated historic property now enjoys two restaurants, a bar, and viewing decks. The food, while rather expensive, is quite good fortunately, but what you are really shelling out for is the impressive view of

Seal Rocks and the Pacific Ocean, doubly dramatic if waves are crashing about. The closest museum is the **Palace of the Legion of Honor** (see Chapter 11), another wonderful place to wait out the weather (the museum has a good cafe). The 18 bus will bring you to both locations.

Finding Activities for Everyone at the Metreon and Yerba Buena Gardens

The **Metreon** and **Yerba Buena Gardens** (see Chapter 11) make up a one-stop rainy-day haven, particularly if you're traveling with your family. Depending on everyone's ages, you don't have to stick together for the entire day. Teens can flex their independence at **Zeum** or in the **Airtight Garage.** The elders, if they aren't needed, can shop, play pool at **Jillian's** (the large restaurant on the first floor), or even dash across the street to the **Museum of Modern Art.** Bowling and ice-skating work for everyone, and when it's time to regroup, you can see what's playing at the movies.

Defying the Weather at the California Academy of Sciences

The **California Academy of Sciences** (see Chapter 11) has abandoned its Golden Gate Park laboratory until 2008 and taken up residence south of Market in a multistoried former garment warehouse at 825 Howard St. (☎ 415-750-7145). Amongst the aquarium, the exhibits, the gift shop, and the cafe, you can find enough to keep you busy until the sun comes back out. You'll also be just down the block from Yerba Buena Gardens (see the preceding section) and about two long blocks from the new **Apple Store** (see Chapter 12) where you can check your e-mail or discover some new tricks for your iPod.

Sightseeing and Staying Dry on the F-Market Streetcar

The **F-Market streetcar** (see Chapter 11) is my current public-transport ride of choice. Grab an umbrella, and then grab a seat for a ride to **The Cannery** (see Chapter 12). Yes, it's really just an enclosed shopping mall, if you want to be blunt and unromantic; but still, it's an *attractive* enclosed shopping mall with some fun things to do with the kids. Take the streetcar all the way toward **upper Market Street** and reward yourself with a late lunch at **Zuni** (see Chapter 10).

Babying Yourself at Nordstrom

See if you can get an appointment for a manicure, a pedicure, and/or a facial at Nordstrom in the **San Francisco Centre shopping mall** at Fifth and Market streets (☎ 415-977-5102). If you have a retinue to deal with, send them to the fourth-floor grill for lunch or a snack. You can find lots of shopping opportunities here as well, although most of the stores are your typical mall flavors. While not quite open at press time, there's also going to be a spa at the **Bloomingdale's Westfield Centre** next to Nordies, along with many more shops and restaurants.

Doing Business on a Rainy Day

A great thing to do is sit around your hotel lobby, or better yet the glamorous lobby at the **Palace Hotel** (2 New Montgomery St.), and complain about the weather. Grab a copy of the *Chronicle* and maybe the *Wall Street Journal* for good measure. Whisper into a cellphone while gripping a cup of coffee in your free hand. Then hail a cab and dash to the nearest Internet cafe to check your e-mail: **Golden Gate Perk,** 401 Bush St. at Kearney (☎ 415-362-3929) has computers if you didn't bring your laptop, and **Café de la Presse,** 352 Grant Ave. (☎ 415-398-2680), has free Wi-Fi. The terminals at the Apple Store get busy, but their use is free. Anyway, if you think the rain is bad, be thankful you haven't been inundated with foggy mornings for 40 days straight. Now you know why anyone who can afford a summerhouse in Napa puts up with the traffic on Friday afternoons.

Chapter 19

Ten Ways to Avoid Looking Like a Tourist

. . . .

In This Chapter

▶ Eating, shopping, and dressing like the locals

▶ Avoiding tourist traps

. . . .

I don't understand why being a tourist is considered so beneath some people. Even my own dear husband scoffs at tourists — or people he presumes are tourists — and when we travel he does his well-meaning best to look like a local. This generally leads to amusing misunderstandings with actual citizens, who ask him something in a language he doesn't understand, or presume he knows where he's going when he hasn't a clue. So, why live a lie, I say. If you're visiting for pleasure and have a keen interest in looking around, you're a tourist. Be proud. Wear that camera around your neck (but maybe leave the bum bag at home). Rattle a map in frustration. Ask a stranger for directions.

Otherwise, memorize the following tips.

Dress for the Weather

This is not *The O.C.* — you cannot tan here. In summer, San Francisco is foggy and cold in the morning, turning to sunshine in the afternoon, with temperatures in the upper 60s or low 70s. I know this because the weathermen repeat the same forecast every morning in July and August. Dress in long pants, not shorts. Wear a sweater over your T-shirt and a jacket over both. You can always tie extraneous clothing around your waist when you enter one of our famous microclimates. In San Francisco, the temperature changes from neighborhood to neighborhood, so if you're shivering in Golden Gate Park, head to the Mission to warm up.

September and October are the warmest months here. If you look good in shorts, wear them then.

Don't Trust Your Map

Those darn hills have a way of interrupting the streets in ways that may not be apparent to the untrained eye. It may look like a straight shot from one part of town to the other, but take into consideration the up-and-down of the steep hills. Telegraph Hill is the worst offender. If you can't go through, you'll have to go around. If you're planning on walking to a particular destination, ask first at the hotel or call ahead to see if it isn't more advisable to take public transit or a cab.

Don't Gawk at Tall Buildings

An article in the *San Francisco Chronicle* noted that San Franciscans do not gawk at tall buildings, although I don't know if that includes skyscrapers in other towns. The author also noted that San Franciscans are breaking their own rule and gawking like mad at the downtown ballpark. So, if you don't want to look like a tourist, don't stare at the Transamerica Pyramid — a quick glance should do — but feel free to drool while admiring AT&T Park. You'll then resemble a local who didn't buy season tickets.

Don't Eat or Shop Like a Tourist

Be picky about where you spend your time and money. Places most residents wouldn't be caught dead in include the Hard Rock Cafe, any restaurant on Fisherman's Wharf, Ripley's Believe It or Not!, and the Golden Gate Bridge on a Friday afternoon.

Wait 'til You Get Back to the Airport to Buy That Delicious San Francisco Sourdough

Don't walk around with loaves of bread wrapped in plastic for the trip home. Around here we buy our baguettes for same-day consumption. Anyway, you can buy that particular brand of bread at the airport, where no one will see you.

Cross the Bridge before or after — but Not during — Rush Hour

Don't cross the Bay Bridge between 3 and 7 p.m. unless you want to be mistaken for a suburban commuter. Anyway, no one, not even the commuters, are actually crossing the Bay Bridge at this time; rather, they're sitting and fuming and occasionally inching their way forward. This is important to remember if you have friends in the East Bay who invite you to come over for dinner.

Don't Stare at the Locals

Don't point/gasp/shriek at the man/woman/other with the attention-getting tattoo/leather chaps/chartreuse wig no matter how unusual he/she/it appears. That would be unseemly.

Don't Shout at People You Suspect Don't Speak English

Don't raise your voice or speak extra slowly to your waiter if you suspect he doesn't speak English. In fact, he does speak English. He's merely trying to turn your table as quickly as possible.

Do the Farmers' Market Thing

Hang around the Ferry Plaza Farmers' Market on a Saturday morning. Have breakfast, circle the stalls, eat all the samples, buy something ßnonperishable to take home.

Remove Any Incriminating Evidence

Remember the plastic nametag you attached to your lapel upon entering the Moscone Convention Center? It's okay to remove it now.

Chapter 20

The Top Ten Gifts for Cheapskates

In This Chapter

▶ Bridging the gap with Golden Gate souvenirs
▶ Sweetening the return with fortune-cookie souvenirs
▶ Spreading the fruits of love with gifts of jam

1 don't know about you, but buying gifts for the folks back at the ranch who know I've been on vacation is sometimes more a chore than a pleasure. Besides the fact that no one in the Western world *really* needs another T-shirt, those souvenirs add up (and subtract from my shoe allowance). Understanding, however, that some people expect a little something, here is my list of portable, fun, San Francisco–related gifts — and they're (almost) all under $10.

Playing Bridge

Not to be outdone by the museum gift shops, our own Golden Gate Bridge hawks a variety of branded items sure to remind your nearest and dearest of one of the wonders of the modern world. I particularly like the $6 **Golden Gate Bridge playing cards,** printed with trivia about the construction and history of this landmark. A close second is the $7 **Golden Gate Bridge kitchen towel,** the gift of choice from thrifty shoppers like my cousin Irene. If you run out of time and can't get to the gift shop, you can actually purchase these things online at `http://store.goldengate.org`.

Riding High

This truly is a cheapskate souvenir, but being a practical sort, I find it elegant in its simplicity and usefulness. For a mere $5 at the Powell Street or Hyde Street Cable Car ticket booths, you can purchase one of four **limited-edition souvenir cable-car tickets.** The cards each picture a historic cable car and are good for two-thirds of the fare of a one-way ride. Collect all four, and someone with a scrapbook will treasure them.

Smelling Salts

The Ferry Building Marketplace is full of places to find great gifts, but go on a Saturday when the Farmers' Market is in full tilt. Behind the building look for the Eatwell Farms booth and check out the $5 jars of **lavender salt** or **rosemary salt.** They smell divine and add extra oomph to salads and roasts. Your friends who cook will be most impressed.

Bringing Good Fortune

The biggest producer of fortune cookies in town is **Mee Mee Bakery,** 1328 Stockton St., between Broadway and Vallejo streets in Chinatown (☎ **415-362-3253;** www.meemeebakery.com). Hand over $9.75 and you can delight someone with a **giant fortune cookie.** Okay, at roughly 5 inches in diameter, maybe it's not an actual giant, but it's still fairly large. Mee Mee also sells bags of chocolate- and strawberry-flavored fortune cookies for $6.50 per pound, and almond cookies for $4.50 per pound. If you want to splurge on something more creative, for about $25 per 100 cookies, the bakery will put your own custom fortunes inside the crispy little devils.

Lighting the Way

Intellectuals and all your friends who belong to book clubs will be thrilled to receive anything from **City Lights,** San Francisco's iconic bookstore in North Beach. For those keeping to a budget, check out the very cool $8 **black-and-white posters** featuring the storefront, or Jack Kerouac and Neal Cassady looking rather James Deanish.

Writing Clearly

You can't have too many postcards, but picking them out can be stressful. After all, postcards are like greeting cards — they say something about the person who spent 20 minutes deciding between the one with the cat and the one depicting Einstein. Save your friends grief and gift them with a book of **30 San Francisco postcards** featuring the photographs of Michal Venera. At $9.95 this is a deal. Find *San Francisco 30 postcards* at **Chronicle Books Metreon Store,** 101 4th St. (☎ **415-369-6271**), or **Cody's Books** at 2 Stockton St., near Market Street (☎ **415-773-0444**).

Spilling the Beans

You may not believe this, but B.S. (before Starbucks), people in the Bay Area were drinking strong, delicious coffee! And many continue to do so. They purchase it at any of a number of **Peet's Coffee & Tea** stores, including the newest one in the Ferry Building (see Chapter 10), the shop in the Russ Building at 217 Montgomery St., or in the Marina at 2156 Chestnut St. A gift your coffee-loving pals will truly appreciate is **a pound of Peet's French Roast,** my husband's favorite — this stuff is so strong it can bench-press the competition. At $11.95 per pound, you've crossed the cheapskate limit, but not by much. Besides, it's worth it.

Ringing Your Bell

Useless ornaments . . . ah, where would commerce be without snow globes, pewter models, and plastic barista figurines? Well, San Francisco can supply its fair share and at the top of my list is a spiffy **tin cable car.** A mere $8.75, this little beauty actually moves using friction, and ting-a-lings like the real thing while skittering over the linoleum. These are among the many fine doodads available online and at the **Cable Car Museum** gift shop, 1201 Mason St. (☎ 415-474-1887; www.cablecar museum.org). Admission to the museum is free and it's open every day from 10 a.m. to 5 p.m.

Nibbling Bliss

San Francisco has long attracted chocolate makers to its shores, not for any reason I know of, but there was Ghirardelli to start and Joseph Schmidt (of the beautiful truffles) and most recently a former doctor and a former winemaker who have together produced some serious dark chocolate under the Scharffen Berger label. Free one-hour tours of the handsome brick factory, located in Berkeley at 914 Heinz Ave. (☎ 510-981-4050; www.scharffenberger.com), are offered by appointment daily at 10:30 a.m., 2:30 p.m., and 4:30 p.m. for people 10 and older. Scharffen Berger sells two gifts that I, for one, would be genuinely pleased to receive; the $8 **cylinder filled with chocolate-covered champagne grapes,** or the $6 **rectangular acrylic package of a dozen 5-gram squares** (the mint flavor, if you're wondering).

Spreading the Love

Ten bucks may not seem like much to spend on a gift, but how often do you fork over that kind of money for a small jar of jam? Berkeley's June Taylor does not make ordinary preserves from ordinary fruit; thus her divine products created from organic fruits in small batches do not sell for chicken feed. And that's why an 8-ounce jar of her **white nectarine conserve** or **tangerine marmalade** (among many flavors that will cause your bread to sit up and take notice) is such a thoughtful and extravagant offering. June Taylor's jams can be purchased at Yum (see Chapter 13), and the Ferry Plaza Farmers Market. If you take a walk through Crissy Field (see Chapter 11), you can get them at the Warming Hut, too.

Appendix

Quick Concierge

. . . .

Fast Facts

American Automobile Association (AAA)

The office at 150 Van Ness Ave. in the Civic Center provides maps and other information for members traveling by car. Call ☎ 800-222-4357 for emergency service or ☎ 415-565-2012 for general information.

American Express

The office is at 455 Market St., at First Street (☎ 415-536-2600), open Monday through Friday from 8:30 a.m. to 5:30 p.m., Saturday from 9 a.m. to 2 p.m.

Area Codes

The area code for San Francisco is **415**; for Oakland, Berkeley, and much of the East Bay, **510**; for the peninsula, generally **650**.

ATMs

ATMs are easy to find, especially downtown but also on any main business corridor.

Babysitters

Your hotel concierge can probably arrange for a babysitter. Otherwise, try American Child Care Service (☎ 415-285-2300; www.americanchildcare.com). Its rates are $19 per hour with a four-hour minimum plus $20 agency fee.

Camera Repair

Discount Camera at 33 Kearny St. (☎ 415-392-1180) is convenient to Union Square

and it sells and repairs photographic equipment. It's open from 8:30 a.m. to 6:30 p.m. Monday through Saturday and 9:30 a.m. to 6 p.m. Sundays (for sales only, no repairs).

Convention Center

The Moscone Convention Center, 747 Howard St., between Third and Fourth streets (☎ 415-974-4000), is within easy walking distance of the Montgomery Street Muni and BART stations.

Credit Cards

To report a lost or stolen card, contact Visa at ☎ 800-336-8472; American Express at ☎ 800-221-7282; MasterCard at ☎ 800-307-7309; Discover at ☎ 800-347-2683; or Diners Club at ☎ 800-234-6377.

Dentists

Call the San Francisco Dental Society for 24-hour referrals (☎ 415-421-1435).

Doctors

Saint Francis Memorial Hospital, 900 Hyde St., between Bush and Pine streets (☎ 415-353-6000), offers 24-hour emergency-care service. The hospital's physician-referral service number is ☎ 415-353-6566. Your hotel can also contact on-call doctors. Before receiving any treatment, check with your health-insurance company to find out how emergency treatment is handled when you're out of your provider area.

Earthquakes

California will always have earthquakes, most of which you'll never notice. However, in case of a significant shaker, you should know a few precautionary measures. When you're inside a building, seek cover; do not run outside. Stand under a doorway or against a wall and stay away from windows. If you exit a building after a substantial quake, use stairwells, not elevators. If you're in a car, pull over to the side of the road and stop — but not until you're away from bridges, over-passes, telephone poles, and power lines. Stay in your car. If you're out walking, stay outside and away from trees, power lines, and the sides of buildings. If you're in an area with tall buildings, find a doorway in which to stand.

Emergencies

Dial ☎ 911 from any phone for police, an ambulance, and the fire department.

Hospitals

San Francisco General Hospital, 1001 Potrero Ave. (☎ 415-206-8111), accepts uninsured emergency patients, but the wait can be long and uncomfortable. The patient referral and assistance number is ☎ 415-206-5166.

Hot Lines

In case of emergency, here are a few num-bers to have at hand: Poison Control Center, ☎ 800-876-4766; Rape Crisis Center, ☎ 415-861-2024; Family Service Agency, ☎ 415-474-7310.

Information

The San Francisco Convention and Visitors Bureau is in the lower level of Hallidie Plaza, 900 Market St., at Powell Street (☎ 415-391-2000).

Internet Access and Cafes

You can check your e-mail while on the road at Golden Gate Perk, 401 Bush St. (☎ 415-362-3929), or Quetzal Internet Café, 1234 Polk St. (☎ 415-673-4181).

Liquor Laws

You can't drink or purchase alcohol legally if you're under 21. All the clubs, bars, supermarkets, and liquor stores ID anyone who looks younger than 30 (try not to be offended if you don't get carded). Bars don't serve liquor from 2 a.m. to 6 a.m.

Maps

The visitor's bureau (see "Information" earlier in this section) has maps of the city, or stop by the California State Automobile Association (see "AAA" earlier in this sec-tion) if you're a member of AAA.

Newspapers/Magazines

The major papers are the morning *San Francisco Chronicle* and the afternoon *San Francisco Examiner.* They are distrib-uted from sidewalk kiosks and boxes. The free weekly *San Francisco Bay Guardian* includes excellent events listings. Find it in cafes and in sidewalk boxes around the city. *San Francisco* magazine is the monthly city magazine. You can find it at newsstands everywhere.

Pharmacies

Walgreens has taken over the city, and you should be able to find one almost any-where. Call ☎ 800-WALGREEN for the address and phone number of the nearest store. Around Union Square, Walgreens is at 135 Powell St. (☎ 415-391-4433), open Monday through Saturday from 8 a.m. to midnight and on Sunday from 9 a.m. to 9 p.m., but the pharmacy has more-limited hours. A branch on Divisadero Street at Lombard has a 24-hour pharmacy.

Police

Call ☎ **911** from any phone. No coins are needed. The nonemergency number is ☎ 415-553-0123.

Post Office

Dozens of post offices are located all around the city. The closest to Union Square is in Macy's department store, 170 O'Farrell St. (☎ 800-275-8777).

Radio Stations

Find KQED, our National Public Radio affiliate, at 88.5 FM. News and sports may be found at KCBS 710 AM.

Restrooms

Dark-green public bathrooms are on the waterfront at PIER 39, on Market Street near the cable-car turnaround on Powell Street, and by the Civic Center. The restrooms cost 25¢ and are clean and safe. Also try hotels, department stores, museums, and service stations. Restaurants usually let only patrons use their bathrooms.

Safety

Walking around alone late at night is never a good idea. San Francisco is relatively safe, but it still has its share of muggings and more-heinous crimes. Areas to be particularly careful in include the Tenderloin; the lower Haight; the Mission District anywhere between 16th and 24th streets east of Mission Street; lower Fillmore Street;

and South of Market, particularly on Sixth and Seventh streets. Keep your wallet in an inside coat pocket and don't carry around wads of cash. Try to avoid using ATMs at night.

Smoking

Since January 1998, smoking has been prohibited in bars. Smoking in restaurants and public buildings is also illegal, which is why you see so many well-dressed people loitering on the sidewalks during their coffee breaks.

Taxes

A sales tax of 8.5 percent is added to all purchases except snack food. The hotel and parking garage tax is 14 percent.

Taxis

Outside of Union Square, expect to have trouble hailing a cab on the street; you'll have to call for one instead. Try Yellow Cab (☎ 415-626-2345), Veteran's Cab (☎ 415-648-1313), Desoto Cab (☎ 415-970-1300), or Luxor Cabs (☎ 415-282-4141).

Time Zone

California is on Pacific Standard Time, three hours behind New York.

Transit Information

Calling ☎ 415-817-1717 connects you to all transit organizations.

Weather Updates

While in town, turn to one of the news stations on the radio (try KCBS 710 AM). Otherwise, www.sanfrancisco. citysearch.com lists comprehensive forecasts.

Toll-Free Numbers and Web Sites

Airlines

Air Canada
☎ 888-247-2262
www.aircanada.ca

Alaska Airlines
☎ 800-426-0333
www.alaskaair.com

American Airlines
☎ 800-433-7300
www.aa.com

America West Airlines
☎ 800-235-9292
www.americawest.com

Continental Airlines
☎ 800-523-3273
www.continental.com

Delta Air Lines
☎ 800-221-1212
www.delta-air.com

Hawaiian Airlines
☎ 800-367-5320
www.hawaiianair.com

Midwest Express
☎ 800-452-2022
www.midwestexpress.com

Northwest Airlines
☎ 800-225-2525
www.nwa.com

Southwest Airlines
☎ 800-435-9792
www.iflyswa.com

United Air Lines
☎ 800-864-8331
www.united.com

US Airways
☎ 800-288-2118
www.usairways.com

Major hotel and motel chains

Best Western International
☎ 800-528-1234
www.bestwestern.com

Clarion Hotels
☎ 800-CLARION
www.hotelchoice.com

Comfort Inns
☎ 800-228-5150
www.hotelchoice.com

Courtyard by Marriott
☎ 800-321-2211
www.courtyard.com

Crowne Plaza Hotels
☎ 800-227-6963
www.crowneplaza.com

Days Inn
☎ 800-325-2525
www.daysinn.com

Doubletree Hotels
☎ 800-222-TREE
www.doubletreehotels.com

Econo Lodges
☎ 800-55-ECONO
www.hotelchoice.com

Fairfield Inn by Marriott
☎ 800-228-2800
www.fairfieldinn.com

Hampton Inn
☎ 800-HAMPTON
www.hampton-inn.com

Hilton Hotels
☎ 800-HILTONS
www.hilton.com

Holiday Inn
☎ 800-HOLIDAY
www.basshotels.com

Howard Johnson
☎ 800-654-2000
www.hojo.com

Hyatt Hotels & Resorts
☎ 800-228-9000
www.hyatt.com

ITT Sheraton
☎ 800-325-3535
www.sheraton.com

La Quinta Motor Inns
☎ 800-531-5900
www.laquinta.com

Marriott Hotels
☎ 800-228-9290
www.marriott.com

Quality Inns
☎ 800-228-5151
www.hotelchoice.com

Radisson Hotels International
☎ 800-333-3333
www.radisson.com

Ramada Inns
☎ 800-2-RAMADA
www.ramada.com

Red Roof Inns
☎ 800-843-7663
www.redroof.com

Residence Inn by Marriott
☎ 800-331-3131
www.residenceinn.com

Ritz-Carlton
☎ 800-241-3333
www.ritzcarlton.com

Rodeway Inns
☎ 800-228-2000
www.hotelchoice.com

Super 8 Motels
☎ 800-800-8000
www.super8motels.com

Travelodge
☎ 800-255-3050
www.travelodge.com

Westin Hotels and Resorts
☎ 800-228-3000
www.westin.com

Wyndham Hotels and Resorts
☎ 800-822-4200 in continental U.S.
and Canada
www.wyndham.com

Where to Get More Information

Area tourist information offices

San Francisco Convention and Visitors Bureau

P.O. Box 429097; 900 Market St., San Francisco, CA 94142-9097 (☎ 415-391-2000; www.sfvisitor.org).

Call or write the Convention and Visitors Bureau if you'd like to receive a nifty booklet with lots of useful information, including maps and a calendar of events. Of course, the slant is toward the advertisers, so take those glossy ads lightly. There is a $3 mailing charge. If you have a fax and a touch-tone phone, use the toll-free number for automated 24-hour fax service and "fast facts."

Napa Valley Conference and Visitors Bureau

1310 Napa Town Center, Napa, CA 94559 (☎ 707-226-7459; www.napavalley.com).

This is the second-busiest visitor center in California, which either says something about our fondness for wine or something about the beauty of the area (or both). They'll send you a free brochure and a list of hotels on request; for $10 (plastic accepted) they'll mail you a 120-page magazine, suggested itineraries, and a handsome map of the area.

Information on the Web

www.sanfrancisco.citysearch.com

A comprehensive, regularly updated site devoted to all things San Francisco, including arts, entertainment, dining, and attractions, with links to the hotel reservation network.

www.sfbg.com

The *San Francisco Bay Guardian* site with event listings and the lowdown on nightlife.

www.sfgate.com

The *San Francisco Chronicle* Web site. Read all about it.

www.iglta.org

A Web site for gay and lesbian travelers.

www.sanfran.com

The Web site for *San Francisco* magazine. Includes dining recommendations and timely entertainment suggestions.

www.gocitykids.com

The Web site for families wondering what to do. Lots of helpful info. Membership fee.

Print resources

Frommer's San Francisco

This guide covers all 46 square miles in great detail, including background on the sites, personalities, and neighborhoods that make San Francisco "everybody's favorite city."

Frommer's San Francisco from $90 a Day

For the budget-minded traveler who doesn't want to compromise the quality of the experience, this guide offers advice on the best values and free and almost-free things to see and do.

Frommer's Irreverent San Francisco

A pocket-size guide that that's both funny and informative; offers unusual and eccentric experiences (as well as information on hotels, restaurants, accommodations, and attractions) in the City by the Bay.

Frommer's Memorable Walks in San Francisco

This guide covers 12 easy-to-follow walking tours through San Francisco's most charming neighborhoods. Includes detailed maps.

Index

See also separate Accommodations and Restaurant indexes at the end of this index.

BUSINESS, CAREERS & PERSONAL FINANCE

0-7645-5307-0   0-7645-5331-3 *†

Also available:

✔Accounting For Dummies †
0-7645-5314-3

✔Business Plans Kit For Dummies †
0-7645-5365-8

✔Cover Letters For Dummies
0-7645-5224-4

✔Frugal Living For Dummies
0-7645-5403-4

✔Leadership For Dummies
0-7645-5176-0

✔Managing For Dummies
0-7645-1771-6

✔Marketing For Dummies
0-7645-5600-2

✔Personal Finance For Dummies *
0-7645-2590-5

✔Project Management
For Dummies
0-7645-5283-X

✔Resumes For Dummies †
0-7645-5471-9

✔Selling For Dummies
0-7645-5363-1

✔Small Business Kit For Dummies *†
0-7645-5093-4

HOME & BUSINESS COMPUTER BASICS

0-7645-4074-2   0-7645-3758-X

Also available:

✔ACT! 6 For Dummies
0-7645-2645-6

✔iLife '04 All-in-One Desk Reference
For Dummies
0-7645-7347-0

✔iPAQ For Dummies
0-7645-6769-1

✔Mac OS X Panther Timesaving
Techniques For Dummies
0-7645-5812-9

✔Macs For Dummies
0-7645-5656-8

✔Microsoft Money 2004 For Dummies
0-7645-4195-1

✔Office 2003 All-in-One Desk
Reference For Dummies
0-7645-3883-7

✔Outlook 2003 For Dummies
0-7645-3759-8

✔PCs For Dummies
0-7645-4074-2

✔TiVo For Dummies
0-7645-6923-6

✔Upgrading and Fixing PCs
For Dummies
0-7645-1665-5

✔Windows XP Timesaving
Techniques For Dummies
0-7645-3748-2

FOOD, HOME, GARDEN, HOBBIES, MUSIC & PETS

0-7645-5295-3   0-7645-5232-5

Also available:

✔Bass Guitar For Dummies
0-7645-2487-9

✔Diabetes Cookbook For Dummies
0-7645-5230-9

✔Gardening For Dummies *
0-7645-5130-2

✔Guitar For Dummies
0-7645-5106-X

✔Holiday Decorating For Dummies
0-7645-2570-0

✔Home Improvement All-in-One
For Dummies
0-7645-5680-0

✔Knitting For Dummies
0-7645-5395-X

✔Piano For Dummies
0-7645-5105-1

✔Puppies For Dummies
0-7645-5255-4

✔Scrapbooking For Dummies
0-7645-7208-3

✔Senior Dogs For Dummies
0-7645-5818-8

✔Singing For Dummies
0-7645-2475-5

✔30-Minute Meals For Dummies
0-7645-2589-1

INTERNET & DIGITAL MEDIA

0-7645-1664-7   0-7645-6924-4

Also available:

✔2005 Online Shopping Directory
For Dummies
0-7645-7495-7

✔CD & DVD Recording For Dummies
0-7645-5956-7

✔eBay For Dummies
0-7645-5654-1

✔Fighting Spam For Dummies
0-7645-5965-6

✔Genealogy Online For Dummies
0-7645-5964-8

✔Google For Dummies
0-7645-4420-9

✔Home Recording For Musicians
For Dummies
0-7645-1634-5

✔The Internet For Dummies
0-7645-4173-0

✔iPod & iTunes For Dummies
0-7645-7772-7

✔Preventing Identity Theft
For Dummies
0-7645-7336-5

✔Pro Tools All-in-One Desk
Reference For Dummies
0-7645-5714-9

✔Roxio Easy Media Creator
For Dummies
0-7645-7131-1

* Separate Canadian edition also available

† Separate U.K. edition also available

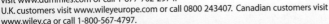

SPORTS, FITNESS, PARENTING, RELIGION & SPIRITUALITY

0-7645-5146-9   0-7645-5418-2

Also available:
- Adoption For Dummies
  0-7645-5488-3
- Basketball For Dummies
  0-7645-5248-1
- The Bible For Dummies
  0-7645-5296-1
- Buddhism For Dummies
  0-7645-5359-3
- Catholicism For Dummies
  0-7645-5391-7
- Hockey For Dummies
  0-7645-5228-7

- Judaism For Dummies
  0-7645-5299-6
- Martial Arts For Dummies
  0-7645-5358-5
- Pilates For Dummies
  0-7645-5397-6
- Religion For Dummies
  0-7645-5264-3
- Teaching Kids to Read
  For Dummies
  0-7645-4043-2
- Weight Training For Dummies
  0-7645-5168-X
- Yoga For Dummies
  0-7645-5117-5

TRAVEL

0-7645-5438-7   0-7645-5453-0

Also available:
- Alaska For Dummies
  0-7645-1761-9
- Arizona For Dummies
  0-7645-6938-4
- Cancún and the Yucatán
  For Dummies
  0-7645-2437-2
- Cruise Vacations For Dummies
  0-7645-6941-4
- Europe For Dummies
  0-7645-5456-5
- Ireland For Dummies
  0-7645-5455-7

- Las Vegas For Dummies
  0-7645-5448-4
- London For Dummies
  0-7645-4277-X
- New York City For Dummies
  0-7645-6945-7
- Paris For Dummies
  0-7645-5494-8
- RV Vacations For Dummies
  0-7645-5443-3
- Walt Disney World & Orlando
  For Dummies
  0-7645-6943-0

GRAPHICS, DESIGN & WEB DEVELOPMENT

0-7645-4345-8   0-7645-5589-8

Also available:
- Adobe Acrobat 6 PDF
  For Dummies
  0-7645-3760-1
- Building a Web Site For Dummies
  0-7645-7144-3
- Dreamweaver MX 2004
  For Dummies
  0-7645-4342-3
- FrontPage 2003 For Dummies
  0-7645-3882-9
- HTML 4 For Dummies
  0-7645-1995-6
- Illustrator CS For Dummies
  0-7645-4084-X

- Macromedia Flash MX 2004
  For Dummies
  0-7645-4358-X
- Photoshop 7 All-in-One Desk
  Reference For Dummies
  0-7645-1667-1
- Photoshop CS Timesaving
  Techniques For Dummies
  0-7645-6782-9
- PHP 5 For Dummies
  0-7645-4166-8
- PowerPoint 2003 For Dummies
  0-7645-3908-6
- QuarkXPress 6 For Dummies
  0-7645-2593-X

NETWORKING, SECURITY, PROGRAMMING & DATABASES

0-7645-6852-3   0-7645-5784-X

Also available:
- A+ Certification For Dummies
  0-7645-4187-0
- Access 2003 All-in-One Desk
  Reference For Dummies
  0-7645-3988-4
- Beginning Programming
  For Dummies
  0-7645-4997-9
- C For Dummies
  0-7645-7068-4
- Firewalls For Dummies
  0-7645-4048-3
- Home Networking For Dummies
  0-7645-42796

- Network Security For Dummies
  0-7645-1679-5
- Networking For Dummies
  0-7645-1677-9
- TCP/IP For Dummies
  0-7645-1760-0
- VBA For Dummies
  0-7645-3989-2
- Wireless All In-One Desk Reference
  For Dummies
  0-7645-7496-5
- Wireless Home Networking
  For Dummies
  0-7645-3910-8